†ROUBLE IN MIND

BOB DYLAN'S GOSPEL YEARS
WHAT *REALLY* HAPPENED

Clinton Heylin

LESSER
GODS

Photo Insert:
Photos by Marty Katz and Chris Bradford
Cover Design:
Michael Doret

FIRST PUBLISHED IN THE UNITED STATES OF AMERICA IN 2017 BY:
Lesser Gods, 15 W. 36th St., 8th Fl., New York, NY 10018,
an imprint of Overamstel Publishers, Inc.
PHONE (646) 850-4201
www.lessergodsbooks.com

DISTRIBUTED BY: Consortium Book Sales & Distribution,
34 13th Ave. NE #101, Minneapolis, MN 55413
PHONE (800) 283-3572
www.cbsd.com

FIRST EDITION NOVEMBER 2017 / 10 9 8 7 6 5 4 3 2 1
PRINTED AND BOUND IN THE U.S.A.
ISBN: 978-1-944713-29-4

LIBRARY OF CONGRESS CONTROL NUMBER: 2017943990

To Debbie Gold.
She was a friend of mine.

INTRO:
BEFORE THE FLOOD

I never felt like I was searching for anything. I always felt that I've stumbled into things or drifted into them. But I've never felt like I was out on some kind of prospector hunt, looking for the answers or the truth . . . I never went to the holy mountain to find the lost soul that is supposed to be a part of me . . . I don't feel like a person has to search for anything. I feel like it's all right in front.

—BOB DYLAN TO DENISE WORRELL, 1985

Caveat emptor: I am an evangelist. That is to say, when it comes to the evangelical part of the Dylan canon—what in mediaspeak has been defined, rather misleadingly, as the gospel years (i.e. 1979-81)—I'm a believer. Not a trace of doubt in my mind.

From the moment I heard a live performance of "Covenant Woman" from the November '79 Warfield shows at a one-day Dylan convention in Manchester the following month, I knew the man had (re)connected to the wellspring of his art when that ol' sign on the cross began to worry him.

As I have long argued, in person and in print, the consummate songwriter composed a body of work in the period 1979-81 which more than matches any commensurate era in his long and distinguished career—or, indeed, that of any other twentieth century popular arist.

But unlike that other seminal starburst of inspiration, the one between 1965 and 1967, the afterglow of this cerebral explosion is barely reflected within the grooves of the trilogy of albums CBS released in real time: *Slow Train Coming* (1979), *Saved* (1980) and *Shot Of Love* (1981).

Perhaps it's because Dylan's heart really wasn't in the process of making records at the time. He did, after all, suggest in an interview designed specifically to promote the third album in said trilogy, that his primary interest was playing "songs which [a] re gonna relate to the faces that I'm singing to. And I can't do that if I['m] spending a year in the studio, working on a track. It's not that important to me. No record is that important." Said interview appeared on a CBS promo album.

The epicenter of Dylan's artistry at the cusp of the decades—as it had been in the mid-seventies—was the stage; surely one reason why, starting in November 1979, he took an acetelyne torch to the 1978 set-list and began afresh. As he said at the time on his one radio interview, quoting 2 Corinthians, "All things become new, old things are passed away."

To howls of protest that couldn't help but remind one of the folk-rock furor thirteen years earlier, he delivered the same unrelenting Good News/Bad News message night after night, while each night becoming born again as a performing artist in front of the aghast eyes and ears of Dylan apostates.

Just as from September 1965 to May 1966, the shows which ran from November 1979 to the following May saw the gospel gauntlet thrown down nightly. Dylan delivered an unceasing barrage of biblical glossaries set to the soundtrack of a heavenly choir and a band of unbelievers riding the musical tide all the way to New Jerusalem. But this time there was no near-death experience to deflect Dylan from his chosen path. He would continue beating his ecumenical drum most of the time for the next eighteen months.

For much of this period, his was very much a voice in the wilderness. Much of the media, and a large percentage of his hardcore fan base, simply switched off. The North American gospel shows—All Saints' Day '79 at the San Francisco Warfield excepted—tended to receive only local reviews, and rarely drew ones interested in reporting the facts.

As for the shows themselves, journalists delighted in reporting that this "voice of a generation" couldn't even sell out intimate theaters. Even the eight English shows in July 1981 struggled (and failed) to sell out, barely three years after people were camping out for 72 hours just to get a single ticket for six Earl's Court shows.

(Those arch-arbiters of fan demand, the bootleggers, were also switching off just as Dylan's muse was switching on again, deeming demand to be insufficient from a demographic of wavering disciples.)

So although Dylan played some ninety-eight shows between November 1979 and December 1980, all but a handful of which were still being taped by hardcore collectors, not a single vinyl bootleg was released in real time; and this, from the most bootlegged rock artist of all time. As for official album sales, the cliff Dylan fell off in 1980 with the catastrophic *Saved* was one it would take him seventeen years to scale again.

So, on the face of it, hardly the sort of period where a thorough revisit would send ripples of excitement through the Dylan world in 2017. And yet, when at the start of the year Dylan's long-time manager hinted to a *Rolling Stone* reporter that the next *Bootleg Series* (lucky thirteen!) would reexamine the gospel years afresh, the fan sites were abuzz with anticipation.

Because, as a Nobel poet once put it, "Everything passes, everything changes." And three decades on, an official release (or two) of a judicious sample of one or two legendary residencies in San Francisco, Los Angeles, Toronto, Montreal or London ranks high on most Bobcats' bucket lists.

Ranking higher still for those whose focus is the studio oeuvre is a set that also affords a thorough reexamination of the two dozen songs Dylan wrote in the six months leading up to the *Shot Of Love* sessions. With 20/20 hindsight, the album bearing that name—even though it has real moments—stands as perhaps the most underwhelming Dylan studio collection of original songs to date, with maybe three performances on the official *Shot Of Love* worthy of inclusion on the double-album it should have been: the title-track itself, a "Property Of Jesus" that aside from a remix could hardly be bettered, and "Every Grain Of Sand."

The good news—praise the Lord of Happenstance—is that the period 1979 to 1981 turns out to be among the best documented eras in Dylan's six-decade–long career as a recording/performance artist.

The explanation for this resides in two events dating back to January 1978: the purchase of a brand-new, state-of-the-art, eight-track tape machine made by Otari, the MX-5050, shortly after Dylan had signed a five-year lease on a rehearsal studio in downtown Santa Monica.

These serendipitous twists of fate meant Dylan could begin to record most rehearsals at his newly leased studio; demo songs he wished to copyright; as well as run tapes of all the shows he was to perform during a 115-date world tour. The rehearsal studio, known privately as Rundown, throughout this period would even serve as a sometime-recording studio for the two albums which bookend the Rundown era, *Street-Legal* and *Shot Of Love*.

Indeed, Dylan soon grew so comfortable with his Santa Monica "home studio" setup that he rekindled a work ethic last seen in the happy days spent in the Big Pink basement in West Saugerties, New York, with the last standing band he kept on retainer, the mostly-Canadian Hawks, back in 1967.

Having put together the second standing band of his career in September 1979, it should come as no great surprise that the dividing line between tour rehearsals, album sessions and copyright demos for the next two years would be as fuzzy as one of Fred Tackett's effect-pedals; or that the aesthetic of the basement tape should be so readily revived by its instigator twelve years on, with a set of musicians no less accomplished than The Band and perhaps even more sympathetic to Dylan's way of working on the hoof.

In those two years, the body of work Dylan and his band captured at Rundown Studios, between tours (and albums), is in many ways more impressive than the one he and The Band managed from their 1967 country retreat. The breadth of material tackled, if presented in its entirety, would certainly challenge that now available on the official "basement tapes" *Bootleg Series*.

At least *Trouble No More*—the next *Bootleg Series*—more than hints at a Rundown facsimile of the "lost" album Dylan could have recorded in the fall of 1980—but didn't! Frustratingly, when Dylan did finally enter the very same rehearsal studio where he demoed an album's worth of new songs six months earlier, to begin the new album, in March 1981, he had already discarded half a dozen strong compositions and begun to bastardize the lyrics to two defining post-conversion masterpieces, "Caribbean Wind" and "The Groom's Still Waiting At The Altar."

By the time Dylan relocated to Chuck Plotkin's Clover studio in late April 1981 to begin work on *Saved*'s successor in earnest, he was well on his way to making an album that was one-third filler ("Heart Of Mine," "Lenny Bruce," "Trouble") but just one-third killer. Yet Dylan himself would compare *Shot Of Love* with 1965's *Bringing It All Back Home,* which to his mind once provided a similar "breakthrough point."

Perhaps not surprisingly, the two ensuing tours—a summer tour of Europe and a fall tour of the States—would signal a rerouting of the holy slow train. By second tour's end, few vestiges of that preternatural commitment to his newly-wrought gospel material remained.

When the second anniversary of his landmark November 1979 West Coast residencies came around, Dylan was still on the road, heading for the Florida swamplands. Yet all that he had embraced when baptized by Vineyard pastor Bill Dwyer was not washed away.

He would soon fuse the sensibilities he was reaching for on *Shot Of Love* on the no less apocalyptic *Infidels* (1983). But that is another story, from another time and place. This trenchant tract confines itself to straddling the great divide which separates the smooth-as-silk *Slow Train Coming* from the bear's-arse monitor mix that is *Shot Of Love*, covering all bases between.

It connects the dots by drawing on a wealth of new information, much of which has not been in the public domain before. Hopefully, it will achieve its primary goal: to serve as a testament to the inspiration faith can bring when aligned to genius, making a case for a wholesale reevaluation of the music Dylan made during his so-called religious period. With the release of an 8-CD Deluxe *Bootleg Series*, the three studio albums will no longer be the be-all and end-all of the gospel years, and we are a whole lot closer to knowing what really happened, artistically. As always with Dylan, it turns out that the more we understand, the more we can enjoy . . .

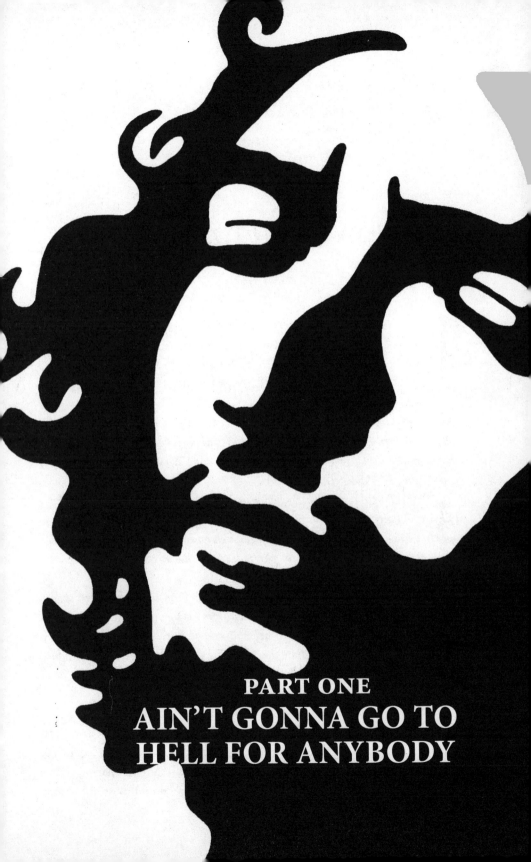

PART ONE
**AIN'T GONNA GO TO
HELL FOR ANYBODY**

THE SLOW TRAIN TO NASHVILLE . . .

Just writing a song like ["Slow Train"] probably emancipated me from other kind of illusions. I've written so many songs and so many records that I can't address them all, . . . [but] on its own level, writing that . . . was some kind of turning point for me.

—BOB DYLAN TO JOHN DOLEN, FORT LAUDERDALE, 1995

December 2nd, 1978. He moved with the quiet determination of a zealot as he made his way unobtrusively into the inner reaches of Nashville's Municipal Auditorium for that night's concert. 'Cept the concert was some hours away and the band was only just starting its soundcheck.

On this tour, the soundchecks had usually proven to be worth catching. After a full year of touring, there was little need to work on the songs in the current set; so once the sound was in some kind of shape, the eleven-piece band would usually play follow the leader on either a new song he had written that day or a cover or a country standard, or a blues vamp.

Tonight, much to the delight of the zealot who had snuck into the rafters shortly before disentangling his cassette tape recorder from his shoulder bag, they began an unfamiliar song with a clear, defined structure and an instantly memorable burden, "There's a slow train coming around the bend." The zealot pressed record, determined to document a new Dylan song, wholly unaware he was witnessing the birth of an entirely new Dylan . . .

Unfortunately for posterity, Brian Stibal may have had the zeal and determination of a believer back then, but he lacked the technical nous required of a first-rate archivist. Though he filmed (on 8mm) and recorded Dylan at various junctures during the second half of the 1970s—while also editing and writing most of the content of the world's first Dylan fanzine, *Talkin' Bob Zimmerman Blues*[1]—his videos were usually marred by a hand so unsteady he filmed mostly ceilings while his audio tapes generally sounded like something rescued from Hitler's bunker after it was flattened.

As such, for the past thirty-nine years all that any self-respecting Dylan "expert" really knew was that Dylan had debuted a song called "Slow Train" at the soundcheck to the December 1978 Nashville show. That is, until a fastidious young tyke at the Dylan office, doing excavations for yet another *Bootleg Series*—this one covering the gospel years—found a cassette marked "Slow Train—Soundcheck." Surely not?

Sure enough, this "Slow Train" would prove to be that four-minute work out of the song at the Nashville Municipal Auditorium, with half-formed yet intelligible lyrics directed at someone "who thought I was blind" and who "couldn't make up [her] mind," set to a distinctly *Street-Legal*esque arrangement of the now-familiar "Slow Train" melody.[2]

What was already unmistakeable was the power of that burden, which consciously tapped into Dylan's personal iconography, something he would knowingly reference at a number of shows in late 1980, delivering variants of the following rap:

> *"When I was a young kid growing up I used to sit around all the time, the trains used to roll through town three or four times a day. And I used to watch them trains just wondering where they were going. And one day I knew I was gonna go where those trains were going."*

Between November 1979 and the following November 1980, it would be prefaced by more sulphurous sentiments, but only after the "holy slow train" Dylan first referenced on the *Highway 61 Revisited* sleeve was hijacked by a Christian fellowship for whom interpreting The Bible's notoriously elliptical meanings was child's play.

Back in early December 1978, Dylan did not find the task quite so easy. He had been reading and rereading the Gospel According to Matthew for the past fortnight, dropping in a nightly reference during a dramatically rewritten "Tangled Up In Blue."

---

[1] Later abbreviated to *Zimmerman Blues*, and then, for the tenth and final issue, *Changin'*.
[2] Just as another innocuously marked cassette, listed as "Legionnaire's Disease—Billy Cross," has turned out to be Dylan's original Detroit soundcheck performance.

Such a choice of reading matter was a telling one. Matthew had written his gospel for his fellow Jews, in order to convince them that Jesus was the Messiah foretold in the Old Testament; each chapter and verse almost ticking off a checklist of messianic prophecies the young Jesus fulfilled.

Matthew is also a work that, as the noted scholar A.N. Wilson has written, "reflects the tension which saw the new religion—what we call Christianity—being fashioned from the old—Judaism. It is by paradox an intensely Jewish, and an intensely anti-Jewish work—indeed it is the great Ur-text of anti-Semitism."

This innate contradiction probably troubled Dylan, who for the past fortnight had been seeking a rational explanation for an experience he had, on the road to Miami, via Damascus:

Bob Dylan: Some people say they just heard a voice on a lonesome road, other people say they were in the middle of a football game; some people were in the men's room of a Greyhound bus station. You don't have to be in any special situation [to hear Jesus calling]. [1981]

He certainly wasn't in a "special situation." In his case, he "heard a voice" in a hotel room in Arizona, of all places. It was November 18th, 1978, and he was not feeling at all well. In fact, he was feeling worse than the night before, when he had forced himself to get through a show in San Diego, something he confided to a more select audience in the same town a year later:

Last time I was here in San Diego, it was about a year ago, I was coming from someplace [else] and I was feeling real sick when I came through here. I was playing, I don't think it was this place—Anyway, towards the end of the show somebody out of the crowd—they knew I wasn't feeling too well, I think they could sense that—and they threw a silver cross on the stage. Now, usually I don't pick things up that are thrown on the front of the stage. Once in a while I do, but most times I don't. But I looked down at this cross and I said, "I got to pick that up." I picked up that cross and I put it into my pocket. It was a silver cross, maybe so high—and I brought it backstage and I brought it with me to the next town which was off in Arizona. Anyway, when I got back there I was feeling even worse than I had felt when I was in San Diego, and I said, "Well, I really need something tonight," and, I didn't know what it was. I was used to all kinds of things, and I said, "I need something tonight that I never really had before." And I looked in my pocket and I had this cross that someone threw up on stage . . . in San Diego. And I put that cross on.

In 1980, Dylan would twice openly admit to a mystical element to the hotel room experience, telling the *LA Times*' Robert Hilburn in November, "There was a presence in the room that couldn't have been anybody but Jesus . . . I truly had a born-again experience, if you want to call it that." While to Australian journalist Karen Hughes, the previous May, he confessed, "Jesus put his hand on me. It was a physical thing. I felt it. I felt it all over me. I felt my whole body tremble. The glory of the Lord knocked me down and picked me up."

Indeed, he grew increasingly unapologetic about his conversion, even belligerent, when met with skepticism. At an impromptu German press conference in July 1981, he gave the assembled media both barrels: "Jesus did appear to me and is King of Kings and Lord of Lords and He <u>did</u> die on the cross for all mankind . . . Born again, that's what they call it. It's pretty scary to think about . . . I'm not preaching . . . It's spiritual—it's not complicated."

And yet, for a man who had been wholly changed from all he had been, in a hotel heartbeat, there was precious little external evidence he had been on the receiving end of this Blakean vision of the Lord of Lords. Or maybe the subtle changes just passed the American media by.

At a show in Fort Worth, seven days after San Diego, he was photographed wearing a new piece of stage jewelery, a not-so-small silver cross. And he was now prefacing "Señor" every night with an extended rap, an apocalyptic vision involving a man with eyes of fire on a slow train smoking all the way to San Diego. Meanwhile, the eternal femme fatale in "Tangled Up In Blue" was nightly reading chapter and verse from the prophetic Jeremiah. Away from the arenas, he was also asking all sorts of questions of one young black singer in his band with whom he had formed a close bond:

Helena Springs: He was having some problems once and he called and asked me, and they were questions that no one could possibly help with. And I just said, "Don't you ever pray?" . . . And he said, "Really?" And he asked me more questions about it, and he started enquiring. You know . . . he's a very inquisitive person.

Unbeknownst to Springs, he was also trying to change his way of thinking about the album he planned to make when he came off the road. He had stockpiled quite a few songs since *Street-Legal*. But they seemed to largely comprise "a man talking to a woman, who is just not treating him properly"—which was his exact description of "Stepchild," the one new song he was playing nightly—only minutes after soundchecking "Slow Train."[3]

Allen appears to have been the last US journalist to catch a glimpse of the pre-born–again Dylan. She caught a man planning big changes in how he managed his career—one of which would directly impinge on the studio legacy of his gospel years. Asked about his previous studio methodology, he admitted, "Years ago, I used to do the song live before you ever made a record, so ... I got into just taking the songs into the studio before I was too familiar with them and making the record, and as time went on it would evolve into something else. So I'm gonna try harder next time ... to make a more accessible record."

He also seemed to be thinking about doing a theater tour as the persistent, presumably pretty lady wondered what he thought would "happen when no one wants to pay to see Bob Dylan anymore." Dylan's reply was startlingly prescient, "I guess I'll have to play smaller halls."

By then, Dylan had already recorded "Slow Train" in the studio for the highly "accessible" album of the same name. Throughout the intervening months his every move would remain shrouded in speculation, with a smattering of media misinformation.

That Dylan himself was already thinking three steps ahead was confirmed by another meeting he had on a very busy day in Nashville. One of his 1978 backing singers (and future bride), Carolyn Dennis, had arranged for him to meet her best friend, the singer Regina McCrary, whose father was a preacher. McCrary herself was a fine gospel singer.

According to McCrary, the two immediately agreed that should the chance arise, she would "go on the road ... with him," just as soon as he took to the road again. In fact, when she did get the call just four months later, it was to work on *Slow Train Coming*, before becoming the only perennial component of a gospel group that would serve as the vocal backdrop to everything he recorded and performed between 1979 and 1981.

That gospel choir would also initially comprise Springs and Dennis, the last two vestiges of the '78 sound. For now, the pair were wailing their way through the two and a quarter hour show that was the 1978 set, beginning with a honking, full

---

[3] That journalist was probably Lynne Allen. References in Allen's published *Trouser Press* interview to an Atlanta conversation have led to some doubt this Nashville conversation was also with her, but the Dec. 2nd interview has been attribted to her. Incidentally, when Allen's interview finally appeared the following May in the American music monthly, *Trouser Press*, it was beneath the headline, "Interview with An Icon," accompanied by a remarkably Christ-like image of the poet-singer—see Chapter 1 heading.

band arrangement of Tampa Red's "She's Love Crazy" and ending with the opening song on *Street-Legal*, the epic "Changing Of The Guards."

Tonight in Nashville, the cameras would be rolling. For the one and only time on the 1978 tour, an official camera crew would film part of the show for a TV special (the so-called "Rome TV film"). Had the footage been broadcast in real time and not in 1979, Dylan's more perceptive fans may well have realized something was afoot, based simply on the way he tore into "Changing Of The Guards" like it was a harbinger of things to come. It was almost as if his subconscious self had known all along where he had been heading these past twelve months. And it wasn't Lincoln County Road:

> Eden is burning.
> Either get ready for elimination,
> Or your heart must have the courage,
> For the changing of the guards.

1. PULLING BACK ON THE REINS
[December 1978 – April 1979]

INTERVIEW WITH AN ICON

Bob Dylan grants an audience

It would have been easier if I had become a Buddhist, or a Scientologist, or if I had gone to Sing Sing.

—BOB DYLAN TO KAREN HUGHES, MAY 21, 1980

That was all part of my experience. It had to happen. When I get involved in something, I get totally involved. I don't just play around on the fringes.

—BOB DYLAN TO ROBERT HILBURN, 1983

Dylan's close reading of Matthew's account of the Sermon on the Mount, not for the first time—he had referenced it in 1974's "Up To Me"—had not stopped him from writing another song from the vantage point of "a man talking to a woman, who is just not treating him properly."

The song he would soundcheck in Greensboro just five days after soundchecking "Slow Train" in Nashville took the famous dictum from that sermon—"Whatsoever ye would that men should do to you, do ye even so to them" [7:12]—and turned it into an admonishment of Her: "If you do right to me, baby/ I'll do right to you, too," sounded very much like it came from the same pen as "Is *Her* Love In Vain?" (to use the original title).

Nor did the appearance of "Do Right To Me Baby" at the final show in Miami in a heavy-metal disco guise set off any alarm bells in the audience, the song sitting easily enough alongside the likes of "Stepchild" and "We'd Better Talk This Over." As for any gospel tinge the tune might have contained, it was resolutely headed off at the pass by metalhead guitarist Billy Cross, for whom Lessismore was a castle in Denmark. As to whom Dylan was directing the song's sentiments, here was a man who thought Monogamy was a board game.

For most of 1978 Dylan had delighted in sending up speculation about his love life with band introductions that cast every girlsinger as his muse. The Miami show was no different as he announced to the audience, "On [the] one side, my ex-girlfriend Helena Springs. I like to eat and Helena doesn't like to cook. In the middle [is] my current girlfriend, Jo Ann Harris. She is sweet, too. [And] on the other side, the true love of my life and fiancée, Miss Carolyn Dennis."

Coming from a man who always liked to blow smoke, it was an amusing smokescreen. Dennis would end up as Mrs. Dylan, though not for another decade, while Springs was more of an on-off girlfriend than a former girlfriend. Only Jo Ann Harris seems to have remained wholly immune to the rock star's charms.

But when the tour ended, it was to another female figure hovering in the background that Dylan returned, someone who had been waiting (im)patiently for him in LA, where she had been sharing an apartment with another of the singer's sometime-girlfriends, actress Sally Kirkland.

Actress Mary Alice Artes had already been accorded a cryptic credit on *Street-Legal*, listed simply as Queen Bee. She had been buzzing around Bob since late 1977. And she was very much his type:

David Mansfield: Mary Alice Artes was one of these dynamic personalities that Bob's probably attracted to in general, and if they're black, so much the better— she was really powerful. She could look really sexy, dress really sexy, without ever exuding sex, but meanwhile being one of those really competent mothers who would shower you with all this love and attention, and . . . tell you what you should do, and slap your bottom to get you off doing it. She would have been like the perfect Jewish wife.

Although Artes did her best to stay resolutely in the shadows, a series of press reports the following summer credited her with sparking Dylan's conversion to the born again creed. But on the two occasions when Artes was subsequently tracked down by Dylan researchers, she insisted, to Howard Sounes, she "cannot lead anyone to the Lord," and to Scott Marshall, that if the Holy Ghost wanted him to find out about Dylan's story, then he should try and talk to Dylan—a curious portrayal of the Holy Spirit as a believer's press agent.

Artes's terse comments to both parties made it very clear she was still a believer. But as to whether she was the "very close friend [who] mentioned a couple of things to me and one of them was Jesus"—Dylan's November 1980 description of his precious angel—she wasn't (and isn't) saying. Thankfully, there seems little doubt she was the one; or that Dylan returned to LA for a rethink, only to discover Artes had already changed her way of thinking—according to one contemporary report, refusing to live in sin as a result. Her own personal quest had led her to the Vineyard Fellowship, a small evangelical sect based entirely in California, led by a charismatic convert in the Pauline mode:

Ken Gulliksen: At the end of [a Vineyard] meeting [Artes] came up to me and said that she wanted to rededicate her life to the Lord . . . That morning she did rededicate her life to the Lord. Then she revealed that she was Bob Dylan's girlfriend and asked if a couple of the pastors would come, there and then, and talk to Bob.

The Vineyard could not have been wholly unknown to Dylan. At least three members of the 1978 touring band had succumbed to its charms in the past year: David Mansfield, T-Bone Burnett and Stephen Soles, though both Mansfield and Burnett personally insisted they had no hand in bringing Dylan to the fellowship. Nonetheless, all three threw themselves into church activities with a little more aplomb than the notoriously circumspect new convert:

David Mansfield: TBone was the first one to go through this experience, and Stephen sort of followed him, and I eventually did, too. TBone has more than a bit of preacher in him and was probably hammering at all of his friends in the ways that he could be most effective—arguing Christian apologetics. But there was this revival going on—there was a certain time when we were all going to the same church, and Bob would be way in the back incognito, [while] TBone, Stephen and I were all playing in the church band.

So it really does appear that Artes found Jesus independent of Dylan and/or his musical circle, and then told her would-be boyfriend the good news. If Dylan, two years on, can be believed, his reaction was surprisingly offhand, "The whole idea of Jesus was foreign to me. I said to myself, 'I can't deal with that.' . . . But later it occurred to me that I trusted this person and I had nothing to do for the next couple of days, so I called the person [from Vineyard] back and I said I was willing to listen about Jesus."

The person he spoke to when he called the fellowship seems to have been Bill Dwyer. According to Dwyer, "He called our office because of some things going on" in his personal life, which flatly contradicts Dylan's account. He would insist: "A lot of people think that Jesus comes into a person's life only when they are either down and out or are miserable or just old and withering away. That's not the way it was for me. I was doing fine." The songs Dylan had begun writing rather suggest not. The pastor himself, when interviewed by Joel Gilbert, confirmed that the initial discussion with Dylan addressed some personal concerns:

Bill Dwyer: We had some pastors [who] had musical backgrounds and they went up and talked to him. It was very down to earth: Do you need help in your life?

[Do] you have a sense of something more, [and want to] invite the Lord in? Are you aware that your own sins have created a lot of guilt and shame in your life, and [do] you want to get free of that? . . . The thing that was going on with the Vineyard in those days was not in any way coercive, it was not ecstatic. Most of the people [who join the fellowship] . . . cry out to God, "I need a Higher Power." Most people come to that place because of a crisis in their life . . . They just talked with him, answered questions that he had. I think they gave him a Bible. [JG]

The reference to "a Higher Power" suggests the kind of person the Vineyard were generally used to dealing with—it, being a term most commonly used not in church but in addiction therapy, as part of the so-called Twelve Step program. For those in a hurry, though, there was the One Step program, and this was the path that, according to Kenn Gulliksen, Dylan embraced that day: "Larry Myers and Paul Emond went over to Bob's house and ministered to him. He responded by saying, Yes, he did in fact want Christ in his life. And he prayed that day and received the Lord."

The Vineyard's choice of Myers, in particular, was a shrewd one. A fellow musician, he knew exactly who Dylan was and what his trip had been, and was adept at dispensing a crash-course in millenialist eschatology that would have made an archdeacon's head spin:

Larry Myers: I was one of two [pastors] who went to see Dylan in Brentwood in very early 1979, at the request of Bob Dylan . . . through Mary Alice Artes. There we met a man who was very interested in learning what The Bible says about Jesus Christ. To the best of my ability I started at the beginning of Genesis and walked through the Old Testament and the New Testament and ended in Revelation. I tried to clearly express what is the historical, orthodox understanding of who Jesus is . . . There was no attempt to convince, manipulate or pressure the man into anything. But in my view God spoke through His word, The Bible, to a man who had been seeking for many years. Sometime in the next few days, privately and on his own, Bob accepted Christ and believed that Jesus Christ is indeed the Messiah.

Myers seems to suggest that Dylan's conversion was not as instantaneous as Gulliksen implied at the time. Dylan's own memory of the meeting was that he had approached it with an open mind, "I certainly wasn't cynical. I asked lots of questions . . . like, 'What's the son of God? What's all that mean—dying for my sins?'" He had been asking questions like this in song since at least 1962's "Long Ago, Far Away";

most tellingly on the 1967 masterpiece, "Sign On The Cross," which depicted the penitent sinner worrying that he would arrive at the pearly gates only to find "the door it might be closed."

In January 1979, the open door in this Homer's mind did not remain ajar for long. And once it was closed, it stayed closed for some time. Asked point blank, in 1984, whether he was still "a literal believer of the Bible," Dylan confirmed he was. And when questioned as to whether both Old and New Testaments were "equally valid," said that to him they were. Two years later, he was still asserting a literal interpretation of chapter and verse:

Bob Dylan: For me, there is no right and there is no left. There's truth and there's untruth, y'know? There's honesty and there's hypocrisy. Look in the Bible: you don't see nothing about right or left. Other people might have other ideas about things, but I don't, because I'm not that smart. I hate to keep beating people over the head with the Bible, but that's the only instrument I know, the only thing that stays true. [1986]

A change had come. And if Dylan's truth-seeking had previously embraced many mansions, the Vineyard Fellowship was an evangelical house of God, with a capital E. To Vineyard members, this did not equate with fundamentalism. As David Mansfield says, "It was as intense as what was going on in fundamentalist circles, but it was culturally from an entirely opposite place"; a distinction lost— with some cause—on all nonbelievers and a fair few believers. To quote John Green, author of *Religion and the Culture Wars*:

Fundamentalists tend to read the Bible literally. Many evangelicals don't actually read it literally. They're willing to understand that there's metaphor and poetry in the Bible . . . It's just that the truth expressed in that metaphor and poetry is without error.

The more salient spin the Vineyard pastors put on the Scriptures—which helped to sell the fellowship's idea "of who Jesus is" to Dylan—was the radical notion that the prophecies in the Book of Revelation were just about to become historical fact. Whether he was told as much on that first visit, or was only exposed to such outlandish eschatology at a later date, Dylan had signed up to a particularly fierce form of Christianity.

As David Mansfield suggests, another key component in their pitch to the pop icon was the fact that "a big part of the fellowship of that church was music." This was bound to appeal to a man who who would later insist, "I find the religiosity and philosophy in the music . . . I don't adhere to rabbis, preachers, evangelists . . . I've learned more from the songs than I've learned from any of this kind of entity."

For now, Dylan remained at the mercy of "rabbis, preachers *and* evangelists!" And though he had never really been a practicing Jew, it was the first of these who soon balked at the idea that they had lost one of their own. As Helena Springs later recalled, "People were mad at him, the Jewish people were [particularly] mad at him because he became a Christian. [For him,] it was like he was exploring Christianity."

Once his nearest and dearest knew of the change, the pressure on him became intense. Dave Kelly, a fellow musician and believer, remembers it well, "The pressures that his mother was putting on him to submit to these very high rabbis from the Orthodox Judaic—it was like a war going on."[4]

According to Kelly, there was one specific occasion, probably in early 1980, when "three or four rabbis, including [leader of the Chabad-Lubavitch movement,] Rebbe Menachem Schneerson, . . . turned up . . . They felt he had taken the time to study Christianity . . . So their position . . . was that they felt like he should give them a chance."

Dylan may initially have given the impression of going along with these emissaries, as was his wont. Certainly his publicist, Paul Wasserman, remembers, "[At] this period . . . there were all these very religious Jews in the background, who . . . were hanging out . . . Dylan would also study the Torah with them . . . He didn't close his mind to anything."

But for now they were fighting a losing battle. The Vineyard now had "dibs" on Dylan, and they were not about to let go. Within a matter of weeks—or even possibly days—they had persuaded him to sign up for their unique brand of Bible-teaching at a School of Discipleship. Perhaps he thought it might have a similar effect to the school for painting he attended for three months in 1974, a key that had unlocked *Blood On The Tracks*:

Bob Dylan: I went to Bible school at an extension of this church out in the Valley in Reseda, California. It was affiliated with the church. [1985]

Bob Dylan: At first, I said, "There's no way I can devote three months to this. I've got to be back on the road soon." But I was sleeping one day, and I just sat up in bed at

---

[4] Beattie herself qualified Kelly's claim, insisting that when these rabbis called her up, she would tell them, "If you're [so] upset, you try to change him."

seven in the morning and I was compelled to get dressed and drive over to the Bible school. [1980]

Larry Myers: [He] studied in the School of Discipleship under Kenn Gulliksen, and at least four other competent pastor-teachers, including myself. We met in a comfortable conference room that was part of a suite of offices . . . There was a real estate firm occupying the first [i.e. ground] floor suite of offices. Bob attended the intense course of study along with other students for three and one-half months.

Ken Gulliksen: It was an intensive course studying about the life of Jesus; principles of discipleship; the Sermon on the Mount; what it is to be a believer; how to grow; how to share . . . but at the same time a good solid Bible-study overview type of ministry.

Bill Dwyer: All of our ministry at the Vineyard was based on Bible studies. That was a primary focal point. Every Sunday we taught the Bible. We told everybody carry your Bible, read your Bible every day. We started our actual Bible school and [students] would go three, four hours in the morning. I taught one of the classes. Kenn taught one of the classes, Larry Myers taught one of the classes. It was intensive. The word of God is what we wanted to get across. The Bible class was usually about a dozen students so it was very interactive. We treasured the Scriptures, so we might study the Book of Exodus—the children of Israel coming out of slavery—and the application might be, "You once were in slavery to sin. You've come out of Egypt in the spiritual sense and you're going to the Promised Land." We would teach every book in the Bible from Genesis to Revelation. It was very Bible based. At the same time we weren't very fundamentalist, in the sense that [that creed] was very black and white, very legalistic, very hard line. It was [more], This is the Word of God and these words . . . bring life to you. [JG]

The foundation stone of this fellowship was the notion that the believer is literally born again, and initially Dylan was unapologetic about the label being applied to him. He articulately explained to DJ Dave Herman, in the widely-syndicated July 1981 London interview, that one is "born once . . . with the spirit from below. Which is the spirit that you're born with. 'Born again' is born with the spirit from above, which is a little bit different." He was even more forthcoming to Australian writer Karen Hughes, the night the gospel tour reached the end of the road:

Bob Dylan: Being born again is a hard thing. You ever seen a mother give birth to a child? Well, it's painful. We don't like to lose those old attitudes and hang-ups. Conversion takes time because you have to learn to crawl before you can walk. You have to learn to drink milk before you can eat meat. You're reborn, but like a baby. A baby doesn't know anything about this world and that's what it's like when you're reborn. You're a stranger. You have to learn all over again. God will show you what you need to know. [1980]

In later years, though, the term seemed to get his hackles up. When Hilburn used it in a 1983 interview, he dismissed it as "a hype term. It's a media term that throws people into a corner and leaves them there. Whether people realize it or not, all these . . . religious labels are irrelevant." And to *Time* reporter Denise Worrell, he would be blunter still:

Bob Dylan: I don't want to talk about what I . . . became because that sets people off into role playing. You can't lead people by role playing, and you can only muddle things up. So, whatever it is that I am manifests itself through what I do, what I say, not by what title I want to put on myself, or other people may want to put on me. That's why I've stayed away from all that stuff. I mean, I know you can call somebody "born again" and then you can dismiss that. As long as you can deal with it on a level of a cartoon, you can dismiss it. [1985]

But this antipathy for the phrase would come only after years of being metaphorically beaten about the head with this particular crown of thorns. At the time, he was caught up in the whole experience, and the experience locked him into the present like nothing had since he attended Norman Raeben's art classes.

Inevitably, old habits still died hard. Personal interactions with his fellow students were sporadic at best. As Bill Dwyer would recall, "He was there, he came to my class, he interacted with other students. But he was still Bob Dylan— he dressed like Bob Dylan. [I was almost tempted to say,] 'Take off the glasses, the leather jacket and the beret for a minute.' But he did all the assignments."

Likewise Terry Botwick, another teacher at the school, recalls, "He was a sincere and honest seeker, trying to understand and learn. What struck me about him was how deeply interested he was. My only frustration was keeping up with his questions. I'd go over five to six subjects each week, an Old Testament book like Isaiah 28, and he would've read ahead to chapter 43."

In *Stairway to Heaven [1986]*, Davin Seay and Mary Neely gave an account of these classes, describing how, "during class breaks, Dylan would often walk into the parking lot in back of the prefab building, dressed against the brisk morning air in a leather jacket and stocking cap, to smoke Marlboro cigarettes and talk with his girlfriend." This one reference confirms he and Artes were for now wrapped up in a joint covenant.

But Dylan also had his participatory moments, as when a fellow student at the School of Discipleship related a dream the previous night, in which "the members of the class were gathered in an upper room . . . [but] one corner of the room had been left unfinished, exposing insulation padding, ducts, and a tangle of dangerously frayed electric wiring . . . The dreamer was frightened, until an unidentified man assured him that only boldness was required. Encouraged, the dreamer thrust his hands into the wiring and pulled. It fell away, and through the hole in the roof, fresh, clean water began to flow."

It was a "nodding and smiling" Dylan who used the good book to interpret the dream, as he was being taught to do, quoting 2 Corinthians 5:17: "Old things are passed away, and all things are made new."

But if Corinthians was being interpreted in a way familiar to other Christian sects, the Book of Revelations was treated in a wholly different way—becoming an almost sci-fi version of the End of Days. The Vineyard's take on this allegorical work by St. John the Divine would color Dylan's view of the Bible for half a decade or more. And it all derived from a book published as recently as 1970, called *The Late Great Planet Earth*, written by Hal Lindsey (with the help of C.C. Carlson).

Lindsey himself had a direct connection with the fellowship dating back to at least the mid-seventies, though he retained his independence, staying focused on his consistently misguided conviction that he had correctly interpreted St. John.

As Larry Myers begrudgingly admitted, after Lindsey's prophecies proved to be all sound and fury, "Bob, along with several million other people, read Lindsey's *The Late Great Planet Earth*. We also taught on some of [its] themes in the School of Discipleship." Myers also confessed he was already aware that "Bob had a long-standing interest in some of the great themes of Biblical prophecy," and as such was ripe for receiving the full Lindsey litany. And according to shallow Hal, the Antichrist was already abroad in America as the clock ticked down to a second millenia:

> Men today vainly seek after peace while they reject and shut out of their lives the
> Prince of Peace, Jesus Christ . . . The spirit of "Antichrist" reigns in the governments

of the world, for Christ is said not to be relevant to the problems we face. Peace is available to the individual today as he invites Christ into his heart and allows Him to reign upon the throne of his life. But the Bible teaches that lasting peace will come to the world only after Christ returns and sits upon the throne of David in Jerusalem and establishes His historic kingdom on earth for a thousand years.

Lest one thinks *The Late Great Planet Earth* was some obscure religious tract, Lindsey's work had sold millions before Dylan avidly read and believed it. In 1979 a film of the same name was being readied for release.[5] Yet Lindsey was simply the latest in a long line of misguided autodidacts who believed they had found the key to unlock St. John the Divine's poetic flights, turning the allegorical into the prophetic. Lindsey did so by interpreting the restoration of Israel in 1948 as the beginning of the countdown to Apocalypse:

Keep your eyes on the Middle East. If this is the time that we believe it is, this area will become a constant source of tension for all the world. The fear of another World War will be almost completely centered in the troubles of this area. It will become so severe that only Christ or the Antichrist can solve it. Of course the world will choose the Antichrist . . . The United States will not hold its present position of leadership in the western world; financially, the future leader will be Western Europe. Internal political chaos caused by student rebellions and Communist subversion will begin to erode the economy of our nation. Lack of moral principle by citizens and leaders will so weaken law and order that a state of anarchy will finally result. The military capability of the United States, though it is at present the most powerful in the world, has already been neutralized because no one has the courage to use it decisively. When the economy collapses, so will the military. The only chance of slowing up this decline in America is a widespread spiritual awakening.

This is why, as late as 1981, Dylan was insisting to Neil Spencer that he thought "everything that's happened is like a preview of what's going to happen." Though he never actually came out and cited Lindsey or his book/s, there was a period when much of what he was saying—particularly between songs—was a thinly-veiled commentary on *The Late Great Planet Earth*. Of these, the most disturbing would come the night he returned to Tempe—where he had first received a personal vision

---

[5] The film, when it appeared later that year, had enough of a budget to enlist Orson Welles to narrate it. However, when more extreme interpretations were required it was Lindsey who appeared on camera, looking like a James Taylor album cover.

of Jesus—and decided to open the School of Discipleship to students of the University of Arizona, delivering an impromptu keynote lecture:

> Let me tell you that the Devil owns this world. He's called the God of this world. Now . . . I like America just as much as everybody else does. . . . But America will be judged. [Because] God comes against a country in three ways. First way He comes against their economy. Did you know that? He messes with their economy the first time. You can check it all the way back to Babylon, Persia and Egypt. Many of you here are college students, aren't you? Well, you ask your teachers about this now. I know they're gonna verify what I say. Every time God comes against a nation, first of all He comes against their economy. If that doesn't work, he comes against their ecology . . . He did it with Egypt. He did it with Persia. He did it with Babylon. He did it with the whole Middle East. It's a desert now. It used to be flourishing gardens. [And] if that don't work, He just brings up another nation against them. So one of those three things has got to work. Now Jesus Christ is that solid rock. He's supposed to come two times. He came once already. See, that's the thing. He's been here already. Now, He's coming back again. You gotta be prepared for this. Because no matter what you read in the newspaper, that's all deceit. The real truth is that He's coming back . . . You just watch your newspapers . . . maybe two years, maybe three years, five years from now, you just watch and see. Russia will come down and attack in the Middle East. China's got an army of two hundred million people. They're gonna come down to the Middle East. There's gonna be a war called the Battle of Armageddon, which is like some war you never even dreamed about. And Christ will set up His kingdom . . . and He'll rule it from Jerusalem. As far out as that might seem, this is what the Bible says.

Nor was this rap some one-off abberation on Dylan's part. As we shall see, he would return to the theme of the End Times repeatedly in the months after the Tempe shows, usually as a prelude to "(Hanging On To A) Solid Rock," a song played at every show between November 1979 and November 1981, by which time it was a shell of a former shell.

If Dylan had only recently accepted that Jesus was real, he had long believed the Devil was working his mischief on mankind. As early as 1963, a handwritten draft of "Masters Of War" was accompanied by a crude drawing of a figure standing by the grave of some unnamed master of war (presumably there to "make sure [he's] dead"), with a guitar in his hand and, tellingly, two cloven hooves. And throughout 1978, he had immersed himself afresh in the concise canon of Robert Johnson, the Delta blues icon whose work seemed most infused with the fumes of hell, not to say a more-than-nodding personal acquaintance with the Devil.

As such, he was more than ready to be debriefed on the works of the Devil when he had thrust into his hands the second installment in Lindsey's contentious canon, published in 1972, also with the help of C. C. Carlson, under the provocative title, *Satan Is Alive And Well On Planet Earth*. If anything, this book had an even more profound effect on his worldview than Lindsey's debut diatribe. He seemed particularly struck by one of the Devil's nom de plumes that was new to him, the meaning of which warranted an entire section of *Satan Is Alive etc.*:

Satan's second title is "prince of the power of the air." Before a person becomes a Christian, he is spritually dead and ruled by this prince . . . Satan is said to be the prince and power behind the atmosphere of the thoughts of this world system that are hostile to God. Before we believe in Jesus Christ and are born spiritually, we are unwittingly dominated by this atmosphere of thought. As "prince of the air," Satan rules over the thoughts of the world system. He originated the concept of brainwashing long before human rulers used it to manipulate prisoners of war. In this role Satan injects his treachery into the educational system, the philosophy, the mass media, the arts, the style, and the culture. He will use a lake of truth to disguise a pint of poison. His deceptions about life and its purpose are lethal. Any flirting with the ways of the world can lead to spiritual adultery (James 4:4). When we think that he is the ruler over all of these thought forms and realize the ways in which we are bombarded every day by these sources, we begin to see how deadly the world system can be. At the same time we begin to understand the importance of the promise of 1 John 5:4: "For whatever is born of God overcomes the world; and this is the victory that has overcome the world—our faith. And who is the one who overcomes the world, but he who believes that Jesus is the Son of God?"

Again, one doesn't have to look far to find an onstage equivalent from Dylan, delivered to believers and nonbelievers alike from the last carriage of the holy slow train. This time he was in Buffalo, New York, in April 1980, and once again the cameras were rolling (Ron Kantor shot the concert from onstage, up close and personal):

How many of you out there know that Satan is called the God of this world? Prince of the power of the air? He's a spiritual being. How many of you do know that? Anybody? Now Jesus Christ defeated that power at the Cross. Who knows that? These are dangerous times. A lot of people think Jesus was just some kinda meek person who

came around on Earth and they hung Him for being so meek. But that's not true . . .
Sometimes [when] I go on and on, they say "Bob, don't preach so much." Anyway, Jesus
did say, blessed are those that mourn for they shall be comforted. [Except] it doesn't say
exactly that. It says, "Blessed are those that mourn for only they shall be comforted."
Some Bibles say, "Blessed are those that hunger and thirst after righteousness for they
shall be satisfied." But it really means only they shall be satisfied. Now He says all these
things. [Yet] if Satan is the God of this world, all these things don't seem too strong and
true. They don't seem to be good principles to live by because Satan doesn't like that.
We're talking about Satan now as a spiritual being. He's not somebody you can see, but
he can possess you.

Even when Dylan no longer felt that the stage was the right forum for
proselytizing his newfound faith, he was prepared to use the same printing presses
Lindsey himself had requisitioned, informing a skeptical editor that Satan is only
too real during an August 1981 *NME* cover story:

Bob Dylan: People don't know who the enemy is. They think the enemy is
something they can see, and the reality of the enemy is a spiritual being they can't
see . . . You would think the enemy is someone you can strike at and that would
solve the problem, but the real enemy is the Devil. That's the real enemy, but he tends
to shade himself and hide himself and put it into people's minds that he's really not
there and he's really not so bad . . . The struggle against oppression and injustice is
always going to be there, but the Devil himself is the one who creates it . . . [But] I can't
beat the Devil. Only God can. He already has.

The false messiah was to remain a theme in Dylan's songwriting long after his
so-called evangelical phase, being captured most appositely on his 1983 composition,
"Man Of Peace," a song he was still singing on the Never Ending Tour and a subject
he directly referenced in a September 1985 interview with Bob Brown:

Bob Dylan: There is a lot of false prophets around . . . That's the trouble, people say
they think they know what's right, and other people they get people to follow them
because they have a certain type of charisma. And there's always people willing to
take over, you know. People want a leader—and there'll be more and more of them.

As late as 1991, Dylan was still doing battle with the great deceiver and
still talking about "two kinds of thoughts in your mind . . . good thoughts and

evil thoughts . . . Some people are more loaded down with one than another. Nevertheless, they come through. And you have to be able to sort them out, if you want to be a songwriter."

Not surprisingly, the Devil played a leading role in several of the songs Dylan was writing in the winter of '79. Of these, "Trouble In Mind" seemed to Paul Williams, "easily the most naked of Dylan's recent songs . . . seem[ingly] a catalog of the singer's own troubles, his fears, guilts and doubts,'" save that it turned out they had all been planted there by a spiritual being:

> Satan whispers to ya, now I don't wanna bore ya
> But if you get tired of that Miss So-and-So,
> I got another woman for ya.

In January 1979, he remained a songwriter, first and foremost—even if most of the songs he felt impelled to write drew directly from a particular saying he had been shown in school:

"Gotta Serve Somebody"—And if it seem evil unto you to serve the Lord, choose you this day whom ye shall serve. [Joshua 24:15]

"I Believe In You"—Unto you it is given in the behalf of Christ, not only to believe in him, but also to suffer for his sake. [Philippians 1:29]

"No Man Righteous"—As it is written, there is none righteous, no, not one. [Romans 3:10]

"When You Gonna Wake Up"—Be watchful, and strengthen the things which remain, that are ready to die: for I have not found thy works perfect before God. [Revelations 3:2]

"When He Returns"—For yourselves know perfectly that the day of the Lord so cometh as a thief in the night. [Thessalonians 5:2]

"Ye Shall Be Changed"—In a moment, in the twinkling of an eye, at the last trump: for the trumpet shall sound, and the dead shall be raised incorruptible, and we shall be changed. [1 Corinthians 15:52]

Here are the core songs of his conversion, and each appears to date from the weeks of daily Discipleship. Yet two of these songs would not even make the first gospel album. "No Man Righteous" would be passed over because Dylan was never entirely happy with the studio versions, while "Ye Shall Be Changed" was largely a synopsis of chapter 11 of *The Late Great Planet Earth*, called, ironically, "The Ultimate Trip" and dealing with the Rapture. Its sentiments were disturbing, nay certifiable, even for a new convert.

It may well be this song to which Dylan was alluding in 1984 when, talking to fellow Christian Bono about *Slow Train Coming*, he admitted, "I've written some songs that [frightened me]. The songs that I wrote for the *Slow Train* album did that . . . I didn't plan to write them . . . I didn't like writing them, I didn't want to write them."

He'd certainly never written a song like "Ye Shall Be Changed" before, one mired in the fantastical notion that true believers will be taken up to heaven when the Pangs of the Messiah begin. If he shied away from revealing these thoughts on album, and never played "Ye Shall Be Changed" live, his thinking carried on along similar lines well into the eighties:

Bob Dylan: All that exists is spirit, before, now and forever more. The messianic thing has to do with this world, the flesh world, and you got to pass through this to get to that. The messianic thing has to do with the world of mankind, like it is. This world is scheduled to go for 7,000 years. Six thousand years of this, where man has his way, and 1,000 years when God has His way. Just like a week. Six days work, one day rest. The last thousand years is called the Messianic Age. Messiah will rule. He is, was, and will be about God, doing God's business. Drought, famine, war, murder, theft, earthquake, and all other evil things will be no more. No more disease. That's all of this world. What's gonna happen is this: you know when things change; people usually know, like in a revolution, people know before it happens who's coming in and who's going out. All the Somozas and Batistas will be on their way out, grabbing their stuff and whatever, but . . . they won't be going anywhere. It's the people who live under tyranny and oppression, the plain, simple people, that count, like the multitude of sheep. They'll see that God is coming. Somebody representing Him will be on the scene. Not some crackpot lawyer or politician with the mark of the beast, but somebody who makes them feel holy. People don't know how to feel holy . . . People are going to be running to find out about God, and who are they going to run to? They're gonna run to the Jews, 'cause the Jews wrote the book. [1985]

For Dylan, as for most Jews, the restoration of Israel held particular resonance. The son and grandson of Jewish emigres from East European pogroms at the turn of the century, he had visited Jerusalem's Wailing Wall in 1971 as he turned thirty, and so naturally found solace in the idea, propogated by Lindsey, that Jesus spoke for Jews and Christians alike. In 1989, Lindsey would suggest in his third millenialist potboiler, *The Road to Holocaust*, that he had been looking to a Judaic audience all along:

> In writing *The Late Great Planet Earth*, I had the Jews constantly in mind. I prayerfully and deliberately sought to present my prophetic case in such a way that it would especially appeal to them. It has been published in more than fifty foreign editions and has been instrumental all around the world in bringing tens of thousands of Jews to faith in Jesus as their Messiah. I run into them everywhere. They continue to write to me from virtually every part of the world. The first Prime Minister of Israel, David Ben Gurion, was reading it shortly before he died. Since everything in his room has been kept the way it was before he died, a copy of *The Late Great Planet Earth* remains on his desk. A friend of mine who is one of Israel's top military commanders passed out hundreds of copies of the Hebrew translation to the Israeli Defense Forces, even though he personally hasn't as yet believed in Jesus as the Messiah.

Another worrying contagion was an anti-Arab subtext to much of Lindsey's rhetoric, one which Dylan seemed to embrace, reflected in at least two 1979 raps. At the penultimate Warfield show, he prefaced "Solid Rock" by commenting on "the situation in Iran. The students rebelling. Even over here, they're rebelling. [I hear] they won't let the Iranian students into the whorehouses in Nevada now." It was a line he probably delivered with a wry grin, but this time he wasn't joking. Nor was he in any doubt as to who the infidels really were when he found himself back in San Diego:

> *If you read the newspaper, all kinds of terrible things [are] happening. People in Turkey [are] revolting; and Russians don't have any food, all that trouble in Ireland. And you certainly know about Iran. They got a funny bunch of people over in Iran. They got a religion called Muslims. But you know the Bible says, "Vengeance is mine, sayeth the Lord." So anything that goes against the Bible can't be all that together, right? But we don't care about any of that, we're not bothered by it, we're not dismayed. We know this world as we see it is going to be destroyed. Christ will set up His kingdom in Jerusalem for a thousand years; we know that's true.*

If the suggestion that even Muslims shall be judged on that dreadful day was a logical by-product of Lindsey's apocalyptic worldview, when it prompted a couplet like one in the newly-rewritten "Slow Train"—"Sheiks walking around like kings/ Wearing fancy jewels and nose-rings,"—it prompted howls of protest from liberal-minded reviewers.

Dylan was now drawing a line in the desert sand and the Arabs were on one side and recently converted Jews and Gentile Christians were massing on the other. As for himself, he had become changed from the selfish creature he once was, being baptized at the home of a Vineyard pastor or disciple (according to Al Kasha). One passage in *Satan Is Alive And Well On Planet Earth* was doubtless imprinted on his mind the day he was formally welcomed into what Larry Myers calls "the larger church, which includes all believers in Christ":

> Paul's exhortations to the believers to be filled with the Spirit [Ephesians 5:18], to walk in the Spirit [Galatians 5:16] and to walk by faith [2 Corinthians 5:7; Hebrews 11] all refer to the same principle of the believer coming to the conclusion that he can't live for God. He must trust the Holy Spirit to live the Christian life in and through him. For many Christians the realization that the Holy Spirit wants to and is able to live the Christian life through them is such welcome news that when they begin to experience victory instead of defeat, they are literally overwhelmed . . . The baptism of the Spirit is mentioned many times in the New Testament, but it is only defined in one place, 1 Corinthians 12:13: "For by one Spirit we were all baptized into one body, whether Jews or Greeks, whether slaves or free, and we were all made to drink of one Spirit." This verse simpy tells us that the baptism of the Spirit is that particular ministry of the Holy Spirit which joins us into a living union with Christ and His body, the Church. This happens to each person the moment he places faith in Jesus Christ as Savior . . . When a person is baptized in water, it is a public testimony of his faith that he was taken by the Holy Spirit at salvation and joined into living union with Jesus. This identifies him with Christ in His death, burial and resurrection (Romans 6). In the baptism of the Spirit, each believer, at the moment of his conversion, is totally identified with Christ in His death, burial and resurrection and with that one body which is Christ's body here on earth, of which He is the head (1 Corinthians 12). The ritual of water baptism is a symbol of the inner baptism of the Spirit which has already taken place at the moment the person was born again.

Three raps from May 1980 confirm that Dylan took his newfound responsibilities as a member of this "larger church" seriously. At the first of two shows in Akron, Ohio, he told the crowd, "The Devil's already been defeated. All you gotta do is accept it [and] be baptized with the Holy Ghost. You will have the power. I'm not talking about water baptism, I'm talking about the Holy Ghost baptism." The following night he was more explicit, explicating the distinction: "John the Baptist baptized with water. Jesus he baptized with fire and the Holy Ghost. If you ain't baptized like that right now, you just run out of here and get baptized like that."

A couple of days earlier, he had addressed a Pittsburgh crowd in similar terms, in what sure sounded like a public admission of his own baptism, "Once you get baptized that way, you've been baptized." By then, there was no doubt he had become imbued with "'the inner baptism of the Spirit," having devoted an entire album to his new relationship with Christ, one made when he was a fully-ticketed passenger on the holy slow train.

2. FROM SHEFFIELD TO SANTA MONICA
[March – August 1979]

"WHEN HE RETURNS" SONG TITLE

MUSCLE SHOALS SOUND STUDIOS

ARTIST Bob Dyla[n]

ENGINEERS

DATE 5/4/79

REEL NUMBER	TAKE NUMBER	LOCATOR NUMBERS	COMMENTS	
11				
	①	0-540	W/BAND	
	②	540-989	PB HOLD	
	③	1009-1490		
	④	1490-1670	↑PARTIAL	
	5	1686-1770	↑PICK-UP	
	6	1770-2093	"	
	⑦	2115-2300	↑PARTIAL HOLD	
	⑧	2300-2615	PICK-UP	

WHEN HE RETURNS (CONT.) SONG TITLE

MUSCLE SHOALS SOUND STUDIOS

ARTIST Bob Dy[lan]

ENGINEERS

DATE 5/4/7[9]

REEL NUMBER	TAKE NUMBER	LOCATOR NUMBERS	COMMENTS	
12	⑨	90-573	HOLD — (PULLED)	

Austin Scaggs: Am I crazy to love Street Legal *[and]* Slow Train Coming. . . ?
Bob Dylan: Not at all. I can play those songs, but I probably can't listen to those records. I'll hear too many faults. I was just being swept along with the current when I was making those records. [2004]

I found myself writing these songs and after I had a certain amount of them, I thought I didn't want to sing them, so I had a girl sing them for me at the time . . . Carolyn Dennis was her name. I gave them all to her and had her record them, and [did] not even put my name on them . . . I wanted them out, but I didn't want to do it, because I knew that it wouldn't be perceived in that way. It would just mean more pressure. I just did not want that at that time.

—BOB DYLAN TO BONO, 1984

If Dylan was already wondering whether the revelation that he was a Christian "would just mean more pressure," he did not have to wait long to find out. As he later told Hilburn, he had consciously held off telling people for a short while: "I didn't want to reflect on the Lord at all because if I told people and then I didn't keep going, they'd say, 'Oh well, I guess it was just another one of those things that didn't work out.' . . . But I did begin telling a few people after a couple of months and a lot of them got angry at me."

When he did finally confide in those (he thought) knew him well, the reaction was, "like He was just another prophet . . . one of many good people. That's not the way it was any longer for me." Not surprisingly, the experience—surely the one alluded to in the first two verses of "I Believe In You"—drew him closer to fellow Christians like Helena Springs and Mary Alice Artes, who was for now still Queen Bee.

Dylan's publicist, the devoutly irreligious Paul Wasserman, clearly remembers Springs bringing "Dylan in to [see] a lot of gospel groups and things like that." He felt, "She was a little bit off her rocker . . . [with that] 'Jesus loves you'-type stuff." As a good Catholic girl but a non-Vineyard convert, she remained an independent Christian voice, like Carolyn Dennis.

As regards how long Dylan's fleeting notion of letting the latter record his new songs lasted, one can only speculate. But the fact that he set up a record label—Accomplice Records—in January 1979 suggests he was really looking to find the right rostrum for his former backing singers—not just Dennis, but also Springs, who had an album's worth of songs she had written with Dylan in the past year.

But opportunity would not knock for either Springs or Dennis for a while. They would be too busy rehearsing and recording with the whirlwind that was Dylan. By early March, he had decided not only to do the songs himself, but to live up to a promise to Jerry Wexler, the iconic Atlantic producer whose middle name was Soul, to let him produce the next album.

Dylan and Wexler had history, once ostensibly coproducing a Barry Goldberg album back in 1973, when rumors were rife that Dylan was about to sign to Atlantic. (Wexler later suggested Dylan was there but hardly coproduced.) And some time in 1978, Dylan had popped in—at least twice—to Cherokee Studios in LA, when Wexler was recording Etta James' comeback album, *Deep In The Night*, to confer with the producer:

Jerry Wexler: That afternoon in Cherokee. Bob told me he'd been writing on the piano. Since Dylan famously composed on guitar, I was intrigued. He walked over to the piano and played a series of chord progressions with the enthusiasm of a child. I thought it was great. Then, back in New York a few weeks later, Bob asked me to produce his next album . . . Naturally, I wanted to do the album in Muscle Shoals—as Bob did—but we decided to prep it in LA

So does the timeline work here? Only partly. It was certainly not "a few weeks later" when Dylan reconnected with Wexler. The James album was in the shops before Dylan even embarked on his 1978 US Tour. But the meeting had set Dylan thinking about recording something more soulful—hence, presumably, his Nashville job interview with Regina McCrary.

To Dylan's mind, Muscle Shoals was probably still the studio Spooner Oldham fondly described to Joel Gilbert, when it was all "mono there. That meant as a piano player, I knew if I made a mistake and I had to stop, everybody had to stop. So you have to learn to make everything work—a mistake becomes a beautiful thing . . . [Dylan] liked [that] organized but spontaneous feeling."

Unfortunately for Dylan, Wexler didn't work that way any more. No one did. In fact, Jerry's latest project had been A&Ring and producing the second album from a bunch of English rookies who couldn't decide whether they wanted to sound like J.J. Cale or John Cale—those sultans of eastern swing, Dire Straits.

When *Communique* cracked it for the Geordie crew Stateside, Wexler hit on the outlandish idea of adding Mark Knopfler's guitar to the sweet soul sound he planned applying to his fellow Jew's harp, convinced that Knopfler's "subtle guitar mastery . . . would inspire and push Bob in a couple of different directions." It was apparently all part of a patented working method developed over many years:

Jerry Wexler: Occasionally I would bring in another player and [challenge] the other people there [at Muscle Shoals] to get what I call the aesthetic rub. Instead of three plus one equals four, you get an extra synergy. I said, "Bob, instead of the usual complement of players, I'd like to bring in a guitar-player called Mark Knopfler from Dire Straits." Sly ol' Bob says, "Yeah, he does me better than anybody." We were in LA, [so we] went to the Troubadour[sic][6] one night when Dire Straits were there, to see them perform, and we met Mark.

Convinced that Dylan knew who the hell this folically-challenged guitarist was, Wexler began to prep the awestruck novice, informing him, "Don't play Mark Knopfler, play Albert King." Whether Dylan ever shared Wexler's vision of Knopfler-does-King, he was content for now to go along with the producer's instincts. He later admitted on a 1985 radio show it was "Jerry [who] recommended him to play on that album . . . [So] I went down to see him and I thought he sounded sort of like me—not really, but a little bit."

Having damned the hot young guitarist with faint praise, Dylan proceeded to play Wexler and Knopfler songs full of praise—for the Lord. Up to this point Wexler insists he "had no idea what the content was going to be—[or] that it would be wall-to-wall Jesus! But I couldn't have cared less." Knopfler, though, was not so unfazed. That night he phoned his manager, Ed Bicknell, to confess real concerns, "All these songs are about God." He nonetheless threw in a few suggestions as to how these Godly songs might go:

Mark Knopfler: Bob and I ran down a lot of those songs beforehand. And they might be in a very different form when he's just hittin' the piano, and maybe I'd make suggestions about the tempo or whatever. Or I'd say, "What about a twelvestring?"

Also there at these informal sessions at Dylan's own studio was Barry Beckett—who had been Wexler's regular sidekick and coproducer for some time, and was a fine musician in his own right—as well as Tim Drummond, the solid rock on which Dylan would bass his touring band's sound for the next two and a half years:

[6] It was actually the Roxy, on March 29th, 1979.

Barry Beckett: Jerry . . . really didn't know what songs they'd been rehearsing until he got there. I didn't either. We hadn't heard the songs . . . So that [first] day I met him . . . we ran down the songs. Drummond was there, Mark Knopfler was there . . . Dylan was playing keyboards . . . Normally you would think he would play guitar, but he played keyboards, and he was writing in a different musical direction . . . The lyrics took on more of a blues phrasing . . . So he ran down "[Gotta] Serve Somebody" and when I heard those lyrics, I said, "Oh my goodness, this is great." [SM]

Also probably there at Rundown, if not that first day, was Helena Springs, who remembers, "We did the album first . . . He did most of the organizing and arranging of what he wanted to do, [but] we did a lot of rehearsing." Whatever "organizing and arranging" was required before the start of sessions—and there was only four weeks between Dylan meeting Knopfler and the first *Slow Train* session—by the time Dylan arrived in Sheffield, Alabama he had cut the songs to twelve—i.e. an album and a couple of B sides.

If the repository of Dylan papers in Tulsa, Oklahoma accurately reflects what Dylan had in his locker at this point, just two other songs were ever under consideration, "Am I Your Stepchild?," a nightly standout on the Fall 1978 tour depicting a decidedly unChristian woman, and "Ain't Too Proud (To Repent)."[7] Neither song would be Alabama bound, which was where Muscle Shoals Studio was located, and where a preapproved band of gold standard musicians were awaiting Dylan's imminent arrival.

As with all things Dylan, the dust of rumor about who was to play at the sessions, and what purpose they might serve, was already swirling around Sheffield. The Shoals' assistant engineer Scott Huffstetler "was under the impression that he wasn't really gonna do everything—just a few things." At least his bosses had explained Dylan "was coming into the studio to do this album that was gonna be 'gospel music.'"

Meanwhile, five thousand miles away, the gossip section for English music weekly, *Melody Maker*, seemed better informed about what was about to go down, reporting in mid-April that "the final details of the recording schedule have now been worked out, and [Mark] Knopfler and [Pick] Withers plus other musicians—including Richard Tee on keyboards—join Dylan in the studio for the first two

---

[7] It is possible that the tune to this "lost" Dylan song could be reconstructed. A song listed as "Ain't Too Proud To Beg"—which it most certainly isn't—was taped when an off-mic Dylan auditioned guitarist John Pechickjian in September 1979.

weeks of May, then take a break before starting the revised [Dire Straits] European tour on May 23."

If something evidently happened to fabled black pianist Richard Tee, who was probably putting the finishing touches to his solo album, *Strokin'*, the rest of the report proved spot on, down to timetabling "the first two weeks of May." The report even seemed to provide enough detail for a small gaggle of Dylan fanatics to congregate outside the studio, including, according to Huffstetler, "this really weird woman . . . [who] claimed she was his wife Sara Dylan, yet she had shoes that were completely worn out [and] had duct tape wrapped around her shoes and feet."

A relaxed Dylan seemed to take it all in his stride. As Huffstetler told Scott Marshall, "When they'd have a break on the sessions, he would walk up front, he would walk around. He wasn't a huge conversationalist, but . . . to come out of the studio, walk out front and [stroll] down to the river . . . was nothing for him."

Brian Stibal, the man who first documented the title track's birth, was among those waiting patiently, and he was able to "speak with him a couple of times there, and if his manner when we talked is any indication . . . *Slow Train Coming* promises to be a fresh, friendly and relaxed album." As it happens, Dylan's demeanor imparted not the slightest indication. The person on *Slow Train Coming*—according to one prominent reviewer, *NME*'s Charles Shaar Murray— "never seemed more unpleasant and hate-filled."

Ironically, CSM also felt the finished album highlighted the very "essence and core of Dylan's art . . . He's never sung more like Dylan than he does here . . . Every note, every phrase is either caressed or cuffed, spat out or thrown away, twisted and shaped for emphasis and irony . . . Far from having his wits addled by religion, Dylan would seem to have sharpened up his act all round." This seems to have been Dylan's—and Wexler's—intention: to dip a bitter liturgical pill in some southern musical molasses:

Jerry Wexler: It was a meticulously produced studio record, because those songs had never been played out . . . Bob might run it down on piano or guitar, just singing and playing the background until we had a rough shape in our minds, then the Muscle Shoals band would start to play it. As soon as it sounded right, Bob and the girls would start to sing. We'd just keep recording until we found the pocket. [1980]

But it would not prove the smooth sail Wexler's comments to *Rolling Stone* imply. In fact, for the first two days (April 30 and May 1), Dylan's working methods rubbed up against Wexler's plans for a smooth, slick record—i.e. the antithesis of all great Dylan albums.

Jerry Wexler: First day, Bob started to play on every take. In Muscle Shoals all they have are some chord charts [with] chord designations by number, until they get into it and play the inbetweens and the pickups and the turn arounds and the syncopation. [Then] you get the rhythm [which] equals pattern. [But] Bob was playing and singing on every one. I didn't know exactly what the protocol was gonna be, [so] we spent the whole day on one song. [JG]

That song was "Trouble In Mind," which needed eight takes, seven of them complete—at six-minutes-plus—the seventh of which was pulled to master for consideration as an album track—or, as it turned out, a single B side.[8]

The following day, there was more of the same. A version of "Precious Angel" came quickly, but would need a lot of fixing up before being deemed releasable; while "No Man Righteous (No Not One)" would occupy most of the six hours they spent in the studio on May Day, before take six got "pulled to master." By now, Wexler had reached a state of near despair, so much so that he confronted Dylan with the news, this just ain't working:

Jerry Wexler: We were staying at a rented house. I stayed there, too. And we played it back—rigor mortis. It was a disaster. Was this what Bob Dylan hired me [to do]? Come up with something like this? We sat down, had a little talk. . . . I finally convinced him to hold off on the vocals until later, when the arrangements were in shape and the players could play their licks around—not against—him.

When all the musicians convened at the studio the following afternoon, Wexler told everyone there had been a change of plan. He had been warned all along that "Bob was uncomfortable wearing headphones," and felt he had arrived at a solution. If the set-in-stone way of making a modern record couldn't be changed, the musicians themselves could meet Dylan halfway:

---

[8] An earlier take of the song, with Dylan leading the way on the piano and Knopfler barely to be heard, features on the *Bootleg Series Vol. 13*.

Jerry Wexler: I had everybody [sit] on the floor, all playing together [in a circle]—no booths, no separation, it's leakage [city], nothing you could ever record 'cause everybody is into everybody else's microphone, but I had an engineer record it on a quarter-track [tape]. We got the first song. In a very short time, they find a pocket, they hit a groove. We stop that. We send them all back into isolation [booths], isolated the amps, put the [head]phones back on and played back what they had just played. They played it a few times with the phones [on], then I took the track out of the phones—take one. They had found the pocket. We made four songs that day. Did you ever hear of anything like that?! It was invention on the spot. [JG]

They cut three songs on May 2nd—"When You Gonna Wake Up," the apposite "Gonna Change My Way Of Thinking" and "Ye Shall Be Changed," with the first two then pulled to the album master reel/s. Everyone was relieved. The following day the roll continued, successfully capturing a reworked "No Man Righteous (No Not One)," "I Believe In You" and the title track.

But Wexler's coproducer, Barry Beckett, still wasn't happy, feeling that "there were a few things we needed to correct." He finally turned to Wexler and said, "We've got to do something about that guitar sound, and mix it [so] we can hear the vocal." Though it is unclear whether he meant Dylan's or Knopfler's guitar, it was probably Knopfler who had to be turned down in the mix so the vocals sat centerstage. And when they did, Beckett—never a huge fan of Dylan's work—was blown away:

Barry Beckett: The sound of his voice wasn't fantastic. It didn't have to be. It was just the way he phrased it . . . the way he had of taking that lyric and making it mean something, according to the phrasing. [SM]

The coproducer had discovered something it had taken as great a technical singer as Tony Bennett to articulate. Asked once if he thought Dylan could sing, the crooner replied, "He may not be able to sing, but he sure can *phrase*." And if Beckett was impressed by Dylan's vocal technique, backing vocalist Helena Springs "was completely impressed with Barry Beckett's contribution to the album, [which] was much more than he had been given credit for. Actually, I think it was much more than Jerry Wexler's."

Apparently, Beckett ended up playing the piano part on the album's devastating closer, the apocalyptic "When He Returns"—and it was probably him who persuaded Dylan to do the song solo in the first place, after an initial attempt to record it with the band failed to inspire.[9]

In a footnote to a laudatory *Rolling Stone* review of the album, Jann Wenner claimed, "According to Wexler . . . Dylan's intention [was] not to sing on the song at all, rather it was to be a lead ensemble by the otherwise backup female singers." After the attempt at a full band arrangement was scrapped, Dylan and Beckett (initially with Knopfler) set out to deliver a vocal tour de force and the perfect closer for an album which depicted a world on the brink.

In fact, the entire May 4th session was highly productive, perhaps because everyone now knew Dylan's idiosyncratic way of working well enough to adapt to ad hoc arrangement quickly, while there was still life there. The four songs that wrapped up proceedings on day five were "Gotta Serve Somebody," "Do Right To Me Baby (Do Unto Others)," "When He Returns" and, as light relief at the end of a long day, "Man Gave Names To All The Animals."

The last of these was one of just two songs on the final album where Dylan took advantage of the girlsingers he had invited to the sessions only for the trio to spend their time, as Regina wryly recalls, "sit[ting] there and wait for the songs to come back that had been recorded that day . . . [so we could] start creating background parts." This "children's song" he may not have originally intended to include:

Regina McCrary: Bob Dylan and Jerry Wexler weren't sure if they were even going to put that song on the record . . . At that time my son Tony was three years old . . . When Bob played "Man Gave Names To All The Animals" . . . my son was falling over on the floor laughing . . . Dylan looked over and saw how my son was laughing and he said, "I'm going to put that on the record."

So that was that—almost. Wexler liked to suggest, "We started Monday. Friday, Bob was out of there—back to New York, or wherever. We did a little sweetening, maybe some percussion, a little guitar. Mixed the record the second week. Done." But once again, Wexler is being a tad economical with the facts.

The overdub sessions began on the 5th, running to the 7th, and after a short break, concluded on the 11th. So they took as long as the actual recordings. Dylan was certainly in Sheffield on the 5th, 10th and 11th, conversing with Brian Stibal and friend on the 5th; having a war of words with Beckett on the 10th, and being

[9] The one time Dylan attempted the song with full band accompaniment, at a show in Cincinnati in November 1981, the results border on excruciating. A full band—probably instrumental only—arrangement was abandoned after a single take at Shoals. See chapter heading.

persuaded to do two vocal overdubs—to "I Believe In You" and "When You Gonna Wake Up"—on the 11th.

Of these, a disagreement about whether to use horns on a particular track was perhaps the most significant. It was the one moment when Wexler's coproducer elected to stand up to Dylan, for the good of the record:

Barry Beckett: I was conservative as far as suggestions. I wanted to make sure that I understood his style before I started interfering . . . [But] he was concerned about using horns . . . There was this song we used horns on, the idea was to strengthen the guitars, not [just] the use of horns per se. There was a sound I was looking for just to help the overall tone of the guitars. And he didn't understand. He thought I wanted to use horns for the sake of the sound itself. And . . . I said, "Just please give me a chance with this. Let me try this." Jerry had to talk him into trying it, because I couldn't talk him into it. He was adamant against using any horns. [SM]

Adding horns to "Slow Train," "When You Gonna Wake Up" and "Gonna Change My Way of Thinking" on the 10th and 11th further sweetened the sound on three admonitory calls to repent and confess, applying a final aural coat to the Shoals shuffle.

Their contribution to "Precious Angel" was more subtle, and less obviously required. Perhaps this was the song where Beckett was looking to "strengthen the guitars"—not that Knopfler needed any more bolstering in the mix. Indeed, a rough mix of the song (dated May 11) places drums and piano higher, perhaps in an attempt to subsume some of those Strait fills.

But the need for a lead track that would generate radio play seems to have led to a belated tweak—perhaps after Dylan's departure; possibly even after a dub of the song was sent to Roger Scott at London's Capital Radio in June to play on the radio, to hear how it fit that station's format.

Of somewhat greater significance was the decision—presumably Dylan's—to resequence the album. The ten-track rough mix which was sent to his New York attorney on the 11th, presumably for copyright purposes, appears to constitute a provisional sequence. It runs as follows:

Side 1: Slow Train/ Trouble In Mind/ Do Right To Me Baby/ Gonna Change My Way of Thinking/ When You Gonna Wake Up
Side 2: Precious Angel/ I Believe In You/ Gotta Serve Somebody/ Man Gave Names To All The Animals/ When He Returns

This works slightly better than the final album. It begins with the title track, puts most of the Bible-bashers on side one, places the natural lead track as side two's opener while retaining "When He Returns" as album closer. It also includes "Trouble In Mind," perhaps the most personal song recorded that week.

Of the other two songs recorded, "Ye Shall Be Changed" never seems to have been under serious consideration, with neither of the two extant versions being pulled to master nor subject to overdubs. Indeed, the first take rather rambles and Dylan stumbles over the second bridge; while the second take—the one on *Bootleg Series Vols. 1-3* and *Vol. 13*—still sounds more like a pretender than a contender.

"No Man Righteous (No Not One)" is an entirely different matter. It was a song he spent most of the second day at Shoals working on, and even after he pulled a complete version to the master reel/s, returned to forty-eight hours later with an entirely new approach, which required Knopfler to overdub guitar and Beckett acoustic piano.

Though it was the latter version—with some Cooderesque slide guitar and a half-spoken vocal—which was originally due to appear on a four-disc *Bootleg Series* in 1991, the piano-driven version from May 1st was the one on the master reel when the album was sequenced, and should have got the vote, if only for the way he sings, "In a city of darkness there's no need of the sun."

As it is, there was never likely to be enough room on the record to include both—or as it turned out, either—"Trouble In Mind" and "No Man Righteous." So for the next thirty-eight years, fans were left with the choice of Jah Malla's cover version or an audience bootleg from the final Warfield '79 show, one of just two live performances on the gospel tour.

By omitting this message song—with its unambiguous couplet, "When I'm gone don't wonder where I be/ Just say that I trusted in God and that Christ was in me"—Dylan ensured that speculation about his personal theology, already rife in the media, would continue unchecked. Indeed, it was shortly after Dylan's return to LA in May, that his long-time publicist asked for a meeting to discuss this looming PR disaster:

Paul Wasserman: The whole press was printing the Christian story and I said, "Bob I got to have a meeting with you . . . I don't know how to handle it." He said, "Well, what's your problem?" . . . "I don't know how to deal with the press, who ask me questions about you and religion." He said, "Give me an example." "Well, Bob, are you a born again Christian?" And he looked at me and said, "What do you mean [by] born again?" [SM]

Once again, Dylan was determined to let the music speak for itself. There would be no public announcement, no press release to the effect that he had seen the light. Not that this stopped the speculation, or the *NME* coming up with surely the best headline of the ensuing silly season, "Dylan and God—It's Official," for a report which included Wasserman's account of his meeting with Dylan, described as "cryptic *even* for Dylan," during which the singer informed his employee that "all my albums have contained religious overtones," suggesting Wasserman should "get the first one."[10]

Just to muddy the waters further, the various international offshoots of CBS made their own minds up as to what constituted an advance single, with the US releasing "Gotta Serve Somebody" (a minor hit), the UK releasing the blazingly commercial "Precious Angel" (a complete flop) while France put out "Man Gave Names To All The Animals" (a major smash). All three would be backed by a slightly truncated "Trouble In Mind," trimmed of the final verse which wondered aloud, "How long must I suffer, Lord/ How long must I be provoked?"

He would not have to wait long to find out. The last week in August, the reviews started to roll in. It was a mixed bag even when given the benefit of nonbelieving doubt. Chris Bohn in *Melody Maker*—who still felt that *"Slow Train Coming* reeks of complacency, not contentment"—was obliged to admit that when Dylan "does . . . convince us of [his] humility . . . the impact is awesome . . . [And] Dylan's strongest affirmation comes in the splendidly sung final track, with the self-explanatory title, 'When He Returns.'"

Likewise, Charles Shaar Murray in *NME* was taken aback at the way "Dylan takes a severe, sulphurous Old Testament line on the New Testament, communicating little of the joy, warmth and salvation often found in Black American gospel music," but still had to conclude that if "Bobby has found God . . . neither of them are pissing about." Meanwhile, Hugh Fielder in *Sounds* gave the album five stars, and Dylan a metaphorical high five:

> You can argue the toss about Dylan's religious conversion until the cows come home but at least the man is being assertive once again . . . He's cut the crap and the innuendo and got down to what for him are the basics right now. [And] the religious element doesn't need to intrude more than you want to let it.

---

[10] A fair point, given the inclusion of "Gospel Plow"and "Jesus Make Up My Dying Bed," to give the latter its real title.

But the *Rolling Stone* review penned by the editor himself, Jann Wenner, took everyone by surprise. It came after the fortnightly rock bible consistently dismissed Dylan's best work of the Seventies with wide-of-the-mark reviews of *Pat Garrett & Billy the Kid* by Jon Landau, *Blood On The Tracks* by Dave Marsh and *Street-Legal* by Greil Marcus. Wenner, though, gave the new album a critical kudos Dylan never expected. Of course, he still couldn't stop himself from including, in an opening salvo of self-justification for his magazine's wayward critical record to date, a ludicrous assertion:

It takes only one listening to realize that *Slow Train Coming* is the best album Bob Dylan has made since *The Basement Tapes* . . . In the Seventies, Dylan's situation turned almost paralytic, both for himself and his audience. Five or six superb songs weren't enough to overcome this long, stagnant interval of doubt and reconsideration . . . [Now] Bob Dylan has, at long last, come back into our lives and times, and it is with the most commercial LP he's ever released. *Slow Train Coming* has been made with a care and attention to detail that Dylan never gave any of his earlier records . . . For the third time in his long career, Dylan has turned to a full-time producer . . . [because] once again [he] has something urgent to sing . . . Mark Knopfler tears into phrases and attacks with a fearsome skill, his licks . . . derived mainly from Albert King . . . At the urging of various personal friends, [Dylan] went to Bible-study classes led by a fundamentalist preacher. And, boy, without a doubt, this record is chapter and verse. The album's religious content is [all] pervasive . . . [But,] musically, this is probably Dylan's finest record, a rare coming together of inspiration, desire and talent that completely fuse strength, vision and art. Bob Dylan is [also] the greatest singer of our times. No one is better. No one, in objective fact, is even very close . . . More than his ability with words, and more than his insight, his voice is God's greatest gift to him. So when I listen to "When He Returns," the words finally don't matter at all . . . I am hearing a voice.

For once, a *Stone* review mattered. Wenner, like Fielder, had given the master interpreter an all-important thumbs-up; which was as much as Dylan could hope for, as he set about rehearsing for a series of shows which would remove all element of doubt as to his eschatological position, and would shake the very foundations of America's cultural consensus. His was a message formulated, or so Dylan now believed, before the foundation of the world.

3. LOVE & HAIGHT
[September 11 – November 1, 1979]

FROM: NAOMI SALTZMAN– BOB DYLAN'S OFFICE – NEW YORK CITY   *Arthur*

ARRANGEMENTS as of 10/11/79   SATURDAY NITE LIVE –10/20/79

TRANSPORTATION: Main group: coming from Los Angeles: American Airlines, Flight 40
PLANES   Leaves LA 10:00 a.m. – Arrives Kennedy 6:10 p.m. (OCTOBER 18)

                Others: Regina Havis– from Nashville: American Airlines, Flight 248
                Leaves Nashville 2:25 p.m.–Arrives LaGuardia 5:19 p.m. (OCTOBER 18)

                (Other people not coming in with main group will be announced)

TRANSPORTATION
FROM KENNEDY: Cars will be provided by Saturday Nite Live (Laurie Zaks).

                Jock McLean of CBS will also meet group. We have requested
                that provisions be made for an equipment case approximately
                60" long by 36" wide.

REHEARSAL BEFORE   Probably not possible Thursday night, but Jock McLean
SHOW: will hold space and match equipment neccessary for Saturday
                Nite Live performance at Studio Instrument Rentals for Thursday
                night. Arthur Rosato will coordinate with S.N.L. & C.B.S. & S.I.R.

HOTEL: Navarro Hotel, 112 Central Park South, New York, NY 10019
                Telephone : (212) 757-1900

SAT.NIGHT LIVE REHEARSALS
BEFORE SHOW: Probably Friday, October 19 at 11:00 a.m.; and any others to be
                advised by Jeanine Dryer of S.N.L.

REFRESHMENTS AT   S.N.L. will provide SOFT DRINKS, TEA WITH REAL LEMONS, COFFEE, FRUIT,
REHEARSALS & SHOW: AND CHEESE. NO ALCOHOL!

OTHER REQUIREMENTS: S.N.L. – At least 25 towels will be available and full length
                mirrors in all dressing rooms.

EQUIPMENT NEEDED: Arthur Rosato has made these requests directly to Jeanine
                Dryer and has spoken with S.I.R. He will also advise Jock McLean.

OTHER REQUESTS :   A minimum of two video cassette copies to be given to Naomi
                Saltzman for Bob Dylan.

SONGS TO BE PERFORMED: 1. GOTTA SERVE SOMEBODY
                          2. to be advised
                          3. to be advised

ADMISSION TO PERFORMANCE: 20 tickets to be provided to B.D. Naomi Saltzman will give
                Laurie Zaks a list; hopefully by Friday 10/19/79.

CUE SHEETS & CREDITS: To be discussed with Jeanine Dryer

UNION CONTRACTS: To be signed by all of group at S.N.L. 10/20/79. NS will
                be there to help handle Bob's and artists' agreements.

CONTACTS:	NAME	COMPANY	OFFICE#	HOME#
	NAOMI SALTZMAN or	BOB DYLAN OFFICE	(212) 473-5900	260-0667
	DIANE LAPSON	NEW YORK CITY		233-1860
	BARBARA MOLDT	BOB DYLAN OFFICE	(213) 399-9105	
		LOS ANGELES		

Usually I put together bands that wouldn't be together otherwise, but this time it seemed like that this band is just born to be together with me.

*—*BOB DYLAN TO TIM BLACKMORE, JUNE 12, 1981

As the plaudits for *Slow Train Coming* began to roll in, Jerry Wexler was quick to point out, "We furnished Bob with a band. It was something that we projected and thought might work." And it had. But it was never going to be a long-term option, with Dylan just itching to get back on the road and spread the word. In fact, for much of the ten days it took to make the album, Dylan was—to his mind—just papering over some glaring sonic cracks. He had a sound in his head, and the one on the album was not it. He wanted more true grit, and went looking for a set of musicians who could extract it.

As always when operating close to the center of his creative fulcrum, key components of the sound were in his head and he had specific people in mind. The girls—or some girls—were a given, though Carolyn Dennis was temporarily unavailable. Nor would she share a stage with Helena Springs, perhaps seeing her as a rival for Dylan's affection.

As per, the sound Dylan wanted began with a beat. The rhythm section came first, as it did in 1965-66 and 1975-76, his two most inspirational tours to date, with Tim Drummond the one element of the Muscle Shoals sound Dylan definitely envisaged keeping, building a band from the bass up, as he had when Rob Stoner was his bandleader.

When it came to the perfect foil, both Drummond and Dylan wanted Jim Keltner, who had recorded with Dylan back in 1971 and 1973 and now made his living as the go-to LA session drummer. A famously reluctant touring musician, persuading Keltner to join the new revue would be Dylan's first task. Thankfully, he let the music do the talking:

Jim Keltner: Bob would say, "You wanna come down and play," and it was actually for auditions. I would go down and I would hang around and play, knowing that I wasn't going to do the tour, but I would go down just to have the opportunity to be around him. And then at the end of the day he would say, "Well, whaddya think?" And I'd say, "I can't really go on the road," and they'd move on and find a drummer. That happened at least a couple of times. [But] in '79, when the same thing occured, I went down again and I listened to the music and I heard the whole [of *Slow Train Coming*]. I went upstairs to Bob's room and knocked on the door. He answered and I said, "Listen! I'm aware of [where] you're going. Whatever you want to do, I'm with you." . . . I stayed with him for two and a half years.

The other foundation stone he put in place for "this band [that was] just born to be together," was someone Dylan had once known only from his contribution to songs as seminal as "Mustang Sally" and "When A Man Loves A Woman." When they shared the Shoals studio, he quickly realized how much organist Spooner Oldham brought to the whole vibe, and asked Drummond to put out feelers to see if this personally diffident musician wanted to join the caravan of souls:

Spooner Oldham: After they finished the album, I understand Bob said something like, "Well, I'm gonna need a keyboard player for this tour, [to play] this kind of music." Tim Drummond mentioned my name . . . so Bob called me and asked if I'd be interested in touring for a few weeks.

There was no mention of Oldham, though, at the end of July, when at least one music paper reported that Dylan was putting together "a new small band which might include Jim Keltner, Tim Drummond and Billy Cross." But Dylan had already discounted Cross. By September, he had a shortlist of more sympathetic guitarists—Cross having surely failed his own audition back in Miami, with the guitar solo on "Do Right To Me Baby." Three days of guitarist auditions, September 11-13, saw Dylan and the core trio run down a ragbag selection of songs with Fred Tackett, Wayne Perkins, Rick Ruskin and the mysterious John Pechickjian—in that order:

Fred Tackett: Tim recommended me as someone to check out. [He] and Jim Keltner, the drummer, and Spooner Oldham, the great piano player, were [already] rehearsing with Bob. They were playing with a lot of different guitar players.

In all likelihood, Tackett was always Drummond's preferred choice. For the luckless Perkins—who had not only auditioned for the post-Taylor Rolling Stones back in 1975, but ended up playing on the better half of their 1976 album,

Black & Blue—it was another near miss. For Rick Ruskin, who had played with
the Reverend Gary Davis, the session proved particularly daunting. Dylan not
only played the *Slow Train Coming* songs—which he could have prepped for—
but would also run down "No Man Righteous" and "Ye Shall Be Changed," which
required radar.

But it was the final auditionee, the largely unknown John Pechickjian, who
ended up in pole position. During the lengthiest of auditions, Dylan tried every
which way to trip the young tyke up—attempting a song he never finished, "Ain't
Too Proud To Repent," and at least three new songs which were still works in
progress: "Covenant Woman," "Blessed Be The Name" and "Hanging On To A
Solid Rock." He was even expected to play along on a couple of half-formed song-
ideas: "Chosen To Follow" and "Holy Land."

Dylan was wholly disinterested in running down any pre-*Slow Train* songs
with any of these potential new recruits. Evidently, Dylan was pressing on. As it
is, when rehearsals began in earnest twelve days later, Pechickjian was installed as
the new guitarist.

Strangely enough, one guitarist who was not auditioned in any shape or form
was Dave Kelly, a blues guitarist who was already on Dylan's radar having "worked
as a producer on at least three gospel albums on which Tim Drummond had
played bass." Kelly, a fellow Christian, soon became an integral part of the setup,
without ever being considered for the band itself. To Dylan's mind, he served an
equally crucial function: personal assistant, which required not only a musical
background but a shared faith:

Dave Kelly: I was involved in . . . the Vineyard Fellowship with Master Ken
Gulliksen . . . He wanted somebody that would go on the road that understood the
kind of thing he was going through, 'cause he was surrounded by people who were
antagonistic to that kind of thing. So he wanted some buddies . . . and amazingly
enough, he had already heard of me . . . So he knew that . . . I had a musical
background . . . I didn't know really what I was supposed to be. I was just told that
he needed someone he could talk and relate to for a while . . . So Bob said to me . . .
"Look, I need someone to talk to the guys, the crew and the band. Right now I
don't want to defend my faith; I don't want to have to explain to them what's going
on. So I want someone to be there and if need be, explain to them what's going
on." . . . I found out that Dylan's assistant was Arthur Rosato, who . . . was the one
indispensable person around Dylan during this time. It seemed most people after
three or four months got fired. I don't think Dylan likes having people around a

long time. He likes to keep it fresh with new people. But Arthur was always with him. And Arthur was one of the people Dylan wanted me to talk to. Arthur didn't understand what was going on . . . So I would talk to him a bit about Dylan's faith.

However changed the new Dylan had become, it seems he never considered putting together a band of fellow believers. In fact, he seems to have gone out of his way to recruit musicians on strictly musical grounds. His faith had not scrambled his mind such that he couldn't see the need to provide a musical epiphany first.

As a result, some of the more skeptical musicians would roll their eyes behind Dylan's back at some of the goings-on; bandleader Drummond seems to have been the chief mischief-maker. As Kelly suggests, "He was [often] really sending it up when Bob was out of the room." Journalist Harvey Kubernik also remembers hanging out with Drummond at the November Santa Monica shows, when he commented, "The Priest on the tour['s] arriving . . . We call him the God Bother."

Dylan was not oblivious to the way Drummond delighted in his own unregenerate sinner status. One night in Seattle he sarcastically interjected into his nightly band introduction, "We're living on borrowed time. One of the first people to tell you that would be our friend on bass guitar, Mr. Tim Drummond."

But the boss knew only too well that the unbelieving bassist's contribution to his finest-ever touring band was without peer. Drummond also became key to whipping that band into shape in the six weeks Dylan had set aside before taking his potentially unpalatable message from place to place.

That a lot was going to be required of everyone became plain on day one: September 25th, 1979. No need to brush up on the Dylan songbook; Born-Again Bob intended to do an entirely new set, half of which would be songs no one knew—not even the man himself, who was still writing and rewriting verses, dropping lines and moving phrases around as rehearsals revved into gear.

To make the musical brew an even more unholy mix of sinners and saints, he constructed a band that was not just bass, drums, lead guitar, and keyboards, throwing three girlsingers and a horn section into the sonic stew. It was quite a musical melting pot for a man who generally liked to wing it, and was disappointed when any others failed to follow his lead.

But the last time he had attempted something similar—the "big band" *Desire* sessions back in June 1975—two entire days of sessions ended up scrapped and the eight-piece pub-rock outfit Kokomo were sent packing before Dylan stripped things down again. A similar change of heart would occur during these rehearsals but for now the entire gospel repertoire acquired balls of brass.

In those early weeks of rehearsals, Drummond, Keltner and Oldham would have to earn their stripes by keeping the other cadets in line. Of the others, only Helena Springs had any experience of working with the maverick musicmaker.

The first two days of rehearsal were a baptism by fire, Dylan throwing song after new song at the novice elements. It really was a case of sink or swim as Dylan introduced an album's worth of songs just as soundman Arthur Rosato finally fired up the Otari on the 26th. The Otari would also be put through its paces, providing a unique document of Dylan's working methods one cassette at a time.

Cassette dubs would be made of all the new songs, to be sent to New York for copyright purposes. However, these were only ever reference recordings, which meant the results were usually dubbed to cassette and the original eight-track tape reused. As a nod to the basement tape aesthetic, he only ran tape when he felt they could do the song whole. This was not Twickenham film studios and Dylan was not looking to let it be:

Arthur Rosato: I operated the tape and mixed the sessions. I was an audio engineer for Bob and The Band when I first started working with him, so it was in my background. We usually taped any arrangement that was complete—not to say that we edited anything, but I would roll tape whenever it seemed like an arrangement was close. The purpose was to have a record on something other than someone's boom-box recording. We always transferred the songs, no matter how close to the actual finished version, to cassette. At that point it was out of my hands. Barbara Moldt may have transcribed them or just sent them to New York for transcription.

Fortunately, the last of the true believers had hit a vein of songwriting as rich as the one he struck in the Big Pink basement. On the very first day of these get-down-to-it rehearsals, three of the songs were dispatched to lawyer Naomi Saltzman to file the requisite copyright registration—"In The Garden," "Blessed Be The Name" and "Stand By Faith." All three were based on epithets from the good book:

"In The Garden"—Being born again, not of corruptible seed, but of incorruptible, by the word of God. [1 Peter 1:23]

"Blessed Be The Name"—Blessed be the name of God for ever and ever: for wisdom and might are His. [Daniel 2:20]

"Stand By Faith"—Because of unbelief they were broken off, and thou standest by faith. [Romans 11:20]

Of the three, "Stand By Faith" was most promptly forgotten. Indeed, it sounds like the impromptu clapalong call-to-convert its title suggests—a Southern Baptist take on 1973's "Rock Me Mama" (on which Keltner had played). The last song of the day, it was never done again. Oddly enough, he did not copyright the song preceding it. Another seemingly impromptu example of Bob and the girls trading lines, "I Hear Jesus Calling" possibly had more promise yet became another lost teenage prayer.

"In The Garden" and "Blessed Be The Name" were both cut from hardier cloth. Both would feature in the live set, the former at every show in the gospel years and beyond; the latter on almost every show through February 1980, without ever being committed to record, replaced in the end by the turgid "Are You Ready?" Which is a shame, because "Blessed Be The Name" was precisely the type of song critics accused Dylan of no longer writing, a joyous paean to the Lord above.

With "In The Garden," Dylan finally wrote something that shaped a crucial part of the gospel narrative into a message-song which was both evangelical *and* redemptive. He later expressed amazement he could have written something so much like "a classical piece. I don't know how in the world I wrote it, but I was playing at the piano, closed my eyes and the chords just came to me. I can hear it being played by a symphony orchestra or a chamber choir."

Even if he felt the song had come direct from above, this seems to have been one of those lyrics he ran past the pastor he had been assigned by the Vineyard Fellowship, who wished to ensure he stayed in the scriptural straitjacket they had stitched for him:

Ken Gulliksen: He shared his music with Larry Myers, one of the pastors who had originally ministered to him. I freed Larry to go with Bob as much as possible. Bob asked him to come with the band on the road, so that Larry would be there to lead them in prayer and Bible study, and to minister to him personally. He and Bob became very close, and trusted each other. Larry was often the backboard for Bob to share the lyrics.

As long as Dylan continued to live and love in LA, he was at the mercy of Myers. So he spent much of the summer in the Midwest. While his record label again scratched its collective head on how to market their favorite maverick, he was in quiet seclusion on the Minnesotan farm where he had previously written the bulk of *Blood On The Tracks* and *Street-Legal*. Now he was using his remarkable poetic gift in the service of Christ. And verily, the songs poured forth as if he did indeed have a direct line to his Maker.

So productive had he been in the summertime that he had two more song-ideas he wanted to show the band on the 26th, both of which showed a great deal of promise as and when Dylan finished the lyrics. "Covenant Woman" only had dummy lyrics, while "Ye Shall Be Changed" was a reimagining of the song he had recorded for *Slow Train Coming*, with a new melody and chorus: "In the twinkling of an eye/ When the last trumpet sounds/ The dead will arise/ and step out of the ground."

For all the death and damnation that still suffused many of the songs, Dylan was clearly having a blast. As someone who never learned how to sing within himself even at rehearsals or soundchecks, near the end of the day he ran down five *Slow Train* tracks with his new band. Every single take had an inner fire that made the album versions sound like someone had been pulling back on the reins. And playing a full part was new guitarist John Pechickjian, whose contribution to the title track alone suggested a young Robbie Robertson.

Dylan had a different texture in mind, though, and two days later, when rehearsals resumed, Pechickjian had been put out to pasture. Tackett stepped in to fill the void after Drummond, acting as Dylan's designated foreman, offered his own musical opinion. Although Dylan decided to defer to Drummond, there were still some hoops his friend would have to jump through before he got the gig:

Fred Tackett: Tim Drummond and Jim Keltner were real close friends and I worked with them a lot on other people's albums, and they were just auditioning guitar players . . . and they called me up to come down there . . . We just kept going down there in Santa Monica, where Bob had a studio. We were rehearsing and he was getting ready to be on *Saturday Night Live* . . . Finally, just about two days before, Bob calls me at home and says, "Well, I want you to come and do this tour with me." I said, "Sure. Have your manager call me up and we'll talk about the money." Bob goes, "I don't have a manager." . . . So next day, after rehearsal, we had to go into his office and talk about money . . . He said, "Well, what do you get?" "Well, Bob—" I said. He goes, "Shhhh." So I have to whisper . . . "Well, see Bob,

I normally get blah blah blah . . ." And he would pull away and look at me, like, "WHAT! Are you kidding me?" . . . It was like all designed to make me squirm. I [finally] got the job, worked with him for about three years and it was just really a great deal. But I got it just by going down and playing with him for three weeks—until he had to hire somebody.

In fact, Dylan knew he was going to retain Tackett's services pretty quickly. He just wasn't about to let him know what they were rehearsing for, or how long he had signed up for. From this point forth, Dylan had the team he needed to weave his new tapestry, after Mona Lisa Young was drafted in to deputize for Carolyn Dennis and her husband Terry assumed the musical director role. It was quite a band, and hang the cost.

Tackett's first day, September 28th, saw another lengthy rehearsal. Dylan nonchalantly chucked song after unfamiliar song at his chosen musicians, rarely losing them. First up was "Hanging On To A Solid Rock," Dylan trying a number of tempos and grooves, and at least one verse dropped from the song before its live debut: "One law for the flesh/ One law for the spirit/ No one can drink from two cups/ No one said, it's easy not to slip up."

After such frenetics, they slowed things down on a run through of "Covenant Woman" with all the verses in place but Dylan calling out the chord changes to the band. Here was a song directly inspired by the chapter and verse he later quoted on the *Saved* sleeve, "Behold, the days come, saith the Lord, that I will make a new covenant with the house of Israel, and with the house of Judah." [Jeremiah 31:31] It was already a keeper, whose stature would only grow throughout the rehearsal process.

But not everything worked as well, at least to Dylan's mind. A series of attempts to recast "Ye Shall Be Changed" failed to convince him it would suit the forthcoming salvation ceremonies. The few new, intelligible lines suggest the song is now directed at a former unbeliever, who is traveling "on a morning train/ going nowhere again," unaware that he "will die" or that "God is mighty and He rules from on high."

The new melody is gorgeous and Dylan did not give up on the song entirely, but he had another major new song he wanted to spring on his vital new band. "What Can I Do For You?," a song of deep humility, was inspired by a line from Job [5:7], "Yet man is born unto trouble, as the sparks fly upward." Dylan had evidently already shown the basics to Oldham, who counterpoints Dylan's idiosyncratic riffing as the rest of the band do their best to pick up their cues.

For now it's still swimming in lava, with only its supplicatory refrain as a raft. They will not return to the song for another fortnight, by which time Dylan will have finally found the words to say, "I am your servant, Master." Instead, he resumed work on "Ye Shall Be Changed," a song two girlsingers last heard in Muscle Shoals, when it used to go like that. After a brief pause, he revisited "Solid Rock," "Blessed Be The Name" and "In The Garden," none of the trio quite catching fire the way they had two days earlier.

Yet Dylan was not done for the day, or inclined to stop springing surprises on the put-upon players. Reclaiming the piano stool, he plonked out a simple but effective set of chords while coaxing the girls into sharing another highly evocative refrain, "I'm pressing on to the higher calling of my Lord." ("I press toward the mark for the prize of the high calling of God in Christ Jesus" [Philippians 3:14].) The effect was immediately uplifting.

After just two serious days of rehearsal, the auguries were propitious. They needed to be. Dylan had convinced himself he could sell out a handful of shows in Texan arenas, scheduled to take place in just three weeks' time. Presumably, he planned to relive the triumph of September 1965, when he had breezed into Austin and Dallas with The Hawks to play two sell-out shows on the back of forty-eight hours' rehearsal, garnering great reviews and kick-starting the most momentous tour in rock history. But this was not 1965, and *Slow Train Coming* was not *Highway 61 Revisited*, and Dylan gave in to the inevitable.

By month's end, *Rolling Stone* were reporting that "Dylan had reportedly booked a fall tour of the US but then canceled all but the San Francisco dates. Tickets for one show—on October 18th in Houston—went on sale but were then withdrawn . . . [allegedly] because of lack of ticket sales. A spokesman for Concerts West . . . [insisted] the concert was canceled because it conflicted with Dylan's *Saturday Night Live* performance."

In fact, tickets for the 12,000-seater Tarrant Convention Center in Fort Worth had also gone on sale, before it was also canceled. Already the question Lynne Allen had asked Dylan in December hung like the sword of Damocles: Could he tour again so soon and with such a contrary message, and sell out arenas?

A rethink was required—not least to allow time to refine the set. Rehearsals resumed on October 2nd with a return to some of the *Slow Train* songs. Perhaps startling new arrangements, with a horn section reinforcing the messianic message with blasts of brass on "When You Gonna Wake Up," "Slow Train," "Gonna Change My Way of Thinking" and "Precious Angel," could help sell out those arenas.

Certainly the effect was positively transformative. For the next ten days Dylan would focus on working up arrangements which allowed the brass to complement the basic band, who were still looking for a way into the new songs themselves. Not surprisingly, the results included a couple of car crashes.

Attempts to shoehorn the brass into "Covenant Woman" and "Pressing On" were accidents waiting to happen. Thankfully, the *Slow Train* songs—even those not so embellished at the Shoals sessions—were markedly improved by some extra musical muscle. Versions of "Slow Train" and "Gotta Serve Somebody" (both on *Bootleg Series Vol. 13*) show a Dylan rising to the occasion, snapping into the lines with a gusto that had as much to do with the joy of making music as the fervor of faith. Equally infused with the cup of inspiration were "Gonna Change My Way of Thinking" and "When You Gonna Wake Up," both of which needed all the help they could get to browbeat would-be believers.

Yet after this exhilarating day, there was a six-day break before rehearsals—or the recording of rehearsals—resumed. By now Dylan was ready to apply a layer of brass to "Solid Rock" and "Blessed Be The Name," two songs which seemed to naturally lend themselves to affirmative horns. Indeed, it looked like Dylan intended to make the horn section work for their supper, as almost every song got staves of brass.

New songs of salvation continued to pour forth as rehearsals remained unencumbered by "old songs." As Dave Kelly informed Chris Cooper, Dylan might "jokingly go into old songs at the end of the day, [just] not his [own] stuff ... He wouldn't sing them, he'd just play twelve-bars and stuff like that. But he did write an awful lot of [new] stuff and he did try them [all] out. There must have been twenty songs that he pooled from to do the tour . . . He'd go into his little room and come out with a new song."[11]

Sure enough, when he returned to rehearsals, it was with something called "Knockin' On The Door (Calling)," a first cousin to "I Hear Jesus Calling." The following day, he again tackled the recast "Ye Shall Be Changed," only to decide it would remain on the backburner; and on the 10th, he resumed asking "What Can I Do For You?"

It was now ready to take its place on the rostrum, just not with the trumpets of Jericho, even as Dylan daubed "Pressing On," "In The Garden," "Blessed Be The Name," "Covenant Woman" and "Solid Rock" with the same musical palette as the *Slow Train* songs. But just when it seemed Dylan had fallen in love with the horns, he pulled the rug away from under them. Due to fly to New York for an

---

[11] The one old song he definitely did at these rehearsals was an old folk song he revisited on a couple of occasions in 1981 with the band, "Barbara Allen" (Child Ballad 84).

all-important TV appearance, Dylan suddenly asked his personal assistant what he thought of the horns:

Dave Kelly: There was an intensive period of rehearsals beforehand . . . They started with a five- or four-piece horn section . . . They were supposed to go with the horns on one side and the girls on the other. He had percussionists—Ras Baboo, the Jamaican guy . . . [So] it was about a week before we went on the road. He actually sat down on a sofa . . . and said, "What do you think? The horns or the girls? . . . We can't have both. Financially, it's just ridiculous" . . . I thought the girls were adding [a lot] sing[ing] with him, where[as] the horns were not doing a lot. The next day I came in and there were no horn players. I don't think he did it because of what I said . . . All through the tour he did it with me, and lots of other people. [He'd] just bounce the idea off you that he's already got, and if you confirm what he thinks, then he does it.

If finance was a factor—which it must have been on what was going to be a theater tour—someone close by thinks his boss's primary concern remained a musical one. Listening back to a tape of the horns and girls, sans the singer, convinced the man missing that the horns merely increased the likelihood of a musical straitjacket:

Arthur Rosato: Bob doesn't write horn charts, so when the horns appeared he asked them to just play along. The horn players [we]re not used to doing that, so they scrambled trying to find parts and Bob was a little disappointed that they just didn't jam, as it were. So not wanting to make it a big deal, he just moved on.

When Dylan turned up to resume rehearsals, minus the horns, he immediately sprung another new song on the band, no longer having to think about another musical layer. "Saving Grace That's Over Me," his second song of supplication in as many weeks, suggested he was finally fusing two great pillars of his faith: the grateful servant and harbinger of doom. He even revisited a sense of his own mortality—"By this time I'd-a thought I would be sleeping/ In a pinebox for all eternity."

However, before they could really begin working up an arrangement for this plaintive prayer to his guardian angel, the whole band had to pack their bags and fly three thousand miles east to record Dylan's first national studio TV appearance in four long years, on the hit comedy show, *Saturday Night Live*. Having now canceled shows in Texas, it would be the only dress rehearsal to a fortnight of shows in San Francisco, and it was going out in front of twenty million viewers, making an already irascible Dylan nervous as hell:

Dave Kelly: He hated [*Saturday Night Live*]. All I heard for a week was how bad it was, and how terrible the people were there . . . I think his own personality clashed with them. They were such egotistical people at the time . . . I think his manager, Jerry Weintraub, pushed him into doing it.

It was bad enough that his own three songs—"Gotta Serve Somebody," "I Believe In You" and "When You Gonna Wake Up"—would be sandwiched between the usual skits and spoofs, MC'd for the evening by the iconic Python comic and coauthor of *Life of Brian*, Eric Idle. But then Dylan found out he was expected to run through the set no less than three times, each performance only serving to make Dylan progressively more uptight:

Spooner Oldham: The rehearsal for *Saturday Night Live* happened on the set. The way they did it back then was midafternoon you'd come into the studio so the cameraman could get a fix on where you're standing, and you actually played what you were going to do that night . . . Then you do it for a second time . . . later that same afternoon, and then the third time is the live one. [SM]

There had already been a full rehearsal the previous day at Studio Instrument Rentals, during which Dylan decided which two songs would accompany "Gotta Serve Somebody." So there was an awful lot of hanging around in the days between Dylan's arrival at JFK at 6:10 p.m. on Thursday, October 18th, and his departure from the same airport at noon on Sunday the 21st.

Which is perhaps why the actual performances on *Saturday Night Live*—which were indeed live, as Elvis Costello had previously proven—seemed a little stiff; a self-conscious Dylan forcing himself to deliver his first message-songs in a decade and a half to an expectant nation. The one song that scaled the heights was "I Believe In You," perhaps because he really did feel the *SNL* crew wanted to drive him from town. They sure didn't want the killjoy around, spoiling their fun.

As for Dylan, he couldn't wait to get back to LA to resume rehearsals. The decision to can the horns, made in the interim, meant he was up against it, getting the stripped-down songs into shape in a single week before opening night at the Warfield Theatre, which promoter Bill Graham had rescued from wrack and ruin.

Graham was also up against it just to get the place ready for the grand unveiling. As Dylan's tour manager, Dan Fiala, recalls, "The [Warfield] had literally been a movie theater, and they had to redo it to accomodate live shows. They had to put sound systems [in] and lighting and dressing rooms and all that stuff . . . to turn it into a music venue."

Meanwhile, Jerry Wexler turned up at Rundown to hear how the rehearsals were progressing. He had a vested interest, after all, having provisionally agreed to record the new songs once they were road-tested. According to Kelly, "Jerry Wexler [was] telling them they weren't ready . . . [But] they tried lots of different things. Bob was really in charge of that, he'd get the [band] to change the tempo, the style . . . He was even telling the girls how to sing." Dylan was also feeling the pressure to include some older songs—and from a most unexpected quarter, his pastor:

Larry Myers: I did assure him that I considered his old songs to be Truth songs, and that he should certainly feel free to sing them if he wanted. I personally felt that he should, but he chose to do what he wanted to do, pure and simple.

Graham, too, was pleading for "just one old song." But, as Fiala soon learned, "He doesn't really take artistic direction from anyone. All you can do is provide him with technical and financial information." Some things hadn't changed, and wouldn't change, conversion or no conversion. Deep down, he was still the same man. And no matter how much he was feeling the pinch, he didn't think twice about bringing yet another new song to the first post-*SNL* rehearsal, which was on the 23rd.

"Saved (By The Blood Of The Lamb)" was one song he had written which even the Shakers might have embraced, thanks to its hallelujah chorus and full tilt bass-led riff (contributed by Tim Drummond, who was rewarded with a co-credit). It also completed the new repertoire, Dylan slotting both "Saving Grace" and "Saved" into the set list before a full-blown runthrough on the 24th, in this order:

Gotta Serve Somebody/ I Believe In You/ When You Gonna Wake Up/ When He Returns/ Man Gave Names To All The Animals/ Slow Train/ Precious Angel/ Saved/ What Can I Do For You?/ Covenant Woman/ Gonna Change My Way Of Thinking/ Saving Grace/ Solid Rock/ Do Right To Me Baby

Also rehearsed that day, for the first time on tape, was the six-song opening set by the girlsingers, beginning with "If I've Got My Ticket" and concluding with

"This Train." The following day, it was more of the same: a runthrough of the girls set before Dylan reexamined the first half afresh. Only then did Dylan devote the rest of the day to working out the kinks in a born-to-boogie "Saved," two songs of confession—"What Can I Do For You?" and "Saving Grace"—and a stripped-down "Covenant Woman."

One last Rundown rehearsal, the day before they flew to San Francisco, rather than confirming the order of things, was a throwback to earlier rehearsals. Dylan spent precious time getting "Saved" up to speed and giving "What Can I Do For You?" harmonica bookends. He even threw the band one last curveball by attempting "No Man Righteous," an afterthought from the past, before wrapping up proceedings with the stately "In The Garden."

It was time to reveal the word of God before an audience of fans and critics on All Saints Day. Even before Judgement, though, Dylan was on the receiving end of one more rebuff. Checking into the York Hotel on Halloween, he received an unexpected premonition of the reception his new music was about to be accorded:

Dave Kelly: The night we booked into San Francisco, George Harrison was in that hotel . . . They have been the best of friends, but the minute Bob checked in, George checked out! . . . He actually ran away. Bob could not understand it.

The following morning, the whole band assembled at the theater to indulge in one last soundcheck before the curtain rose and the Titanic set sail. It would be their only sustained soundcheck, and it gave Dylan one last chance to work out the order of the show, which would give Neil Young's fabled Tonight's The Night Tour a run for its money in the "paid for your ticket so don't complain" stakes.[12]

If "Covenant Woman" was the only unreleased song in the first half, coming after seven consecutive *Slow Train* songs, the ninety-minute set concluded with five brand-new songs, all just as beholden to the Scriptures as those on the new album. Finally, an encore of "Blessed Be The Name" and "Pressing On" rammed home Dylan's new message:

Bob Dylan: In 1979 I went out on tour and played no song that I had ever played before live. It was a whole different show, and I thought that was a pretty amazing thing to do. I don't know any other artist who has done that, has not played whatever they're known for. *The Slow Train* record was out and I had the songs to the next

---

[12] Young famously performed a completely new show in autumn 1973, then encored with a song "you've already heard." It was the one he had opened the show with.

record, and then I had some songs that never were recorded. I had about 20 songs that never had been sung live before . . . Nobody seemed to pick up on that. [1985]

Dylan knew all too well that he hadn't confirmed in print or press release his closely guarded decision to play only songs written in the last twelve months. Sure, it was "a pretty amazing thing to do." It was also making a rod for his own back. Even at Newport and Forest Hills, he had met his fans halfway. Not now.

The reaction from the fans and critics on that first night would set the tone for six months of shows and define the likely critical reception when *Slow Train*'s companion album, *Saved*, was released the following June. Not for the first time, fans were left wondering. Certainly for the poor sinners in his band the first Warfield show was a baptism by fire the likes of which none of them would ever (want to) see again:

Fred Tackett: There were a group of people that were very upset, to put it mildly . . . I remember somebody had a sign that said, "Jesus loves your old songs, too!" [But] then, there were a lot of religious people that were really into it.

Tim Drummond: Bob stuck to his guns. I told him that I'd stay with him until the tits fell off the Statue of Liberty, after seeing what he went through. They were one degree short of buying fruit off the sidewalk and throwing it at him, throwing it at the stage.

Jim Keltner: The audience didn't know what to make of it. A lot of them were thinking it was going to be a typical Dylan show, and so they were all out there with their pot and ready to party, ready to rock 'n' roll, and so they would yell and scream. They'd holler at him, they'd curse. Right next to them would be a family, "Bob, we love you, we love your new music." It was the weirdest thing.

If in the beginning there was the word of God, then the word of mouth at the beginning of the Warfield residency would soon drown out any and all utterances from those who heard something remarkable developing across the next fortnight.

Dylan, having spent six weeks preparing meticulously for this moment, had set the agenda. But it was not the one the fourth estate had in mind. Indeed, as the man said from the same stage, a year later, "When we came here last year, we came in with a show and the newspapers, they distorted it, they slandered it." The experience would prompt a post-conversion "Positively 4th Street," "Yonder Comes

Sin" ("Jeremiah preached repentance to those who would turn from hell/ But the critics all gave him such bad reviews . . ."). He was about to find out just how Jeremiah felt, and what it was like to be a prophet without honor in his own land. And no one was offering to take his crown of thorns.

4. ROCK 'N' ROLL DOWN TO THE PIT
[November 1 – 16, 1979]

The Gospel according to Bob Dylan

Bob Dylan
Warfield Theater
San Francisco
November 1st, 1979
By Robert Palmer

THE NEW BOB Dylan tour began on a chilly Thursday evening at the Warfield Theater, a cozy 2200-seater in San Francisco's Tenderloin district. Outside, grizzled panhandlers solicited; holdout hippies, whose cassette players blared "Gotta Serve Somebody," tried to scavenge tickets; and dozens of porno theaters and sleazy topless

Dylan and his new group came on without a break, opening with "Gotta Serve Somebody." Their ninety-minute set consisted of the entire, *Slow Train Coming* album plus seven unrecorded songs in a similar vein, and while the unrelenting sermonizing grew tedious, the music was top-notch. The band — Fred Tackett on guitar, Spooner Oldham and Terry Young on keyboards, Tim Drummond on bass and Jim Keltner on drums — provided attentive backing in a Southern soul-gospel groove. Tackett's fingerpicking and lead-guitar fills were sensitive and fluid, Oldham and Young were appropriately churchy, and the rhythm section provided a tremendous kick. Given some time to play together and Dylan's open-ended

Bob Dylan's God-Awful Gospel

By Joel Selvin

These are strange times. Gas costs a dollar a gallon, someone built a pyramid in San Francisco. And Bob Dylan converted to Christianity.

The ironies flew fast and furious Thursday at the Warfield Theater, where Dylan took the capacity crowd by surprise with an opening-night performance composed exclusively of his singing praises to the Lord.

He never touched the likes of "Blowin' in the Wind," "Don't Think Twice," "Mr. Tambourine Man," "I Shall Be Released," "Just Like a Rolling Stone" or any of the many other songs that secured his fame and allowed him to sell out each of his 14 Warfield shows far in advance, with tickets scaled sky-high at $15 and $12.50 apiece.

The audience, given that, behaved with admirable restraint. Catcalls and boos, to be sure, echoed throughout the 2200-seat former vaudeville palace. But

San Francisco Chronicle

Keltner on drums, Tim Drummond on bass, Spooner Oldham on keyboards and Fred Tackett on guitar. Dylan rounded out the band with a four-member gospel group to provide background vocals. The three ladies in the group — Helena Springs, Regina Havis and six

Sounds 15-12-79

OH CHRIST IT'S DYLAN

BOB DYLAN
Fox Warfield Theatre, San Francisco

DYLAN has always been the master of changes, following his muse wherever it led him regardless of fashion. Resurrection however is more than a change. There's a depressing ring of finality to it. Dylan has swapped his muse for the Lord — the prophet becomes a servant, the poet a preacher.

Dylan isn't touring, just playing 10 dates at the relatively tiny Fox Warfield theatre in San Francisco (2,200 seats). Reasons unspecified. A special preview or maybe just a whim.

Outside the pavement swarms with evangelists with designs on your soul. Inside things ain't that different. When Dylan isn't singing about the personal significance of his rebirth, he's after your soul. Which induces the kind of h e m m e d - i n claustrophobia that results from being button-holed by a drunk who is determined to have you for a confessor.

Dylan has continually denied that he's a leader, continually refused to press a moral. Until now. With God on his side, he's dodging his duty if he does anything else.

The evening begins with the appearance of Regina Havis, one of three black gospel singers who back Dylan tonight. She begins to narrate the story of an old woman to the projection of the Lord. She breaks into gospel and the other ladies join in. They run through five gospel tunes of the 'Fire Next Time,' 'This Train' variety backed by a piano, handclaps, tambourines.

Baptism, fire and brimstone, fundamentalist American religion. The tone of the evening is set. The audience is familiar enough with the set-up to enjoy it even if they've come to see Dylan. Nobody will call out "Judas" tonight.

Dylan appears, dressed in leather jacket, accompanied by an L.A. studio band — Jim Keltner on drums, Tim Drummond, bass and band conductor, Spooner Oldham on keyboards and Fred Tackett on guitar. Tackett plays Mark Knopfler's solos from 'Slow Train' note for note. Competent enough, they are never allowed to stretch. Gospel is communal but Dylan insists on remaining centre star.

Which gives the evening a grim formality. He launches into 'You Gotta Serve Somebody.' Dylan doesn't smile all night. There's no sugaring of the dose.

There's not a single pre-'Slow Train' song. It's as if Dylan tied up the past in the Budokan album, looked at the size of it, gave it its due and then took the only total transformation train in the station. Reborn, his past is dead, the dog days of a sinner who's finally found the light.

All the new songs pursue the conversion further into Bible-belt territory 'What Can I Do For You?', 'Saved By The Blood Of The Lamb', 'Hanging Onto A Solid Rock Made Before The Foundation Of The World'.

Trouble is, in accepting Christ, Dylan's taken up the hackneyed language of fundamentalist religion. Both musically and lyrically he no longer uses religious themes they use him.

The tools of Dylan's trade are in excellent shape: the voice more dramatic. But the subject matter is narrowed, and gospel a groove that gets repetitive. Especially when it lacks joy. Dylan's religion is close to paranoia, with its tales of broken friendships and its finger pointing at the oddest targets from Arab oil sheiks to women who talk too much.

He performs all of 'Slow Train'. Halfway through he leaves the stage to Regina to sing 'The Man From Galilee'. 'I really wanna hear it so bad,' he mumbles.

Two encores, the last entitled 'Pressing On', with Dylan at the piano. He explains how you can't prove the Lord to unbelievers. 'How can you explain an experience within?'

It's a hook, line and sinker job. Faith is the oldest drawn line in the book and Dylan's crossed it.

He finishes standing centre stage chanting 'Pressing On' clapping his hands, eyes closed, looking uncomfortable. The audience are either accepting or confused.

I prefer the poet to the preacher but with Jesus on the mainline who needs fans? MARK COOPER

RECORD MIRROR

They always [repeat] something that's reported in the newspaper . . . It's always misinterpreted in some way. Like, the last show we had out was [called] some kind of gospel show. Well, it was—because most of my stuff, [okay,] all of my stuff, at that time was influenced or written right off the Gospel. But that was no reason to say it wasn't a musical show . . . They just [wrote about] one side and they forgot to say that it also had different aspects, rather than just [say I was] preachin' from The Bible. A lot of people may read something like that and say, "Wow, I can read my own Bible. I don't have to get it preached at me," you know. That's when they decide[d] not to come."

—**BOB DYLAN TO PAUL VINCENT, NOVEMBER 1980**

Bob Dylan: *I wanted to keep touring in '79. But I knew that we'd gone everywhere in '78, so how you gonna play in '79? Go back to the same places? . . . At that point, I figured, "Well, I don't care if I draw no crowds no more." [So] a lotta places we played on the last tour, we filled maybe half the hall.*
Kurt Loder: *And you don't think that was because of the material you were doing?*
Bob Dylan: *I don't think so. I don't think it had to do with anything. I think when your time is your time, it don't matter what you're doin'. It's either your time, or it's not your time. And I didn't feel the last few years was really my time . . . The people who reacted to the gospel stuff would've reacted that way if I hadn't done "Song To Woody." [1984]*

The negative publicity was so hateful that it turned a lot of people off from making up their own minds, and financially that can hurt if you got a show on the road. The first time we went out on that tour, we had something like eight weeks booked. Two of the weeks were in San Francisco. In the review in the paper, the man did not understand any of the concepts behind any part of the show, and he wrote an anti-Bob Dylan thing. He probably never liked me anyway, but just said that he did. A lot of them guys say stuff like, "Well, he changed our lives before. How come he can't do it now?" Just an excuse really. Their expectations are so high, nobody can fulfill them. They can't fulfill their own expectations, so they expect other people to do it for them. I don't mind being put down, but intense personal hatred is another thing. It was like an opening-night critic burying a show on Broadway. This particular review got picked up and printed in all the newspapers of the cities we were going to . . . even before tickets went on sale, and people would read this review and decide they didn't want to see the show. So . . . it took a while to work back from there. I thought the show was pretty relevant for what was going on at the time.

—DYLAN TO SCOTT COHEN, 1985

Next morning we would go to this little restaurant next to the gig [venue] and he'd buy all the papers and we'd read the reviews, and you would not believe that these people were at the show . . . Yeah, there were some people that walked out, but they were small by comparison with people that were there."

—DAVE KELLY TO CHRIS COOPER

It's my perception that Bob has always enjoyed stirring up a little dust. Makes life more interesting, plus it stirs interest and sells records . . . [But] I have not been in the middle of anything quite like this before or since. The atmosphere . . . at the Warfield was charged with electricity that was palpable.

—LARRY MYERS TO SCOTT MARSHALL

On January 3rd, 1974, the part of the world media assigned to cover seismic cultural events convened at the Chicago Stadium for Bob Dylan's first tour in eight long years. The almost universally laudatory reviews set the tone for a 40-date tour that was essentially a victory parade for battles fought a decade earlier.

The music on that tour, though, was as jet-lagged as this year's model; and in future Dylan decided to find his musical feet before the culture vultures could gather. His next three tours opened far enough out of town—Plymouth, Mass.; Lakeland, Florida and Tokyo—for most reviewers to take the hint.

But the prospect of fourteen shows in that home of hippiedom, San Francisco, at a 2,200-seat theater, with his overtly Christian album riding surprisingly high in the charts and no prior pronouncements as to what to expect, was too great a bait for a worldwide music press to pass up.

Whatever happened, this would be a news story. Not surprisingly the three major English music weeklies, America's one omniscient fortnightly music paper and every Bay Area daily and weekly decided to dispatch a correspondent or at the very least print a syndicated review.

It was something Dylan surely anticipated. What he couldn't have anticipated was that the syndication of particularly negative reviews from local reviewers would do lasting damage. The ones from the *Examiner's* Philip Ellwood and freelancer Michael Goldberg were bad enough, but the one from the *Chronicle's* Joel Selvin, a well-respected old-school rock critic, was worse.

Selvin's rather unforgiving review ran not only in various US dailies but in *Melody Maker*, where at least it didn't appear under the misleading headline the *Chronicle* copy editor applied to it: "Bob Dylan's God-Awful Gospel." How he must have chuckled when he came up with that doozy! At least Selvin was paying attention, even quoting the one comment Dylan made from the stage accurately, and appositely, as the critical gloves came off:

The ironies flew fast and furious Thursday at the Warfield Theatre, where Dylan took the capacity crowd by surprise with an opening-night performance composed exclusively of his singing praises to the Lord . . . The audience, given that, behaved with admirable restraint. Catcalls and boos, to be sure, echoed throughout the 2,200-seat former vaudeville palace. But mostly, the audience sat in stunned silence for the two-hour show, greeting the close of each of the seventeen songs with modest, polite applause . . . Taciturn and remote as ever, he spoke to the audience for the first time when he bid them good night. "I hope you were uplifted," he said . . . [He was] backed by an unobtrusive quartet—surprisingly undistinguished considering the extraordinary excellence of his past accompanists . . . By the time he breezed through the [four] opening numbers . . . it became abundantly apparent that the evening would be devoted to religious studies, not rock and roll. Genius may be pain, but this guy is not feeling any pain. Anesthetized by his new-found beliefs, Dylan has written some of the most banal, uninspired and inventionless songs of his career for his Jesus phase.

Though no dean of Bay Area rock criticism—an honor surely reserved for Ralph J. Gleason, cofounder of *Rolling Stone* and friend of Dylan's—Selvin insists he entered the theater with an entirely open mind and a profound appreciation of Dylan's work to date, only to find, "There was an undercurrent of hostility in the audience. I certainly picked up on that, and spoke for that element in my review. He was asking for it and he knew it."

That "undercurrent of hostility" wasn't just coming from critical enclaves. Dylan had left a pair of tickets for Lawrence Ferlinghetti, the owner of City Lights Books, someone Dylan once considered as his own publisher. "Larry" took along a City Lights clerk and art student, who remembers they left early:

Raymond Foye: We left towards the end of the show. Ferlinghetti said to me, essentially, "The whole point of the sixties was that we were free of all these old prejudices and ideologies. That's what we struggled for: you don't have to serve anybody." He was fairly upset. As an Irish Catholic ex-altar boy from Lowell, Mass., I too had had my fill of all that . . . I remember the crowd response as fairly mixed. It was a disturbing experience because Dylan was so obviously possessed and his intensity definitely had an edge of hostility to it. "If you're not with me you're against me," that was the vibe.[13]

It gradually dawned on everybody at the Warfield that night there were going to be no old songs. It seems even legendary promoter Bill Graham, having put his neck on the line and an entirely refitted theater at Dylan's disposal, had been unaware all old things were passed away. Tim Drummond actually remembered, "standing right there with Bob when Bill said, 'Please, Bob, just sing one old song.' And Dylan wouldn't. And then Bill said, 'Oh, I don't care, I'm going to retire anyway.'"

But Graham did care, and he was quietly mortified by the reviews the show received on that first night, going as far as phoning up Robert Hilburn at the *LA Times*, begging him to come up to see the following night's show. It proved a smart move, and a gesture neither Graham nor Dylan forgot:

Robert Hilburn: I often went out of town to interview (chiefly) or review important acts that came to town, probably once a month at least, frequenty to San Francisco . . . Oddly enough, however, I didn't go to the opening show at the Warfield. I don't know why. Maybe it was because he wasn't doing an interview and I was hoping he would agree to talk later during the long engagement and I'd fly up for that. But I got a call the day after the opening from Bill Graham, the powerful San Francisco promoter, who said the local papers killed the show, which really angered him because he thought the show was terrific. He said something to the effect, "You've got to come up and see this. I guarantee it'll be a good story." So, I did fly up that day and wrote about the second show.

Unfortunately, by night two the first-night reviews were already wreaking havoc. Perhaps the most damaging allegation of all—largely because it was grossly exaggerated—was that people were walking out in their hundreds, and that those who did not, were roundly booing their old friend Bobby. West Coast critic Michael Goldberg wrote a particularly snide account which appeared first in *NME*, still the hippest music weekly on the planet:

[13] According to Dave Kelly, Ken *"One Flew Over The Cuckoo's Nest"* Kesey was "also there and came to the shows and he would be backstage a few times. He had a new UFO/alien-type book he was pushing."

Of course, everyone suspected that a good portion of the service . . . oops, I mean, show . . . would consist of Dylan's *Slow Train Coming* material. What no one imagined was the brash gesture he would actually make; because during the two-hour performance, Bob Dylan completely turned his back on his past and didn't play a single song recorded before the last album . . . "I've already been to church," one member of the audience shouted. Many others booed . . . The audience wasn't particularly thrilled . . . when the women sang six spirituals, accompanied only by piano. [Soon] their displeasure became verbal. Sarcastic shouts of "Jesus loves you!" echoed throughout the theater and people began to leave . . . Most didn't even wait for the first encore. Only four or five hundred remained and they pushed up close to the stage and shouted for Dylan's return as if it was the Second Coming."

The accusation that people left early in numbers clearly rankled Dylan, who chose to send up those who made this accusation at a number of shows in the new year, notably at Hartford in May, where after five songs he said, "Anybody left yet? They tell me everybody leaves at these shows. It's a little hard to see out there."

Back at the Warfield, the shock was still palpable. Callow English reporter Mark Cooper, writing for the *Record Mirror* on his way to becoming the executive producer of BBC Four Music, was one of those appalled, "There's not a single pre-*Slow Train* song. It's as if Dylan tied up the past in the *Budokan* album . . . All the new songs pursue the conversion further into the Bible-belt territory . . . [but] both musically and lyrically he no longer uses religious themes, they use him." At least Cooper had the integrity to admit the majority of paying attendees were "familiar enough with the setup to enjoy it, even if they've come to see Dylan. Nobody will call out 'Judas' tonight."

It was primarily the critical community which had a problem with what they heard, though even that select body had dissenters in their ranks, more than a little ashamed at the closed minds those fellow scribes had nailed shut. Gail S. Tagashire, sent by the *San Jose Mercury News* to report on proceedings, directed most of her scorn at those who were booing and apparently leaving in their droves:

Leave all those prejudices outside the door, if you don't mind. Forget everything that Bob Dylan's done in the past . . . The show he's offering (that is the word) at the Fox-Warfield Theatre through mid-November is a far more believable one than last year's version, thank God . . . [He] is not some pained imitation of Neil Diamond, but a Dylan singing from a hurt in the heart, from somewhere deep within himself . . . This one's for real. It's honest and true. Judging from Thursday night's audience, however, this is an opinion from the minority. There were loud boos . . . [and] over half the first-floor audience walked out, but there were scores of those who stayed hoping for a third encore . . . People who had paid $13 and $15 apiece, who had expected to hear songs from a bygone era were shouting "Highway 61" and "Maggie's Farm" and "Mozambique"[!] between numbers. Even ruder creeps were yelling, "Where's Bob Dylan?" . . . And yet one doesn't have to embrace Christianity to get through this Dylan. If his audience simply accept humanity, that alone would be enough. Unfortunately, not many on opening night had had lessons in being humane.

Yet even Tagashire shared a belief that the Warfield was half-full by concert's end. It was like the media's own Rapture in reverse, seeing "hundreds" of nonbelievers disappearing into the ether. At least Robert Palmer, in his *Rolling Stone* review of opening night, saw nothing of the sort:

[Initially] there were snide comments from the audience—"I went to church this morning," "How about some sin?"—but once [Regina] Havis and the other vocalists began singing an uptempo spiritual, the resistance seemed to melt away . . . The end of the concert was greeted with both applause and boos, but there were surprisingly few emotional outbursts. As the audience filed out quietly, they were confronted with the words "You've Gotta Serve Somebody," writ large across the back of the illuminated marquee.

Another reviewer, who took the radical step of attending more than one show before filing a full-page review in the weekly *San Francisco Bay Guardian*, was Leslie Goldberg, who reported on the contrast between opening night and subsequent nights. He also had his own explanation for some of those empty seats on evening one:

Not all the seats were filled when the ushers closed the doors, like guardian angels at the gates of heaven, denying passage to those who arrived too late . . . Many people had barely sat down when three gospel singers tromped onto the stage . . . [When] Regina began the show by telling a peculiar tale about an old woman trying to visit her dying son . . . the audience didn't like the parable one bit, any more than they liked the songs that followed, including an eerily apocalyptic, yet musically infectious, "It's Gonna Rain" . . . As the women sang, accompanied only by a gospel piano player, someone kept drunkenly shouting, "Rock and roll!" . . . [So] Jesus himself couldn't have looked more vulnerable, more lonely, more naked than Bob Dylan did onstage that night . . . It was as if Bob Dylan had already prepared a part for the audience and the audience, without actually realizing what they were doing, played it to the hilt. It was a good thing no one had thought to bring the rotten tomatoes.

Another witness who caught multiple shows was Larry Myers who actually "rode to and from Warfield with [Dylan] and the band, hung out before the shows and after, sometimes alone with Bob, sometimes with Bob and the band." He remembered on that first night, in particular, the girlsingers' opening set bore the brunt of the ire rising up from those who felt they had handed over $15 under false pretense:

Larry Myers: As their set progressed, some in the audience grew impatient and began yelling for Dylan to come on—not usual treatment for opening acts. They continued undaunted until they were finished. By now the audience was really on the edge of their seats . . . The singers would move to their places and Bob would go to his, and Tim Drummond would count down—three, four—and on the downbeat the spots would come on and "Gotta Serve Somebody" would start . . . Song after song, no in between song patter, just the music . . . all new music. After a while, some would start yelling for their old favorites . . . Toward the end of the show I suppose a few walked out, but what I remembered most was seeing the audience sitting and listening intently. [SM]

If the pastor refuted reports of large numbers walking out, Myers had his own axe to grind. Perhaps people were just taking a breather from all the Bible-bashing in the lobby, as was Dylan's former guitar tech, Joel Bernstein, who ran into Fellowship follower T-Bone Burnett, who had come to provide some moral support. Not everybody backstage appreciated the Vineyard presence, not even fellow Christians:

Helena Springs: I remember a lot of people [there] were . . . from the Vineyard in Los Angeles. It's kinda like a cult, a Jesus-type cult . . . A lot of them [were] pressuring him a lot about a lot of things . . . Like if he'd drink some wine . . . They were not allowing him to live. They were just . . . too much of a headache. One time he said to me, "God, it's awfully tight [in here]," and I said, "Yeah, it seems to me like you gotta get out from under it a bit." I felt a lot of pressure [myself] from those people. And also he found a lot of hypocrisy from those people. A lot of the Jesus people . . . were saying one thing and doing another. He mentioned that to me, too . . . God, we had a lot of talks about it.

What almost none of the contemporary reviews mentioned was the way that, by the end of opening night, Dylan achieved at least some kind of rapprochement with those for whom the message was hard to swallow. It took two of the more sympathetic reviewers there that night, the *Bay Guardian*'s Goldberg and the father of American rock criticism and founder of *Crawdaddy*—who was there that first night simply as an interested observer and lifelong Dylan fan—to describe a truly moving second encore in detail. It came after prolonged applause; something most scribes seemed to miss, or miss out, of their reviews:

Paul Williams: The applause went on and on, maybe because people thought if they could bring him out once again he'd do an old favorite, but mostly because people really liked the show and were glad to see him, in spite of everything. [Finally] he [came and] sat at the piano, almost out of sight, accompanying himself singing, "I'm just pressing on to the higher calling of my Lord" . . . his best singing of the night, super—[then he] got up. We assumed he was walking off for the night, but he came around the piano and then made his way to the mic at the front of the stage. He beckoned, and other band members started to come back on. Dylan seemed really pleased, it was like he was discovering to his surprise that a good part of the audience had liked the concert, were with him, weren't just calling out for old songs. He clapped his hands together a few times, and went on with the song.

Leslie Goldberg: As a good three-quarters of the crowd stumbled grumpily out of the theater, a few refused to leave right away, clapping stubbornly. The house lights were already on . . . when Dylan suddenly reappeared . . . Accompanied by the band, Dylan sat down at the piano while the small disciple-like crowd stood awestruck. As he sang . . . directly, passionately, "Still Pressing On For My Lord" [sic], an aching desire and yearning for something truly beautiful and holy welled up within the almost empty hall. It was a moment completely stripped of pretension. And what was left was utterly and undeniably human.

The media fallout from the momentous evening was immediate. And just like when Dylan went electric at the Newport Folk Festival in July 1965, no one could agree on how many booed, how many left and how many stuck it out. Dylan himself phoned up his publicist, Paul Wasserman, to ask him for Joel Selvin's home phone number.

Wasserman thought nothing of it, knowing how in the past his boss "would call people up once in a while, to correct them but also to thank them. I knew Selvin had reviewed the show, so I figured it had something to do with that." Dylan neither wanted to thank Selvin, nor correct him. Instead, he was phoning up to tell him his license to review future Dylan shows had been revoked. Unfortunately, Joel missed the call in person, but his wife took the message and passed it on to the stunned scribe.

Meanwhile, Robert Hilburn was on the plane to San Francisco, anxious to see and hear what all the fuss was about. Arriving at the unfamiliar theater by cab, he remembers sensing "some tension in the theater before the show, [now that] the audience knew what to expect after the reviews and word of mouth of opening night; some disappointed fans were selling their tickets for the second show outside the theater and there were lots of people, favorable to the gospel theme, to buy them . . . [That night] the audience was overwhelmingly supportive. Dylan seemed relieved, relaxed." Hilburn loved the show/s he saw, giving Dylan his first important positive press from the US media since Wenner's *Slow Train* review:

Prepare yourself . . .

Dylan sang seventeen songs in his 95-minute set at the 2,200-seat Warfield Theatre here, and none was older than 1979. That means he didn't do "Blowin' In The Wind" or "Like A Rolling Stone" or even "Knockin' On Heaven's Door." Nine of the selections were from Dylan's new *Slow Train Coming* album; the others were unrecorded tunes that will presumably be on his next LP. The common link in the material was the fundamental Christian viewpoint that the rock star reportedly embraced in recent months . . .

Some booed the absence of old Dylan songs. Others, displeased by the religious emphasis, walked out. One frustrated patron near the end of the show shouted an obscenity. Reviews of the first show were scathing . . .

By Friday [the 2nd], the Warfield Theatre was a buzz . . . Was the show as bad as the newspapers had said? Would Dylan ease up on the spiritual tone? . . . But Dylan didn't retreat from the opening night format . . . Occasional yells of "We want Dylan!" and "Rock 'n' roll!" could be heard between songs . . .

A few people did leave early, but there was no general uprising as was reported on opening night . . . Dylan and the band also turned in a stronger performance Friday, said fans who also were at Thursday's show . . . Towards the end of [the] show, he [really] loosened up—especially on such joyously celebrative gospel-rockers as "Blessed Is The Name Of The Lord Forever." He was even so frisky that he even took a wry stab at an old nemesis—the press. When someone in the audience shouted something affectionate at him, Dylan said, "You'll be all right if you don't read the newspapers." Dylan's Saturday show was a triumph . . . One doesn't have to accept Dylan's views to enjoy the concert any more than one has to adore jazz music to enjoy Joni Mitchell's new Mingus album. The joy is seeing an artist in top form and Dylan, on this tour, is a man with his artistry aglow.

The shows Hilburn caught had tightened a couple of notches on opening night, when an undercooked "Saved" and a stuttering "In The Garden" suggested the band was still a day or two away from hitting their musical marks. As the residency progressed and Dylan loosened up, the battle of wills became a fairer fight. Everyone soon knew there would be a whole lot of Jesus and a lot more rock 'n' roll.

And just in case anyone arrived at the theater still unaware of the theme of the evening, there was now a motley crew of Jesus freaks outside, hustling for tickets. As Kelly notes, "There was every kind of cult you could imagine, but they all stayed and they all loved it . . . Lots of people came back . . . I think they knew they were going through an historical event. The first time was a shock, the second was to take it all in."

Amid the throng mingled members of Jews for Jesus, an organization anxious to affiliate themselves with the most famous modern convert. They were handing out their own, tangerine-orange leaflets emblazoned with the inflammatory message, "The Times They Are (Indeed!) A-Changin'—the times can change for you, too—you've just gotta choose whom you're gonna serve," and quoting Joshua 24:15, "Choose you this day whom ye will serve." It seems they at least had Dylan's tacit blessing:

Mitch Glaser: We received this phone call from someone in Dylan's entourage. He said, "Bob really wants you to hand out pamphlets at his concerts." So being a cynical New Yorker . . . [I suggested we] put this person to the test. We called this person back and we said if you have eight tickets for us at Will Call [on the first night] then we'll know this [message] is true. And we'll hand out tracts at all the [other] concerts. We went up to Will Call and, lo and behold, the tickets were there. We went in and we had great seats, and it was the most phenomenal concert. We went back and we wrote a gospel broadside called The Times They Are A-Changin' and we presented the message of Jesus through the previous lyrics of Dylan, because we didn't really have all the lyrics to the new songs. And by the next night we had a dozen people outside the Warfield Theatre handing these things out. There was very little antagonism. Everyone was trying to figure out where Dylan was at. They wanted us to help [them] understand Dylan. [JG]

Dylan, though, was not quite as engaged by the Jews for Jesus message as Glaser suggests. One of Dave Kelly's "jobs after the shows was to go out there and engage in the conversations. There'd be little clusters of people with pamphlets . . . and I'd take one from each of them . . . [But Bob also] wanted me to . . . make sure they don't convince anyone that he's believing the same thing they believe."

If Dylan was not about to personally engage with a group whose message seemed more naturally akin to his than the Vineyard, he clearly felt a kinship with the outsiders to whom his Lord had preached a couple of millenia earlier. But how could he reach out to such a demographic, as he felt he should?

His, after all, was a very messianic message—both socially and spiritually. As he told Hilburn the following year, "When I walk around some of the towns we go to . . . I'm totally convinced people need Jesus. Look at the junkies and the winos and the troubled people. It's all a sickness which can be healed in an instant. [But] the powers that be won't let that happen."

This really was not so far from the sentiments in "When The Ship Comes In," a song he penned after being refused entry to a hotel based on how he looked. (As the man said, "You know they refused Jesus, too—you're not him.") In San Francisco, he found an outlet for such concerns, down the street from the York Hotel:

Dave Kelly: There was a little "greasy spoon" type restaurant near the hotel, and he'd go in there and sit and talk to the locals for hours, with no one else around. He loved that chance for normal contact with people. He loved to meet people who were not shattered by his presence . . . The girls [also] took him to a black church one time that they [said] he really loved. He got up and was dancing and clapping . . . This was during the Warfield shows.

Meanwhile, back at the Warfield, the shows were going from strength to strength. The band kicked into gear and everyone—onstage and offstage—embraced the experience. It seems any backbiters and unbelievers who attended the first three shows gave up trying to change Dylan's way of thinking and simply voted with their feet:

Spooner Oldham: I remember night one, two and three was a mixed reaction as far as the audience . . . Half the audience would applaud after each song and half would boo . . . After the first three nights, all the rebels didn't come back or [they] accepted it. It calmed down and everybody seemed to enjoy it more—although it was sort of enjoyable even when it was weird, 'cause it was challenging to face that kind of audience. You knew the music and message was nothing but good news, so you couldn't [allow yourself to] be bothered by that. [SM]

Dylan, too, finally started making his chosen band feel like brothers in arms. Even if not every musician was a disciple to the cause, most were perfectly prepared to thank the Lord. As Fred Tackett says, "He felt like he had a calling to do what he was doing and he was very sincere about the religious thing at the time . . . [So] we would have little prayer meetings before every show . . . We'd all hold hands . . . We got to be really close." This bonding process would bind them together for four times as long as the Rolling Thunder Revue. Dylan did not even retire to a darkened room after these shows but rather invited everyone back to his place:

Spooner Oldham: Most people ended up in Bob's room talking about the show . . . I guess maybe they were just enjoying the camaraderie of being a band, 'cause a lot of the [girl]singers hadn't been on the road before.

The evening didn't necessarily end there, either. Dave Kelly recalls how, on occasion, "After the concert[s] there would be another concert for three hours downstairs . . . The girls were usually the instigators of that and it would sometimes go on for hours."

The girlsingers remained the only members of this traveling band on the same page as Dylan, somewhere around 2 Corinthians. Soon, that spiritual bond the singers shared began to translate to the band, turning them into believers—at least for the duration of each show. The music they were playing was certainly God-given. As Dylan's drummer told journalist Harvey Kubernik at the first concert in LA:

Jim Keltner: San Francisco was really happening after the first night. It's beautiful now. Bob is a powerful man. We go on stage knowing the audience will let us play.

You saw them standing at the end of the show. It's an experience. I feel younger and very lucky to be a part of this situation. I'm having one of the times of my life.

Keltner's comment contributed to a generally positive piece in *Melody Maker* on Dylan's gospel show from Kubernik, who "laugh[ed] at music critics like Greil Marcus who doubt the sincerity of Dylan's new direction." A brief feature in *Rolling Stone* took a similar tack, recording the thoughts of Bill Graham, who had feared losing his shirt after adding a second week of shows, and now agreed it had been a life-affirming experience:

> We are all used to nostalgia, but this was something completely new . . . From night
> to night, the show keeps getting stronger and stronger. It is awesome. I am a Jew, and
> I am deeply moved by what this man is doing. It's a very profound public display of
> personal convictions.

Dylan would never forget Graham's gesture. He referred to the faith the promoter showed at the following year's Warfield residency, during which he gave "Bill Graham . . . a lot of credit . . . because when we came here last year, we came in here with a show and the newspapers . . . slandered it . . . That's enough for most promoters in the business just to cancel out the rest of the shows, but Bill didn't do that."

The singer would also find time at this second residency to acknowledge another voice who tried in the aftermath of the original 1979 shows to shift the debate away from the "controversy," to what really mattered: an artist at the peak of his performing powers, singing with the conviction of faith harnessed to a music machine that was firing on all cylinders.

Paul Williams had lost his way in the seventies, rarely writing about the rock music genre he helped define in its infancy, but the experience of eight Warfield shows had renewed his resolution to write about what he truly cared about—the most vital art-form and art-ist of his age. Williams also wanted to put some fellow critics through the grinder as he began penning a slim monograph on these shows, *What Happened?*, a self-conscious allusion to a 1977 book Presley's bodyguards wrote, hoping (and failing) to save their former boss from himself:

> [The reviews] had such a measurable impact on so many of the people I've met who
> weren't at the concerts (partly because the reviews were picked up and parroted by
> radio disc jockeys) . . . [But then] critical response in the influential media to most

of Dylan's major work in the last six years has been overwhelmingly negative . . .
This year the critics, and some of the people in the audience (fewer each night) were
upset because he didn't do any old songs. Last year, when he did a show that was
almost entirely old favorites (carefully chosen from the whole range of his career),
he was widely attacked for having changed the arrangements! It seems there are a
whole lot of people out there who are so hopelessly mired in their own long-gone
adolescence that they have no interest in living art at all; they want their performers
to be time machines for them . . . [But by the fifth night,] things had reached the
kind of pull-out-the-stops energy level I associate with Dylan's 1966 tour with The
Band, or the Rolling Thunder shows. And Dylan had relaxed and opened up to the
point where he was really getting into it, holding the long notes, allowing his voice
to soar and bite and growl and carress . . . No more calls for old songs. Instead the
showstopper had become "Hanging On To A Solid Rock" . . . On the third night [sic],
with the band really cooking and the audience getting more and more enthusiastic
(and showing it) with every song, Dylan grinned for a split-second into the wild
applause after "Saving Grace" and told us, "Don't read any more newspapers." The
audience . . . howled its approval.

The admonishment on the *second* night, to not "read any more newspapers,"
signaled a change. He had decided to meet his audience halfway, not by making
concessions in the material but by explaining what was going on his head—an all-
time first. As he informed Robert Hilburn, six months after preaching the word
of God nightly:

Bob Dylan: If someone really wants to know [the message], I can explain it to
them, but . . . I don't feel compelled to do it [anymore]. I was doing a bit of that last
year on the stage. I was saying stuff I figured people needed to know. I thought I was
giving people an idea of what was behind the songs. [1980]

For followers of this man, here was a unique opportunity to hear what made
that mind tick. And it was not one he was ever likely to repeat. As he said in 1986,
after reverting to type, "I usually say everything I have to say through the songs. I
mean, it would be pointless for me to go out and say how I feel about this and how I
feel about that—I could never articulate [it] this well."

Starting part way through the Warfield shows, there was a six-month window
when this was not the case, so much so that some of what he felt a burning need
to share became things he would later regret saying. Once he began prefacing

the songs with "stuff I figured people needed to know," it seemed like there was no off switch.

The first song he felt a yen to explain was the unreleased "Hanging On To A Solid Rock," which as Williams noted, soon became a showstopper every night, and an excuse to talk about the "End Times" every other night.

And on the fourth night for the first time Dylan talked about how "we're living in the end of the end of times." By November 6th, he wanted everyone to know, "In the last days of the end of times, you're going to need something strong to hang on to. This song is called 'Hanging On To A Solid Rock Made Before The Foundation Of The World.' You're gonna need something *that* strong."

By the ninth, increasingly sure of his hold on the Warfield audience, he asked the auditorium if they shared his concerns, "We are living in the last of the end of times. I know everybody agrees with that. All right, shout if you agree with me." The reaction only further convinced him to spread—and, indeed, quote—the word of God.

The following night he set "Solid Rock" in context by directly quoting, almost correctly, chapter eighteen of what was fast becoming his favorite book, Corinthians, "The Bible says that preaching of the cross is foolishness to those who perish, but to those who are saved, it is the power of God."[14]

In fact, Dylan's penchant for (mis)quoting the Bible suggested someone who was not a natural-born preacher. His wariness of the type had been given voice in song back in 1961, with his early tour de force, Lord Buckley's "Black Cross," where the preacher was the kind of bigot who would hang a black man for owning books and because "the son of a bitch never had no religion." He was still sending them up in the semi-improvised bridge to 1967's "Sign On The Cross."

Yet two days after quoting Corinthians One from the Warfield stage, he was quoting Timothy Two, in what may have been a thinly-veiled dig at those who took the tag, "City of Brotherly Love" literally: "And the last days of perilous times shall be at hand and men will become lovers of their own selves." [2 Timothy 3].

Again, he asked for a response from the crowd: "He works by faith not by sight, right? Is that right? You see, we're living in the end of times now. Are we living in the end of times? Is that right?" Though the reaction was half-and-half, three days later he went back to Corinthians, quoting, "If the gospel is hid, it is

[14] The King James translation of 1 Corinthians 1:18—the edition Dylan preferred—reads, "For the preaching of the cross is to them that perish foolishness; but unto us which are saved it is the power of God."

hidden to those that are lost." [2 Corinthians 4] He also referenced Revelation, in terms smacking of Lindsey:

We read about all the trouble [in] Iran, Great Britain, Russia, Red China and the United States. But we're not going to be bothered by all that, because we know the world is going to be destroyed and we look forward to the approach of the second coming. So we're hanging on now to a stronger rock. One made before the foundation of the world. That real, that true.

By now, regular attendees knew such harangues were coming, and met suggestions "that Jesus is coming back," with affirmative shouts of "Praise be to God!" By the final night at the Warfield, Dylan had taken on the appearance of a fire 'n' brimstone preacher, peppering several song intros with testimonies to his faith.

It was probably not coincidence that it was also the best of the Warfield shows; in fact, one of the best performances of a long, illustrious career. So, when he prefaced "Saved By The Blood Of The Lamb" with a heartfelt message that "Satan's called the God of this world, that's true, and it's such a wonderful feeling when you've been delivered from that," it was a prelude to the most spirited version to date as the band also got to grips with their holy mission, conveying that "wonderful feeling" with every ounce of their unbelieving being.

If Dylan was reveling in the band dynamic, he couldn't resist making his first joke in a fortnight at their expense. Debuting "No Man Righteous (No Not One)"[15], he informed the sympatico audience, "We're gonna do something right here that we haven't done before. This is a song that nobody knows. Nobody in this band even knows it—that's how I can tell who really wants to stick with me and who doesn't."

In fact, such were the waves of positivity rising up from the pit that he allowed himself another dig at doubters—in this case, those working for his own record company. Rather than prefacing "Solid Rock" with a litany on the world's woes, he hinted at some of his own: "This is a song we been working in on, and we hope to record sometime . . . They hold my records so long, you know . . . [so] you might hear it a month from now, maybe a year from now. But whenever you do [hear it], remember you heard it first right here." Cue whoops of approval. He received similar affirmation during another now-familiar rap, transferred tonight to before "Slow Train":

We read in the newspaper every day what a horrible situation this world is in.

---

[15] One of just two live performances from Dylan, the other coming in Hartford, CT on May 7th, 1980.

Now, "God chooses the foolish things in this world to confound the wise."[16] *We know this world is going to be destroyed, we know that. Christ will set up His kingdom in Jerusalem for a thousand years where the lion will lie down with the lamb. Have you heard that before?* [Some applause.] *Have you heard that before?* [More applause] *I'm just curious to know, how many believe that?* [Rousing applause.] *All right! This is called "Slow Train Coming." It's been coming a long time and it's picking up speed.*

This pugnacious performance of "Slow Train"—included on *Bootleg Series Vol. 13*, with the rap trimmed—had been "picking up speed" for the past fortnight. Tonight it steams all the way to New Jerusalem. Nor does it travel alone. Definitive, or near-definitive performances of "When He Returns," "Covenant Woman," "Saving Grace" and "What Can I Do For You?" show Dylan had found the music to accompany his message and that, far from revising that message to make it more palatable, he was ramping up the rhetoric just as his own busload of faith was idling out of neutral and heading down Route One to a homecoming party at the Santa Monica Civic Auditorium, a stone's throw from Rundown.

[16] The quote, a favorite of Dylan's, comes from 1 Corinthians 1:27—"God hath chosen the foolish things of the world to confound the wise."

5. '65 REVISITED
[November 18 – December 9, 1979]

Whatever label is put on you, the purpose of it is to limit your accessibility to people. There had been so many labels laid on me in the past that it didn't matter anymore, at that point. What more could they say? You'd never hear me saying that stuff is religious, one way or the other. To me, it isn't. It's just based on my experience in daily matters, what you run up against and how you respond to things."

—BOB DYLAN TO EDNA GUNDERSEN, 1989

Robert Hilburn: What was it like to be adored at times and booed at others—like on the Slow Train Coming tour in the 70s?
Bob Dylan: I was booed at Newport before that, remember. You can't worry about things like that. Miles Davis has been booed. Hank Williams was booed. Stravinsky was booed. You're nobody if you don't get booed sometime. [2001]

Though Dylan knew he had turned the pop world on its axis last time he had been roundly booed, it had taken a year of solid touring and a motorcycle crash to convince former fans he had been right all along. Hoping to avoid the crash this time, he recommitted himself to that long and lonesome road less than a year after the end of a 115-date world tour. Shows were booked into Advent, reaching almost to the Mexican Border.

As in 1965, the tour focussed initially on the West Coast, using LA as its hub. Four shows at the Santa Monica Civic Auditorium, which sold out in less than a day, served as a further reminder of his critical and commercial heyday. He had played there twice in 1965, at the beginning and end of that particular media storm, debuting the more acoustic side of *Bringing It All Back Home* in March, before introducing the roar of The Hawks in December.

This time he was playing the shows to benefit a nondenominational Christian charity, World Vision, raising money for Cambodian relief, before disappearing into the hinterlands to spread the gospel there. Not surprisingly, followers from the fellowship turned out in force. Hilburn recalls, "The Santa Monica show audience was even more supportive. By then, of course, the disenchanted knew to stay away. I remember people lifting their hands up—as a sign of spiritual support or agreement—as he sang."

If there was any of the negativity that don't pull you through, it came from a Hollywood-based media too apathetic to take a trip north. *Sounds'* LA correspondent Sylvie Simmons, who had always preferred Leonard Cohen, came to the show with a closed mind and left with a cold heart but only after "wrestling with my conscience whether to walk out on one of the most tedious Sundays of my earthly existence."

She barely made it through "half a dozen new songs with the same religious theme . . . more funereal and simplistic than before and not even a nod or a wink to the old heathen stuff," before heading for the bar to work on a killer riposte to yet another religious nut. All she could come up with was, "If Bob Dylan is aiming to get crucified by the press on this tour, he's going about it the right way."

To Dylan's mind, Simmons was just another journo on "a one-way ticket to burn." There were far more prominent voices in the LA media. And he already had its most powerful critical voice on his side. Unlike in 1965— when he *was* the epicenter of pop culture—and the *LA Times* could barely raise itself to mention the man, in November 1979, its rock critic got two pops at the gospel-rock cherry. If anything, Hilburn enjoyed the first Santa Monica show even more than the second Warfield:

Where the rock singer [Dylan] spoke almost exclusively through his music in the all-religious program up north, he prefaced several songs Sunday with expressions of his new-found faith . . . [He] introduced [one] song with these words, "Some people call Satan the real God of this world. All you have to do is look around to see that's true. But I wonder how many of you know that Satan has been defeated by the cross . . ." When hundreds in the capacity audience in the 3,200-seat Civic cheered, Dylan smiled, looked at his vocal trio and said, "Well, it doesn't look like we're alone tonight." . . . The enthusiasm showed that Dylan's tour has moved from near disaster to triumph in less than two weeks . . . The only boos Sunday were when the audience feared Dylan wouldn't return for an encore . . . What appeared to some observers to be a near suicidal career move two weeks ago is already turning into a victory for Dylan. America's most acclaimed songwriter of the rock era has again dumbfounded his critics . . . Before this tour, Dylan seemed headed for the same artistic impasse that ultimately trapped Elvis Presley. The audience adoration of his past made movement difficult for Dylan, but by refusing to be bullied any longer by the 60s crowd, he has again asserted his own vitality. That's what makes this tour "born again" in more ways than one.

One of Hilburn's rival scribes felt equally positive about the whole evening, and was even more enthused after a close encounter of the third kind:

Harvey Kubernik: Jim Keltner arranged for myself and [The Knack drummer] Bruce Gary to have backstage access . . . Kris Kristofferson walked into the room and every chick swooned and all the guys went over to Kris, leaving me, Bob, Bruce and Helena Springs together. I muttered something about "In The Garden" . . . sound[ing] like an outtake from *Abbey Road* . . . Bruce got [Helena's] phone number. We all went out to eat at the Sundance Cafe later that week.

Unbeknownst to a distracted Dylan, Gary's interest in Helena—which would become both professional and personal—would play its part in convincing her to quit the gospel revue at the earliest opportunity; while Gary himself, having auditioned for Dylan in December 1977, pre-Knack, would join the same revue at its last departure point, just before the wheels came off in November 1981.

In the period between, Gary tried to stage-manage Springs's evolution into a solo artist, beginning with setting up and producing a session to record the most commercial of the dozen or so compositions Dylan and Springs had written together in 1978.

"More Than Flesh And Blood" was a song Dylan had soundchecked on a number of occasions that year and included in the original US '78 set list, but never performed. At the time of its composition, Dylan did not seem to know the true name of the "adverse" spirit who sets man against (wo)man, and wrecks relationships. But by the Santa Monica shows he was in no doubt, using the phrase "flesh and blood" in his opening night "Satan is real" rap:

[With] Satan, we wrestle not against flesh and blood, it's all happening on a spiritual level. ["Like A Rolling Stone!"] *Satan is called the God of this world and, as you look around, you see proof he really is the God of this world. . .*

When he invoked Satan's name the reaction bordered on Southern Baptist, the audience testifying loudly from the plush recesses of the Civic Auditorium. On the second night, when Dylan suggested, "Satan is called the God of this world . . . Anybody here who know that?" he was met with loud cheers. When he continued, "That's right, he is called the God of this world and the prince of the power of the air," someone audibly shouts, "He sucks!" A delighted Dylan responds, "That's right, he does!" duly delivering the holiest "Slow Train" to date.

By the final night, he knew he was in the bosom of fellow believers and if he wanted to proselytize, any doubting Thomases would be shouted down. It prompted another pre-"Slow Train" sales pitch for *Satan Is Alive And Well*:

The God of this world is blind to many people. Satan is called the God of this world. He owns the media. Everything about the media, he owns . . . [He] causes disturbance to your mind, while America is on its way down [to] becoming a third-rate power. We can't help that. There's nothing we can do about that. But we can know what is going to happen, and . . . this world is going to be destroyed. That's been coming a long time . . . Christ will set up His kingdom in Jerusalem for a thousand years. I want you to know that—because you got a choice.

The pitches just kept coming, most of them for a decent edition of the King James Bible, a book he now might quote from at almost any point. Thus, on the second night, after the usual band introduction, he admonished the audience, "Remember now, you wrestle not against flesh and blood but against principalities and power—and the ruthlessness of the darkness of this world, spiritual wickedness in higher places. So, if you're down, that's why you're down," thus demonstrating he knew the Book of Ephesians [6:12] almost as well as the four Gospels. Nor did he forget the statutory namecheck from 1 Corinthians [10:12], preceding "When You Gonna Wake Up":

I don't know what kind of God you believe in, but I believe in a God that can raise the dead . . . [In] trying to bring good news, so many people are so conditioned to bad news, they don't know good news when they hear it. That's right. So we want you to know one thing: God don't make promises that He don't keep. And "let he who thinketh he stand take heed, lest he fall."[17]

But the longest rap at the second Santa Monica show—a particularly impassioned evening of evensong—was again reserved for "Solid Rock." This time, he branched out to the book of Isaiah—the one widely assumed to be the one he drew from on "All Along The Watchtower," in 1967, when first he dipped into the apocalyptic books of the Bible for lyrical source material. Romans, too, was invoked in another apocalyptic account of the end of days:

---

[17] 1 Corinthians 10:12—"Wherefore let him that thinketh he standeth take heed lest he fall."

You know we're living in the last of the End Times. I don't know if anybody's told you
that before, but I'm telling ya . . . How many of you believe that? You should know that.
Anyway, we're not worried about all that. We see hostages being taken here . . . drugs
being outlawed there . . . All these sad stories that are floating around . . . And we're
not worried about any of that. We don't care about no atom bomb, 'cause we know this
world is going to be destroyed, there's no other way, and Christ will set up His kingdom
in Jerusalem for a thousand years. When the lion lies down with the lamb, you know
the lion will eat straw on that day. Also, if a man doesn't live to be a hundred years old,
he will be called accursed.[18] *That's interesting, isn't it? . . . And if any man have not the*
spirit of Christ in him, he is a slave to bondage.[19] *You know bondage? I know you all*
know bondage. So you need something just a little bit tough to hang on to. The name of
this song is called, "Hanging On To A Solid Rock, Made Before The Foundation Of The
World." And if you don't have that to hang on to, you'd better look into it.

For a man who had generally resorted to a little artificial stimulation to
conquer chronic stage fright, the gregariousness of Born-Again Bob took some
fellow believers by surprise. The born-again singer Pat Boone—who was rumored
(incorrectly) to have held Dylan's baptism by his swimming pool—called the show
"one of the gutsiest things I've seen in my life. I wanted to shout, 'Hey, listen—for
a generation he asked the questions, and now he's giving you the answers. Why
don't you just listen?'"

Dylan needed no encouragement to amplify the meaning of his songs, or their
scriptural source/s. At the third show he gave his own idiosyncratic account of
Jesus's arrest in the Garden of Gethsemane before delivering an anthemic "When
They Came For Him In The Garden":

Jesus was in the Garden [when] they came to get Him. Peter, who was . . . there with
Him. [Peter] was always saying things. When he didn't know what to say, he'd always
say it. Anyway, Peter took out his sword and he cut this man's ear off . . . Jesus says,
"Hold it Peter. Don't you think that if I pray to my father, he would give me twelve
legions of angels to take care of this matter. This cup that's coming to me, I must drink
it." Anyway, I just [want to] give you a little idea of Peter. Peter's the man, He said,
"Upon this man, upon this rock, I will found my church." . . . But when Jesus did go

---

[18] Isaiah 65:20—"There shall be no more thence an infant of days, nor an old man that hath not filled
his days: for the child shall die an hundred years old; but the sinner being an hundred years old shall
be accursed."
[19] Romans 8:15—"For ye have not received the spirit of bondage again to fear; but ye have received the
Spirit of adoption, whereby we cry, Abba, Father."

to the cross, He did defeat the Devil. We know this is true, we believe it, and we stand
on that faith.

Yet still Dylan did not do "Stand By Faith," or any other song that had fallen at
the last hurdle in rehearsal. From the first Santa Monica show to the first Memphis
show in February 1980, the set would be set in stone. Only the raps changed or
became subject to extemporization.

At the final Santa Monica show came one of the stranger raps. It came before
Mona Lisa Young sang "God Uses Ordinary People"—usually an excuse for Dylan
to snatch a quick "fag"—which he used on this occasion to explain the meaning of
Passover, which Bobby Zimmerman had been brought up to believe was a Jewish
holiday. But Dylan had been tutored by his Christian teachers to believe the same
thing was about to happen again, and real soon, with a modern Pharoah in the role
of the Antichrist:

God uses ordinary people . . . all the time. All those guys in the Old Testament, Joshua,
Moses, Abraham, Gideon, they were all ordinary people. They weren't superheroes.
In fact, Moses did not want to go back to Egypt, and get the people out, because he
knew he was an ordinary person. [But] God told him to go back and tell the Pharaoh
to let those people go. Pharaoh didn't want to let those people go . . . and said, "No
way, Moses, I can't let those people go, they're building my pyramids." Moses said to
Pharaoh, "Well, God say that your rivers are gonna dry up, if you don't let those people
go." The Pharaoh didn't pay any attention [to that] and his rivers dried up. Then Moses
said, "Frogs are going to crawl across your streets." Still didn't make any difference to
Pharaoh. Frogs crawled everywhere. There was no place they could look where they
didn't see frogs. Hail started falling, as big as basketballs. People [are] dropping like
flies. Many, many plagues came down. Finally God said to Moses, "Moses, you go
tell Pharaoh, that every first-born son is gonna die, if he don't let those people go." . . .
But Moses figured if all the first-born sons are going to die, what about the Hebrew
children? Are they going to die, too? And God said, "Moses you just put the blood sign
on every door." So, when the angel of the Lord passed over, he saw the sign of blood on
the door of every [Jewish] house, and he didn't touch those houses. Now, you need the
blood on you. Because of what is going to be happening in the world, coming up, you
need the blood on you.

As this particular rap began to evolve over the next few shows, Dylan finally got
around to explaining how a sign on the door became the sign on the cross, "So if they

had the sign of blood on the door, they lived. And that's why John the Baptist, when he saw Jesus coming, said, 'Behold, the lamb of God who taketh away the sins on the world.' If you don't know Jesus, you better check into it. He's real."

By the time he gave this particular testimonial—a mere week after the last LA revival meeting—Dylan had seen his faith and sermonizing skills sorely tested by two "collegiate" audiences in Tempe, Arizona.

Compounding the difficulties he was to face the minute he left La-La land, *Newsweek* decided they hadn't told enough lies about Dylan in their October 1963 hatchet-job. A report in the December 17th issue claimed "Dylan often couldn't fill even small halls on his recent Western tour—and five hundred marched out in San Diego when he shunned such secular chestnuts as 'Lay Lady Lay.'" The periodical also delighted in suggesting that he was being met invariably with "catcalls, then a few boos."

As is the *Newsweek* way, the weekly sprinkled just enough half-truths to give the piece a certain veracity. The one part that *was* true was that Dylan was struggling to "fill even small halls" once he left the Californian coastline. Even in Tucson, where he filled a five-figure arena a year earlier, the *Arizona Daily Star* reported that on opening night only "1,500 people showed up, [little] more than half the capacity of the . . . Music Hall."

In fact, three nights at Salt Lake City's Performing Arts Center (November 30 to December 2) were canceled due to poor ticket sales, leaving a gaping hole in the tour schedule. After San Diego on the 28th, the band would now be cooling their heels in LA until two shows in Albuquerque, New Mexico, on the 4th.[20] Likewise, a third show in Tucson on the 10th proved unnecessary. The fall tour now ended on December 9th, after two shows in Albuquerque and two in Tucson.

Dylan's fanbase—and finances—were taking a hit like never before. And he responded in Tempe with all the fiery fury he could muster, once it became apparent he had been dropped slap-dab in the valley of nonbelievers. It did not take long for him to notice, as shouts of "Subterranean Homesick Blues" and "Rock 'n' roll!" ricocheted around the Gammage Center, even before he got to "Slow Train."

At this point Dylan asked the lighting man to turn up the lights. As a momentarily non-plussed Fred Tackett recalls, "Bob said he wanted to see what the people looked like who were yelling stuff. We played a couple of songs with all the lights on."

---

[20] A provisional "third" Albuquerque show on the 6th was also canceled when the promoter realized shows on the 4th and 5th would more than satisfy demand.

Sure enough, proof resides on tapes of the show—and there are at least three, two audience tapes (the worst of which comes from nearby a nest of noisy nonbelievers) and a fine soundboard—all of which capture Dylan laying into one vociferous heckler in the crowd after "Precious Angel":

> *Turn the light on that man over there. You know, when John the Baptist saw Jesus coming up the road, he said, "Behold! The Lamb of God which taketh away the sin of the world." Now, . . . in San Francisco, we opened there about a month ago, about three or four people walked out because they didn't like the message. But we're still here now. Don't you walk out before you hear the message . . . "The Lamb of God which taketh away the sin of the world." Don't know how many people understand that. I'm curious to know, how many of you understand that?*

The mixed response confirms he is a long way from LA. His next pronouncement suggests someone equally removed from realpolitik, as he decides to address the current political crisis raging around the taking of fifty-two members of the US embassy as hostages in Tehran, three weeks earlier. If a botched attempt at rescue would duly cost Jimmy Carter the presidency. Dylan's "solution" came straight from a nondenominational division of Marvel Comics:

> *The Shah of Iran, he's in the hospital now. Who knows what he's doing there in that hospital. He's walking around, looking out the window. Meantime, fifty or sixty American hostages are being held somewhere [in the desert] because this man plundered [his] country, murdered a lot of people and escaped. Now they want him to come back. Now, here's what Jesus would have done. Jesus would have gone back. See, that's what Jesus did. He . . . took all the hostages back. Now, of course, we're not expecting the Shah of Iran to do anything like that. 'Cause he's just human.*

As the show rumbled on, Dylan began to warm to his theme: it was the end of the world, and he felt fine. After all, he had a solid rock he could call his own:

> *Don't be dismayed by what you read in the newspapers, about what's happening to the world. Because . . . the world as we know it now is being destroyed. I'm sorry to say it, but it's the truth. In a short time—I don't know, maybe in three years, maybe five years, could be ten years—there's gonna be a war . . . called the war of Armageddon. It's gonna happen in the Middle East. Russia will come down and attack first. You watch for that sign.*

After Dylan retired to rest and recuperate, he was more than a little shaken by the sheer vehemence with which he had been greeted by Arizona's academy. That he blamed the students and teachers from the nearby State University is clear from the few public pronouncements he later made about the battle of Tempe.

Talking to the *Sunday Times'* Mick Brown on the 1984 tour, he accused "the so-called intellectual students [of] show[ing] their true monstrous selves." And if there was any doubting whom he had in mind, a protracted polemic to Cameron Crowe—who was compiling the sleeve notes for 1985's five-album retrospective, *Biograph*—gave Dylan an opportunity to vent his wrath in a forum he could control:

Bob Dylan: College kids showed the most disrespect . . . I mean, it was fierce . . . We'd play the so-called colleges, where my so-called fans were. And all hell would break loose: "Take off that dress!," "We want rock 'n' roll!," lots of other things I don't even want to repeat, just really filthy mouth stuff. This really surprised me, that these kids didn't know any better, all from good homes and liberal-minded, to boot . . . I was happier with the pimps and the hookers . . . During the gospel tours I saw what the nation's universities were about. It was extremely fascinating. It used to be that people would boo my backup band . . . Now they were shouting abuses at the girls that were singing with me . . . I was a little embarrassed for these people but I didn't let it show. [1985]

He clearly wanted to get this off his chest, preferably in a way that a skeptical media could not distort. This could well have been why he first talked about the experience at a show in Toronto five months after Tempe, when a camera crew was there to film a TV special that, sadly, never came to pass.[21]

On one occasion, at a concert in Toronto the following April, Dylan not only revisited Lindsey's disingenuous dialectic but the reaction it engendered in Arizona, in what was—surely not coincidentally—the night he paid for a local camera crew to film the show, thus capturing on celluloid this five-minute midrash on Old and New Testament prophecies:

In the Bible it tells you specific things in the Book of Daniel, and in the Book of Revelation, which just might apply to these times. It says certain wars are soon gonna happen. I can't say exactly when, but pretty soon . . . So at that time, it mentions a country to the furthermost north and it has [as] its symbol: the bear. It's also spelt R

---

[21] Widely bootlegged from a VHS dub, the show is for now the best visual record of this tour, despite the limitations of the three-camera setup.

O S H in the Bible. Now, this was written quite a few years ago. [Yet] it can't really but apply to one country that I know. Unless you know another country that it can apply to? I don't. Then there's another country, I can't remember what the name of it is, but it's in the eastern part of the world and it's got an army of two hundred million foot soldiers. Now there's only one country that that could actually be. Anyway, I was telling this story to these people. I shouldn't have been telling it to them, I just got carried away. And I mentioned to them . . . Russia is gonna come down and attack the Middle East. It says this in the Bible. I been reading all kinds of books my whole life, magazines, books, whatever I could get my hands on, and I never found any truth in any of them. But these things in the Bible they seem to uplift me and tell me the truth.

That night in Canada he recalled an occasion "about four months ago" when he was playing "someplace, it was a college campus, I forget exactly where, Arizona, I think . . . Anyway, I read the Bible a lot, you know, I mean it just happens I do and . . . it says certain things in the Bible that I wasn't really aware of until just recently." He proceeds to describe an audience full of "higher learning people," who teach their students "all these different philosophies like Plato and . . . Nietzsche and those people."

Dylan decided they could benefit from one more lecture. What would follow would be his most protracted (and eschatologically unsound) account of the Apocalypse According to Lindsey since that second night at Tempe:

So I said, this country is gonna come down and attack, and all these people, there must have been 50,000 . . . [voice of band member: "If there was one."] [Okay,] there was . . . maybe 3,000, [but] they all just booed. You know, like they usually do. They just booed. I said Russia's gonna attack the Middle East and they all went "boo." They couldn't hear that, they didn't believe it. And a month later Russia moved their troops into Afghanistan, and the whole situation changed. I'm not saying this to tell you that they was wrong and I was right, or anything like that. But these things that is mentioned in the Bible I pay mighty close attention to. ['Cause] it does talk about this man here called Antichrist. Now we've had a lot of previews of what the Antichrist could be like. We had that Jim Jones, he's like a preview. We had Adolf Hitler, a preview. Anyway, the Antichrist is gonna be a little bit different than that. He's gonna bring peace to the world for a certain length of time. But he will eventually be defeated, too. Supernaturally defeated.

Unlike in Tempe, the fourth night Toronto crowd would take this all in their stride. But, back in November, he had to deal with a crowd in no mood to hear the message through and determined to get its money's worth. And if he felt he had been in the wars on night one, it was a mere skirmish compared to the second onslaught:

> *How many people here are aware that we're living in the end of times right now? How many people are aware of that? Anybody wanna know that? Anybody interested in knowing that we're living in the End Times? All right, how many people do know that? Just, yell out or do something. How many people don't know that? Well, we are. We're living in the End Times.* [*"The Times They Are A-Changin'!"*] *That's right. I told you "The Times They Are A-Changin" twenty years ago. And I don't believe I've ever lied to you. I don't think I said anything that's been a lie. I never told you to vote for nobody. Never told you to follow nobody . . . What you're gonna need is something strong to hang on to. You got drugs to hang on to now. You might have a job to hang on to now. You may have your college education to hang on to now. But you're gonna need something very solid to hang on to when these days come. Let me tell you one more thing, when Jesus spoke His parables, He spoke them to . . . all these people . . . Everybody heard the same parables. Some people understood them and some people didn't. But He said . . . the same thing to everybody. He didn't try to hide it, He just said it. Those that believed it, believed it and understood it, and those that didn't, didn't. That's right . . . You talk to your teachers about what I say. I'm sure you're paying a lot of good money for your education now—so you better get one.*

With hecklers this determined, he was always fighting a losing battle. For once, an aethiest cabal gave as good as it got from the lapsed agnostic. They might have done even better if they'd known the titles of the songs for which they were shouting. When someone kept shouting for "Everybody Must Get Stoned," Dylan explained the true meaning of that song's dual layered burden:

> *I'll tell you a story about that now. When Jesus saw this woman, they all wanted to stone her. Because she was an adulteress. So they come by and they wanted to stone her. And they said to Jesus . . .—they wanted to trick Him—"What say you? What do you say there, should we stone this woman? Because she has been an adulterer?" And He says, "Well, let him who is without sin cast the first stone." They all just dropped their stones and they walked away. And then He said to the woman, "Woman, you're free now. Go and sin no more." And the woman left.*

When the song request was merely repeated, he snapped, "I'll tell you about getting stoned! What do you want to know about getting stoned?" The section of the audience who thought they were going to get a show similar to last year's arena-friendly greatest hits resorted to bellowing—in time-honored fashion—the mantra, "Rock 'n' roll." It sparked a verbal spat between performer and would-be rock 'n' rollers that made the fuming folkies of 1966 (for whom the phrase rock 'n' roll had always been anathema) seem positively circumspect:

> Pretty rude bunch tonight! You all know how to be real rude. You [all] know about the spirit of the Antichrist! Does anybody here know about that? Well, the spirit of the Antichrist is loose right now. Let me give you an example. You know, I got a place out [West]. Somebody stopped by my house . . . There's many false deceivers running around these days. [But] there's only one Gospel! The Bible says anybody who preaches anything other than that one Gospel, let him be accursed. ["Rock 'n' roll!"] Anyway, a young fellow stopped by my house one time and wanted to so-called "turn me on" to a certain guru. I don't want to mention his name right now, but he has a place out there, near LA. And [so] he gave me this taped cassette . . . ["Rock 'n' roll!"] . . . If you wanna rock 'n' roll, you can go down and rock 'n' roll. You can go see Kiss, and you rock 'n' roll all your way down to the pit!

Hoping he had seen off the infidels' insurrection, Dylan resumed his portrait of another false Messiah—this one catering largely to gullible hippes—but it was all in vain. No one was listening. Eventually, he again asked someone to shine a light in the dark, "Turn the lights on in here. I want to see these people. Turn some lights on. Give them some light. Put them in the light." Temporarily cowed by the prospect of some mightily pissed Christians (a few of whom can be heard shouting back) forgetting to turn the other cheek, the hecklers quietened down long enough for Dylan to complete his account of the fake guru who was telling his disciples:

> "What life's all about is to have fun . . . I'm gonna show you now how you all can have fun." And he had a big fire extinguisher there and he put colored water in this fire extinguisher, and he'd spray it out on the people. And they all laughed and just had a good time. They took their clothes off. They were overjoyed to be sprayed by this man. And a little while after that, he . . . said that God's inside of him and he is God. I want to tell you this because there's many of these people walking around. They might not come right out and say they're God, but they're just waiting for the opportunity. There

is only one God! Let me hear you say who that God is? [mixed shouts] Their God makes promises he doesn't keep.

Before Dylan can steam into "When You Gonna Wake Up," though, another heckler makes one last plea for some "Rock 'n' roll," prompting Dylan to show all such hecklers their future cards—aces backed with eights:

You still want to rock 'n' roll? I'll tell you what the two kinds of people are. Don't matter how much money you got, there's only two kinds of people: There's saved people and there's lost people. [Applause] Now remember that I told you that . . . I may not be through here again, you may not see me [again, but] sometime down the line you'll remember you heard it here, that Jesus is Lord. And every knee shall bow to him.

The "When You Gonna Wake Up" Dylan finally got to deliver that night, after an unprecedented eight-minute rap, would have woken a coma patient, while subsequent shouts of "rock 'n' roll" would be met with shrift so short it was more like five o'clock shadow.

But Dylan had not yet had the last word. One particularly determined purveyor of the Tempe rock 'n' roll chapter may well have traveled the relatively short distance to Tucson because, a fortnight later, somebody audibly shouts for rock 'n' roll before "Slow Train" at the Community Center on December 8th. It prompted Dylan to spit out, "I know all about rock 'n' roll. I been rock 'n' rolling when you was in diapers . . . Do you know about the end of times, though? I'm just curious. I know you know about rock 'n' roll, but do you know about the end of times? The last days?"

Outside of California, large elements of the audience were simply not listening when the girlsingers sang, "It's gonna rain/ Won't be water, but fire next time." In fact, it was the hostility which greeted the girls' set which initially fired Dylan up in Tempe:

Regina McCrary: I remember one or two times that the crowd, when I walked out on stage, these people were like, "Who is that? That ain't Bob Dylan." . . . I think [the reaction in Arizona] was what really blew him away—that it was a college crowd . . . Normally, the audience when I went out telling the story would listen and they would respond. They would be into it. This crowd wanted Bob Dylan. They were real rowdy. Dylan was really disappointed.

As late as 1985 Dylan was still complaining about the reaction McCrary sometimes received when she "would open these shows with a monologue about a woman on a train. She was so incredibly moving. I wanted to expose people to that sort of thing because I loved it, and it's the real roots of all modern music, but nobody cared." It would be fair to say the reaction was usually, er, mixed.

Dylan's assitant recalls they actually "heckled [the girls] at the Arizona shows." Indeed, Kelly takes the view that Dylan was left with little choice but to meet them head-on, "In Arizona he had to talk. I don't think they were walking out but they were definitely heckling. They were insisting on the old songs . . . At the first one I thought he was going to put his guitar down and leave, but he stayed and talked to them, like a new song he'd written on the spot for them."

At the second Tempe gig—the one and only time Dylan did not do an encore on the gospel tour—he made one last attempt to get through before "In The Garden."[22] It had been an encounter he would never forget and it would color his mindset for the rest of the tour. In this final rap he is possibly alluding to finding Jesus himself in Tempe, a year earlier:

We have time for one more. I wonder what it will be. I think it will be this one. Remember now, don't be deceived by what gets inside. You know, even Jesus was deceived by one of His own men. Just like Jesse James, He was deceived by someone He invited into His house. Anyway, we're gonna play this one and beat on down the road now. Remember what I said, if you ever hear it some other time, that there is a truth and a life and a way. So you may not get it now. It may not be the next week. It may not be the next year or so. But remember, the next time it happens.

The revelation he experienced a vision the night after San Diego on the '78 tour he would reserve for his return to the bordertown, the night after Tempe. Again, he was given a rocky ride but he kept his nerve, at one point seemingly responding to a request, "Someone shouted out . . . 'Solid Rock.' 'Hanging On To A Solid Rock Made Before The Foundation Of The World,' is that the one you mean?" All requests for older fare, though, continued to be stonewalled, much to the growing frustration of local writer John Mood, who later questioned Dylan's sincerity and reveled in his own ignorance in a 1994 *San Diego Reader* article:

[22] It is possible that Dylan cut short both Tempe shows simply because he was not feeling well. A report in the Arizona Republic (Nov 29th) reads: "It was touch and go there for a while on Sunday night. Bob Dylan had complained of a cold and made some noise like he might call off Sunday's show unless he could see a doctor. He was talked into taking the stage when he was asured a doctor would be waiting backstage to treat him."

It was a completely uncompromising concert. None of his older stuff, just the Christian tunes. But what was really awful were the little pissant sermons he regaled us with between songs. Dylan, who hadn't spoken ten words in the half a dozen concerts I had heard before! Here he was, going on and on, talking his head off about Jesus, about how the last time he was in San Diego he was down and blue and some kid put a cross on the Sports Arena stage and how he thought about the kid caring, blah blah blah. It was so embarrassing my wife went out to the lobby to get a stiff drink . . . She was immediately interviewed by someone from Channel 8. We saw it that night after we got home . . . For the only time in my life, I booed a performer.

Thankfully, in California there remained enough believers who loved what they were hearing to encourage Dylan to press on. The girls onstage were also a willing chorus, even between songs. In San Diego they could barely wait to start "Blessed Be The Name" as Dylan concluded his band introduction by reiterating, "We want to give all praise and glory to God tonight," before reminding the audience, "We'll be back here tomorrow night." He knew neither show had sold out, spiritually or materially.

A six-day break in Los Angeles followed—after Salt Lake City decided it already had its own Christian cult, thank you very much. Dylan, meanwhile, decided that if this was going to be 1966 revisited, he was going to take a leaf from that oft-consumed document and record the reactions of fans leaving the shows for posterity—and perhaps as a promotional tool.

Unlike the Channel 8 news piece, he was looking to present both sides, good and bad responses. And so, in Albuquerque he placed a small recording crew outside the Kiva Auditorium to ask fans if they liked the show. The reactions proved just as polarized as the ones Bobby Neuwirth captured outside Manchester's Free Trade Hall in 1966 and those he had already encountered in Arizona, especially from those scurrying out before the encores:

"I love Bob Dylan and I had no idea it was going to be like this. And it's really a drag. He wouldn't play any of his old songs. It was a total let down and I'm never gonna listen to Bob Dylan again."

"I thought it sucked. I think they should advertise what they're gonna play for fifteen bucks."

"He should've played his old songs and [instead] he acted like he was doing us a favor when he was singing the songs. I was really disappointed."

He had finally found a way to directly address all those requests for old songs, which he slipped in before another "Slow Train" started smoking down the tracks:

If you look at the Middle East, they're heading for a war. That's right, they're heading for war. There's gonna be war over there . . . maybe five years, maybe ten years, could [be] fifteen years, I don't know, but remember, I told you right here. I told you "The Times They Are A-Changin'" and they did! I said the answer was "Blowin' In The Wind" and it was! And I'm telling you now, Jesus is coming back, and He is! There is no other way to salvation. I know around here you've got a lot of gurus . . . You've got a lot of people just putting a mess on you in all kinds of ways, you don't even know which way to believe. There's only one way to believe. There's only one way, the truth and the light. Now it took me a long time to figure that out . . . I hope it doesn't take you that long. But Jesus is coming back to set up His kingdom in Jerusalem for a thousand years. I don't know if that's news to you. I know you don't read it in the newspapers. But it's the truth, . . . if you're saved, you're saved. And if you're lost, you're lost.

As for those who thought they could detach the music—which most reviewers had realized was top-notch—from the words, he had another little speech prepared, a thinly-veiled dig at said reviewers:

I was reading something somebody said, "I like the music, but I can't get the message. I like the music, but it's the message I can't get." That's like saying, "I like the eye, but the nose, I just can't quite place. The ears are okay, but the neck just don't work." You know, some of you people got to be responsible for what you say.

The first night in Albuquerque, enough of the audience stayed with him to prompt him to say, "I'm glad you all got to come," pre-encore. The fellow Christians who stayed for the encore were also caught on tape leaving the show, and though many confined themselves to a "Praise the Lord!" or a "It was great!," others reveled in the opportunity to tell it like it is. One happy-clappy fan said, "He's coming right out and saying it. He's not keeping it in." Another attendee was particularly delighted that he stuck it to the Tucson chapter of Rockers:

"I think it's great he stands up for what he believes in. When he started, there was some people in front of us shouting for 'Rock 'n' roll,' and at the end they were [just] sitting there. I think he pulled it off pretty good."

But the local ex-fans had some thoughts they wanted to get off their chests, too, including one lady who took the idea of Dylan as Judas to a whole other level: "I can tell you what I think. It was disgusting. Dylan wasn't there! He really should have put a bullet in his brain five years ago."

The heckling continued on the second night, according to the *Albuquerque Journal*'s reporter, Denise Tessier, who heard shouts of, "Is this a revival meeting?" and "I've heard all these stories before—in Bible class!"

Maybe Dylan had started to realize he was losing the media war. Perhaps this is why, when he picked the phone up in his Tucson hotel room two nights later, and the person on the end of the line identified himself as a radio reporter, he did not slam the phone down or tell him to put it where the Son don't shine. Rather, he agreed to answer some questions. The lucky radio reporter had caught the recalcitrant rock star in a rare moment of openness, thus securing the one and only interview of the year:

Bruce Heiman: The interview actually became a reality because of personal enterprise . . . I narrowed a list of hotels where he might be staying. The first place I called was an historic boutique hotel called the Arizona Inn. I knew I couldn't call asking to talk to Bob Dylan . . . So, I asked for Bob Zimmerman, and he picked up on the first ring . . . Had I been a more seasoned journalist and interviewer at the time, I most certainly would have done more research, challenged him a bit, and broadened the scope of the interview . . . I hosted a call-in/interview program, *Tucson Talk*. Madalyn Murray O'Hair, who founded the [American Atheists] organization, was a guest on the show. And during the course of our interview, she mentioned plans to picket the concert . . . I remember being . . . somewhat surprised that when we did chat he was pleasant, personable, and even complimentary of the initiative I employed to get through to him . . . I remember when he answered the phone, I asked his permission to roll the tape and record the interview. And, he said, "Sure. Since you were so resourceful in finding me, how can I say no?" [SM]

What perhaps worked in Heiman's favor was his almost complete ignorance of the general tenor of the reviews to date. All he really knew when he began rolling tape for his seven-minute scoop, was what he had read on a press release from a so-called voice of reason:

Bruce Heiman: We got a press release from the Tucson chapter of the American Atheists and they said in response to your recent embrace of the born-again Christian movement, they plan to leaflet your upcoming concert . . . The American Atheists is a worldwide group headed by Madalyn Murray O'Hair, and they have a chapter here in Tucson, and I think basically what they are talking about is your stand in the past and the type of music you played with the message you tried to get across and the music you're playing today and the different message you're trying to get across.

Bob Dylan: Well, whatever the old message was, the Bible says, "All things become new, old things are passed away." I guess this group doesn't believe that. What is it exactly that they're protesting?

BH: Well, I think what they're against . . . there's another statement that they make. It says . . .

BD: Are they against the doctrine of Jesus Christ, or that He died on the cross or that man was born into sin? Just what exactly are they protesting?

BH: Well, the Atheists are against any sort of religion, be it Christianity . . .

BD: Christ is no religion. We're not talking about religion . . . Jesus Christ is the way, the truth and the life.

BH: There's another statement they made that maybe you could shed some light on. They said they would like to remind Dylan fans and audiences that one's right to say something does not per se lend any validity to the statement. So, in essence, what they're saying is that you have followers who are going to be at the concert and are going to listen to the message of your music.

BD: Right. I follow God, so if my followers are following me, indirectly they're gonna be following God too because I don't sing any song which hasn't been given to me by the Lord to sing.

BH: OK. So I think that was one thing that they were concerned about. Do you have any idea what they mean . . . see, they believe that all religion is repressive and reactionary.

BD: Well, religion is repressive to a certain degree. Religion is another form of bondage which man invents to get himself to God. But that's why Christ came. Christ didn't preach religion. He preached the truth, the way and the life. He said He'd come to give life and life more abundantly. He is talking about life, not necessarily religion . . .

BH: They say that your songs now expound passive acceptance of one's fate. Do you agree with that? I'm not exactly sure what they mean by that.

BD: I'm not exactly sure what they mean by that either. But I don't feel that that is true. But I'm not quite sure what that means—"passive resistance to mans' fate." What is mans' fate?

BH: I don't know. These aren't my ideologies. These are just a group of Atheists.

BD: Well, this ideology isn't my ideology either. My ideology now would be coming out of the scripture. You see, I didn't invent these things. These things have just been shown to me and I'll stand on that faith, that they are true. I believe they're true. I know they're true.

BH: Do you feel that the message of your music has changed over the years from music which talked about war to music that now talks about Christianity?

BD: No. There's gonna be war. There's always war and rumors of war. And the Bible talks about a war coming up which will be a war to end all wars . . .

[Discontinuity in tape.]

BD: . . .The spirit of the atheist will not prevail. I can tell you that much. It's a deceiving spirit.

BH: Why do you maintain that it won't prevail?

BD: Is it anti-God? Is an atheist anti-God?

BH: Yes. I'm trying to think . . . I interviewed Madalyn Murray O'Hair a couple of weeks ago and she said that it is anti-religion, anti-God. I think that she was saying that anyone who believes in a supreme being is, to use her word, is stupid. So they are against anything to do with religion.

BD: Uh-huh!

BH: Sometimes it's hard for me to grasp exactly what they are saying.

BD: Well, a religion which says you have to do certain things to get to God, they're probably talking about that type of religion which is [faith] by works: you can enter into the Kingdom by what you do, what you wear, what you say, how many times a day you may pray, how many good deeds you may do. If that's what they mean by religion, well that type of religion will not get you into the Kingdom, that's true. However, there is a master creator, a supreme being in the universe.

Out there in agnostic Arizona, on local FM station KMEX, Dylan had just answered all the big questions the national media had been trying to prise out of him for the past six months, and getting nowhere. Here was a series of statements as plain as day and as clear as glass. It would have been difficult for even *Newsweek* to spin a sentence like "Jesus Christ is the way, the truth and the life." As for those holding out hope that he might relent and play some old songs, "I don't sing any song which hasn't been given to me by the Lord to sing," closed the lid firmly shut.

As for the idea that he was now part of a religious conspiracy, he was unequivocal, "Religion is another form of bondage . . . Christ didn't preach religion." Which again was almost chapter and verse from Lindsey's *Satan Is Alive And Well*: "Christianity isn't a religion; Christianity is a personal relationship with God through Jesus Christ and His finished work. It's not [about] our trying to gain God's approbation by what we do."

For someone who did not believe in "faith by works," Dylan was sure going out of his way to spread the Gospel from place to place. No matter how many times he left Sodom and Gomorrah behind—and the twin shows in Tucson again proved something of a haven for hecklers and heretics—he simply refused to look back.

6. WHERE I WILL ALWAYS BE RENEWED
[January – February 1980]

MUSCLE SHOALS SOUND STUDIOS

SONG TITLE: SAVED
ENGINEERS: GREGG Hamm
ARTIST: BOB.
DATE: 2/13

REEL NUMBER	TAKE NUMBER	LOCATOR NUMBERS	COMMENTS	
4	1	8 - 206		SATISFIED MIND R
	2	206 - 606	SAVED PB	
		SAVING GRACE		
4	1	27	FS	2/13/
	1	61		
	1	96 - 610	— PULLED —	
	2	623 - 1175	— PULLED — PB	
		PRESSING ON		
	1	22 -	FS	
		79 - 669		KEEP PB 1518

MUSCLE SHOALS SOUND STUDIOS

SONG TITLE: PRESSING ON
ENGINEERS: GREGG Hamm / MB
ARTIST: BOB D
DATE: 2/13/

REEL NUMBER	TAKE NUMBER	LOCATOR NUMBERS	COMMENTS	
5	1	15 -	FS	
	1	27 - 313	TALISMAN ?	

Gospel music is about the love of God. And commercial music is about the love of sex.
—BOB DYLAN TO KATHRYN BAKER, 1988

Everybody is entitled to lead a private life. Then again, God watches everybody. So there's nothing really private, there's nothing we can hide . . . [from] the power that created you [and I].
—BOB DYLAN TO EDNA GUNDERSEN, 1989

I know a lot of country and western people . . . sing, very often, "You can put your shoes under my bed anytime." And then they turn around and sing, "Oh Lord, just a closer walk with thee." Well, I can't do that, That's right, you cannot serve two masters. You gotta hate one and love the other. You can't drink out of two cups.
—BOB DYLAN, BEFORE "IN THE GARDEN"
AT THE AKRON CIVIC THEATER, MAY 18, 1980

When the gospel band reconvened at Rundown on January 7, 1980 for a couple of days' rehearsing before hitting the trail again in Oregon and Washington with three shows in Portland and Seattle respectively, Dylan had an idea for his first new song in a couple of months. Called "Drinkin' Out Of Two Cups," it took its inspiration from a line in 1 Corinthians 10:21: "Ye cannot drink the cup of the Lord, and the cup of Devils." Now, it was just a riff. In fact, this would be the last ever heard of the idea, perhaps because it was a little too close to real life for the born-again singer. He had just lost Helena Springs at the end of the fall tour, after a full-blown fight:

Dave Kelly: Halfway through the tour one of the girls disappears . . . They had a big row and he told her to leave. They were pretty close . . . She was definitely single. [Their relationship] was only a rumor until the big split up, when it became pretty obvious . . . [She was] a very hot-headed lady. None of us really got on with her . . . I had heard that they had made up again, but I never saw her after December '79 . . . I remember her throwing things around the room and Bob [just] standing there.

It had never been entirely clear where his relationship with Springs ended and the one with Artes began—or how much overlap there ever was. From the outside, it seems like it was Artes who probably saved his life—hence, his description in "Slow Train" of a backwoods girl who "sure was realistic/ She said, Boy, without a doubt, have to quit your mess and straighten out/ You could die down here, be just another accident statistic." Whereas Helena is perhaps a more credible candidate for the precious angel who at one point, at least, was "the queen of my flesh . . . the lamp of my soul, girl, and you torch up the night."[23]

Helena's absence from the band that January prompted a most uncharacteristic rap at the second Seattle show, and it came before "Precious Angel." If the singer was planning to stick to one cup from now on, it seems he sure was missing someone:

> I was talking with someone last night who travels around and [she] said . . . she was riding in a cab once. Cab driver turned around in the cab and said, "Did you hear Bob Dylan's a Christian now?" This girl said, "Oh, I think I have heard that. How does that relate to you? Are you a Christian?" And the driver said, "No, but I been following Bob now for a long time." And the lady said, "Well, what you think of his new thing?" And he said, "Well, . . . I think that if I could meet that person who brought Bob Dylan to the Lord, I think I might become a Christian too." This here song is all about that certain person.

But if Dylan thought a passing comment at a Northwest show was likely to pass without media comment, he was mistaken. To *Seattle Times* reviewer, Patrick MacDonald—who took his job so seriously he attended all three Seattle shows—"the most important question to emerge from the concerts was: Who is the woman?" He even contacted Dylan's New York office, only to be told they were as confused as him, "There are apparently several women involved. Nobody here knows who they are."

One employee, his publicist Paul Wasserman, knew his boss better. When asked whether Dylan's conversion was due to the influence of new women in his life, he told a Toronto journalist, "Bob's over 21. He knows what he's doing. Besides, he has had a lot of women telling him a lot of things." One of these women was soon reported to be on the receiving end of a substantial largesse, Dylan being seen in a Seattle jewelers purchasing an engagement ring allegedly worth $25,000.

---

[23] According to lyrics that appear online, the line is actually, "You're the lamb of my soul, girl, and you touch up the night." It turns out Dylan has his own pirate publisher of bad quartos, name of Google.

(Dylan would later suggest he wrote "Caribbean Wind" after "thinking about living with somebody for all the wrong reasons." Given his newly-found Christian values, he surely did not mean living in sin, a.k.a. drinking from two cups. Hence, perhaps, the rhetorical line, "Would [he] have married her? I don't know, I suppose.")

Rolling Stone picked up on the engagement-ring story, also asking the office to comment, but "no one . . . could offer a clue [as to] the intended recipient." Evidently, he was keeping his employees as much in the dark as the Dark Lady herself.

Instead, the only official comment coming out of Seattle that snowy season came from Dylan's manager, Jerry Weintraub, who wrote to *Rolling Stone* to inform them that the three "undersold" Seattle shows actually generated 8,485 ticket sales from a compound capacity of 8,928, and that, "as far as [Weintraub could] ascertain . . . from people on the road with Bob Dylan, the audience did not walk out. In fact, the tour is doing very well." What prompted the letter was Mr. Macdonald's review of the first Seattle show—which was once again picked up by the wire services:

> Hundreds walked out during the course of the [first] concert. A few left after only a few songs. Perhaps eighty to a hundred headed for the doors in the middle of the show when Dylan turned the stage over to backup singer Regina McCrary . . . Hundreds more left before the first encore and about a third of the house was gone for the second. Very few of the songs elicited more than polite applause. There wasn't even a standing ovation at the end, and there was no attempt to rush the stage during the encores.

What was not picked up by the same services was MacDonald's more measured review of all three shows in the weekend edition of the *Seattle Times*. In this, he qualified his account of the seemingly disastrous opening night, contrasting it with the positive reaction Dylan received at the other shows:

> The [religious] theme was received with enthusiasm by the crowds on the second and third nights . . . He was almost talkative in the second and his performance was more loose and joyful. It was the best show of the three . . . But the first night, where perhaps a majority of the crowd were old Dylan fans rather than new believers, many couldn't accept his new philosophy and said so by turning their backs on Dylan and walking out.

Likewise, a positive review of opening night in Portland on the 11th, by John Wendeborn in *The Oregonian*—under the headline, "Crowd Pleased With New Dylan"—had generated almost no reaction out of state. And yet, according to Wendeborn:

> There was no outbursts of requests for his older material, the stuff that helped a generation of youth in the 60s discover its collective self. As an entertainer, Dylan still had virtually nothing to say verbally. He didn't need any spoken words. His lyrics alluded to his philosophy, but his music drilled the freshness home with a passion that needed no fundamentalist fire and brimstone.

After twenty-hours spent cooling his heels in a snowed-in hotel, Dylan again allowed the music to speak itself, save for the by-now-usual reminder during the band intros. to "give all the praise and all the glory to God tonight. We believe in a God that can raise the dead."

But it seems that whatever Dylan (or his employees) did, they could not stem the tide of negativity swirling around these shows as far as the media was concerned. In a move designed to project the views the shows generated in a positive light, Dylan now had the post-gig interviews from Albuquerque (with at least one "fake" interviewee interposed) made into a radio ad for the upcoming shows.

The ad in question began with a disgusted apostate complaining, "I was kinda disappointed. I wanted to hear rock 'n' roll. Rock 'n' roll! I heard Bob Dylan singing gospel," only to then segue into a series of testimonies as to how good the band were and the show was. Unfortunately, even if the ploy worked, the show it initially advertised—on the 10th—ended up canceled, not because of poor sales:

Spooner Oldham: We had very bad weather several days running. We were on a bus and it was like a storm system was just hours ahead of us . . . [In] Portland, Oregon, we were driving into the city that evening to our hotel, the power was out on that side of town. It was total darkness. There was a lot of snow and the wind was howling. My thoughts . . . that evening were . . . There's no way it can happen. But the next evening we were there and everybody else seemed to be there . . . chains on their cars and four-wheelers. [SM]

As a result, it took Dylan a show or two in windswept Oregon to really warm up. But once he did, he again began interspersing songs with mini-sermons and sardonic asides, commenting at one point during the second Portland show[24] how mentioning Jesus seemed to set some people off:

> *The deity of Jesus just drives people crazy sometimes. Some people love Him and want to throw roses. You can only step in front of the stage and you wouldn't believe it! Some people hate Jesus and they throw toilet rolls at us. Jesus separates all people. [But] The Bible says, "If any man should preach you another gospel, let that man be accursed."[25] Those are strong words.*

In fact, just as in Seattle, the best of the three Portland shows was probably the middle one, when he felt decidedly talkative, prompted in part by an outburst "of requests for his older material," which was dealt with in an uncharacteristically senstive way. After he gave the game away by describing "In The Garden" as "one more hymn," someone audibly shouts from the crowd, "We still dig you, Bob!" Other inaudible shouts follow, but it seems to be the first of these to which Dylan responds when he says, "Well, I know I have a fond remembrance of the old too, you know. [But] the old has passed away. All things are become new."

Where Portland and Seattle were markedly different was the level of resistance he met. At the second Seattle show, there were still some audibly resisting the message. Before "Gonna Change My Way of Thinking," in response to a shout of "This is bullshit!," Dylan asks, "Some of [you] people out there don't like the Lord [or] don't know the Lord? What is it? Don't you like the Lord or don't you know the Lord? Which one of those is it?"

He also felt prompted to suggest "those of you who have never read the Book of Revelation" should "watch out . . . every time you see that word *unilateral* in the newspapers." During the band introductions, he told the waverers, "When Jesus died it was not the end, it was the beginning of the end. And we're right upon it now. You know we are."

At the third and last of the Seattle shows, he continued to interrogate the audience, asking aloud before "In The Garden," "How many here are with the Lord and how many aren't with the Lord? How many? . . . I'd like to say for the rest of [you], that we believe in a God that can raise the dead."

---

[24] The canceled show on the 10th was rescheduled for after the Seattle shows, on the 16th, making the two three-night residencies almost bleed into one. Certainly, a legendary Seattle-based taper also considered the Portland shows fair game.
[25] The quote comes from Galatians 1:8—"Preach any other gospel unto you than that which we have preached unto you, let him be accursed."

He also gave "Slow Train" its starkest preface in a while, "There's a slow train coming. Coming out in the open, coming out there, just so you know what I'm talking about tonight." And when "Solid Rock" generated its usual standing ovation at the end, rather than taking a bow, he wanted to know, "Are you all applauding for Jesus? ['Cause] Jesus is gonna turn this world upside down."

He was warming to his message again. And yet, at the following night, back in Portland, he retired into his shell between songs, even if he continued to deliver every line of lyric as if they were burning coals. In fact, after Portland the tour almost disappeared into a Midwest mist as it ventured across Washington, Colorado, Nebraska, Missouri, Tennessee, Alabama and West Virginia, where it would wind up on February 9th. One band member concluded it was part of a deliberate policy:

Fred Tackett: They were [mostly] places that Bob hadn't played in maybe sixteen years, a lot of them . . . So he was very clever. We didn't ever play New York City or LA [sic]. We always played out [in] Louisville, Kentucky or Knoxville, Tennessee, places where people don't see Bob very often.

The two shows in Spokane, Washington, were so far off the beaten track that even the tapers couldn't be bothered to make the trek. They missed a Dylan determined to play around with the *Slow Train* arrangements, notably on a "Gonna Change My Way Of Thinking" where lines stretched and snapped back with an aplomb last seen in the days of Rolling Thunder. It was perhaps this very arrangement that prompted the now-settled guitarist to offer his boss some advice—and be firmly put in his place:

Fred Tackett: I think he was probably singing better at that period of time than he'd sung in many years. I mean, he really sang great. I have tapes of those shows where he's just doing incredible things. I remember one thing he did [was] back-phrasing, where he'll start to play a song and won't start singing right away. He'll wait and start singing and playing catch-up, trying to catch up before the next chord comes . . . I remember after a show, I said, "Bob, you were really out on a ledge tonight. I didn't think you were going to make it by the time we got to the next chord." . . . And the very next night, we did the song and he did the exact same thing again.

The first Spokane gig saw another impassioned preface to "In The Garden." Alluding to the messsage of the previous song, "What Can I Do For You?,"

Dylan asked the town's unarchival attendees, "You all got somebody you're doing something for? Good. Well, if you get into trouble, it says in the Bible, 'He who calls on the name of the Lord shall be saved.'[26] That's all you got to do. Just you remember that, if you don't hear that again . . . Actually it just starts there. After that, amazing things begin happening to ya. Oh yeah, it's true."

After Spokane, it was time to leave the coastal states behind and head into the hinterlands. For the next fortnight, the tour would loop south, zigzagging from west to east, stopping off only in cities that could sustain two- or three-night theater residencies. Denver, Colorado, was one such city. It was a place he had been visiting since skipping school in 1960, when it had been the part it played in Kerouac's *On The Road* which drew him there and a gig as a piano player and a well-endowed older lady which kept him there.

And its Beat association had recently been reinforced when Allen Ginsberg and Anne Waldman established the Jack Kerouac School of Disembodied Poetics in nearby Naropa in 1974. The prospect of three shows at Denver's intimate Rainbow Music Hall was bound to prompt the now-Buddhist Ginsberg to enter Dylan's orbit for an evening of soul-searching—and so it proved. He brought along a Naropa party of would-be beatniks to the third performance, an experience he enthused about when the topic came up the following January:

Allen Ginsberg: As an aesthetic mood, it's a marvelous mood, in terms of exploring American music and making it his own and reviewing it. Two, it was one of the most integrated shows that I've ever seen. Five blacks and five whites on stage. Three: he seemed to be trying to get out of himself. Transcend himself into something else; which I thought was healthy. Another thing I noticed was that his lyrics were the only world-heard lyrics that mentioned Kissinger and made an outright comment . . . I think the implication was that Kissinger was in the service of the Devil. Not that I believe in the Devil, but it was nice to hear Dylan being so outspoken. [1981]

On a personal level, though, the whole thing proved more unnerving. His friend for the past sixteen years had changed, and when he ventured backstage to say hi, their conversation, he later recalled, "was pithy. I said that I remembered that Blake's Christ was Forgiveness and Mercy, not Judgement and Wrath. And Dylan said, 'Sure, but He is coming to judge.' . . . Dylan meant an apocalyptic judgement, but that's not so far-fetched. He's saying that our evil has gotten so

---

[26] Romans 10:13 says, "For whosoever shall call upon the *name of the Lord shall be saved.*"

thick that it's going to come back on itself . . . His [new] songs are [all] about the end of days, about the classic situation of repent-before-it's-too-late."

As always, Ginsberg preferred to give Dylan the benefit of the doubt. But he was unquestionably disturbed by the things he heard, and concluded, probably astutely, that "Dylan is reacting with a kind of terror to what's going down in civilization, and [to] being a prophet and [is] taking it very seriously." Perhaps Dylan's one onstage pronouncement that night was partly directed at his fellow lapsed Jew, "I wanna tell everybody here to stay out of those cults . . . ['cause] there's only one Gospel. Don't you be fooled now."

Not that the Denver shows were the wholly joyless affairs Allen's account might suggest. The previous night, Dylan enjoyed the groove on "Man Gave Names To All The Animals" so much, he threw in his own call-and-response to the girls' "In the beginning" burdens, calling out, "When?" twice and then, "Is that so?" He also decided the animal which wasn't "too small and wasn't too big" was a dog.

Dylan seemed to be enjoying himself, as were the band. Tackett later told *The Bridge*, "Nobody in the band was . . . overtly Christian, but while we were doing it, we were into it because we could see that was where Bob was coming from, and everybody wanted to push his message."

As the traveling religious revue rolled eastward, the pressure eased off. The reviews also seemed to grow steadily more positive. After Denver, it was two nights in Omaha, where *Daily Reporter* reporter Chuck Nash gave the show a righteous thumbs up:

Dylan came to Omaha in 1978 and the Civic Auditorium sold out in 45 minutes. [The] Jan. 26 [sic] concert was held at the smaller but much more beautiful and acoustically better Orpehum Theatre. It was announced one week before it was to be held and fell about 200 seats short of being sold out . . . Never before have I witnessed such a display of spectators. There were "Jesus people" with Bibles tucked tightly under an arm, enabling themselves to pass out flyers . . . [while] long haired groupy-types dressed in faded jeans and army jackets quickly scurried down the aisles . . . Few showed that they thought the music unacceptable and I heard no shouts for "Mr. Tambourine Man" and "Like A Rolling Stone." At one point, Dylan announced, "We're not going to do any old songs tonight, so if that's what you want you can leave right now." . . . He has chosen to minister to the people through his music . . . Unfortunately [there were] some [who] took offence to being ministered to by their former spokesman . . . but the music was terrific . . . When the concert was over Dylan received two encores and would have gotten more had he been willing to perform longer.

Alhough Nash accurately reported Dylan's rebuke to those who wanted "old songs," he failed to mention the occasion Dylan accepted the mantle of prophet he had been offered a number of times previously. It came as he laid the ground for an increasingly splenetic "Solid Rock":

Years ago they used to say I was a prophet. I used to say, "No, I'm not a prophet." They say, "Yes you are. You're a prophet." I said, "No it's not me." ... Now I come out and say Jesus Christ is the answer. They say, "Bob Dylan's no prophet."

In Kansas, Dylan was again on the receiving end of some unexpectedly positive press. The review in the *City Times* from Leland Rucker apparently struck such a chord with Dylan—who continued reading all the press, good and bad—that he briefly considered including it in an insert to the next album, along with a handful of other reviews. Appearing in the paper the day of the third Kansas show, the review may even have prompted some recalcitrant souls to give eternal peace a chance:

For those expecting a run-through of old hits, there might have been disappointment. Likewise, those thinking he would try to convert the audience Billy Graham-style might have been disillusioned. But for those interested in a magical musical experience, the results were spectacular. The tone of the show was gospel and blues, from the black female vocal quartet that opened the show to the last inspirational rock song. As in the past, when Dylan gets involved in an idea or concept, he does so with complete abandon ... There were a few calls for oldies, and it takes a rare performer not to fall back on familiar melodies in concert. [But] for me, this was a wise move; Dylan has performed and recorded his older songs enough times by now to not continue to have to rely on them ... All the mention of Dylan's conversion and/or personal beliefs is purely academic. Put quite simply, he is making some of the best music of his entire career. Judging from the abundance of new material, he is obviously enjoying it, and the enthusiasm is contagious. The audience cheered wildly from beginning to end, especially at the recognizable cuts from *Slow Train [Coming]*, and I heard no boos or catcalls throughout the more-than-two-hour performance.

By the last day of January, when Dylan and the band pulled into Memphis for a three-night stay in a city whose name was even more evocative of rock 'n' roll than Kansas City, he had just eight more shows in which to definitively whip the songs into shape as a return to Muscle Shoals loomed.

It was the first big "music city" they had played since LA, but the regime remained unchanged. By now, Dylan was concentrating on the music, his only real comment to the Memphis first-night crowd being to remind them, "We'll be here tomorrow night. Come on back if you can."

Bypassing Music City USA, the tour instead went from Birmingham to a two-night pit stop in Knoxville, Tennessee, where they had a special guest backstage. Regina, the daughter of a preacher man, had invited her Nashville-based father to the show; who, as Spooner Oldham recalls, "led the prayer that night, join[ing] in our group. Mostly, it was just a closed group thing . . . the band would gather together for a minute and hold hands in a circle and someone . . . would say a prayer." If Reverend McCrary prayed for a good show, he got one. Once again, a review in the local university *Journal*, by Kathy Boyd, heard only good news at the February 5th Civic Auditorium gig:

> Surprisingly enough, the mixture of strong rock rhythms and gospel lyrics worked. In fact, it soared. Dylan, who has survived transitions from folk to protest to rock to country and back again, has made another amazingly successful transformation, not only in his music, but apparently in his life. His gospel message and his rock and roll music both came through clearly [on] Tuesday night . . . Most of the crowd in the auditorium did concur; unlike other places on Dylan's current tour, here there was no booing or walking out.

Nor, it seems, were there (m)any shouts for old songs in Knoxville. But two nights earlier in Birmingham, Alabama, a persistent soul's call for "Lay Lady Lay" resulted in Dylan laughingly dismissing the request, "Ha, ha, I don't do that anymore. I don't even know why I did it in the first place."

Given that he hadn't sung the song in 1975 or in 1978, his two most successful recent tours, it is hard to see why this particular request kept coming up, it being hardly a favorite of serious Dylan fans. And this would not be Dylan's most damning dismissal of Country Bob's biggest hit.

He had other songs he could relate to, and these included—as of the penultimate show in Charleston, West Virginia (February 8th)—a brand-new original, "Are You Ready?" Replacing "Blessed Be The Name" as first encore, the song was the stick to "Blessed Be The Name"'s carrot, taking a battering ram to the riff he had been using as a backdrop to the nightly band introductions and attaching a bunch of questions a passage in Luke raised: "Be ye therefore ready also for the Son of man cometh at an hour when ye think not." [12:40]

This new song suggested the singer was looking to make the stick and carrot equal partners in the album he would now record. For the first time in a long and distinguished career, Dylan planned to go straight from the road to studio.

He would leave Charleston on the morning of the 10th, flying directly to Nashville, from where he, Drummond and the girls were collected and driven to Muscle Shoals by studio assistant Dick Cooper who remembers "stopp[ing] for burgers in Pulaski, Tennessee, birthplace of the Klan. So there we were, three white boys and three gorgeous black chicks in spandex and sequins. The white waitresses out front were outraged; the black cooks in the back were delighted. It was a helluva scene."

Waiting for them in Sheffield were coproducers Jerry Wexler and Barry Beckett, anxious to resume their commercially-successful association. But at least one Dylan veteran thought his boss was making a big mistake:

Arthur Rosato: We didn't go home. We went straight into the studio. [We thought,] "We're never gonna get home." 'Cause Muscle Shoals is as far away as you could possibly be from anything. It was tiring. And Wexler didn't really have a clue how to work with Bob, either . . . [Here] you have a real famous producer and a guy who's never been produced, and they just don't know how to work together.

The decision to stop off and record a sequel to *Slow Train* after months of playing the songs live was certainly not some whim on Dylan's part. He had hinted at trying such an approach as far back as December 1978, telling the gal from *Trouser Press,* the day he soundchecked "Slow Train," "I got into just taking the songs into the studio before I was too familiar with them and making the record."

Dylan also told an audience as far back as the fifth November '79 show, that they would be "hear[ing] some songs that we're gonna be recording in February or March," reviving an ethos he had abandoned around the time he went electric. This time the intention was crystal clear. As Jerry Wexler said on the album's release, "The [*Saved*] arrangements were built-in, because the band had been playing the songs live. Most of the licks are their own licks, which they perfected on the road, as opposed to the Dire Straits confections on the last album, which were all done in the studio.

And Wexler knew what was coming. He had visited Dylan during initial rehearsals in October 1979, to hear all the new songs. Presumably he had then gone away with tapes of the new songs, waiting for the call to come, suspecting that this time it would be done Dylan's way:

Jerry Wexler: Whatever we did was live. Bob might run it down on piano or guitar, just singing and playing the background until we had a rough shape in our minds, then . . . as soon as it sounded right . . . we'd just keep recording . . . Bob knew what he wanted, and Bob was right. It was just our job to get it, to realize his intention. People don't appreciate Dylan's musical aspect . . . But he's got so much music in him. [1980]

As far as Dylan was concerned, they had spent three months prepping the material for the next album—the reverse aesthetic to the one adopted on *Street-Legal*, an album he essentially wrote before assembling the tour band in November 1977 but, with a single exception (played twice), refrained from teaching to the musicians until they began recording it in late April 1978. The result, if one could believe the US music press, was an album that sounded like a demo. Well, this time, no one— not even Greil Marcus—could accuse him of being ill-prepared or underrehearsed.

He certainly arrived in Sheffield fresher, and several hours ahead of, the rest of the band. According to one key musician, the bulk of the band (and the few members of the crew Dylan knew he needed) had no choice but to travel by bus with the gear—a five hundred mile, eight-hour ride.

This failed to faze them. Spooner Oldham, the only one returning home, remembers, "We essentially went in there and repeated our live performances. It went pretty smoothly. Everybody had fun." Most of the musicians were just delighted to be finally getting the parts they had "perfected on the road" on permanent record:

Fred Tackett: We were on tour, and we literally just drove in with the bus. Played a concert, drove in to the Muscle Shoals to a Holiday Inn, put our bags in the room and got up the next morning and went to the studio . . . We'd go there in the morning and stay there all day, have dinner, come back and stay all night till we were done . . . We had a very warm welcome. We set up the gear and played the songs a few times. We recorded everything. There was very little overdubbing of any consequence . . . I think I overdubbed a couple of solos on "Saved," that's [all] . . . We did this for a few days and then we got in the bus and took off for the next bunch of shows [sic] . . . That was *Saved* . . . Bob said, "You guys mix it and send me a copy of it."

The very approach which had exasperated Wexler at the first two *Slow Train* sessions was exactly the one now adopted: recording the songs live without headphones, with minimal overdubs, to try and capture that live feel. At least one musician seemed to feel there was a more obvious way to capture that live feel—record the songs *live!* It was a view Dylan would only come around to after he heard the finished studio mix. By then it was too late. The album was in the schedule and he was back on the road:

Jim Keltner: I think that it's a pity those songs were recorded in the studio, instead of live. There was a show in Seattle when we got a standing ovation after "Solid Rock" for almost five minutes. It was so extraordinarily powerful, and the people just flipped out and I'd never seen that before, ever. Now if you could get something like that on a recording of that song, instead of going into the studio and have a producer completely produce it to death, then you'd really have something . . . Jerry Wexler was one of my idols [but] we got this sound that was so clean. I think that maybe they were trying to revisit the sound of *Slow Train*. And you can't do that with Bob . . . It didn't want to be anything like *Slow Train Coming*. It wanted to have a big, open, live, exciting sound to match the praise [in] the songs. And it didn't happen. It didn't come across [on] tape.

Keltner was particularly unhappy with the way his drums were recorded, making them sound dull and lifeless. Finally, Rosato stepped in and removed all the tape a rookie engineer had put around them. But it wasn't just the man at the drum kit who was scratching his head. Dylan seemed equally frustrated as he tried every which way to inject life into the recordings.

The first day was again spent working on a single song, "Covenant Woman." The third take—which is included on *Bootleg Series Vol. 13*—tries a half-spoken, half-sung delivery that recalls *New Morning*, searching for that intimacy of tone this torch-ballad had enjoyed early in its onstage existence. But this was not the version pulled to master—and the one that was, take seven, would not end up on the album. Nor would a complete take #9 (number nine . . .) So much for session one.

Not everyone had yet to shake the dust off their feet. Maybe a rousing "Solid Rock"—a la Seattle—would kick things into gear. On the 12th, three solid hours were spent working on this rabble-rouser but just seemed to compound Dylan's sense of frustration. Not only had something been lost, the singer was taking his gift for granted. As Paul Williams wrote in his excoriating review of *Saved* in *One Year Later*:

The meaning of "Solid Rock" is not "I've got a solid rock to hang onto" . . . although that's what it's come to mean in its later performances . . . The deeper original meaning has to do with being suspended, dangling as it were, that instant of awareness when one realizes that the only thing attaching us to the earth, to the world, is the will of God. All is Illusion, except for this solid rock (of ages) from which I am suspended, on which I depend (penderez, to hang) . . . the rock that was here long before any of this illusion was created and that will outlast it all.

Which sounds like prime cut hokum with a dash of delusion until one rewinds to the last Warfield and hits play. Paul's as right as can be. Perhaps a search for Arthur's tape from November 16th might have helped put the Muscle back into that trademark Shoals sound. It also might have put the kibosh on a lackluster "What Can I Do For You?," apparently cut that day in a single take. Again Paul Williams took a baseball bat to the aesthetic underlying this tired retread of a once great song:

On "What Can I Do For You?," which is either a song of total humility or else it's nothing, an indication of the problem with the whole vocal (the attitude of the vocal) can be found when Dylan sings, "I don't deserve it but I sure did make it through." This bit of boasting shifts the focus of the song; the original lyrics and performance here conveyed the subtly (but extremely) different message that "I didn't deserve to survive, but You chose to bring me through and so my life is Yours, please help me find a way to begin to show my devotion." Instead, the new vocal almost suggests that Dylan made it because he was smart enough to buy a ticket on the right train. Ouch.

Dylan finally took out his frustrations on a rambunctious "Saved," which was more like it—and deemed good enough to be pulled to master, though he would return to the song after taking a break and introducing the first cover of the sessions.

If a quick prayer meeting was out of the question, a seemingly impromptu rendition of Jack Rhodes' country classic "Satisfied Mind" came close enough for jazz. Suddenly, Dylan's intimate voice clicked as he rekindled the memory of a song he used to sing back in 1961, long before the likes of Joan Baez, The Byrds, Fairport Convention, Tim Hardin and John Martyn gave it the folk/rock treatment.

Riding the wave, he signaled the band should carry on where they had left off before the break, launching into a positively Pentecostal "Saved" which nudged close to five minutes in its original guise.[27] He had finally found a way into the album, taking the roof off the studio and letting the spirit of the Lord in for the first time since they checked into a local Holiday Inn.[28]

Now was the time to press rewind and revisit "What Can I Do For You?" and "Solid Rock"—but instead Dylan called time on the day's work. When they resumed the following afternoon, he chose instead to tackle "Saving Grace" at a time when his lady muse had been caught short and had again left the building.

Nonetheless, two complete takes *were* pulled to master; the one Dylan and/ or Wexler preferred perfectly encapsulating Williams 1980 description of the whole album, "The songs sound tired to me, unconvincing—the arrangements are uninspired—the band plays with obedience rather than fire."

Still hoping to find some of twelfth night's spirit and fire, he decided now was the time to tackle "Pressing On," perhaps the biggest challenge he would face at these sessions. Here was a song which lent itself to live performance. It would have to be wholly rearranged to work on record. A first take ran to six minutes, and even though it petered out, almost caught alight. (It can be heard on *Bootleg Series Vol. 13*.) This time he persevered and after five more takes had the one he wanted—*Saved*'s stately, majestic highlight.

Now was the time to revisit "Saving Grace." Instead, they concentrated on "In The Garden" and "Are You Ready?," with the latter requiring the most work—not surprisingly—for the least return. The song itself simply did not warrant the effort, save perhaps as a bonus B side on a Bible belt-only 45. But Dylan had seemingly run out of songs he wanted to record, and so he and his coproducers agreed to reconvene the following day, a Friday, to decide what was worth keeping:

Jerry Wexler: This sounds very Biblical in tone but on the fifth day, we reexamined everything we'd done and wound up recutting two songs. We recut "Covenant Woman" and "Saved." They were both really good improvements. It was pretty much Bob's instinct to redo them . . . He didn't think we had done his vocals and the instrumental tracks to the best of our potential. We did a little touching up. In five days it was ready for mixing. [1980]

The truth be told, *Saved* wasn't remotely ready to be mixed, if it was Dylan's

---

[27] Though this is the take on *Saved*, it would be trimmed of a "longer, slower" ending.
[28] Michael Krogsgaard in his own sessionography dates the attempts at "Saved" and "Satisfied Mind" to the 13th, ignoring the session-sheet for the song, reproduced in *Dylan: Behind Closed Doors* some time before his own work. It clearly says the 12th.

intention to capitalize on the surprise success of *Slow Train Coming*, his second-best–selling album (after *Desire*).

Yet a great deal of thought had gone into the project. He even knew exactly the cover art he wanted, having had another of his visions, which he revealed to artist Tony Wright, the man he commissioned to realize "this vision of Jesus, of the hand coming down and these hands reaching up. And he [told me] that at the same time he had this vision, he saw the whole album."

The album as compiled simply did not stack up alongside the material as performed live, let alone its smooth-talking predecessor. As Paul Williams cuttingly observed, "Dylan has never rehearsed that much before making a recording, [but] on the evidence of the album, it didn't work." Again, Mr. Crawdaddy was bang on the critical coin.

Dylan's shifting attitude to the whole ethos behind *Saved* can perhaps be summed up by comments he made the year after its release, of which perhaps his exchange with Paul Vincent on a San Diego radio station in November 1980 was the most telling. Firstly, he informed Vincent that "over the course of a year—[I spend] maybe six days in the studio."

When Vincent pressed him further, saying that he had been told "you heard a cut from *Saved* on a Minnesota radio station and didn't care for the mix," Dylan revealed he now felt, "It was mixed wrong. I don't know, it didn't sound right to me anyway . . . I must've told somebody [that] at that time, who was working on the album."[29]

In a radio interview the following June, Dylan went as far as to suggest that, on "the past two albums, I used producers to organize everything in the studio for me and to come up with some ideas and . . . to help me sort out the songs and make some sense out of what I do . . . And [to] be responsible for the sound of it." He just reserved the right to reject the results.

Shortly after the album appeared, Wexler told *Rolling Stone* it had been Dylan's instinct "to redo" "Covenant Woman," and also to add some overdubs on "Saved." ("Saving Grace" and "Are You Ready?" both also have different guitar-parts on a mix reel, suggesting they too were "redone." The latter was also given both a Spooner Oldham and a Barry Beckett organ overdub.) How bad (or good) was the "Covenant Woman" take seven, "pulled to master," we may never know. The "master comp. reel" on which it featured appears to have been lost. But it is hard to believe the album take could be an improvement.

---

[29] There seems to be at least one earlier album mix. A mix-reel featuring side one of the album in the Sony vaults has been marked D.N.U. (Do Not Use).

Saved would give Dylan a particularly tough lesson in record-making; one he was still not ready to take on board. Only five years later would he provide an articulate disquisition on what went wrong, to *Musician*'s Bill Flanagan—without the word *Saved* being mentioned once, "When I started to record they just turned the microphones on and you recorded. That was the way they did it back in the sixties. Whatever you got on one side of the glass was what came in on the controls on the other side of the glass. It was never any problem."

Nor did this loaded album-title come up in conversation with the agenda-driven Joe Queenan in 1991, when Dylan gamely admitted, "There's some songs buried on my records that are good songs that just aren't performed well." He had just described *Saved* in a nutshell.

If Paul Williams' theory held, it was precisely "the fact that Dylan and the band . . . had been performing these same songs virtually nonstop for more than three months," which ultimately made the album such a tepid affair. Yet how does one then explain the incandescent nature of a song he played a fortnight later on national TV. It was one he had been playing every single night on tour, had previously recorded in the studio, rehearsed with a horn section and debuted on TV the previous October.

The song in question was "Gotta Serve Somebody," and the performance the night Dylan picked up his first ever Grammy Award was as good as any when cameras had been trained on him. It was certainly far too good for the invariably lame spectacle that was, and is, the Grammys.

Dylan really did not want to be at the Shrine Auditorium and when he bumped into Robert Hilburn earlier in the day, he told him so. As the *LA Times* columnist reported, he asked "why he agreed to perform on the [Grammy Awards] TV show. Dylan replied, 'I thought it would be a chance for people to hear my music.'" It was certainly that, even if the whole experience proved rather daunting for some of the musicians:

Fred Tackett: The thing that was the scariest about playing at the Grammys was the rehearsal. There were huge white poster boards in all the seats with the names of who was going to be sitting there later that evening. [SM]

The list of attendees included Kris Kristofferson and Johnny Cash, who were both there—at least in part—to lend moral support to their good friend who had finally joined them selling good news. As for the "rehearsal" which terrified Tackett, there were at least three of them: one on the day before, due to start at

11:15 am; a "full show run-through" the morning of the broadcast, Dylan's segment being recorded between 9 am-10 am.; and a so-called "dress rehearsal" the same afternoon, starting at 1:30 pm.

Something that happened at the first of these rehearsals probably prompted Dylan to not only give his all, but also screw with the micromanaged event at a time when they would be powerless to stop him:

Spooner Oldham: You do a rehearsal in the afternoon prior to the [Grammys], for the cameraman and the sound man. [While we were] doing that, somebody in the production staff asked Dylan . . . would he cut the tune short for production purposes. In other words, it was like four minutes and they wanted it three. And he said no. [SM]

Dylan didn't just say no. He set about delivering a performance the evening of the 27th that would go on to the crack of doom. Not only was he back to his blistering best, but just when it seemed the song must end, he stepped back to let Tackett take a lead, before locating a harmonica from somewhere inside the penguin suit he was wearing for the occasion, proceeding to blast the news straight on through.

And still he found the time and energy for just one more chorus, on which he spelled it out for all to hear—not "it may be the Lord," but "it *can* be the Lord!"

The whole thing clocks in a coupla seconds shy of six minutes thirty, making that "nobody" in the production staff rue the day he asked Dylan to truncate his whole reason for performing at the Shrine.

Though it would be a long time before Dylan put himself through a similar rehearsal/run-through palaver—and when he did, on the David Letterman show March 1984, the broadcast would be unrecognizable from rehearsals—he had done what he had set out to do, given people "a chance . . . to hear my music." And to all those who had eyes and all those who had ears, it was obvious he was still inspired—and inspiring.

One sour milk puss watching the wheels turn and glowering at the screen from his bunker in the Dakota building, overlooking New York's Central Park, was John Lennon who, truth be told, had never really forgiven Dylan for parodying "Norwegian Wood" by writing a better song, "Fourth Time Around," to the same idea. So when he sent "Bob and Sara" a personally inscribed copy of his first solo album, *Plastic Ono Band*, he had drawn a large arrow and a very large circle around the line, "I don't believe in Zimmerman," in order to draw Dylan's attention to it.

And now, Lennon gave vent to another primal scream as he set about writing an existential riposte to his friend's newfound faith, called "Serve Yourself"—though in the end his nerve failed him and he removed the song from the appositely-named *Double Fantasy*. As such, Dylan would not hear the song until after Lennon had been shot—by a man who it was later suggested had also been stalking Dylan—and his own belief in the Us-and-Them aspect of the song Lennon set out to spoof had become tempered by time.

So when Lennon's old publicist, Elliott Mintz, asked Dylan about Lennon's song in 1992, the songwriter insisted, "It didn't bother me, it intrigued me. Why would it affect him [in] such a way? Like, who cares? It was just a song."

Twelve years earlier, "Gotta Serve Somebody" had been anything but. It was the opening salvo in a show which would shift every which way over the next year and a half without ever losing its central message: "Choose you this day whom ye shall serve." The solid rock on which that show would be hung, at least until Independence Day 1981, was what the Grammy committee considered The Best Male Rock Vocal Performance of 1979. They were only one year out.

7. THE DAEMON HATER
[April – May 1980]

"So ... what's so unusual about that? Dylan's always played harp on his albums ..."

RECORD WORLD AUGUST 9, 1980

Born-Again Dylan Leaves Audience Behind

By BERNARD HOLLAND
Post-Gazette Staff Writer

Some of Dylan's religious feeling takes on attractive musical forms. "When You Gonna

Dylan may not judge himself holier tha thou, but he is certainly holier than most of th

Charles Young: During your Christian period there seemed to be an element of self-righteousness. Is that a fair perception?

Bob Dylan: Yeah, that's a fair perception. But . . . self-righteousness would be just to repeat what you know has been written down in scripture some place else. It's not like you're trying to convince anybody of anything, you're just saying what the original rule is, and it's just coming through you. But if someone else can get past you saying it and just hear what the message is, well then it's not coming from you, but through you. And I don't see anything wrong in that. [1985]

When people don't get threatened and challenged . . . in some kind of way, they don't get confronted, never have to make decisions, they never take a stand, they never grow. [Instead, they] live their lives in a fishtank, stay in the same old scene forever, die and never get a break or a chance to say goodbye. I have views contrary to all that. I think that this world is just a passing-through place and that the dead have eyes and that even the unborn can see, and I don't care who knows it. [You] know, I can go off on tangents.

—BOB DYLAN, BIOGRAPH NOTES, 1985

Somewhere in Canada there was a guy with a cross, walking around the theater. I don't know if he was for us or against us. I also [saw] musicians who made a bunch of money playing old Dylan songs to the people in line for the shows.

—FRED TACKETT TO SCOTT MARSHALL

In the summer of 1979, Dylan had retired to his Minnesotan farm to spend time with his children, as he had in the summers of 1974 and 1977—equally troubling times—which inspired *Blood On The Tracks* and *Street-Legal*, his two best seventies collections.

But he still ventured out on occasion and when he attended a Twins baseball game, he was spotted by Jon Bream, a local journalist who had interviewed him the previous year. They talked informally, with Dylan admitting he was thinking of playing "some concerts this fall," but "no formal tour, no big arenas."

He also confided in Bream his frustration at his record label who were again being tardy with the release-schedule on the appropriately-named *Slow Train*

Coming. He told Bream, "The single was supposed to be out in June. I don't understand why it isn't out yet. I hope the album is out by Christmas."

This was to become a familiar mantra in the gospel years, with both *Saved* and *Shot Of Love* taking more than three months to appear. Dylan's sixties albums had generally appeared in the shops within four to six weeks, usually coinciding with touring activities. Not in 1980, they didn't. It seems CBS were in no hurry to release *Saved*. In fact, according to one Dylan insider there was even some doubt as to whether they would follow through:

Dave Kelly: I think CBS put a lot of pressure on him. I don't think they liked . . . the album *Saved* . . . I don't think they wanted to put it out. Seems like I remember at one point, they weren't going to release it. I think the Grammy Bob received helped a lot. But by the second album they were like, "Oh no, you're going to continue this Jesus stuff?" . . . Bob was very frustrated with his record company because they were trying to control . . . what he sang about, what he recorded, and he wasn't about to have that happen . . . One of the things he said to me was: "I can record it but they don't necessarily have to release it. But I'm going to record the album I want." [SM]

And he had. However, now it seems even he was having doubts whether he had made the album he had planned in his head. Even before he heard it played on the radio, his thoughts turned to the possibility of recording the songs live—six months too late. At the same time, he began to think about putting together a TV In Concert, à la 1976's *Hard Rain*, that would put Born-Again Bob in the living rooms of a nation of skeptics.

An ideal opportunity was about to present itself, too. He was due to play his first four-night residency since the Santa Monica Civic at Toronto's intimate Massey Hall, with every night sold out, starting April 17th. However, the cost of filming and recording multiple shows would have to come out of his own pocket. CBS, in the role of Roman governor, washed their hands of the idea early on, rejecting the live album he delivered and refusing to fund a concert film:[30]

Dave Kelly: He was contemplating issuing a live album . . . From the beginning, *Saved* should have been a live album . . . but the record company were not

---

[30] A seven-song tape compiled from the final two Toronto shows, purporting to be that live album, has been bootlegged extensively. Oddly enough, it omits the three new songs Dylan was playing at these shows.

interested. They wouldn't put any money into it . . . It was a good idea, but it was too late. I do recall there were cameras at some shows, but I was too busy making him hot tea with lemon and honey.

Dylan would not be dissuaded, recording the last three Toronto shows on multitrack, and filming the last two. He also assembled the band at Rundown the week before, in order to spend three days rehearsing some songs, specifically three he had written in the past two months—"I Will Love Him," "Ain't Gonna Go To Hell" and "Cover Down (Pray It Through)"[31]—all of which he intended to introduce into the set, telling the band at one point, "We're gonna do these three songs somewhere."

All three songs were shaped in rehearsal, with the girls' contribution being a gorgeous choral intro to "Ain't Gonna Go To Hell" that was so beautiful Dylan duly dropped it from the song by the time he reworked it in November 1980. If Dylan was always willing to coopt such arrangement ideas, he was still not sure which lines he planned to include in the three songs.

Some would be lost in the rehearsal process, though not the line in "Ain't Gonna Go To Hell," "I can make believe I can fall in love with anybody." Sounded like a familiar pattern was still being repeated. But "I can read the leaves of time as well as anybody," an idea he perhaps already sensed could be revisited, was shelved. Likewise, one lost line in "I Will Love Him" should have stayed in, "I thought he was a storybook myth, but I was wrong."

With so much to organize, and with three songs to break in, the decision was made not to professionally record the first Toronto show, even after a prolonged soundcheck, knowing it would also be the one all the press would attend. Dylan even took the opportunity to tell Toronto, "I know you're gonna read in the newspapers tomorrow that everybody walked out. You tell them the truth now," something *Toronto Star*'s Peter Goddard reported verbatim, while confirming, "There were only a few in last night's audience of what appeared to be veteran Dylan fans who walked out."

That didn't stop payees shouting for "something old, Bob!" Michael Lawson in his *Ottawa Citizen* review noted that such requests started "only twenty-five minutes into Dylan's set, [as] the usual obnoxious element at every rock concert started hollering demands between breaks in tunes. 'Jesus loves rock 'n' roll,' someone shouted."

[31] "Cover Down"s subtitle has invariably been listed as "Breakthrough," but on the two occasions Dylan introduced the song in Toronto, he clearly says, "Pray It Through."

Likewise, Jonathan Gross commented in his *Toronto Sun* review on how "the frustrations of a vocal minority began to drift down from the upper reaches of Massey Hall . . . [But] Dylan was quick to put the disgruntled nonbelievers in their place: "'Lay Lady Lay'? You should have been here ten years ago. Why should I play something that I don't believe in?"

Goddard also recalled the same retort, observing that it had actually been fifteen years since he last played the Massey, though for this old-hand it felt "there was more than just fifteen years separating him—and us—from that event. At least this time around Goddard felt resistance evaporate as the show went on:

> It's still theater, of course, but now the play seems for real. And the moment last night's audience realized that, after he'd ignored repeated requests for old songs, after it was evident that gospel music and the Gospel were the subjects of the night, you could detect what amounted to a collective psychological sigh. The pressure was off. [Just] enjoy . . .

Only one reviewer seemed to side with the skeptics. Paul McGrath in the *Toronto Globe & Mail* described a crowd who "sat bewildered while he threw everything but the Gnostic Gospels at them in an attempt to provoke some participation . . . He's playing for and about Jesus now, and the fans don't know how to handle it. They came to be entertained." McGrath's copy was unoriginal, though the *Globe* headline got full marks for wit, "Old-time religion but no old-time Dylan."

As far as Dylan was concerned, the 17th had been a warm-up show. Between the songs he was also just warming up, despite offering his one and only explanation of the song title, "Cover Down (Pray It Through)"—"You get up in the morning, you got to cover down."

He also mentioned two fellow songwriters, one of whom had made it to the show—"I'd like to say hello to a friend of mine, Gordon Lightfoot, one of my favorite songwriters . . . Ain't gonna go to hell for anybody—I know Gordon feels that same way, too"; one of whom was touring another part of Canada:

> I saw the newspaper last night that The Who were playing in, I think, Vancouver. Pete Townshend apologized to all the fans. He said to them, "We'll never leave you alone again." You just think about that for a minute. There is one who will never leave you alone. I just don't think that it's Peter.

On that first night, it was just the two new songs—"Cover Down" and "Ain't Gonna Go To Hell For Anybody"—though the latter, with its memorable multiple refrain, was still recognizable enough for Gross to describe it as "a rocker with an appeal so strong you have to like it even with sermonizing lyrics." Gross began to wonder "just how chatty Dylan is [going to be] through the rest of his four-night stand."

Well, Dylan had a whole lot more about Jesus he wished to say. And he had other things he wanted "to say about such things as ghetto bosses, salvation and sin, lust, murderers going free, and children without hope—messianic kingdom-type stuff, that sort of thing—[stuff] people don't like to print."[32] But he would only say them when the press had moved on.

Not that the lawyers for the Toronto dailies would have allowed them to assign column-inches to some of the things he had to say at the following shows. On the second night he skirted dangerously close to slandering a psychic by the name of Jeane Dixon:

> Does anybody know who Jeane Dixon is? Some psychic. Kinda interesting. She was talking about a Superman coming . . . She said, . . . about three, four years ago, he's gonna be coming in like 1981—and he was gonna settle all the world's problems. Do you know about any of this stuff? . . . Well, she was questioned on where she got all this information. A snake revealed it to her. She said it was a serpent, actually. Well, we remember who the serpent was. Anyway, the serpent will be crushed under the foot.[33]

Mrs. Dixon had warranted a whole chapter (called "Angels of Light") in *Satan Is Alive And Well On Planet Earth*. Lindsey called her "perhaps the best known psychic of modern times with an impressive list of amazing predictions, some of which have come true and were fairly detailed. [But] in her book, *The Call to Glory* . . . Mrs. Dixon claims, 'It is my belief God has given me a gift of prophecy for His own reasons, and I do not question them.'"

Lindsey the master-decipherer had discerned that the lady was no clairvoyant. Dylan's intervention, though, was as baffling as it was unexpected. Even if Spooner Oldham believes that "he was just connecting his own views with what he was singing," the stakes had now been raised. He was now recording the shows for a potential live album. By the following night, he was filming, too.

At the show on the 19th, Dylan reined himself in, confining himself to reading aloud a letter from a fan in the form of a prayer, "When there is no light that is

---

[32] This was Dylan's description of verboten subjects, to *Spin's* Scott Cohen, five years later.
[33] Romans 16:20—"And the God of peace *shall bruise* Satan *under* your *feet*."

shining, Jesus shines through/ When the road is lonely and winding, Jesus comes for you."

Though it is not known who wrote the poem, or how they got it to Dylan, he concluded the main set at the final Toronto show by requesting fans, "to write to me now and tell me what you're thinking. Any of you got any questions you just write them in there, send them in. Prayer requests, questions, any of that."

Somebody called Steve had already somehow managed to get a Variorum edition of the Bible to Dylan at his hotel, prompting the singer to pen a heartfelt thank you to the sender—who rewarded his trust by trying to sell the letter in auction, a couple of decades later. The letter read in part:

> We are up in Toronto singing and playing for about 3,000 people a night in a downtown theater—The Spirit of the Lord is calling people here in their beautiful and clean city but they are more interested in lining up for *Apocalypse Now* than to be baptized and filled with the Holy Ghost—Wanna thank you for that Bible as it is helpful in discovering a few phrases from and shedding more light on what the King James version reads. . . . You will be strong in the Lord and seeing that looks are deceiving, you will work miracles that way—He has called you to be a saint and your responsibility is to Him and Him alone—Be praying and not looking back no more—press on toward what is ahead—I send love to you and will pray for strength and more strength for ya.
>
> —Always In the name of Jesus Christ Son of God, Manifest in the flesh, Bob Dylan.

The letter confirmed he was meeting resistance at the shows, even as the final night saw Dylan forcing himself to focus on the message as the cameras rolled.

If "I Will Love Him," which had appeared in the set the previous night, contained an explicit reference to Lindsey's countdown to Armageddon—"Talking 'bout the state of Israel from nineteen forty-eight"—he wished to be more explicit. And so, after beginning a rap about how "the natural mind . . . can't comprehend loving your enemy—that seems like a foolish thing to do. However, the supernatural mind can comprehend that, so when Jesus says, 'Love thy neighbor as thyself,' he wasn't exactly saying roll over and play dead," Dylan suddenly began to "tell you a story. About four months ago we were playing some place. It was a college campus." Thus began the tale of Tempe.

By the end of the five-minute rap, he had worked himself up to a point where he was ready to tell Toronto, "I don't know what you got to hang on to but I got something called a solid rock to hang onto . . . manifested in the flesh, and justified in the spirit, seen by angels, preached on in the world."[34] The resultant song shook the very foundations of Massey Hall.

Leaving the locals to watch *Apocalypse Now*, Dylan checked into his Montreal hotel on the 21st, pending another four-show residency at the equally resplendent Theatre St. Denis, starting the following night. And after his night off, he carried on from where he had left off, still using his King James Bible when he needed chapter and verse to work himself into a liturgical lather:

Jesus died on Calvary. You may think, why should a man have to die on Calvary? Way back when, the keys to the world were given to someone called Lucifer. You remember the Rolling Stones had a song called Lucifer—[or] something like that. I don't remember the exact title . . . Anyway, he's always around. He's still around. The only way for the keys to come back was by Jesus going to the cross. Now you might think that's a strange thing for me to say, but it has been revealed to me that it is The Truth. Satan, we now call Lucifer. He's called the God of this world, prince of the power of the air. He's called all sorts of things but he's really the Devil, no more, no less than that. And he's a spiritual being. You can't see him, but he can control you and if he can't control you, he'll want to destroy you. So what do we have to fight Lucifer with? What did Jesus do by going to the Cross? He rendered him helpless. That is why I say, "The weapons of our warfare are not carnal, but mighty through God in pulling down strongholds, casting down imaginations against every high thing that exalts itself against God."[35]

This time, though, the reviewers barely mentioned Dylan the preacher man, save for a single snotty reference from Bruce Bailey in the *Gazette*, who felt "it would have been better if Dylan had left the preaching to Oral Roberts." Bailey wasn't perturbed by the new songs, taking the view that "the lyrics that we used to get [from him] weren't much more complex than the National Research Centre's Official Time tone," a jaw-dropping display of critical illiteracy. For Bailey, "It was a good, heart-stopping show, leaning on the funky-gospel back-up . . . [and] probably some of his best musical work so far—if you ignore the lyrics. And that, really is no loss."

The *Gazette* had previously reported on a rapturous reception opening night, writing in the news section about people "leaving their seats . . . before he had

---

[34] 1 Timothy 3:16—"God was manifest in the flesh, justified in the Spirit, seen of angels, preached unto the Gentiles, believed on in the world, received up into glory."

[35] Dylan is (mis)quoting 2 Corinthians 10—"For the weapons of our warfare are not carnal, but mighty through God to the pulling down of strong holds; casting down imaginations, and every high thing that exalteth itself against the knowledge of God."

finished performing . . . But they weren't going out the door. They massed below the stage of the old St. Denis Theatre, and later yelled out for encores." Stephen Gauer's review in the *Ottawa Journal* was equally positive, though he was unable to "ignore the lyrics," as Bailey suggested:

> Last night, at the Theatre St. Denis, as Dylan played the first of four Montreal concerts, he held an audience spellbound with ninety minutes of his new music. That new music is a celebration of his newfound Christianity; it's a rallying point for his creative energies and the focus for some exciting gospel rock and roll . . . It's only when the lyrics descend to the level of Sunday school lessons do the shortcomings of the new music make themselves felt.

Once again, Dylan shrugged off the negative review/s and got down to business. As "Cover Down" and "Ain't Gonna Go To Hell" went from strength to strength, "I Will Love Him" made its second and last appearance on night two in Montreal. If the message, "I will love him, I will serve him, I will glorify his name," seemed conducive to such concerts, the loss of "Blessed Be The Name" and the nightly inclusion of the tub-thumping "Are You Ready?," slanted the shows in the direction of dire warnings about the End Times. And the nightly raps reflected it. Sandwiched between "Ain't Gonna Go To Hell" and "Cover Down" on the last night was certainly one of Dylan's more sarcastic outro/intros:

> *I ain't gonna go to Hell for anybody—like a vision of what's coming. Anyway, in this "liberated world" I wanna offer you this song . . . Well, you heard about the Pharoah's army trampling through the mud . . .*

If the lyrics to "Cover Down" suggested he had rediscovered obliqueness, it also implied something bad was gonna happen. Perhaps the places they were performing were bringing out the preacher in Dylan. Or maybe he felt he was playing to quite different audiences to the ones so far:

Bob Dylan: We'd play theaters in The Mission and Times Square districts in some of the larger cities. In the inner cities where industry has moved out and people don't have work, some of the most beautiful theaters are there—the people that would come to the shows [in those districts], they'd be more or less from the neighborhood; prostitutes, pimps, whatever—shady looking characters. I guess they didn't have anything better to do and most of these theaters were right in the heart where they operated. Anyway, in these areas, this particular show went down well . . . They understood what I was doing . . . and they let me know that. [1985]

If the social concerns in his previous lyrics had rarely if ever proffered a solution, now he had one. And his experiences walking among the prostitutes and pimps seemed to inspire him to offer it. At the final Montreal show he decided it was high time he tackled the thorny issue of the female orgasm:

> *There's a form of liberty that's really slavery. They got a way of twisting things all around. Make what's good seem bad and what's bad seem good. I was talking to a young girl the other day who just lives from orgasm to orgasm. I know that's a strange thing, but that's what she's led to do because of these so-called modern times. But she's not satisfied.*

As at Toronto, he again asked a Canadian audience for direct feedback, "If you want us to come back, you write us some letters. Write us some letters anyway." The generally well-received Canadian shows may have convinced him he was slowly winning this battle, if not the war.

The next fourteen shows showed precious little sign of strategic retreat as he weaved his way down the east coast, starting in Albany, skirting the edges of New York, but never storming the citadel—almost recreating the 1975 Rolling Thunder Revue in reverse, which spanned Massachusetts to Montreal. Once again, he was playing theaters where he might expect to encounter his keenest (former) fans. But he was under no illusion as to the likely reception awaiting him. As he said on that first night back in the USA:

> *You know how we always fall into that trap of expecting too much from people. When Jesus rode into Jerusalem a lot of the people were shouting, and broke branches off the trees. "Hail! Hail! The King is coming." They just worshipped and bowed down. But it was the same people who were shouting, "Crucify him!" You may never be too sure. However, Satan's getting ready to weave his masterpiece and you got to have some strong faith coming up, [for] even the very elect will be deceived.*[36]

From Albany on, his between-song banter was back to its belligerent best, Dylan fulminating at those who rejected the message. In New York's state capital, he again talked between songs and after getting nowhere, prefaced one song that

---

[36] Matthew 24:24—"For there shall arise false Christs, and false prophets, and shall shew great signs and wonders; insomuch that, if it were possible, they shall deceive the very elect."

was merely a litany of questions with one more: "D'you wanna be delivered? Jesus will deliver you. You need the law, Jesus'll do that, too. And I know you need a lawyer. He's all that. Manifested in the flesh, justified in the Spirit. Seen by angels. believed, preach to the nations, raise up all men into glory."

Whilst upstate in Albany, it seems he spent some time wandering the scuzzier parts of town while looking deep within himself, before offering the cup of salvation to those most in need: "When you do need some help, when you've exhausted everything else, when you have all the women you can possibly use, when you've drunk all you can drink, you can try Jesus. He'll still be there." In that moment, it seemed like he was talking about his former self as much as the plights of those he'd encountered on the street.

In Worcester, MA, six days later, the first direct crossover point with Rolling Thunder, "Are You Ready?" was once again preceded by the preacher-man railing against society's ills, quoting the good book to back him up:

[Remember the] girl who told you the story about Jesus, about four or five months ago. Anyway, Jesus is the way of Salvation. [The] Bible says, friendship wins worlds. Friend of the world is the enemy of God. I know that's a rough truth, but it is the truth. Friendship of the world is emnity with God.[37]

And the following night, in Syracuse, he was reminding those who had come to see the old Dylan that said person "never did tell you to vote for nobody. Never told you to follow no Guru, never advertised no product for you. Never told you how to dress, how to wear your hair, what to eat or what to drink. In fact, I really haven't told you anything. Now I'm telling you Jesus is the way to salvation." For the more liberal-minded, the man onstage was harder to recognize than the one in white makeup and a Richard Nixon mask in 1975.

Driving across New York state to Buffalo and two nights at the familiar Kleinhans Music Hall, Dylan started considering just how he might spread the word beyond those who came to hear him–and It–in theaterland. By now, he had seen some kinda rough edit of the Toronto shows he had paid to be shot. The three-camera set-up and an inexperienced camera crew had simply failed to really catch friendly fire on film.

Thankfully, experienced film editor and cameraman Howard Alk, a friend of Dylan's for fifteen years, was part of his traveling band and had a solution. He suggested, why not film the two Buffalo shows from onstage, using the same in-

---

[37] He is referencing James 4:4—"Know ye not that the friendship of the world is enmity with God? Whosoever therefore will be a friend of the world is the enemy of God."

your-face approach Alk had used so brilliantly on the 1976 *Hard Rain* film, and then cut that footage into the Toronto performances? He knew just the right film-man, Ron Kantor.

So when, on the first night, Dylan began to talk about the "kinds of things happening in the world today. . . . The Secretary of State just resigned. What do you think about that? Is that surprising? No, that's not surprising. Stranger things have happened than that. Jesus is coming again though, that's the important thing," the cameraman was unfazed. Still he kept filming at his shoulder, camera in hand, as Dylan made his most explicit statement yet about true faith and the established church:

I've been walking around today. I noticed there's many tall steeples, big churches with stained glass windows [here]. Let me tell you one thing; God's not necessarily found in there. [Cheers.] You can't be converted in no steeple [with] stained glass windows. But Jesus is mighty, mighty to save. If He's in your heart, He'll convert you. You don't have to go to no church. Don't you be deceived now. There's only one Christ and you know where to find Him.

"It's what's inside that counts," was the message, and the message it would remain. Even as late as 1986, when asked on Australian TV whether he felt he had been "reflecting a feeling that was abroad in this country by picking up religion as a subject matter," he went to some pains to separate a religious state of mind from church attendance, "We have to be very careful when [we] talk about religion, you know, because religion is more than just *church*."

In Buffalo, Dylan also expressed a hope that "all the people [who] think the message is gonna change, might change or will change have left by now. The message is not gonna change. I believe in the God that can raise the dead." And as a parting gesture, before shuffling off from Buffalo, he readdressed the theme of not going to hell for anybody as the band began to ask, "Are You Ready?":

A lot of people today, they don't believe in Heaven and Hell. They think you just go on forever. They think when they die, that's it. But let me assure you, ladies and gentlemen, that there is a Heaven and Hell. And if you don't believe me, you just die. You'll find out. I never met nobody come back from Hell to tell what it's like.

By now, he was inured to the reviews, many of which he got to read before he played a second show in a city. As he commented in 2004, "I realized at

the time that the press, the media, they're not the judge—God's the judge . . .
And I just figured they're irrelevant." This didn't stop him rising to the bait,
sometimes before the trap was even laid. In Worcester, a two-night pitstop
immediately after Buffalo, he decided to strike first, prefacing "Slow Train"
with a speech which suggested perhaps he was not wholly immune to sticks
and stones:

> *A lot of time these people [who] come and review these shows, working for the*
> *newspapers, they say all sorts of things. Usually, they're not too encouraging, y'know.*
> *These reporters, a lot of them don't know God . . . or they may think they know about*
> *God, they may think of Him as a creator, but that's about as far as it goes. They don't*
> *think of any kind of morality at all, or any judgement.*

By Syracuse, two nights later, he had apparently stopped reading the press
altogether, "I don't know what you read. All I read is the Bible, that's all I read. So
you can quote me on that if you want. Once in a while I look in the newspapers
[but] the Bible says, 'Friendship with the world is enmity with God.' In other
words, [a] friend of the world is [an] enemy of God."

But to those near Dylan there was an underlying theme at the heart of Dylan's
protestations—"awareness of and fear of death." Howard Alk told Paul Williams as
much after reading *What Happened?* that spring. And in Worcester, Dylan came
close to voicing a very personal fear:

> *I'm in a funny position. Most people show me the side they wanna show me. But I*
> *say, you're [all] in the same position. There's only one name that can save you. Only*
> *one person went to the Cross for you. And you can take it or leave it. Now if you don't*
> *believe in a Heaven and Hell, you just die. You'll find out. . . . What did you bring when*
> *you came into this world? What are you gonna take with you when you leave? You're*
> *not gonna take your baggage with you. You're not gonna take your friends, not gonna*
> *take your attitudes, not gonna take your prejudices, your pride. None of that, you're*
> *taking none of that with you. You go all alone.*

He seemed in a particularly reflective mood on opening night in Worcester.
In the now-ubiquitous pre-"Slow Train" rap it almost seemed like he was talking
about himself as he began to muse about how "many relationships have gone
wrong . . . I know just my own self. Children can't get along with their parents.
Parents can't get along with their children. Can't get along with your boss. Can't

get along with wife. Satan's stirring up all kinds of trouble. [Yet] the Bible says that God in Christ has reconciled the world to him."[38]

By the time he returned to the central theme of following a righteous path the following night, he had rediscovered his joie de vivre. After all, he at least had the promise of eternal life, even if half the audience was on a "one-way ticket to burn":

> You see one man dressed a certain way, and another man dressed another way, and somehow you're friendly to the man dressed one way and unfriendly to the man dressed the other way . . . Well, you already judged that person, whether you know it or not. I guess some of you are just wondering, "What is he talking about? Can't make no sense out of this." Well, we're living in dangerous times. I know we all agree about that. [The Bible] says, "In the last days men will become lovers of their own selves. Boastful, proud and arrogant. Unthankful and unholy." Oh yeah, trials and tribulations will come. But eternal life is yours for the asking. Now don't forget: God knows all the secrets, you can't keep nothing from Him. Don't you be deceived now by the mockers of the truth

By now, the sets had settled into a routine, with the between-song raps almost a way for Dylan to generate the necessary messianic fervor, as well as being performance-pieces in their own right.

If he had already expressed his view on those who judge others (cf. "Do Right To Me, Baby"), he was still inclined to judge those preachers who "say how God wants everybody to be wealthy and healthy. Well, it doesn't say that in the Bible," a view he expressed to Mikal Gilmore in 1986, at a time when he included among his Three Pet Peeves, "Preachers who preach the 'Wealth and Prosperity' doctrine." It was in Worcester at the beginning of May 1980 that he first laid into money-changing preachers—and, by default, the politicians who rode piggyback on them:

> Have you noticed how all these people are running for president now? They're gonna save the country [or maybe] save themselves and try to save the country. But you can't save nothing unless you are saved! Jesus said, "Woe to you when all men speak well of you." . . . It's like when people say, "Well, [if] you accept Jesus, everything's gonna be fine." That's not necessarily true. They have a lot of different doctrines they teach . . . They have something called "[The] Prosperity Doctrine." I don't know if you ever heard of it. Lots of preachers going around saying, "Well, it's your right to have a

---

[38] The Bible quote comes from 2 Corinthians 5:19.

Cadillac. It's your right to have a good house. You have a right to have anything you
want." But you can't go over to Romania and preach that way to those Christians.
You can't go to Russia and say that . . . As long as your doctrine is balanced, then
Jesus will deliver you. From anything. Health problems, love problems, money
problems. But the Bible does say, "Cursed is the man that trusteth in man, that
makes flesh his strength"[39]

Of the various between-song spoken pieces he developed by May 1980, it was
perhaps the one which equated rock 'n' roll with the work of Satan that struck
elements of the audience/s as particularly sacrilegious. They had come to see Bob
Dylan with the same attitude they attended Bruce Springsteen, Jackson Browne
and Bob Seeger gigs. All of these singers were now on the end of a tongue-lashing
from a man who first showed them the way, starting with Springsteen in Syracuse
on the fourth day of May, as Dylan segued from "Ain't Gonna Go To Hell" into
"Cover Down" via the pit:

You know the way some time [when] an evil man might die, you see them long
limousines on their way to the funeral. And you know the man is evil. You know it.
And the Minister's trying [to say], "Oh Lord, accept this man." But by that time it's
too late. They try to preach him into Heaven after he's dead. Anyway, . . . pop music
always has been very popular. I know when I was growing up I used to listen to Hank
Williams, Little Richard, Gene Vincent, Wilbraham Brothers, all those people. They
formed my style in one way or another. But I can't help this type of music I play. This
is just the kind of type I've always played. I know a lot of other people who play this
sort of music tell you some strange things. ['Cause] the Devil's taken rock 'n' roll music
and he's used it for his purposes. I know that some people might not believe there is
a Devil. I'm not talking about a Devil with a pitchfork . . . Are you listening to me?
["Yeah!"] Oh, good. Some of you might have heard about a Devil with . . . horns.
That's not necessarily the Devil we know. We're talking about the Devil who was one
time God's chosen servant, his right-hand man. Beautiful angel. We're talking about
that Devil. He's a spiritual being and he's got to be overcome. He has been overcome
by what Jesus did at the Cross. I just want to tell you that. Some of you may not have
ever heard that. [But] we are living in the End Times now. I know we all agree about
that. It's the midnight hour. God wants to know who His people are and who His
people aren't. [Bible] says, "Draw nigh to God, He will draw nigh to you." I saw Bruce

[39] Jeremiah 17:5,—"Cursed be the man that trusteth in man, and maketh flesh his arm, and whose heart
departeth from the Lord."

Springsteen [recently], I love the guy really, [but] Bruce, he's born to run. And unless
he finds something, he's gonna keep a running. And you'll be chasin' him. But you can't
run and you can't hide.

In Providence, he once again stomped on his fellow rock stars as a prelude to
trampling through the mud. This time, he began by asking the audience, "What
we gonna talk about tonight?" before admitting, "I used to know Jimi Hendrix and
Janis Joplin." Thinking he is about to eulogize these drug casualties, the audience
cheered, but not for long:

I used to know all those people who are dead. [And] I tell you, if they knew then what I
know now, they wouldn't be dead. 'Cause Satan has infested the rock 'n' roll world. Ol'
Jackson Browne he's running on empty. Bob Seeger he's running up against the wind.
Bruce Springsteen, he's born to run and still running. [But] some time sooner or later
you gotta come home.

He had carefully disavowed any personal responsibility for helping Satan to
infest the rock 'n' roll world. However, if it seemed that he had forgotten the 1965-
66 electric tours, a time when he was skirting the very precipice of the pit every
night, the opening show at his next holding station, the Bushnell Memorial Hall
in Hartford, CT, showed he had forgotten nothing. It had been fourteen and a half
years since last he played the Bushnell (having played the Civic Center Arena on
Rolling Thunder), but little had seemingly changed:

I know I been through here before. I think I sang [here] some time in 1964 [sic].
Anyway, I was singing some songs back then. I remember I was singing a song called
"Desolation Row." That's right. You're clapping now, you weren't clapping then! No,
you weren't clapping then! I don't know if the same people were there, but it was,
"What's he singing about?" They did not understand what I was singing about. I don't
think I did, either. However, I understand now pretty much what I'm singing about. It
took a while for "Desolation Row," "Maggie's Farm," "Subterranean Homesick Blues,"
all that stuff to really catch on. But it wasn't accepted very well at the time. So I'm
always prepared for adversity. I always have been. But now I'm even more prepared . . .
Walking with Jesus is no easy trip, but it's the only trip, I'm afraid to say. I've seen a
lot of different kinds of other trips. So you may not ever hear that name again. I know
when I was out in the world traveling 'round, I hardly ever heard It myself. Nobody
ever told me that Jesus could save me. I didn't think I needed to be saved. I thought I

was doing just fine. Anyway, . . . there's gonna be a lot of delusion coming at you. You think what's happening now is bad, you just wait.

Geographically, the two Hartford shows represented the closest Dylan would come that spring to his old hunting-ground, New York City. But anyone who thought there might be a concession made to an audience of local believers and out-of-town Bobcats, they were quickly disabused:

Where are we now? In the middle of East Coast bondage, God is waiting to set you free. I know you don't hear too much about God these days, but we're gonna talk about Him all night. We're not gonna talk about no mysticism, no meditation, none of those Eastern religions. We're just gonna be talking about Jesus. The demons don't like that name. I'll tell right now, if you got demons inside you, they're not gonna like it.

It was as uncompromising an introduction to proceedings as the opening night in Santa Monica, six months earlier. Yet the reviewer from the local *Hartford Courant*, Colin McEnroe, led with the headline, "Born-Again Dylan Shines In Bushnell Concert":

"Are you ready?" Bob Dylan sang to the Bushnell Memorial audience of Wednesday night. On his face and his voice was a dire message of eschatological things to come. He crackled with an energy and purpose he hasn't shown in years . . . Dylan has always been a troubled man . . . [so] it comes as no surprise that Dylan's is an intense brand of Christianity, laced with searing apocalyptic visions and roiling struggles between good and evil . . . Whether audience members accept Dylan's newfound faith or not, it's difficult to dispute the quality of the music. It bristles with exuberance and tension . . . A few stody old-time Dylanphiles stomped out during the concert, but most fans remained, old mingling with the new, to scream the star back on stage for two encores . . . Dylan, to crib from a psalm, is making joyful noise unto the Lord.

If the local Hartford press would prove surprisingly positive, Dylan's proximity to New York also brought a more cosmopolitan critic, Australian writer Karen Hughes, who had last seen Dylan in his Sydney hotel room, two years earlier, when she secured the best interview of the antipodean tour by wearing her shortest skirt and her lowest top. This time Hughes was planning a review/feature for the *Village Voice*, the New York weekly that gave Dylan some of his first-ever press. But as

Hughes quickly discovered, the contrast to the 1978 world tour couldn't have been more pronounced, professionally or personally:

> Gone are the darkened limousines, the plush hotels, the sprawling entourages . . . Unobstrusively, even secretly, Bob Dylan has been trailing across America on his most low-key, low-budget tour in years . . . The reason for the tour? Dylan says it's a kind of public rehearsal for his backup band and, more importantly, an "off-Broadway" tryout of new, drastically different songs, some from *Slow Train Coming*, most from *Saved*, and still others yet to be recorded . . . He has [also] undergone a major personality metamorphisis. Instead of asking questions that put you on the spot . . . or playing now-you-see-me-now-you-don't power games, these days he's humble, honest, courteous, patient and less angry.

Even at the first Hartford show, the one that Hughes caught, a section of the audience who might "accept religion when it comes from Dylan because they came specifically to see him . . . [were] los[ing] patience" every time a girlsinger assumed center stage. And, as Hughes reported, each "time, not so many return."

Yet for Hughes herself, the show proved deeply moving, interpreting Dylan's message positively as one of hope over fear and quoting his introduction to Clydie King's rendition of "Calvary," "I know that some of you don't feel free, but you are. I know some of you are just about on the edge but you're free because of what Jesus did at Calvary."

Venturing backstage afterwards, Dylan seemed genuinely delighted to see her, and promised her a more substantive interview later in the tour (a promise he kept), but for now he was "eager for my reactions. How did I like the show? How did the crowd react?" Returning to his hotel with Hughes, he began talking about taking the show to New York, London, Japan and Australia after one more album. Most tellingly, he was "adamant about remaining silent through all channels other than his music."

Hughes departed, delighted by the change she had seen, describing him as looking "a good five years younger than he did two years ago" and sensing a more compassionate human being. She may not have maintained this view had she stayed for the second Hartford show, which saw Dylan push the eschatological envelope as far as it could go without being arrested for a hate crime, a propos "Solid Rock":

> *A long time ago they used to have these Greek plays, pretty long time ago. Nowadays they have people called actors—they're in movies. Back then they had actors too, but*

they called them hypocrites. That's right! There'd be a play with thirty people in it, but actually there'd only be four. They all used to wear masks. They'd all come out in a mask, [says something in a high-pitched voice—Then they] turn around, come back out and talk in another voice. They'd just wear a[nother] mask. So four people could play the part of thirty people. That's a heavy responsibility, keeps you on your toes. Never know who you are. So there's a lot of hypocrites. They're talking, using Jesus' name, but don't you let that put you off, 'cause you're still dealing with the world. Jesus has overcome the world, that's what He did at the Cross. As simple as that. You can make it complicated, but actually if you look at Jesus, you gotta look at the Cross. If you're wondering why all these things are happening these days, [let me explain]. Joshua went to Canaan land and God told him to destroy all the people, every man, women and children there. That's bad! You certainly think he could leave the children, but they was just all defiled. And there was some cities He said, "Don't go in there yet." Joshua wondered why, and God said, "Because their iniquity is not yet full." So when we started out this tour, we started out in San Francisco. It's kind of a unique town these days. I think either one third or two thirds of the population there are homosexuals. I guess they're working up to 100%, I don't know. Anyway, it's a dwelling place for homosexuals. I mean, they have homosexual politics. It's a political party. I don't mean it's going on in somebody's closet. I mean it's political. You know what I'm talking about? . . . I guess the iniquity's not yet full. And I don't wanna be around when it is!

In fact, the second Hartford show generally seems to have been a more antagonistic affair than the first, with Dylan feeling a need to talk to the audience early on. Even before "When You Gonna Wake Up," he was warning skeptics that it would "be about the same show tonight as we did last night. Talking mostly about God tonight, and about the spirit of God. We gonna talk about Jesus, too. If you got any demons in you at all, you're not gonna like that name. You better warn them demons right now, they're gonna be hearing it tonight." When, between "Ain't Gonna Go To Hell" and "Cover Down," he interrogated the audience as to whether the message was getting through, their response suggested it was not:

I know . . . it's not fashionable to think about Heaven and Hell. I know that. But God is not in fashion, anyway . . . But it's hard not to go to Hell, you know. There's so many distractions, so many influences; you start walking right and pretty soon there's somebody out there to drag you down. As soon as you get rid of the enemy outside, the enemy comes inside. He got all kinds of ways. The Bible says, "Resist the Devil and

He'll flee." [But] you gotta stand to resist him. How we got to stand? You listening to me? Anybody [here] know how to stand? How do we stand? Anybody know how? We gotta stay here in town another night. We got to come back tomorrow night, nobody know how to stand. Oh, mercy!

If he was swimming against a tide of liberal affluence playing the relatively well-off East Coast states, he had four more shows in New England—two in Portland, Maine and two on Rhode Island, site of the Newport Folk Festivals—before heading off into the industrial heartlands of Pennsylvania and Ohio.

After the high drama of Hartford, the shows in Portland passed largely without incident—save for a "Slow Train" rap the first night in which Dylan countered, "I know you might look at me and say, 'Wow, he's just lost his mind!' . . . Never told you which records to buy, what programs to watch, how to live, any of that stuff. I'm telling you the truth now."

It was in Providence—as he prepared for seven shows in Pittsburg, Akron, Columbus and Dayton—where Dylan began to develop two raps, the first of which was his own variant on the parable of talents Jesus recited during his Sermon on the Mount, while the second explicated Satan as serpent in the grass within the gates of Eden.

Lacking the oratory gifts of the man Himself, Dylan's Providence parable was merely a work-in-progress as he soon wandered from the point and back to the theme of Satan's hold on the world of rock 'n' roll. In fact, the pre-"Slow Train" rap could almost be a cut-up of three or four raps from the shows to date:

I'd like to say right now, We're not gonna give an altar call tonight . . . But I am gonna try to implant the words of God in you. I know [when] you cast out seeds; you cast out on the wayside. Some seeds they go on to the rock. Other seeds they go into the thorns, then there are some seeds go on the fertile ground. I know some of you are gonna hear this, you're gonna hear Jesus died for your sins and to destroy the works of the Devil and you're gonna rejoice when you hear that . . . Anyway, some of you are gonna hear that word, it's like throwing it out to the wayside. You hear it, but you're gonna leave this room, it's gonna disappear immediately. Others of you are gonna hear it, you're also gonna rejoice. But you're gonna go out there and it's not gonna take any deep root. It's gonna be like putting [it] on a rock. It's gonna be snatched away by the enemy. I don't mean that old enemy Waylon Jennings talks about, and Willie Nelson, and Jackson Browne, and Henry Kissinger, any of those people. I mean the real enemy, that one that wants your soul. [So] some of you are so choked by the riches of this world, the

cares of this world that those riches and those cares are gonna choke this word. I know
all about that. But others, I know, are gonna plant the word in fertile ground. For these
are the last days, these dark times. It's the midnight hour. I know some of you are on the
verge of committing suicide. Some of you think you got it all together; it don't matter.
Jesus came for all nations. Every knee shall bow, every tongue will confess.

Altogether more successful was the Satan-as-snake mini-sermon, partly because once Dylan got onto the topic of the man of peace, who was apparently alive and well and living on planet earth, he was in his element. At the second of the Providence shows, after "Man Gave Names To All The Animals" ended the usual line short, Dylan began asking, "You have many snakes around here, poisonous snakes? That snake was a snake in the Garden of Eden. Seem like just the other day. Anyway, back then the snake walked on hands and legs . . . [and] Lucifer the high angel of God put his spirit inside that snake."

It provided a cue for another midrash on Hal Lindsey's depiction of the Devil as someone who "controls medicine . . . Controls politics . . . Controls literature, education, you name it, he's there. If you're troubled, that's why you're troubled. 'Cause Satan has got you and you don't know it . . . So Jesus Christ did go to the Cross not only for the forgiveness of sins but to destroy the works of the Devil. [raises voice] *Which no man has ever done!*"

He was just getting started. The account of the snake in the garden and his role in world affairs in the late twentieth century would develop into potential jacket copy for Lindsey's next blockbuster by tour's end, every night bringing a variation on the theme but the same unrelenting message. By the second Akron show on the 18th, Dylan was leaving audiences in no doubt where he was heading, and what means of transport he intended to use:

In case you haven't guessed by now, the name of that last animal was a snake. Same
snake that was in the Garden of Eden, same one. In fact, in those days snakes were
walking on two legs, like [some] snakes today still are . . . Anyway, the same snake
that deceived Eve, deceived Adam, who deceived all mankind. A lot of people they're
waiting till they're at the end of the line before they go see Jesus. They just wait till the
very last moment, till they're too old, or too drunk, or too sick. About that time they
decide they're about ready to go see Jesus. We're talking about that woman with the
issue of blood, she spent all her money on doctors. Couldn't get no relief. And finally
she went to see Jesus . . . [And] we're talking about the prodigal son who went home. If
he'd had more money to spend, more bucks, he wouldn't have gone home either. I want

*to tell you something, the Devil's taken rock 'n' roll and made it his music, same way
he's taken free education and made it is his education, same way he's taken medicine
and made it is his medicine. He's called the God of this world, and if you look around
he's just that. Prince of the power of the air, that's what he is. He prowls the airwaves.
Now, I don't know if you know this or not, but that's precisely the reason Jesus went to
the Cross . . . I'm not talking about no religion now, I'm talking about Jesus. The real
Jesus. The one that's coming back.*

If anything, Dylan seemed to build up a third head of steam as he left "East
Coast bondage" behind. Back among "the pimps and the prostitutes," he felt many
of them seemed to like what they were hearing. As he observed in 1985, in the
inner-city areas, "Audiences would be very receptive and even if I say so myself,
wildly enthusiastic—strange, too, because a lot of these people I don't think they'd
ever heard of me before. They understood what I was doing, though, and they let me
know that."

However, in order to reach the swing state of Ohio, full of people who only
made up their minds at the last minute, he first had to pass through Pennsylvania,
specifically a three-night residency at the Stanley Theater in Pittsburgh. At the first of
the shows he soon let 'em know how it was gonna be:

*Somebody out there called Zeke? . . . He [wants to know] why I don't play no old songs.
Now listen, I wanna tell you something. I love those old songs, probably more than
you all do. And because I do love them so much, that's precisely why I don't do them.
Some of those songs were written twenty years ago. I'm not the same person who wrote
those songs, and you're not the same person that heard those songs. Now if you don't
believe that, go look into the mirror. I know some of you are not gonna like what you
see. I know some of you look in the mirror and as soon as you walk away, you forget
what you look like. But God knows what you look like, and He's got every hair on your
head counted, and He's got a plan of salvation through what Jesus Christ did on the
Cross. He not only [went] to the Cross for your sins and my sins, He went to the Cross
to destroy the work of the Devil. Something no man has ever done. Now if you don't
believe that, you ask Him to come into your heart and you'll see it's true. He's knocking
on your door.*

Not surprisingly, this message went down badly with the unchosen, inattentive
many—and in Pittsburgh on night one they were a signficant, vociferous body.
The impasse gave the local press something they could gleefully report, Bernard

Holland from the *Post Gazette* duly describing an audience "dominated by a minority [sic] of howling teenagers, most not even born when Dylan first served as America's resident legend in the 60s. Indeed, Dylan's five splendid black female gospel singers came near to being shouted down by fans impatient for their idol . . . [But] the trouble . . . [really began] when the real nature of Dylan's conversion beg[an] to come out . . . 'We're here to talk about Jesus . . . Anyone don't like it, can leave.'"

Some did take this as their cue, a few of whom were caught on local TV leaving the theater. One particularly perplexed burgermeister complained, "He talked about religion. He preached. That's why I walked out." He did not need to feel so all alone either. The *Pittsburg Press* reporter Pete Bishop—who quoted a goodly chunk of the above rap in his review—also gave the verbal reaction from fans leaving afterwards, which "ranged from 'I liked it' to 'Right on, Brother Bob,' to, 'If I wanted to hear that, I can go to fuckin' church,' to—from a laughing woman outside the theater—'Did you ever see so many sad faces?'"

It was 1966 all over again. Even after an album's worth of new songs and a year of widely-reported shows adhering to this format, the message was not sinking in. Even Bishop's *Press* review, which advised, "Hang onto all your old Bob Dylan albums—you'll probably never hear him sing those songs again," failed to spread the word both sides of the Monongahela.

Perhaps a word from the man himself might clarify things for any steel-town skeptics. So KDKA-TV's news reporter Pat Crosby decided he would stake out the lobby of the Hilton before the second show, and ask Dylan straight. Remarkably, when Crosby approached him, he agreed to explain in two minutes what a year of adverse publicity had not revealed:

Bob Dylan: I can understand why they feel rebellious about it because up until the time the Lord came into my life, I knew nothing about religion; I was just rebellious and didn't think much about it either way. I never did care much for preachers who just ask for donations all the time and talk about the world to come. I was always growing up with "it's right here and now" and until Jesus became real to me that way, I couldn't understand it.

Pat Crosby: So can you understand people's reaction to you when you come onstage and start singing about Jesus and they want the old stuff?

Bob Dylan: Oh yeah, that's right, they want the old stuff. But the old stuff's not going to save them and I'm not going to save them. Neither is anybody else they follow. They can boogie all night, but it's not gonna work.

Dylan's determination to "remain silent through all channels other than his music" had wilted to naught. He had had enough of uncomprehending criticism. When, on the third night at the Stanley Theater, some foolhardy fan shouted for "Lay, Lady, Lay"—the most unrepresentative hit record in Dylan's entire canon and a song he had systematically, even self-consciously, murdered every time he played it live—he began to strum the chords.

Hallelujah! The man was finally caving in to the baying crowd. Or maybe not. Because, as at Forest Hills, he just kept strumming the chords over and over again till the audience calmed down and then delivered the ultimate put down, "You want 'Lay Lady Lay'? You sing it, we'll play it. Go on, sing it!" In that moment, the admiration of his most trusted assistant, a survivor of both Rolling Thunder tours and a marathon world tour, rose again:

Arthur Rosato: He doesn't want to be a performer on command. He wants to play the stuff he wants to play . . . So when we were doing the gospel stuff, he didn't want to be distracted by performing "a show." He really wanted the audience to listen. Some city theater, the audience kept yelling for "Lay Lady Lay" so he just started playing it, got halfway through the opening and said, "I thought you were gonna sing it." . . . It was a tough battle. He was hanging himself every night.

Dylan never forgot the experience. Eleven years later, he still bitterly recalled how "they rejected all that stuff when my show would be all off the new album. People would shout, 'We want to hear the old songs.' [But] you know, . . . at a certain point, it doesn't really matter anymore." And it really didn't. Just as in 1966, he had learnt to feed off any negativity. So imagine his surprise when he reached Akron, home of devolution, and after the third song, as he gauged the likely reaction, there was unexpected affirmation:

Kinda quiet out there. [Prolonged applause]. I know it's not fashionable to talk about Heaven or Hell . . . We're staying at this motel down the road somewhere [and] there's a convention down there. There must be two thousand people, just up all hours of the night. It's hard to get any rest at all. Just carrying on, big people, little people, all sizes and shapes. Well, they seem to have taken over the place, eating and drinking and being merry, having a good time. I know none of those people believe in Heaven and Hell, I can just take a look at them and tell that.

When this black and white worldview was met with hoots of approval, Dylan could barely contain himself. After "Ain't Gonna Go To Hell," he abandoned his usual "demon" rap, instead enthusing, "What a friendly crowd. I'm not used to these friendly crowds no more. Usually the Devil's working all kinds of mischief in the crowds we visit." And when it came time to introduce the girlsingers, which usually led to Dylan admonishing the crowd to "remember that name Jesus," he remarked instead, "Seems like I don't have to tell you about Jesus, seems like you know all about him."

The two shows in Akron would be his Scandinavia '66 moment—rare occasions when he didn't have to fight the crowd and everyone could enjoy an evening of extraordinary music. As the *Akron Beacon Journal* wrote, "Some came of curiosity. Others came out of adoration. [But] what they saw and heard, well . . . it was beautiful."

It seemed like the sixties was back on his mind, too, as for the final two gospel shows—in Columbus and Dayton—he chose to contrast that decade with the dangerous one to come—as foretold nineteen hundred years ago.

In Columbus, he began by (mis)quoting Isaiah 55:11, "The Bible says no word of God comes back void,"[40] before informing attendees, "A lot of you people are God's people and don't know it. D'you see all the race riots that are happening now, volcanoes going off? Well, let me tell you the eighties are gonna be worse than the sixties." The audience lapped it up. Even the local reviewer from the *Ohio State Lantern* seemed to share the bonhomie:

A reformed Bob Dylan sang and preached to a mostly receptive sell-out crowd at Veteran's Memorial Auditorium Tuesday night . . . "All hell's breaking loose," he said between songs, referring to the eruption of the Mount St. Helens volcano and the race riots in Miami. He [then] followed his comments with "I Ain't Gonna Go To Hell For Anybody," a happy song in which most of the band joined in on vocals and clapped their hands.

And in Dayton, still looking to harp on about the End Times, he was even more abrupt about sixties nostalgia: "I remember trying to tell people in the sixties that hard times would come. I told them about it in 1963. Oh, but harder times are coming now. The sixties are gonna be just like a little lamb compared to the eighties. You already see signs of that happening right now as we work our way up to the nineties. You're gonna need something strong to hang onto."

[40] Isaiah 55:11—"So shall *my word* be that goeth forth out of my mouth: it shall *not* return unto me *void*."

Once again, the Dayton audience seemed on the same page of the same 1611 edition as Dylan, prompting the man to joke, after "Man Gave Names To All The Animals," "If you haven't already guessed the name of the last animal was a monkey. Not really. It was a snake."

Dylan's increasing willingness to share his thoughts carried on even after he returned to his hotel for a prearranged rendezvous with Karen Hughes. He had things he wanted to get off his chest, as if he somehow knew this would be his last chance to do so. And Karen Hughes had already proven an attentive and sympathetic listener as a defiant Dylan unburdened himself:

Bob Dylan: Christianity is not Christ and Christ is not Christianity. Christianity is making Christ the Lord of your life. You're talking about your life now, you're not talking about just part of it, you're not talking about a certain hour every day. You're talking about making Christ the Lord and the Master of your life, the King of your life. And you're also talking about Christ, the resurrected Christ, you're not talking about some dead man who had a bunch of good ideas and was nailed to a tree. Who died with those ideas. You're talking about a resurrected Christ who is Lord of your life. We're talking about that type of Christianity . . . It's HIM through YOU. "He's alive," Paul said, "I've been crucified with Christ, nevertheless I live. Yet not I but Christ who liveth in me." See Christ is not some kind of figure down the road. We serve the living God, not dead monuments, dead ideas, dead philosophies. If He had been a dead God, you'd be carrying around a corpse inside you . . . I guess He's always been calling me. Of course, how would I have ever known that? That it was Jesus calling me. I always thought it was some voice that would be more identifiable.

Yet, what should have been the ultimate scoop of the End of days—a candid interview with Christianity's most celebrated recent convert—found few takers and Hughes's interview ended up in an obscure New Zealand daily, not even being picked up by the wire-service. It seems this believer had outstayed his welcome:

Bob Dylan: The reaction on the *Slow Train* tour was disheartening at times. But it doesn't wound you because you get used to the ups and downs. You get to where the praise doesn't mean anything because it's often for the wrong reason, and it's the same with the criticism. [1984]

Somehow, after a year of prodigious activity and outstanding artistry—

The times can change for you, too.

YOU'VE JUST
GOTTA CHOOSE
WHOM
YOU'RE GONNA
SERVE.

YOU'RE GONNA HAVE TO
SERVE SOMEBODY!

"CHOOSE YOU THIS
DAY WHOM YE
WILL SERVE."

JOSHUA 24:15

The Bible promises that if
anyone accepts the Jewish
Messiah, Jesus, he'll be-
come a new person:
• "Therefore, if any man be
in Christ, he is a new
creation; old things are
passed away; behold, all
things are become new."

II Corinthians
5:17

Are you ready to
choose?

FOR A² CHANGE...
Write or call—

ANOTHER COVENANT WOMAN

**KRESHA
WARNOCK**
JEWS FOR JESUS © 1979
60 HAIGHT ST.,
SAN FRANCISCO,
CA 94102
(415) 864-2600

THE
TIMES
THEY ARE
(INDEED!)
A² CHANGIN'

The Times have changed since man gave names to all the animals

Jerry Rubin HAS BECOME AN ACCOUNTANT!

HA!

The Weathermen HAVE GONE 'OVERGROUND'

YIPPEE!

(AND NOT ONLY THAT) BUT YOU CAN NOW AFFORD $15 TO COME & HEAR DYLAN!

Maybe you came to hear the same old DYLAN

who was always singing just exactly what was on your mind. Maybe you're disappointed that he's not singing the same old songs, but then... you see...

he ain't exactly stuck inside o' Mobile with the Memphis blues any more, either.

You see, he's found the answer, my friend, — AND NOT BLOWIN' IN THE WIND, EITHER —

IT'S SOLID

because he's holding on to the

SOLID ROCK that was formed before the foundation of the world.

AND THAT ROCK IS JESUS THE MESSIAH. He has the power to change hearts, c

BOB DYLAN

ON COLUMBIA RECORDS AND TAPES

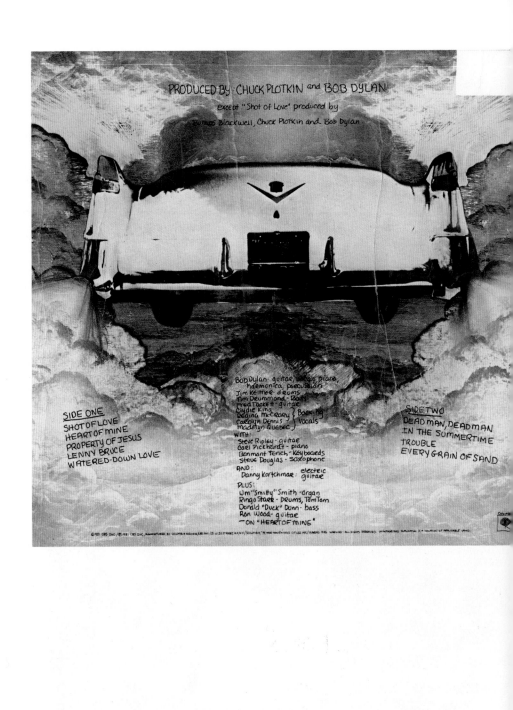

PRODUCED BY CHUCK PLOTKIN and BOB DYLAN
except "Shot of Love" produced by
Bumps Blackwell, Chuck Plotkin and Bob Dylan.

Bob Dylan - guitar, vocals, piano
    harmonica, percussion
Jim Keltner - drums
Tim Drummond - bass
Fred Tackett - guitar
Clydie King
Regina McCreary } Backing
Carolyn Dennis } Vocals
Madelyn Quebec)

WITH:
    Steve Ripley - guitar
    Carl Pickhardt - piano
    Benmont Tench - keyboards
    Steve Douglas - saxophone

AND:
    Danny Kortchmar : electric guitar

PLUS:
    Wm "Smitty" Smith - organ
    Ringo Starr - drums, Tom Tom
    Donald "Duck" Dunn - bass
    Ron Wood - guitar
    — ON "HEART OF MINE"

SIDE ONE
SHOT OF LOVE
HEART OF MINE
PROPERTY OF JESUS
LENNY BRUCE
WATERED-DOWN LOVE

SIDE TWO
DEAD MAN, DEAD MAN
IN THE SUMMERTIME
TROUBLE
EVERY GRAIN OF SAND

Columbia

two albums recorded, six months of solid touring and a controversy at least as profound as the "goes electric" one—Dylan's current activities were slipping down the news columns. Even in Britain, home to his most faithful fans, the gospel tour warranted only the briefest of news stories in *NME* from a still-engaged Nick Kent, whose account ran to a single paragraph:

> His repertoire consists of a few extracts from *Slow Train Coming* plus a bountiful collection of new songs, many of which will appear on *Saved*, his next album and Phase Two of his manifesto railing against sin and urging devotion to Christ as the only way out. This current tour has afforded Dylan the chance to get more voluble with his audiences. He now tends to break into abrupt spurts of sermonizing, informing his audiences that his current stance is no less dramatic a transformation than "Subterranean Homesick Blues" and "Desolation Row."

Evidently, Kent had heard all about the first Hartford show, possibly from Dylan author Michael Gray, who had been there that night. But fourteen years, almost to the day, after he had somnambulently staggered to the end of a debilitating world tour that had shook the very foundations of the pop world, Dylan found himself with another summer off, to recuperate and reenergize, after a heatwave and the commercial failure of *Saved* put paid to a fourth leg of the now-aborted gospel tour.

As is well-documented, in 1966 a partly-enforced eighteen-month break allowed the world to catch up. During this time Dylan would record some of his most therapeutic work, while looking back on a time when he had come close to giving it all up because his message was put through the media mangler and came out chopped to pieces. Even then, when a trusted journalist (Nat Hentoff) asked him what he had to look forward to, his reply had been unambiguous: "Salvation. Just plain salvation."

PART TWO
WATERED-DOWN LOVE

INTERLUDE:
IN THE SUMMERTIME

This is a new song, off our new record . . . This is a song about myself. I was walking right down the road, about ten or twelve years ago now. I wrote this song while looking into the mirror.
—INTRODUCTION TO "DEAD MAN, DEAD MAN," BIRMINGHAM, JULY 4, 1981

Your life doesn't have to be in turmoil to write a song . . . but you need to be outside of it. That's why a lot of people, myself included, write songs when one form or another of society has rejected you.

—BOB DYLAN TO PAUL ZOLLO, 1991

Dylan had been here before, the end of the line, after six months of solid touring, pushing some of the greatest music he ever made in the teeth of nightly resistance. But there are major differences between the summers of 1980 and 1966, which was certainly a time when he was "looking into the mirror" (aka Moviola) and not liking what he saw.

In 1966 he did not sense another creative breakthrough just around the corner—or, indeed, hairpin curve. The songs he had been writing in those months after *Blonde on Blonde*'s completion but before its protracted release were fly-by-night flights of fancy; inchoate hints at a way forward, ultimately a chimera.

Whereas in 1980, he had already loosened the bonds of evangelical orthodoxy with the two songs he performed every show that spring—"Ain't Gonna Go To Hell" and "Cover Down."

Now it was time to break the bonds completely, to fuse past sensibilties with his new-found surety of faith. Gone were the songs written to, and wrapped around, a dictum from the Good Book. Yet he was still standing on a solid rock of faith, not quite ready to abandon his two most recent sermonizing songs.

Indeed, he worked on a new lyrical draft of "Cover Down" in the memo notebook he carried around with him that summer, even as he penned some of his greatest-ever songs.[41] "Ain't Gonna Go To Hell" would also be revamped in a way which suggested former sensibilties were vying with his newfound faith, though that revamp would not occur until the extensive set of rehearsals in fall 1980.

But he would do more than this. The creative breakthrough that in 1966-67 had required a motorcycle accident, months of recuperation, half-hearted attempts to write poetry and playlets and, finally, weeks of rediscovering his muse in a humid basement in Big Pink through playing country, folk and blues standards, in the summer of 1980 simply required Dylan to set sail for parts unknown.

As he told Dave Herman, the following July, "If I can't do something that is telling people . . . you can be healed . . . I'd as soon be on a boat, you know." A few weeks after the end of the third and final leg of the gospel tour on May 21st, 1980, Dylan took his own advice, sailing round the Caribbean in a schooner he had co-purchased the previous year, name of *Water Pearl*. Yet he did not sail this boat alone. His fascination with black girlsingers showed no sign of abating, and his new constant companion was Clydie King, who had only joined the band in April but had quickly become the perfect foil for the frontman, vocally and spiritually.

Just being with this remarkable woman seemed to inspire an inner calmnesss and well-being that even faith had not fully inculcated. It was in such a benign state that Dylan wrote one of his most inspirational songs, "Every Grain Of Sand." In keeping with previous patterns, when this kind of inspiration came, it did so on wings of a prayer. As he told Hilburn in 1991, "It took like 12 seconds—or that's how it felt." But just like the sea he was sailing on, even in "the fury of the moment" there was a great deal going on below the surface:

Bob Dylan: Even a song like ["Every Grain Of Sand"], the simplicity of it can be . . . deceiving. A song like that just may have been written in great turmoil, although you would never sense that. Written but not delivered. Some songs are better written in peace and quiet and delivered in turmoil. Others are best written in turmoil and delivered in a peaceful, quiet way. [1991]

It was the others "written in turmoil" which occupied him most of the time that

---

[41] Though the first verse and chorus remain intact, the remainder of "Cover Down" has been rewritten. This draft resides in the Dylan archives at the George Kaiser Family Foundation in Tulsa, Oklahoma.

summer. "Every Grain Of Sand" appeared in his little notebook three-quarters of the way in, suggesting it was a song seeking resolution after a period of "great turmoil." Yet if he had already embarked on another great artistic journey by the time of his confession, he left a storm of controversy swirling around the other songs he wrote that summer and why it was that every one of them was rejected when it came time to release his statutory annual CBS bulletin.

It was almost like he had conceived, conceptualized and captured on the page an album that explained everything about how he got from A to C, and then burnt the results as an offering to his wilful muse.

It might be tempting to dismiss such an idea if he did not already have form. Back in 1967, he had done the same damn thing and what almost went up in flames in a fire at Wittenberg Road—from which only Garth Hudson's quick thinking saved some of his sublimest songs—was an album's worth of songs that was not merely the bridge from *Blonde On Blonde* to *John Wesley Harding* but an arch of Americana which would cast its shadow over rock's whole direction for the next decade.

Sitting full-square at the epicenter of that poorly-archived, half-forgotten way of killing time was a song Dylan didn't even get around to copyrighting until 1971; the position of which—at the beginning or end of the Big Pink process—is still a source of fierce debate: "Sign On The Cross" was "a song . . . that just may have been written in great turmoil, although you would never sense that."[42]

A song that spoke of being "so misled," the seven-minute sojourn addressed the singer's own struggle to make sense of that old sign on the cross. Twelve years later, it was seized on by some commentators at the time of Dylan's conversion as evidence of his ongoing quest for spiritual affirmation. Yet "Sign On The Cross" is an oddity amid all the bawdy wordplay and irreverent amoralism found on the other material recorded at Big Pink.

"Every Grain Of Sand" is very much the odd song out among those Dylan was writing, and endlessly rewriting, that Carribean summer, the rest of which would be not only "written in great turmoil" but "delivered in turmoil." Dylan was struggling with the same issues that had inspired his conversion in the first place, as he suggested to Herman in their curious interview:

Bob Dylan: If you do walk according to the law, all of the law, well, you'd be a pretty pure person . . . a person who could no doubt move mountains. Most people can't

---

[42] Even those who worked on *Bootleg Series Vol. 11* are not sure of its position. It appears to be an early Big Pink recording, possibly recorded on its own, and maybe even added to the relevant reel at a later date.

walk according to the law, because it's so difficult, there are so many laws, that govern just about every area of your life. [1981]

That struggle led him to compose a series of songs addressing a very personal battle with witchy women—or most likely, woman singular—and to wrestle with them for almost a year, before abandoning the uneven battle to capture "the fury of the moment" in the studio. "Every Grain Of Sand," on the other hand, would prove one song he taught the band on his return to Rundown in September 1980, and then quietly put away, not returning to it until he had fully conceptualized the third album in his so-called religious trilogy, *Shot Of Love*.

By then, he had decided that no matter when exactly the song came to him during this dark night of the soul, it would conclude this particular journey on record. There it stands, a summation of a soul in former torment, earnestly praying that this becalmed moment last for all eternity, his own cosmology of conversion caught in a Blakean grain of sand.

To the world at large, the song would present Dylan as someone who had "come to understand that every hair is numbered." For the rock-solid fanbase who after suffering their own forty days in the wilderness with the unregenerate *Saved*, it would at least offer some hope he had got this belligerent bug out of his system.

Thankfully, having learnt long ago to accept chaos, Dylan just continued writing new songs at a furious pace, continuing a spurt of songwriting the like of which had not been seen since Big Pink, even as he was posting his worst chart position in sixteen years. To his becalmed mind, he was "still on the road, walking towards the Son," waiting for the world to catch up. As ever.

8. WAITING FOR THE NIGHT TO ARRIVE . . .
[June – October 1980]

No Man Righteous –
Pressin on – guitar –
Its All over now Baby blue o
4th time Around o
shes not for you
* picked up a couple of years
* if you could read my mind
yonder comes sin
* willin
serve Somebody –
what can I do –
change my way –
lets keep it between us
Groom still waiting at the Altar
* Rainbow connection
Grain of Sand
Carribean Wind
Cover down –
Slow Train –
makin a liar
Blue Blue River ?
Simple Twist o
* Somewhere over the rainbow
In the garden –
wake up –
Aint gonna go to hell for anybody –
* Sweet Caroline
* show me the way
* Fever
* Goin on
* City of Gold

* Mary of the Wild Moor
* Abraham Martin and John
* Sadsongs and Waltzes
Precious Angel –
Tangled up in blue o
Blowin in the wind o
* Heatwave
* Fallin in love } Reginnia
* Back stairs
Ramona o
~~Simple Twist~~
Covenant Woman –
* What about me – girls
* Going to see the king
I believe in you –
Just like a woman o
* We just Disagree
love in Vain o
Maggies Farm o
Animals –
Do right (changes #4) –
* Do it in love
Solid Rock –
In the garden –
Rolling Stone o
Senor o
Don't think Twice o
you don't know me ?
Saved by the ~~Grace~~ of your love ?
I apologize ?
* This nite won't last forever
lay lady lay o

George Negus: Where do you think that burst of spiritual enthusiasm came from when you were actually recording albums that were genuinely gospel?

Bob Dylan: Oh, I had to do those albums. They were very important and necessary for me to do . . . Because people needed to hear that.

—60 MINUTES, 1986

Having once blazed a trail for his most revolutionary album with incendiary shows of fire and brimstone, and, despite falling off his bike, seeing that album sell steadily for the next eighteen months, Dylan perhaps hoped he had again said all he needed to when he delivered *Saved* to the label in the spring of 1980.

Having previewed the entire album throughout a tour that repeatedly crisscrossed the heartlands, he had surely created the right climate for the commercial acceptance of his ongoing Christian phase.

But whereas *Blonde On Blonde* was the most eagerly awaited album Columbia had on its release schedule in the spring of 1966, *Saved* was an album almost nobody at the label wanted, or knew what to do with—especially after Dylan delivered the finished artwork:

Tony Wright: They were so rude, so nasty about Bob Dylan and said how they weren't going to promote this record, another gospel record . . . I was just astonished to hear these people, highup people at CBS, talking about this man as if he were just [any]one . . . [There was] a "fuck him" kind of attitude. They hated the sleeve.

Coming from a man who for the past two decades had consistently captured the very nuance of an album's contents in its cover-art, the front cover of *Saved* might just as well have been that great big hand raising its middle digit to the record label, the artist's previously loyal album-buying audience and the whole idea of presenting the music inside in the best possible light. Yet four years later, Dylan sought to defend his choice of cover and the confrontation it presaged:

Bob Dylan: I thought the cover was wonderful. In fact, we wanted to have it posted up on Sunset Boulevard, and it cause a big stir. Big bloody hand reaching down. Tony Wright did it. He's a very good artist . . . A person never knows if he's saved or not. It's not for one person to say. I know people who say they are saved, and at a certain moment you may be. But that moment changes from day to day. But at any particular time and place . . . you may feel that that's the case, saved from the fire of damnation. [1984]

CBS's new head of promotion, Paul Rappaport, who had been Dylan's West Coast promotion man for most of the seventies, was genuinely concerned that the singer was doing his own music a disservice by presenting his message in such an in-your-face way. Having worked the radio stations for years, he knew that anything which stopped the DJs from taking the record out of the sleeve and putting it on the turntable would simply ensure that the message stayed in vinyl limbo on the shelves of unplayed albums every radio station had. His solution was simple: release advance copies of the album in a plain white sleeve, almost like it was one of those Dylan bootleg albums that continued to plague the label where he worked:

Paul Rappaport: The original cover is pretty Save-ey. [So] I might have sent that to radio without the cover—it's something I would have done, because I wanted people to hear the music first. I didn't want [them] to make any kinda decision based on a graphic . . . I would not have delivered that album with that album cover, not because I was embarrassed by it, but knowing the way radio brains think . . . I was very into protecting him 'cause I love him. So I was saying . . . "Just play the music in heavy rotation or you're gonna lose my number." . . . I remember talking to people about "Satisfied Mind," because it was pure Dylan, it was a more folky song. Somehow we were able to center people on the music, and tell them, "It's a phase Bob's going through. Make of it what you will, but please listen to the music."

But if Dylan still had CBS's chief cheerleader on board his holy train, his own publicist had decided the album was the last straw. As far as Paul Wasserman was concerned, "*Slow Train Coming* could be [considered] arguably religious in tone, but *Saved*—I threw in the towel then." And if the "arguably religious," musically mellifluous *Slow Train* had snuck past most critics, the benefit of the doubt was not part of any plea bargain Dylan made with the press this time. *Sounds*'s Dave McCullough set the tone:

Saved is remarkable solely because . . . it isn't just plain bad, it's really bad . . . [Dylan] invented half the rock music you listen to today, his influence has been unapproachable and immeasurable. *Saved*, however, is an ugly end. I can't see past it . . . Dylan has stopped communicating.

Although Chris Bohn's *NME* review recognized a shift in Dylan's tone from "the hellfire preachings of *Slow Train Coming*" to "the humbler Sunday school temperament of *Saved*," he considered the results no more than "a solid, functional gospel album, made purely as a celebration of its creator's faith, limiting its audience to those who share it . . . Will he return? Will anybody care? Don't wait up to find out."

The question of whether anybody would care when Dylan finally shrugged off such dogmatic lyrics had become a pressing one. Once again, though, *Rolling Stone* bucked the trend, Kurt Loder finding much to enjoy at this salvation bandstand, even if he questioned its diseased conceit:

Though producers Jerry Wexler and Barry Beckett gave Dylan one of the cleanest sounds of his career . . . the result [on *Slow Train*] seemed curiously embalmed . . . [and] the songs themselves were graceless and chilly in their self-righteous certitude . . . What made the Gospel According to Bob especially tough to take was his hook-line-and-sinker acceptance of the familiar fundamentalist litany and his smugness in propounding it . . . *Saved* is a much more aesthetically gratifying LP than its predecessor, particularly because of the hope (mostly musical, I admit) it offers that Dylan may eventually rise above the arid confines of Biblical literalism . . . "Saving Grace" is . . . a genuinely moving paean to some nonspecific Providence . . . Musically, Saved may be Dylan's most encouraging album since *Desire*, yet it's nowhere near as good as it might have been were its star not hobbled by the received wisdom of his gospel-propagating cronies.

This time, though, a qualified good word from the offices of Wenner Inc., would not save Dylan's latest. The album made a precipitous fall down the UK and US charts.[43] That Dylan was keeping an eye on the numbers was a given, even as he reverted to the no-hype approach adopted for his first post-accident album, *John Wesley Harding*, refusing all interview requests and putting even that planned in-concert TV special on the backburner.

---

[43] *Saved* peaked at No. 3 on the UK charts and remained there for eight weeks, as opposed to *Slow Train Coming* which peaked at two, and stayed in the charts for thirteen weeks. In the US, the disparity was far starker, *Slow Train* peaking at number three and remaining on the charts 26 weeks, while *Saved* managed to peak at 24, and hung around for eleven weeks.

He would twice be asked about the album's commercial failure on European tours, doing his best to put on a brave face at a 1984 Hamburg press conference: "*Slow Train* did all right. [But] I think *Saved* was a little light. Some are big, some aren't, you know." In a more measured July 1981 conversation with Dave Herman, he made a similar comparison, "*Slow Train* was a big album. *Saved* didn't have those kind of numbers," while expressing a personal fondness for *Saved*, "To me it was just as big an album."

At this point, he seems to have remembered that he was doing this interview at CBS's behest, and on their dime, and turned into a company man with a company line, "I'm fortunate that I'm in the position to release an album like *Saved* with a major record company so it would be available to the people who would like to buy it."

Dylan already knew that he had just a single album left on his current deal with the label and unless there was a major change in the way the label promoted his (and their) wares, there was a good chance it might be his last. To which, maybe some at the label were saying good riddance. British pop manager Simon Napier-Bell once told a story of a meeting with Dick Asher, ostensibly arranged to discuss the future of his own act, Japan, interrupted by a call from Dylan:

Simon Napier-Bell: CBS . . . had fired Clive Davis in the wake of a payola scandal. The company was now run by two lawyers—Walter Yetnikoff and Dick Asher. I liked Walter but fell into the half of the company run by Dick—a very dull man indeed. I finally got a meeting with him but had no sooner arrived in his office than the buzzer sounded and his secretary's voice said: "Bob Dylan on line one." "Can I call him back?" Dick asked. "No. He says he wants to talk to you now." Dick was about to have a conversation he didn't want. Eighteen months previously there had been publicity about Jewish-born Dylan becoming a born-again Christian. He'd made a couple of albums full of evangelical zeal but they'd bombed. Now his contract had come up for renewal. Dick especially didn't want to have this conversation in front of me [as he] yelled, "I've told you, Bob—no fucking religion! If you can't agree to that, the deal's off . . ." Bob was arguing the point, but Dick was having none of it. "Look, I'm telling you. There'll be no fucking religion—not Christian, not Jewish, not Muslim. Nothing. For God's sake, man—you were born Jewish, which makes your religion money, doesn't it? So stick with it, for Christ's sake. I'm giving you twenty million bucks—it's like baptizing you, like sending you to heaven. So what are you fucking moaning about? You want twenty million bucks from us? Well, you gotta do what we tell you. And what we're telling you is . . .

No Torah! No Bible! No Koran! No Jesus! No God! No Allah! No fucking religion. It's going in the contract."

The chances such a conversation ever took place are less than zero, but the idea that this was the view of Asher and his ilk when it came to Dylan's Christian work few at the label then deny. It reflected the general "'fuck him' kind of attitude" to which Tony Wright referred. When they printed up the promotional posters for *Saved*, which didn't mention the album title (see photo section), they even used a pre-conversion photo of Dylan playing an acoustic guitar. Pourquoi?

If they imagined that this would deflect Dylan from his preordained path, though, the cocaine really was messing up minds. He intended to continue "doing what I believed I should be doing. Most artists should do some some kind of gospel music. If they don't do something with gospel, I don't really trust that artist, I don't care who he is," a position he was still advocating at an Antipodean Q&A in 1986.

And he would still be insisting that "music should aim for the soul, not the groin," as late as 1990—at the end of a decade when he had once again let his own groin lead him astray most of the time.

In the summer of 1980, though, he was trying to achieve a rapprochement between earthly and heavenly delights; dealing with his inner demons not in therapy, a la latterday Springsteen, but in song. And when he was not reaching for the pantheistic perfection of "Every Grain Of Sand," he was wrestling with his past attraction to witchy women, most notably on a song called "Caribbean Wind":

Bob Dylan: I started it in St. Vincent when I woke up from a strange dream in the hot sun. There was a bunch of women working in a tobacco field on a high rolling hill. A lot of them were smoking pipes. I was thinking about living with somebody for all the wrong reasons. [1985]

Here was a breakthrough as profound as "Mr. Tambourine Man," "Like A Rolling Stone," "Visions Of Johanna" and "Tangled Up In Blue"—and Dylan knew it. What he had perhaps forgotten was that in all four instances, he had had to go back and rerecord each of these songs in order to capture them correctly in the studio, after first attempts at fixing to tape had failed to capture their essence.

This time he hoped would be different. He finally had a band he could spring surprises on, and they would respond with glee not gloom. He couldn't wait to play Keltner, Drummond, Tackett and co. "Caribbean Wind" and "Every Grain Of Sand." Hell, he couldn't wait to play them all of the eight songs he had scribbled into a memo notebook of his daughter's in the following order: "Let's Keep It Between Us," "Caribbean Wind," "Makin' A Liar," a rewritten "Cover Down," "The Groom's Still Waiting At The Altar," "Wild About You Babe," "Every Grain Of Sand" and "Yonder Comes Sin."

It was his third great starburst of new songs in eighteen months, and his most inspired—though not his most inspirational. The songs were at last showing a welcome disparity of approach, although the themes themselves were etched in stone.

There were catchy catechisms on calumnies perpetrated by both sexes ("Makin' A Liar," "Cover Down" and "Yonder Comes Sin"); testaments to the shared love of a pair shunned by society ("Let's Keep It Between Us" and "Wild About You, Babe"); the Augustinian "Every Grain Of Sand"; and, most inspiring of all, a pair of songs about star-crossed lovers on the run from the End Times, "Caribbean Wind" and "The Groom's Still Waiting At The Altar." The last title suggested the narrator wasn't the only one who had previously considered "living with somebody for all the wrong reasons."

It was with these songs in his once-hip pocket that Dylan arrived at Rundown on September 18th, 1980, refreshed and revitalized, ready to delve into the American songbook and his own, to teach his still-standing band a bushel of torch ballads and salty blues from his own blood-stained pen. Here, over the next fortnight, he would rediscover an aesthetic last explored in a West Saugerties basement a dozen years ago.

He began that day by running down all seven originals—the rewritten "Cover Down" being the exception—the total product of a highly productive summer spent mostly in the Midwest and the Caribbean. What he didn't manage, not surprisingly, was to lay down a definitive version of any these songs. This was a getting-to-know-'em session.

Indeed, in the case of "Let's Keep It Between Us," the first lyric in the notebook, only the barest snatch of it is on tape before Dylan starts teaching the band to play "Yonder Comes Sin"; while "Wild About You Babe" lasts barely a minute before Dylan abandons the piano-driven blues with a snort of disgust. It is the last time the song will be heard (of), and it is never copyrighted. Ditto, the first song of the day, "Blue, Blue River," a title Arthur Rosato listed on his song log without the asterisk that indicates a cover version.

Another victim of Dylan's ever perverse attitude to the copyrighting of song ideas—a trait most clearly manifested with The Basement Tapes, some songs from which were still being hastily copyrighted in 2012—was "Makin' A Liar." Yet, even on the evidence of two fragmentary versions on the 18th, it was immediately apparent this was an important, cohesive piece of work and a companion-piece to "Yonder Comes Sin," as "Groom's Still Waiting" was to "Caribbean Wind."

At least this was a song Dylan would return to a couple of times over the next week or so, thankfully recording a full six-minute version (now featured on *Bootleg Series Vol. 13*) some eight days later. By then, the words had been honed and synchronized to real invective from an accusatory voice:

> You tell people . . . you're just being courageous
> On them burning bridges, though your feet are made of clay
> You say you won't be destroyed by your inventions . . .
> And that you really do have the best intentions,
> But you're makin' a liar out of me . . .
>
> You say that ain't flesh and blood you're drinking
> In the wounded empire of your fool's paradise
> With the light above your head forever blinking
> Turning virgins into merchandise . . .
> You're makin' a liar out of me.

Every line stings like the crack of a whip as Dylan itemizes her (or his) falsehoods until the liar—no bride of Christ—stands there, stripped bare. Though on that first day, there is more nuance to Dylan's singing and a more melodic counterpoint, he abandons it after a second taped attempt, saying, "All of a sudden it got too boppy."

Anyway, he has other songs he wants to show the band so he shuffles across the piano stool and begins to plunk out the rudimentary outlines for "The Groom's Still Waiting At The Altar," "Yonder Comes Sin" and—most beautiful of all, introduced to the band with the suggestion, "Let's do this one, it's a ballad"—"Every Grain Of Sand." He would return to them all in the coming week.

The last new song of the day, though, would prove to be something more elusive, as if it was already getting away from him, each line seemingly shifting with the sands of rhyme each time he attempted to impose himself. A song destined to be a legend in its time, it was first logged, incorrectly, as "Blue Blue River." Only when he tries it again, is it correctly logged as "Caribbean Wind." Already, it is clear he has the skeleton keys to unlock this door of perception:

Told her about Jesus, told her about the pain,
She told me about the vision, she told me about the rain,
That had risen from the ashes and abided in her memory.

But if these lines would survive almost intact until its live debut, much of the rest of this prototype would be cast aside in a rewriting process that in the fullness of time would become an exercise in craftsmanship over creativity. Almost immediately lost was the rhetorical question, "Was she a virtuous woman? I couldn't tell"; as was the suggestion he had "met her at a home of a profiteer-type" after "a show in Miami." The original chorus, a mish-mash of mythologies, also didn't last long:

That Caribbean wind blows down from the iron gates of Chinatown
To the royal walls of the hungry Volunteers,
The Caribbean wind still swirls with a flash of gold and a string of pearls,
Bringing me down from the underworld, when heaven was living here.

The very air crackles as Dylan sings lines which still glow "like burnin' coal" thirty-seven years later, even as the meaning of the song dances ever out of reach, much like another song not released officially for thirty-seven years. For "Caribbean Wind" is the "I'm Not There" of the gospel years.

Unlike "I'm Not There," though, he shall return to the wind again and again over the next few days, weeks and months, more appreciative at thirty-nine of just how rare such moments are. In the meantime, Dylan and the band tackle another new song as a backing band to one of the backing singers, who had brought her own song along:[44]

Regina McCrary: I wrote [a] song called "Got To Give Him My All" . . . Actually Bob helped me write it . . . I started singing the words I had already written on my notepad—up to a point—and then I said, "But right here, I mean, I'm stuck. I don't know where to go with it." So Bob took the pencil and pad and he wrote the bridge to the song, and it was awesome . . . Later Bob Dylan, Tim Drummond, Jim Keltner, Spooner Oldham, Smitty, went in the studio that Bob used to have in Santa Monica, which was also our rehearsal hall, and we did a rough demo of it.

---

[44] There are actually a couple of candidates for this song on the early rehearsals, neither with clear accreditation as to its true title.

McCrary's appearance prompts Dylan to put away his notebook and turn his hand to some country covers. It is as if the past two years were but a dream as he steps out of the shower singing Shel Silverstein's "A Couple More Years" and Willie Nelson's "She's Not For You," throwbacks to those 1978 soundchecks he had peppered with country standards.

Something had happened and the band didn't know what it was. They were flummoxed to see the man whom a year earlier had eschewed every attempt to play any old songs, now wanting to play his way through the entire panoply of popular song. And the more MOR the material, the better:

Fred Tackett: We would go in and we'd rehearse really weird songs. We did a Bee Gees song and we did Neil Diamond['s] "Sweet Caroline" . . . We'd record these and Bob'd . . . send . . . Neil Diamond a copy of him doing "Sweet Caroline" . . . We'd rehearse all kinds of songs, but we wouldn't rehearse the songs we were going to do.

Tackett is here referring to the shows they were due to play in six weeks' time. After all, these rehearsals had been ostensibly convened because there was another tour booked, commencing at the Warfield Theatre on November 9th, another fortnight-long residency.

Based on reputation, getting Dylan back on message might not prove so easy. He was having a good time making music he wanted with musicians he trusted and without agenda, working up arrangements to an album's worth of new Dylan songs and some old favorites.

If "Caribbean Wind" was one side of the coin, "The Groom's Still Waiting At The Altar" was the other, a blast of rhythm 'n' blues that cast aside all ball-busting ballads, as he dismisses this lady (of the night?) with the suggestion, "If you see her on Fannin Street"—a notorious thoroughfare in Shreveport, Louisiana, immortalized by Leadbelly—"tell her I still think she's neat/ and that the groom is still waiting at the altar."

His "virtuous woman" has become a fallen woman. The narrator, though, has greater concerns—"Set my affections on things above/ Let nothing get in the way of that love/ Not even the rock of Gibraltar." He for one could hear the countdown on the late, great planet earth. He returned to "Groom" on the 24th and a week later, trying to get a version he could copyright. After that, the song largely disappears from the process, reflecting a way of working that was on the face of it counterintuitive but served him well:

Fred Tackett: Funny thing about rehearsals with Bob was [that] he didn't want you to learn the songs real well. He wanted to have the spontaneity of it . . . He didn't want us to know them, 'cause everybody'd get a little part and everybody'd get an arrangement and it'd be the same way every night. So he would go out and just surprise us and just start playing something and we'd follow on. All kinds of interesting things would happen that way.

So what was the underlying purpose of these September sessions? Perhaps, as one of Dylan's favorite musicians once said, there was "no particular reason for it. We weren't making a record. We were just fooling around. The purpose was whatever comes into anybody's mind, we'll put it down on this little tape recorder." Which is Robbie Robertson's description of the Dwarf Music demos Dylan recorded with The Hawks in the summer of '67.

If, in the fullness of time, those musicians produced "quite a collection of songs," the September 1980 Rundown rehearsals also produced a set of publishing demos, five songs being copyrighted from tapes made on the Otari the last week in September: "Every Grain Of Sand" (the one on *Bootleg Series Vols. 1-3*), "Let's Keep It Between Us" and "Yonder Comes Sin" (both of which have been genuinely bootlegged) and the key songs, "Caribbean Wind" and "The Groom's Still Waiting" (which haven't).

However, unlike the Big Pink demos, very little care seems to have been taken when choosing the best takes for copyright purposes. Only the demo of "Yonder Comes Sin," recorded on October 1st (or possibly September 30th)[45], could be considered definitive, and only by default. Even this version abruptly cuts on the master when it seems like Dylan has at least three more verses he has to do. He never returns to the song again, though those verses would be added to the copyrighted lyric (see *Still On The Road*).

Indeed, the "Yonder Comes Sin" demo seems to mark a line when Dylan finally stopped indulging himself in "fooling around" and got down to rehearsing in earnest for the shows to come. Not that he was about to run down any of the songs that would make up the bulk of what was being advertised as a "Retrospective" show, notably the ones he had written between 1961 and 1978, bequeathing fame and fortune.

Instead, he began running down a long list of covers he had seemingly been yearning to play for years, intent on working up a *Self Portrait Vol. 2* in the

---

[45] Its position at the start of the October 1st tape, without prelude, suggests one should exercise a little caution as to the actual date.

downtime between annual albums of original songs, an arrangement previously formalized in Dylan's 1978 CBS contract.[46]

The second September rehearsal—undated, but probably either the 19th or 22nd—began with Dylan singing his heart out on "Sad Songs & Waltzes," before a perfectly sincere "Somewhere Over The Rainbow" (where a lyric sheet might have come in handy) and finally, "If You Could Read My Mind."

Though a number of covers would carry over to the fall '80 shows, and in several cases be highlights, none of this trio would make the final cut—not even "Sad Songs & Waltzes," another Willie Nelson song he invested with a passion sadly lacking in inconclusive performances of "Gotta Serve Somebody," "Gonna Change My Way Of Thinking" and "What Can I Do For You?" cast off the same day.

A pattern had been set—rehearsals spent working up unlikely covers and Dylan only reluctantly returning to his own repertoire for the odd cursory run-through. And once it was established, it was one Dylan was reluctant to break until he was up against it, the clock having ticked down to another rendezvous with the notoriously fickle fans of San Francisco.

On September 23rd he warmed up for the serious matter of getting usable takes of "Every Grain Of Sand" and "Caribbean Wind" while Ben Keith was in situ, to pedal some steel strings, by taping five attempts at "Rainbow Connection," made famous the previous year by Kermit's ribbet-riven rendition in *The Muppet Movie*. Even after he had got two distinctly different takes of "Caribbean Wind"— including the gorgeous, if unresolved take on *Bootleg Series Vol. 13*—he returned to "Rainbow Connection," on which he was word-perfect.

For the rest of the last week in September, he concentrated on band arrangements for his own new songs, still undecided which of them might qualify for inclusion in "A Musical Retrospective." Perhaps he was waiting for the girls to arrive before he made his selection.

When the girls did finally turn up en masse on October 1st, he immediately sprung "Yonder Comes Sin," "The Groom's Still Waiting" and "Caribbean Wind" on them, before leading everyone a merry dance on several country standards. The girls' presence seemed to remind him he should at least run through the spring '80 tour set. So the day ended with Dylan and the girls going hell for leather on "Ain't Gonna Go To Hell," still with the core lyrics they'd sung in May.

But when sessions resumed the following week, Dylan's attention was

---

[46] The 1978 contract specifically excludes Dylan from delivering more than an album a year. How times change.

once again wavering. He spent one whole session—on the 8th—working up an arrangement (a terrific one, in fairness) for Dave Mason's 1977 radio hit, "We Just Disagree." This one, at least, was a keeper, an occasional survivor in the set till the following October.

Staking a claim to contemporary relevance by playing songs he had heard recently on the radio seemed to him one way to (re)connect with his core audience, but it was not just his choice of covers that left the musicians dazed and confused— it was their relative obscurity. Much of it was less known to—and less to the taste of—Dylan's audience than "Cover Down" or "Ain't Gonna Go To Hell," both as yet unreleased and underrehearsed.

Two days after the "We Just Disagree" marathon, Dylan spent the bulk of another session working on a song called "Goin' On," to which he would return twice during rehearsals. It was the first time he had ever covered a Beach Boys song and what a wacky choice, their most recent single which had charted at a barely warm 83 in the Hot 100.

As far as he was concerned, he was just having fun, fun, fun recording "really weird songs," many of a contemporary hue. Bill LaBounty's "This Night Won't Last Forever," a big hit when covered by Michael Johnson in 1979, was attempted the day after "We Just Disagree," Dylan trying for a little more tenderness than he displayed with "Don't Think Twice, It's All Right," subjected to only its second-ever band arrangement, from which it emerged unwanted, heading for the discard pile.

Whatever radio station Dylan had been tuned to when he heard "We Just Disagree," "Goin' On" and "This Night Won't Last Forever," it perhaps also played some Christian rock, because on the 16th, the day after his second attempt at an arrangement for "Goin' On," he and Clydie arrived at Rundown to record a resplendent acoustic duet on Dallas Holm's 1977 Christian rock ballad, "Rise Again."

It was a song which very personally identified with the crucified Christ and was, as such, a real statement of intent. Unlike "Goin' On" and "Rainbow Connection," this empathic message was one Dylan intended to carry into concert halls, after subtly but distinctly improving Holm's lyric:

> Go ahead, drive nails through My hands,
> Laugh at Me where you stand.
> Go ahead, say it isn't Me,
> But the day will come, you will see.

'Cause I'll rise again,
Ain't no power on earth can turn Me down!
Yes, I'll rise again,
Death can't keep Me <u>buried</u> in the ground.

If "Don't Think Twice" had made an ungainly transition from acoustic to electric, "Rise Again" would face the same fate more willingly. By the end of his Warfield residency, the band arrangement would raise the rickety roof, while Dylan and King's vocals wrapped around the rafters like the red rose and the brier.

But the acoustic "Rise Again" on the 16th would prove a one-off. In fact, the whole session would be a one-off, as Dylan also acoustically revisited two songs he'd last performed in 1961, "Jesus Met A Woman At The Well" and "Mary From The Wild Moor"—with cameras rolling. This was no tour rehearsal. Dylan was trying to record some intimate performances for the not-yet-aborted In Concert he had been trying to sell to TV since April—his last roll of the dice on that project, and the last that would be heard of it.

More pressing was the need for Dylan to bang the drum and play the carny to sell some tickets for the San Francisco shows, all twelve of them, now that the promise of a musical retrospective had whet the appetite of an audience that felt it had been burnt before. As such, on the same day, Dylan and band attempted to record a medley of his songs, old and new, to be used in a radio ad for the shows.

Slowly but surely, economic reality was dawning. Dylan needed to whip the songs he was planning to actually perform into shape and not spend time working up even more new material while the clock ticked down to midnight. Naturally, he responded by ending the session playing the band his latest song, at the piano:

There is a country of light
Raised up in glory, where the angels wear white
Where sickness can't enter, and demons can't bite
There is a city of light.

Called "City of Gold," it was an affirmative song of faith and a perfect companion piece to "Every Grain Of Sand." But when rehearsals resumed the following week, he proceeded to spend more precious time wailing through "Goin' On," "She's Not For You" and the Little Willie John standard, "Fever," than arranging this hymn to hope.

It was 1979 all over again. With a week to go, the final shape of the live set had never seemed more in flux. As then, a week of real tour rehearsals were now scheduled to address these issues head on. On the 27th, Dylan and the whole band convened at Rundown for five solid days at the collective coalface.

It was time to revisit a more familiar repertoire, beginning with "Gotta Serve Somebody," still the starting point for every Dylan show. And it still sounded great. But a woeful "Covenant Woman" followed, suggesting a distinct disconnection from the material he wowed the Warfield with less than a year earlier.[47]

"Covenant Woman" had previously been dropped from the set back in April, to make way for "Ain't Gonna Go To Hell," another song he had seemingly forsaken. But it also reappeared on the 27th in an entirely new technicolor coat and over the next week it would shed most of the April lyric and adopt lines seemingly left over from an early draft of "The Groom's Still Waiting" (he even reuses the image, "Sleeping in the ghetto" as he travels "from Memphis to Austin, New York to Boston").

Over the next four days, Dylan would repeatedly return to the song, sculpting and shaping the new arrangement, sacrificing its slowburn Spring self at the altar of a man who had decided the target for his ire was someone who was "a pretty good girl but you don't look back" as opposed to a man "wailing down the road . . . lost on the trail . . . found below the highway."

If much of the song remained in dummy lyric form, it was not alone. A raucously realigned "The Groom's Still Waiting" involved Dylan throwing out random lines from the blues lexicon, from "ten past midnight" to "Rooster crowing, early in the morning." He just needed the arrangement honed for the handful of original songs he wanted to introduce at the shows.

Still central to that process was "Caribbean Wind," which he worked on multiple times on the 28th. And this time there was not a dummy lyric in sight. He had the words *down*. It was the arrangement which needed work. On this occasion, he slowed it down to a crawl, savoring the words, even enunciating the couplet, "Doorknobs turning, there was heat in my bed/ Street band playing Nearer My God To Thee."

He was almost there. He just needed to change one line in the final verse from, "And like they say, *the show must go on*," to the altogether more self-referential, "The ship will sail at dawn," thus ensuring the street-band's song mirrored the one the band played as the Titanic went down. Just as soon as he tightened the chorus

---

[47] A fascinating violin/harmonica-driven arrangement of the song at the final October rehearsal had real promise but ended up sidelined.

to make "the circle of light" flicker around the "furnace of desire," he would be ready to reveal his latest vision to a world on the brink.

By the time he did, though, the world had already heard about this tantalizing new song. Michael Oldfield—the *Melody Maker* journalist, not the musician from *Hergest Ridge*—had been privy to an afterhours continuation of Rundown rehearsals after a night at the Roxy watching the return of Dire Straits as chart-conquering communiquétors.

It was October 29th, and Dylan turned up at Mark Knopfler's hotel room, not expecting him to be courting a British journalist, but still anxious to play some songs. He even told the stunned Straitman, "We do a lot of old songs now," before proceeding to play him this brand new song. The description by Oldfield of that new song, which appeared on the streets of London the day it made its San Franciscan live debut, whet the appetite among fans the world over who had despaired of ever hearing him write a song *like* "Visions Of Johanna," let alone one as good:

> Bob's raring to go . . . He sits himself on the edge of an armchair and starts another song, possibly titled "Carribean Wind." This is Dylan at his very best: enigmatic lyrics which seem a lot more gritty than we've been been hearing recently, and a simple but beautiful melody. The spell is cast, and it encaptures the dozen or so people who are privileged to hear this private recital.

It seems Dylan had the centerpiece for his new live set, and maybe even a new album that could reverse his fortunes and make up much of the ground *Saved* had eaten up. For now, though: the show must go on.

9. BACK IN BABYLON
[November – December 1980]

CARIBBEAN WIND

Words and music by Bob Dylan

She was from Haiti, fair brown and intense
She was a friend of both bus-boys and presidents
I was playin' a show in Miami at the theater of divine comedy
Told her 'bout Jesus, told her about the rain
She told me about division, she told me about the pain
That has risen from the ashes and abided in her memory
Was she a child, or a woman, I really can't say
Something about her said trust me anyway
As the judge and the jailer were meeting with the man of the hour
It looked like I was sleeping and they thought I was
But I was paying attention like a rattlesnake does
When he hears footsteps tramplin' on the flowers

    And them Caribbean winds still blow
    From Mexico to Curacao
    From Chinatown to the furnace of desire
    And them distant ships of liberty on iron waves so bold and free
    Bringing everything that's near to me, nearer to the fire

Our shadows drew closer 'til they touched on the floor
Prodigal son sitting next to the door
Preaching resistance, waiting for the night to arrive
He was well connected but her heart was a snare
And she had left him to die in there
But I knew that he could get out while he still was alive
Stars on the balcony, flies buzzing my head
Door knob turning, heat in my bed
Street band playing, "Nearer My God to Thee"
We met in secret where the mission bells ring
She said, "I know what you're thinking, but there ain't a thing you can do about it,
    so we might as well agree to agree."

    And them Caribbean winds still blow
    From Mexico to Curacao
    From Chinatown to the furnace of desire

This is a 12-string guitar. First person I ever heard play a twelve-string guitar was Lead Belly. Don't know if you've heard of him. Anyway, he was a prisoner in, I guess, Texas State Prison. I forget what his real name was but people just called him Lead Belly. He was recorded by a man named Alan Lomax . . . great man, done a lot of good for music. Anyway, he got Lead Belly out and brought him up to New York. And he made a lot of records there. At first he was just doing prison songs and stuff like that . . . Lead Belly did most of those kind of songs. He'd been out of prison for some time when he decided to do children's songs and people said, "Oh, why did Lead Belly change?" Some people liked the old ones, some people liked the new ones. Some people liked both [styles]. But he didn't change, he was the same man!

—BOB DYLAN, INTRODUCING "CARIBBEAN WIND," NOVEMBER 12, 1980.

Paul Vincent: You're not preaching to us?
Bob Dylan: No I'm not . . . This is a stage show we're doing, it's not a salvation ceremony.

—KMEL RADIO INTERVIEW, NOVEMBER 18, 1980.

In September 1965, Dylan had flown to Austin, Texas, to play only his fourth-ever professional electric show accompanied by a band with whom he had rehearsed for exactly two nights, the previous week. The reviews were wholly positive and The Hawks, later The Band, never looked back.

In November 1980, for the second time in twelve months, Dylan arrived at the Warfield Theatre in San Francisco accompanied by an equally gifted band with whom he had been rehearsing on and off for six weeks and playing with for the last fourteen months.

And yet, for the second time in 375 days, said band seemed unprepared and underrehearsed on opening night. In fact, West Coast reviewer Ron Gluckman had the timerity (or tinnitus) to suggest afterwards that although "Dylan is in exceptional voice" (which he was not), he was "playing with one of his sloppiest bands ever."

The one thing Gluckman got right in his overview of the residency was that "the local critics blast[ed] the [first] show." Once again, the reviewers seized on the way that fans had been kept in the dark—or even misled—as to the content of the shows. Even local weekly music magazine *BAM's* review played follow the leader-page:

> A few weeks ago word began to circulate that there were going to be some secular themes on [Dylan's] next LP. Then it was announced that Dylan would be putting on a retrospective at the Warfield, featuring songs from every period of his career . . . Tickets for the shows sold briskly and the run was extended for five nights to an eventual twelve. Well, in a move that surprised almost everyone opening night (including Bill Graham) Dylan's idea of a "retrospective" turned out to be five older songs . . . haphazardly dropped into a set overwhelmingly dominated by religious tunes . . . [Meanwhile,] the band was incredibly sloppy and poorly rehearsed, the pacing of the show clumsy, and Dylan seemed to play his older songs only grudgingly . . . The crowd's response was chilly at best—the call for the encore seemed more perfunctory than genuine. All in all, it was a disaster. The next morning, Graham's office was flooded with phone calls complaining about the show.

It seemed Dylan had again miscalculated, failing to address the expectations of an audience that had been courted with radio ads promising a retrospective— while freshly-minted versions of "Mr. Tambourine Man" and "Blowin' In The Wind" played in the background—part of a concerted push that strongly implied a balance would be struck between his born-again material and the songs of a sinner man.

In truth, for the first time in his career, Dylan was struggling to conceptualize the kind of show he envisaged doing. And if proof were needed, it resides in three provisional set lists, one typed, two in either Dylan's or Rosato's hand, pre-Warfield.

One of these divided the set into "religious" songs, seven of them, including "Ain't Gonna Go To Hell," six older songs and a two-song encore, one from *Saved*, the other a rare number one hit for the great American songwriter. A second handwritten set list gave a track order to a sixteen/seventeen-song set beginning with the unnumbered "Show Me The Way," one for the girls to sing, followed by:

1. Rolling Stone 2. Serve Somebody 3. Señor 4. Simple Twist of Fate 5. Ain't Gonna Go 6. Animals 7. Blowin' in the Wind 8. Slow Train 9. Keep Fallin' In Love [a song sung by Regina McCrary at the shows] 10. Love In Vain 11. Solid Rock 12. Ramona 13. Wake Up 14. In The Garden. [Encores - unnumbered:] Pressin On/ Mr. Tambourine Man.

The one thing the above shares with opening night at The Warfield is the balance of material—religious and pre-conversion—which was about the same. He clearly envisaged a show that clocked in at around ninety minutes. Included was not a single song written that summer, nor a single cover version, but he envisaged playing two songs from *Street-Legal*,[48] and encoring with two songs he had barely rehearsed, one of which ("Pressing On") he would never play again.

That the balance he struck on the 9th was askew even a pro-Dylan proselytizer like Robert Hilburn found hard to candy coat. This time he was struggling to put a positive spin on a show which not only lacked the previous year's frisson of controversy but was plain ordinary in every sense of the word:

> Ten of his seventeen tunes were from his last two, gospel-dominated LPs . . . But this time he didn't ignore his pre-1979 material . . . Unlike opening night last year, there was no hostility expressed by the audience toward the gospel tunes . . . [although] most people [had] hoped for at least a 50-50 mixture . . . [However,] the capacity audience quickly learned that Dylan was [still] operating on his own terms. Unwilling to turn himself into a museum piece, he kept the emphasis for [most] of the show on the new Christian numbers, just slipping in an occasional oldie or a surprise . . . [like] two unrecorded songs, one of which ("Ain't Gonna Go To Hell For You" [sic]) seemed only slightly religious in nature, and the other (the R & B-tinged "Let's Keep It Between Us") even less so.

Given that less than a third of the set came from his pre-*Slow Train* repertoire, and one of the new songs was called "Ain't Gonna Go To Hell For Anybody," the fans were entitled to wondering just how sincere was the gesture Dylan was making by playing just "Like A Rolling Stone," "Girl From The North Country," "Just Like A Woman" and "Blowin' In The Wind." And that night all were delivered in a way suggesting he was as divorced from those songs as he had been in 1974, when he shouted their very essence down.

It wasn't just the audience who were mystified as to the motive behind Dylan playing his old songs—and then doing so in such a half-hearted way, far removed from the way they had been in rehearsal:

Fred Tackett: We all wanted to play the old songs, too. But nobody in the band would say anything about it. So I don't know who put the pressure on or what

---

[48] The rehearsal tapes confirm that "Love In Vain" was not the Robert Johnson song but rather "Is Your Love In Vain," which he never played in concert again.

made him decide to do that, but I think it was just a business thing: to make people happy, he started doing his old songs again . . . He never told us why he was doing it . . . [But] I don't remember the audience reaction being that much better because he was playing his old songs.

The muted reaction to songs fans once feared they might never hear again was partially a reflection of the undynamic performances themselves, each song being reined in. Not since the Isle of Wight in 1969 had Dylan invested so little into "Like A Rolling Stone," denuded of the requisite rage he had found so easy to muster on the likes of "Slow Train" and "When You Gonna Wake Up" six months earlier.

Not that this post-conversion pair were served any better. He was finding it just as hard to summon the spirit on more spiritual material. "When You Gonna Wake Up" sounded like it was suffering from narcolepsy, while the opening double whammy of "Gotta Serve Somebody" and "I Believe In You" were an audible downgrade on the V8 performances a year earlier.

Once again, it was left to Bill Graham and his organization to bear the brunt of the ire disgruntled attendees expressed on opening night. According to Gluckman the effect was immediate, "The word gets out. Tickets can be found for $10 for the second night's show, while prices slide as low as $3 later in the first week!" Meanwhile, promoter and performer were prompted to exchange some warm words about the way this needed to go, and the middle ground that Dylan was going to have to find—real soon—if the most influential popular American artist of the post-war era didn't want to end up a sideshow at someone else's salvation ceremony.

Thankfully, Graham's tête-à-tête, a good night's rest and a change of uniform (into unbuttoned waistcoat, slacks, and an open shirt) seemed to do the trick and on night two, Dylan began the long slow climb back to where the high moral ground and middle ground were still part and parcel of the same plot. In fact, the tenth would be the real starting point for one of the most surprising reinventions in Dylan's quixotic career. Having again dismantled expectations on opening night, he then set about rebuilding his live reputation brick by brick.

On night two, he added a delightful "To Ramona" with a touch of the Waylons about it to the main set, and seemed generally more on his game, more willing to throw the odd vocal curveball. But it was the encore, described by a returning Gluckman, which suggested meeting audiences halfway might not be anathema to his art:

For his encores, Dylan does "Blowin' In The Wind" with his band, then performs solo on "This City of Gold" [sic]. Smiling at the end, Dylan says, "Thank you, thank you, I hope you liked that. Good night," but the crowd refuses to let go. A jubilant Dylan bounds back on stage with a harmonica brace in one hand and says, "I hope I can still do this. I saw Bruce Springsteen do it a while back, and it didn't look too difficult." The ensuing "Love Minus Zero/No Limit" is a staggering déjà vu, Dylan strumming the six string while blowing the frenzied, tuneless harp.

Few of the mainstream rock writers went to more than opening night, and even fewer reported on the transformation in Dylan's demeanor and performance-art over the full fortnight of shows. But *BAM* did, reporting that "Dylan, apparently sensitive to a degree about the outcry, included more older songs in successive shows, although the Christian material still dominated. Dylan also mixed [up] the selection of older tunes . . . [and] chatted freely with the audience, explaining why he was doing certain songs, and generally . . . enjoying himself."

Gluckman also reported seeing Bill Graham "stroll[ing] the Warfield lobby after the shows, bubbly with enthusiasm [while] Dylan was in obvious good cheer, as evidenced by an impromptu backstage interview he agreed to." That "impromptu backstage interview" was nothing of the sort. It was a radio interview with Paul Vincent at KMEL, hoping to sell some more seats for the shows scheduled after San Francisco.

But the opinions of rock critics were certainly on Dylan's mind and on night four, before "Ain't Gonna Go To Hell" he announced, "I want to say hello to Greil Marcus, if he's here tonight. I think he's here tonight . . . I guess he's the top rock 'n' roll critic of the era—whatever that is."

Marcus wasn't there that night—though he caught at least a couple of the shows—missing the live debut of "Caribbean Wind," dedicated to another "top rock 'n' roll critic," one that seemed to rate much of Dylan's recent work. If the singer had not forgotten the slam Marcus had given to *Street-Legal*, as wide of the mark as Greil had ever been in a decade of gathering moss, Paul Williams had never wavered.

Although he had retired from the rock fray just as punk happened, Williams had caught the first two and fourth Warfield show, and so saw Dylan emerge from his curmudgeonly chrysalis. He also got to spend time with the man himself, for the first time since 1966. According to Paul, it was "because he liked [*What Happened?* that] he allowed Sachiko and I to spend several hours with him backstage after four of the November [19]80 shows. He even read me the lyrics of a new song, 'Every Grain Of Sand,' [and] told me about another song he was proud of ('Caribbean Wind')."

Not only did Dylan make such an uncharacteristic gesture, he told this commentator on the 10th that if he came to a subsequent show and wanted to drop a note backstage beforehand requesting something specific, he would try to oblige. And so it was that Williams and his lady friend took their seats on the 12th after asking to hear this "song he was proud of," which he had as yet made no effort to debut.

Imagine Paul's delight when Dylan broke off from the established order of the shows to date—"Just Like A Woman" into "In The Garden," the finale of the main set—to tell a story about Lead Belly (see chapter heading) and after delivering its punchline, began talking about "a new song I wrote a while back. I'm gonna try and do it as good as I can. There's somebody important here tonight who wants to hear it."

That "someone important" was Paul Williams, the father of rock criticism, and Dylan's idea of giving "it our best" was to deliver perhaps the greatest live vocal of his career.[49]

Grabbing this tiger of his own making by the tail, Dylan hangs on for grim death through a near-death experience to the promised land. In the process he is obliged to not so much throw the girl with "bells in her braids" overboard as just leave her on dry land:

> I said come on with me, girl,
> There's plenty of room,
> But I knew I was lying,
> And besides, she was already gone.

This singular performance confirms Jann Wenner's wild-eyed assertion, in his rare self-penned *Rolling Stone* record review of *Slow Train*, that in 1979-80 Bob Dylan really was "the greatest singer of our times . . . No one, in objective fact, is even very close." But what did the man whose request had ensured the song was captured in all its ferric fervor while burning with the light of inspiration, think of it all?:

---

[49] The inclusion of the two-track soundboard recording of this trailblazing performance on *Bootleg Series Vol. 13* finally puts into the public domain one of the most revelatory recordings in Dylan's entire canon. The revealing spoken intro, though, wasn't captured complete.

"Caribbean Wind" . . . sounded on first listen like it could join the ranks of Dylan all-time classics; he sang it with tremendous feeling and energy despite frustration at the band's inability to follow him . . . [But that night] was just an incredibly giving evening, the idea of an audience really liking his show is something he hasn't necessarily gotten a surfeit of in the last year or more, and he seemed very pleased at all the positive response.

In fact, Dylan seemed more frustrated with his own performance than the band's, wondering aloud at song's end, "I don't know if you could get all of the lyrics, I don't know if we got that off or not, [but] I know we can do this one," and launching into an impassioned "In The Garden."

Also on the 12th, for the first time at this residency, he delivered some songs debuted at the previous residency with commensurate craft and passion. If the two openers stayed stuck in neutral, the return of "Precious Angel" in a radical new arrangement, complete with a harmonica-wielding Dylan, suggested he had reconnected with his devout muse. If "Covenant Woman" sounded "shattered like an empty cup," "Slow Train" and "In The Garden" again reveled in their evangelist element. The girls also seemed to have come into their own, Dylan now inserting an acoustic/autoharp duet with Regina, a way of having a sly dig at those who wanted the old songs:

All right, we're gonna try something new tonight. Don't know how it's gonna come off, but we'll try it anyway. A lot of people want to know about old songs . . . This is a song I used to sing before I even wrote any songs. But this is a real old song, as old as I know . . . This is what I guess you call one of them old folk songs. I used to sing these kind of songs . . . hundreds of these things. Well, I hope it brings you back, I know it brings me back. This is "Mary And The Wild Moor." I guess it's about 200 years old.

The glorious 12th witnessed a Dylan once again hanging in the balance of a perfect, finished plan. It was a format he now clung to, not only till the end of this jaunt but till this touring band sounded the last reveille.

Playing twenty songs, three more than opening night, he proved once again that no matter how much he changed, he was the same troubadour who turned up in the Village in 1961 and sang this English broadside ballad collected by the great Yorkshire collector, Frank Kidson, at the turn of the century. And before the now-nightly "City of Gold" encore he responded to the audience's prolonged applause by confessing, "I'm glad you even showed up." The criticisms had stung but he refused to feel any pain.

The following night, "Caribbean Wind" was gone. Perhaps Dylan really did think the lyrics needed work. Nor was he finished with the words to the song that replaced it on the 13th, an equally intense "The Groom's Still Waiting At The Altar," Dylan being joined for this and three other songs—all from *Saved*—by Carlos Santana. The experiment was repeated at the next show on the 15th, with an even more inspiring guest guitarist and outcome. This time his introduction spoke of a contemporary bluesman whose impact was almost as great as Lead Belly's:

> *I was playing a club in Chicago, I guess it was about 1959 or 1960 and I was sitting in the restaurant. It was across the street or maybe it was in front of the club, I'm not sure. But a guy came down and said that he played the guitar. He had his guitar with him and . . . I said "Well, what can you play?" He played all kinds of things. I don't know if you've ever heard of . . . Big Bill Broonzy? Or Sonny Boy Williamson? That type of thing. He just played circles 'round anything I could play and I always remembered that. Anyway, we were back in New York, I think it was 1963 or 1964 [sic] and I needed a guitar player on a session there I was doing. And I called [him] up . . . and he came in and recorded an album. At that time he was working in the Paul Butterfield Blues Band. Anyway, he played with me on the record and I think we played some other dates. I haven't seen him too much since then. He played on "Like A Rolling Stone" and he's here tonight. Give him a hand, Michael Bloomfield!*

There he was, shuffling onstage and unleashing, note-perfect, the ringing guitar riff he played to "Like A Rolling Stone" immediately after it emerged from the womb of "La Bamba." If anyone fortunate enough to be there that night thought Bloomfield had nothing left in the tank after this—his personal appearance suggesting such might be the case—he came back all the way, auditioning for the role of best man on "The Groom's Still Waiting." Good as Santana had been, in Bloomfield's master hands, its performance was more Peter Green than Mick Green.

A delighted singer gave the man a most unDylanlike bear hug as he left the stage, unaware that he had just orchestrated Bloomfield's live swansong. The gifted guitarist would be found dead in a locked Mercedes Benz of a drug overdose the following February.

Dylan, though, was just starting to come back to life. The following night he continued his guitarist auditions on "The Groom's Still Waiting," inviting another local hero and closet junkie to share the stage, Jerry Garcia. Unfortunately, Garcia seemed to think the people were there to see him and even when Dylan played song after song he simply did not know, he would not relinquish the spotlight. Afterwards, Fred Tackett had a quiet word with his mightily miffed boss:

Fred Tackett: Carlos played a song—thank you and left. Mike Bloomfield came out, played "Like A Rolling Stone"—thank you—left. Jerry Garcia came out, played and stayed. The whole two-hour show. He didn't know any of the songs and he was higher than a kite . . . We finished the show and Bob said, "I'm never going to have anybody sit in with us again." I said, "Bob, you gotta do it after the whole show's done and you're doing the last song. Then you bring out Jerry Garcia and let him play, but you don't bring him out the first song, 'cause he's liable to stay all night.

As it happens, Dylan was done auditioning guitarists. After three remarkable workouts for a song that never entirely lost its essence, he had decided to shake up the set all over again. Dylan had been playing a riveting piano duet with Clydie King on "Abraham, Martin & John," bringing the house down every night on the line, "Has anybody seen my friend Bobby, can you tell me where he's gone?" A reference to the assassinated Bobby Kennedy. On the 18th, though, he stayed at the piano with his paramour and dispelled all doubt about his current religious position with a compelling "Rise Again."

By the second week of shows, the band sets were also supplemented by a judicious sampling of the best covers from Rundown rehearsals, starting on the 17th with the introduction of Dave Mason's "We Just Disagree" and Shel Silverstein's "A Couple More Years." On the 21st, "Rise Again" itself rose again, this time in a full-band arrangement so powerful that the theater itself seemed to levitate a couple of inches. And, best of all, on the final night (22nd), he decided he would rock 'n' roll all the way down to the orchestra pit, delivering a Little Willie John classic with so much fire it gave the entire audience a temperature. He prefaced it with another back-in-the-day story:

I ran into a girl here on the street a while back and she said I was a strange person and she told me why. She said, "You were born up in a certain area where the ground is metallic." And actually she's right. Where I come from the ground is metallic. As a matter of fact during the Second World War, 90% of all the iron and steel that went into all the ships and boats and the airplanes and all kinds of weaponry . . . came from the area where I always lived. They dug it out of the ground. So there's something to that, I'm sure. But one of the great lakes is called Lake Superior, I don't know if you've ever heard of it. Across the lake is a town called Detroit. And I got to go to Detroit once. I think I was about twelve or so, with a friend of mine who had relatives there. I can't remember how it happened but I found myself in a bingo parlor. There were people coming to eat all day and play bingo all night, and there was a dance band in the back. Where I'm from, I would only hear mostly country music, you know: Hank Williams, Hank Snow, Hank Penny, all kinda Hanks! This was my first time face-to-face with rhythm & blues, it was in Detroit . . . and the man there was singing this song here. I don't think I'll do it as good as he did it, but I'm gonna try. [sings] Never know how much I love ya . . .

Leaving aside the unlikelihood of Dylan hearing the song before 1956, the year it was written, the story has a certain veracity, even if it seems likely to have really been Madison or Minneapolis where he came "face-to-face with rhythm & blues" for the first time. Another rap that alluded to an undocumented, life-changing incident from his past also tapped into something real, albeit with the whiff of a master teller's embellishment. This near-death experience he placed at the point when he was the Prince of Folk wooing its Queen with his talent for songwriting and seduction:

I know everybody here [has] heard of Joan Baez. Well, me and Joan are old friends, and one time, maybe fifteen years ago, she invited me out to her house in Carmel. At that time she was living out there, and she said, "Let's go down to the beach." So that's what we did. We went down to the beach and the waves were comin' in pretty hard that day. They were just crashing up against the rocks, and I think it was about 3:30, 4:00 when we were up there., and she said, "Ya see that cave up there? Maybe you want to go up there." And I looked up and saw this cave. I said, "Well, not really. Can you just give me a reason why I should?" She said, "Well, you may like it up there." That persuaded me to do it. She said, "Just keep climbing." I guess she wanted to climb too. Anyway, there was no water on the beach at all. I went down to the beach and I started climbing up these rocks and pretty soon I was in this cave and things being what they were, I kinda get carried away and just sat there for a while. The sun went down and I was still in the cave and she was nowhere to be found and the water started comin' in. I looked out of the cave and all the waves are crashing in towards the cave and there was no way to get back to the beach except to jump into the water, and eventually that's what I had to do. I just took a big risk and jumped into one of these waves coming in, and sure enough it just carried me back to the beach. Well, I was lucky. But this friend

of mine he did the same thing down in Florida and jumped off a wall. I guess the
timing was wrong, but he broke himself up pretty bad. He sits in a wheelchair now. So
I just want to say hello to him.

The friend who "broke himself up pretty bad" was Larry Kegan, a childhood
chum who had returned from Florida one summer in the late-fifties in a wheelchair.
He and Dylan remained close, and the impact the incident had on Kegan's lucky-in-
life friend never quite left him, while Kegan himself became a familiar sight at shows.

This story had more credibility than certain other raps from the residency.
Once again, after taking a couple of shows to find his groove and win over the fans,
Dylan was becoming positively gregarious. The story he told before "Just Like A
Woman" on the 16th, while Garcia tried to learn the chords, addressed an urban
myth—that the song was about a transvestite—head on:

I was standing out backstage, and this guy came up to me. He said, "You remember
that woman that came up to you about an hour ago with the long red hair?" And I
said, "Yeah, I remember that woman." And he said, "She sure was beautiful, wasn't
she?" And I said, "Yes, she was all right." He said, "That was me."

He had been playing this song every night, as he had "Like A Rolling Stone"
and "Girl From The North Country," both of which went down extremely well,
even if Dylan on the third night concluded the latter by insisting, "That was 'Girl
From The North Country.' Well, I think it was. It sounded like about four different
songs at the same time."

He had also been alternating "To Ramona" and "Simple Twist Of Fate," songs
which were once affectionate portraits of lost love but seemed to have been infected
with the "witchy women" virus, and were all the better for it. On the latter, she was
no longer some innocent naïf. Rather, "She looked at him with that look that can
manipulate/ And forgot about that simple twist of fate," leaving him alone at the
dockside, waiting for the ship to sail at dawn.

On the 17th, he introduced another stonewall classic from the medicine days,
"Just Like Tom Thumb's Blues," a song he had sung exactly twice since 1974. Five
days later, at a memorable final Warfield show, he came back for a fourth encore,
delivering a full-blooded, full-band arrangement of "A Hard Rain's A-Gonna Fall"
that suggested he still thought the end might be Nigh.

He had turned it around and most of the fans attending shows from the
12th on left the theater believing they had got Dylan back again. On the 13th, the

prolonged cries for more, after a devastating "It Ain't Me Babe" at set's end, led Dylan to joke, "I'd love to stay here and play all night but I can't. I've got too many songs, I got to keep some for tomorrow night."

As Ron Gluckman wrote in a review of the entire residency, "By the second week a different word had gone around and nearly everyone in attendance was a veteran of an earlier show. The atmosphere turned to party. Girls danced on nearly every uptempo number and even songs like 'Covenant Woman' drew surprisingly strong cheers."

Dylan was more than meeting the dancing girls half way. But at what cost to his eternal soul? By that final night, just six of the twenty-four songs were now culled from his two Christian albums. And at an interview given days earlier, he seemed to be distancing himself from those albums, telling Robert Hilburn, "I've made my statement and I don't think I could make it any better than in some of those songs. Once I've said what I need to say in a song, that's it. I don't want to repeat myself."

What this didn't really explain was why the commitment to those Christian songs seemed to be diminishing with every passing concert, a criticism even the enthusiast Paul Williams leveled at the man in his own, generally upbeat monograph on this remarkable residency, *One Year Later*:

> Dylan is on the move. These concerts, quite unexpectedly after that disastrous first night, turned into real crowd-pleasers. But there is no possible way that these concerts can be anything but a transition, a door into something very different and, uh, quite unpredictable . . . evolving into something else altogether, and largely I think because none of last year's songs are really clicking except "Serve Somebody," "I Believe In You" and "In The Garden." And it's not a question of the audience being unreceptive. It seems rather that Dylan can't get fired up about those songs right now, he seems mostly to be doing them because if he didn't do them, you'd misunderstand . . . But Dylan was sleepwalking through most of his Christain material (much more so than any of his other material) the six nights we saw him . . . When he sings "Covenant Woman" without any conviction other than his desire to sing a song he knows is a good one, I know something's changed since a year ago . . . He can't be happy doing lackluster performances of his "Jesus" songs just to keep them in the show. And the side of him that is committed to surrendering to the will of God must be a little uneasy at how readily Dylan the performer and star falls back into the routine of having his ego stroked.

When Williams wrote his "j'accuse," he had cause to think Dylan himself might be listening. As he later wrote, "Howard Alk told me Dylan called him up after he read [*One Year Later*] and said, 'It happens every time—when I meet someone who's written something about me that I like, meeting me spoils them and the next thing they write doesn't work.' Or words to that effect. And I agree . . . After hanging out with the singer and having him be so friendly, I was too aware of his presence as a likely reader."

Yet the points Williams was making were wholly valid. The religious songs—"Rise Again" and "Slow Train" excepted—had become the low points of the show, not its high-water mark. And it was the *Saved* songs which seemed to be suffering worst. The title track, performed just once on the 19th, seemed to come across particularly badly. Both "Covenant Woman" and "Solid Rock" sounded stripped of their essence, with the former in particular sounding like he was addressing a succubus, not his Savior.

And perhaps he was. His portrait of the woman who had "told me 'bout division, told me 'bout the pain" in "Caribbean Wind" and "The Groom's Still Waiting" suggested this Madonna had been revealed to be a tramp. Both of those songs certainly contained the passion of the penitent, as did a recast "Ain't Gonna Go To Hell," which was prefaced in Tucson, two nights after the Warfield, with the one vaguely judgemental rap of the entire tour:

> *This is a new song I been working on, trying to get it together, called, "I Ain't Gonna Go To Hell For Anybody." There's a line in it, "Smoke it rises forever." I started working on this song maybe six months ago. Did you read about that hotel that went up in fire, where was it? Las Vegas? I was reading all but a hundred people died. But nobody got burned, they all died from smoke, hmmm.*

In keeping with most performances of the song that November/December, the line, "Smoke it rises forever on a one-way ticket to burn," was just about the only intelligible line—title excepted—in the Tucson performance. Hence, Robert Hilburn's suggestion in his first-night review that the song was only "slightly religious." But if the idea that a song called "Ain't Gonna Go To Hell For Anybody" could be only "slightly religious" tickled Dylan's funny bone, he did not let it show the night he and Hilburn had their heart-to-heart in his San Francisco hotel room.

The singer had some things he had been yearning to get off his chest for the past six months and on November 11th, he finally gave Robert Hilburn the interview his unwavering support in the past year warranted; knowing full well that once it appeared in the *LA Times*, it would be widely syndicated—as indeed it was. Hilburn, who had interviewed Dylan in 1973 and 1978, was the ideal father-confessor, putting Dylan at ease and letting him do all talking:

Robert Hilburn: I don't know if my positive reviews led to Bob finally deciding to talk. I had called his publicist (Paul Wasserman) repeatedly. I tend to doubt it, because usually when an artist is fond of a review he or she will mention it the next time you interview them. Bob never mentioned the two reviews . . . I don't usually go backstage when I review a concert because I don't want to be that cozy with the artist. I want to try to show some independence—and only talk to the artist during a formal interview. But I took my teenage son, a huge Bruce Springsteen fan, to see Bruce at the Los Angeles Sports Arena on a night I wasn't reviewing and I took Rob backstage just so he could get a sense of the backstage color. We didn't go see Bruce or the band; we just stood in the general backstage area. Suddenly Bob Dylan walks up and starts talking. You can imagine my surprise. He said he's going to be doing some gospel shows in San Francisco and I ought to come out and see a few of them. I said, I didn't think the paper would send me unless we did an interview and he said something to the effect that [that] might be possible. I attended the first show of the 1980 Warfield engagement, but Bob said he was too tired afterward to talk and suggested we talk again after the next show. Same thing the second night. But on the day after the second show, I got a phone call to meet Bob at his hotel room at 3 pm. He opened the door himself and started talking about his religious experience before I even asked a question. He seemed to want to finally clarify things. There was no sense of hesitancy. I had never seen him so focused and he was ready to talk about it in depth. This was as far from the elusive, pugnacious man in *Don't Look Back* as you could get. The only other time I saw him as focused—or fully into an interview that he was virtually answering questions before they were asked—was when I met with him in Amsterdam in the early 2000s for nearly nine hours over two nights to talk about the process of songwriting. My favorite part of the gospel interview was when I asked if he started telling friends about it when he went to Bible classes, and he said, "No, I didn't want to set myself up . . . But I did begin telling a few people after a couple of months and a lot of them got angry at me." I then asked, "Did you have any second thoughts when that happened?" and he said, "No. By that time, I was into it. When I believe in something, I don't care what anybody else thinks."

Even today, the interview hardly reads like your average on-the-record exchange, but more like an extension of the persona Dylan was presenting at these shows; someone looking to distance himself not from the Lord Himself, but from some of those who continued to invoke His name for their own ends. After embracing an evangelist creed that interpreted the Bible in a literal, ahistorical way, he was now telling Hilburn, "You can find anything you want in the Bible. You can twist it around any way you want and a lot of people do that."

Having warned a radio interviewer the previous November that Christ was not a religion, he was reiterating the same message, "The basic thing, I feel, is to get in touch with Christ yourself. He will lead you. Any preacher who is a real preacher will tell you that: 'Don't follow me, follow Christ.'" The direct identification with Christ also found in a song like "Rise Again" had stayed strong, while his relationship with the LA fellowship that had freed him from the pit had begun to fade.

A sense of his own mortality—alluded to in the Carmel cave rap—also permeates his driven renditions of "Ain't Gonna Go To Hell" and "Señor." It also made its presence felt on a one-off version of "Knockin' On Heaven's Door," one of two songs he sang with Roger McGuinn, who had played on the original 1973 recording (as had Jim Keltner). He used his introduction to this final Warfield guest appearance to send up the whole idea of "special guests":

I know I speak for myself and everybody in the band when I say we really enjoyed this time at the Warfield. And . . . I sure hope we do get invited back . . . We been here for twelve nights I think, and different people have been stopping down. I wanna thank them all. Jerry Garcia was here. Let's see, Elton John, Bruce Springsteen, Captain Beefheart. They all went through here one time or another. Anyway, got another special guest tonight. We know so many people, you know. I first met this next man almost twenty years ago. He was playing in a group. I don't remember the name of the group, actually, but he went on and started a group called The Byrds, I'm sure you heard of them. Anyway we've . . . been on tours together and all that kind of stuff. I'll bring him out here now. You know who he is . . .

In a genuinely touching moment, the band proceed to play the instantly recognizable intro to "Tambourine Man" not in the Dylan style, but à la The Byrds. Those who had taken first-night reviews at their word had missed something special. Dylan had reclaimed his audience for his own, even as he prepared to return to Tucson and San Diego, where he had laid the ground with a prerecorded radio interview that again confirmed he was pressing on to a newer calling:

Bob Dylan: You can't record every album and have it be a *Saved*-type album, because, you know, you just don't get that many kinda songs all in a row like that. So I'm sure there'll be some difference, but I couldn't say what it would be.

The inclusion of "The Groom's Still Waiting At The Altar," "Ain't Gonna Go To Hell," and "City of Gold" at the San Diego show on the 26th certainly suggested he was still trying to wend his way down the road to heaven, "thick beset with thorns and briers." But he also couldn't resist sending up those who expected every song to be a Bible-bashing sermon.

Having continued reading every misguided review, he prefaced "Mary From The Wild Moor" by claiming, "In Tucson, there was a review in the newspaper that I'd like to get straight . . . [He said] this one here was about Jesus being born in a manger. Well, that's not entirely true. It's just an old Southern Mountain ballad about somebody dying in a snowstorm."

If no such review has turned up, Dylan was at it again in Portland, Oregon, on the final night of the tour, suggesting "Let's Keep It Between Us" was "a song we played last night that a newspaper journalist said was 'Maggie's Farm.' I'm here to tell you it's not 'Maggie's Farm.'"

Just as at the shows the year before, San Diego brought out the raconteur in Dylan, even if the connection with one song he prefaced was not immediately apparent. Telling another strange story from the same drawer as the "is she a woman or a man" rap on the 16th, he turned "Ain't Gonna Go To Hell" into a wedding song of sorts:

When we used to play here in San Diego, we used to stay at the Grand Hotel on Broadway . . . They just closed it last week, so we had to stay at the Holiday Inn. They've got fourteen, fifteen floors on the Holiday Inn. We have very nice views from up there, but on every floor all the balconies connect. So when you go outside your balcony, if you walk across the fence . . . you can go through everybody's room. Looking through windows in everybody's room. Anyway, I was in my room, it must have been three o'clock in the morning, and I was washing my face in the bathroom and . . . I heard somebody come in my room. From the balcony, fourteen floors up. So I went out to see who it was. It was a couple of newlyweds, who had gotten out of their apartment, and had come across all the balconies and walked into my room. With a big bottle of champagne. So I invited them down here tonight and they're out there somewhere tonight. I want to do this song for them. I hope they have a long and happy marriage.

The last five shows of this magical mini-tour would take place after a two-day break, Dylan returning to the Northwest states for the second time this year. But the shows he gave in Seattle, Salem and Portland were as far removed from their earlier kith and kin as the New from the Old Testament, having taken on the epic proportions of a Cecil B. DeMille Biblical blockbuster.

A show that on opening night, three weeks earlier, had run to a mere seventeen songs was by the first Portland show—on the 3rd—a twenty-six song marathon, concluding with another unexpected bonus: an all-acoustic, word perfect "It's Alright Ma," his most withering assessment of modern society's value-system. The show—during which he prefaced a smokin' "Señor" with a dedication to "a young girl I met in Durango, Mexico, 1972. She's out there somewhere, I know . . . Her name is Victoria, she's a happy married young lady now."—was one for the ages.

It seemed like everyone was happily married, save him. And now, the two recent songs that seemingly addressed his marital status, "The Groom's Still Waiting" and "Caribbean Wind," were no longer part of these celebratory concerts. Perhaps they took too much of any psychic energy he needed to conserve to make it through a twenty-six song night.

Not that energy was in short supply as he segued from the revelatory "Rise Again" (who knew he could hit those notes?) to the bluesy "Let's Keep It Betweeen Us," one of just two new originals that had made the twenty-six day journey from opening night to closing time. If his promise to Portland, that "one of these days, I'll record it," would prove to be another white lie, the visceral vocal suggested he was as connected with the song as he had ever been.

Likewise, "Slow Train" remained a nightly stand-out even as "Covenant Woman" disappeared from the set, post-Warfield. In Seattle, he even suggested the former would have been the perfect song for the town's most famous rock casualty. After asking the audience, "Does this sound halfway decent out there?" he insisted he "always like[d] to come to the home of Jimi Hendrix. I met Jimi Hendrix in New York when he was there. Anyway, we're gonna do a song now. I wish Jimi was around now, 'cause I know he'd record it."

The time had now come to recharge batteries, replenish his faith and revisit his Bible. If he could yet find a way to invest the same passion in "When You Gonna Wake Up" and "What Can I Do For You?" with which he continued to bless "Gotta Serve Somebody," "Slow Train" and "In The Garden," he might yet convince his worldwide audience that the gospel years remained an ongoing period of renewal and rebirth.

These shows and the set of new songs they previewed, taken in total, also suggested he had an album of originals (and, indeed, an album of covers) that could yet rank with the best from a recorded legacy second to none.

Of course, persuading CBS to get behind that all-important follow-up to *Saved,* and to support the world tour Dylan had alluded to in his interview with Paul Vincent, might prove his greatest challenge yet. For now, he could simply bask in another improbable resurrection as rock's greatest live performer, in this world or the next.

Once again the band had backed him to the hilt in his hour of weakness. They would not reassemble until early March 1981, by which time Dylan would have another album's worth of songs written, taking him yet further down the road to addressing the many concerns of the songs he had written that summer. Quite how he was going to fit them all onto a single album was a question for another day.

10. RUNNING BACK TO RUNDOWN
[March 3 – April 2, 1981]

shot of love
Grain of Sand
You changed my life
Need a Woman
Borrowed Time
Movin' or ?Wait + See?
Angelina
Is it worth it
Gonna love her anyway
Groom still waiting
Almost Persuaded
In the summertime
you can't make it on your own
Rockin' Boat
the king is on the throne
Fur slippers
Straw Hat
Well water
All the way
More to this than meets the eye
its all dangerous to me
My oriental home
Walking on Eggs
Carribean Wind
Ah Ah Ah Ah
lets keep it between us
She's not for you

When I started to record they just turned the microphones on and you recorded . . . It was never any problem. What you did out front was what you got on the tape. And it always happened that way. Whether you played by yourself or played with a band didn't really matter—there'd be leakage and that stuff, but you were pretty much guaranteed that whatever you did on that side of the glass was going to be perceived in the same kind of way. That was never any problem . . . I kept working that way through the seventies. I didn't realize things had changed! (Laughs.) . . . The problem is, you can't record that way anymore. If you go into a studio now the technology is so different that you might have a live sound that you want and you'll put that live sound down, but it won't sound that way on the other side of the glass. So then you have to contrive the sound to make it sound the way you really want.

—BOB DYLAN TO BILL FLANAGAN, 1985

They didn't have that many producers back [when I started]. The producer was what they called the A&R man. Now you have all these producers who are in themselves stars. And it's their record. I [just] don't think of myself as being told what to do all the time, you know.

—BOB DYLAN TO DAVE HERMAN, JULY 2, 1981

Ever since he acquired the Otari eight-track in January 1978, and installed it at his rehearsal studio, Dylan had been wondering why exactly he couldn't record an album on it, in an environment he had made his own. His own set of ears were telling him that the rehearsal tapes from that world tour sounded terrific, so why did *Street-Legal*—recorded at Rundown using Wally Heider's mobile truck—come out sounding like the bells were cracked and the horns washed-out?

He had been told that recording his way—taking his touring band into their rehearsal studio and cutting an album live, "old school"—wouldn't work, and it hadn't. As he later told Bill Flanagan, "I don't think I knew you could do an overdub until 1978. I just didn't think about it." He still wasn't convinced.

Recording two albums at Muscle Shoals with a professional producer—nay, an R & B legend—hadn't endeared Dylan to the modern methodology one jot and once again the results were, to his mind at least, mixed at best. There had to be a better way and he was determined to find it, especially when he returned to Rundown in March

1981 with yet another notebook full to the brim with new songs, and resumed recording every rehearsal.

There was only one problem. As old hand Arthur Rosato knew, when it came to his boss working on songs, new ones always trumped old ones; no matter what their respective merits might be. Often the only way to keep the man interested was to rework an old song and start anew, with all the risks this approach entailed. Even when it came to a song as near-perfect as "Caribbean Wind," which even Dylan knew was too good to discard readily, he couldn't resist reworking it. Setting aside a whole session—at a famous LA studio—to record the song once and for all, the old failing came to the fore:

Arthur Rosato: It was hell, recording that particular song . . . He would call everybody he knows to come down, so we would have a band of like fifteen people . . . I had the original recording that I did back at [Rundown]. I played that for all the musicians . . . All the musicians loved the song. It had that "Rolling Stone" feel to it. So Bob finally shows up about three hours late, which was pretty much on time for him . . . As soon as the musicians ran through it once he goes, "Nah, nah, nah, that's all wrong." They could see it coming, because they had all worked with him before. "Oh, here we go."

But if what he did to "Caribbean Wind" at Studio 55 was bad, what he did to "Yonder Comes Sin," "Makin' A Liar," "Ain't Gonna Go To Hell," "Cover Down" and "Let's Keep It Between Us" was ten times worse. He ignored them completely. The spine of an album he could have recorded back in the fall was now snapped in half, leaving just "Caribbean Wind," "The Groom's Still Waiting" and "Every Grain Of Sand" scrabbling for studio time in the spring of 1981. Even these, he left on hold for the three weeks leading up to the start of pukka sessions on March 25th.

Instead, he spent time developing a series of new songs which were surprisingly devotional in tone, with titles like "Dead Man, Dead Man," "You Changed My Life," "Yes Sir, No Sir (Hallelujah)" and "Heart Of Stone" (a.k.a. "Property Of Jesus").[50] The one song he worked on extensively, whose title seemed to suggest something cut from more worldy cloth, "Need A Woman," turned out to be an excuse to contrast his devout, faithful woman with all the sluts and trollops he'd previously encountered (and doubtless slept with):

---

[50] The last of these would end up on a copyright-tape with four recordings from October 1980, leading me to assign its composition date to the previous year. Mea culpa.

Need a woman drinking from the same cup . . .
Black, white, yellow, blue, green . . .
A woman who don't make herself up to be seen by other men . . .
I know a virtuous woman is hard to find
but they surely can't be obselete.

He continued working on the lyrics to these songs throughout the rehearsal process, shedding some of the more extreme lyrics, shaping them for public consumption. At the same time, he continued playing around with an instrumental he called "Bolero," which he would continue to rehearse—and indeed record, at the first Clover session on April 23rd.

Nor was it the only instrumental he seemed determined to get down on tape, as is. If his last released instrumental had been for a movie soundtrack back in 1973, he seemed to have a surfeit of simple tunes in his locker, not all of which lent themselves to the lyrics he was writing. Throw in the number of times he jammed with the band until something came along and the end result was a huge stockpile of song ideas that came to naught but needed titles nonetheless, a duty Dylan entrusted to his righthand man:

Arthur Rosato: I would always ask Bob, after he ran through a song that was recorded, "What do you want to call that one?" If it was obviously a riff, he would just say something off the top of his head. If it was an actual song, then he pretty much had a working title.

When the band reassembled at Rundown, after almost three months of downtime, every one was vaguely aware that there was an album in the offing and an opportunity to tour abroad on the table but knew better than to ask what they were rehearsing for. On March 3rd, Dylan apparently wanted to reference those 1978 rehearsals, the first song being "Where Are You Tonight?"

By the second rehearsal, he wanted to show the band what he had been up to that winter, getting them to groove on the likes of "Dead Man, Dead Man," "Gonna Love You Anyway," "Need A Woman" and a lost original crafted out of a single line ("And besides she had already gone") and a half-remembered sliver of melody from "Caribbean Wind." Called either "She's Already Gone" or "Time To Be Rollin' On," it went the way of "Wild About You Babe."

After this, he resumed work on *Self Portrait Vol. 2.* Or was this just his way of putting the band through its paces by sticking a series of pins in the American lexicon of popular song? They tackled everything from bluegrass standard, "The Dark Road is a Hard Road," to Carole King's "You've Got A Friend." By the end, one thing was evident, the band knew Carole King's solo work—and Neil Young's "Old Man"—a helluva lot better than our friend Bobby.

It was not until a rehearsal on March 4th that Dylan finally opened the notebook, but when he did, he returned to "Dead Man, Dead Man," a song which at this stage seemed to have more verses than your average Child Ballad. Over the next fortnight, the rehearsals assumed a by-now-familiar course, deviating at any given moment from an amorphous original to covers of Leon Russell's "A Song For You" or the Four Tops' "Reach Out I'll Be There," rarely sticking with any one song to the bittersweet end.

He had apparently decided that the way to make an album was the one The Beatles adopted for their swansong, *Let It Be*. Perhaps it is even a blessing in disguise that after meticulously archiving the 1979 and 1980 Rundown rehearsals, all but a handful of the two dozen rehearsal-tapes made between March 3rd and March 20th have been mislaid.

After this, another series of rehearsals—which would occupy Dylan and the band on and off until April 2nd—would be designated recording sessions, for an album he already knew would be called *Shot Of Love*. It was with the title track in mind—a song he later described as "my most perfect song. It defines where I am at spiritually, musically, romantically and whatever else . . . I'm not hiding anything"—that everyone assembled at Rundown on March 25th, soundstage one, for the start of a marathon almost as tortuous as The Beatles'.

Just like The Beatles, Dylan seemed determined to work his way through a sheaf of producers, young and old. If The Beatles ended up with a slightly crazed Phil Spector, he hoped to catch a break by recording with the almost-as-legendary "Bumps" Blackwell, whose production on the early Little Richard singles had been his first true sonic love:

Bob Dylan: "Shot Of Love" was one of the last songs Bumps Blackwell produced, and even though he only produced one song, I gotta say that of all the producers I ever used, he was the best, the most knowledgeable and he had the best instincts . . . I would have liked him to do the whole thing, but things got screwed up and he wasn't so-called "contemporary" [enough]. [1985]

The real problem seems to have been a more pressing one—working with Dylan was killing Bumps by degrees. Well into his sixties, he was not a well man. And after two days work, they had managed just four takes of "Shot Of Love," two of them incomplete. Thankfully, the last of these—which ran to five minutes—was a keeper, making it all the way to the opening cut on its namesake long-player. Yet it was the first take, cut on the 25th, that would end up on an April 6th reel of "Early Roughs" (and on *Bootleg Series Vol. 13*), as Dylan became choosy about which one worked.

The next song he had in mind to tackle was another new one, with a tight connection to both "Caribbean Wind" and "The Groom's Still Waiting." If "Angelina" had long been a name to conjure with in Dylan iconography, the song of that name, which he'd already completed lyrically, was the missing jigsaw piece in the Tangled Up In End Times trilogy he'd begun the previous summer.

After completing "Shot Of Love," everyone at Rundown set out to capture "Angelina," which Dylan later described to *NME*'s Neil Spencer as one of "a couple of really long songs . . . Do you remember "Visions Of Johanna"? . . . Well, [it's] like that. I'd never done anything like it before. It's got that same kind of thing to it. It seems to be very sensitive and gentle on one level, then on another level the lyrics aren't sensitive and gentle at all."

If he was placing "Angelina" in some mighty esteemed company, perhaps it was because they were twin siblings of the same death goddess. Certainly this "Angelina" was a temptress who for a while got her talons into the narrator, who was lucky to get out alive. As for the lady, it seems after "she rode a donkey through the crowd," she ended up "wearing a blindfold" in front of a firing squad.

Recorded in two complete takes, after a single harmonica-driven false start, this full-band arrangement would run to eight and a half minutes, which made it as much of a statement for the proto-*Shot Of Love* as "Visions Of Johanna" and "Stuck Inside Of Mobile" had been on *Blonde On Blonde*.

Nor do the comparisons end there. Keyboardist Carl Pickhardt—who has temporarily replaced Spooner Oldham—references that classic organ sound as he kicks things off with a stately organ fugue, soon joined by a choir of angelic girlsingers humming that honeydew melody. With flamenco flourishes from both guitars and a drummer who steadfastly ensures the tempo ebbs and flows with the lyric, it is an ensemble performance that would have made any snakeoil salesman proud. But it is Dylan's vocal which really draws the listener in, compelling him or her to decide where they would "like to be overthrown . . . Jerusalem or Argentina."

With his stellar contribution complete, Blackwell now took his leave of proceedings. Dylan had already decided which key songs he needed to get down on tape immediately. As with the Nashville *Blonde On Blonde* sessions in February 1966, he wanted to get the epic ballads first.

It seemed he had the first two pieces of his jigsaw. Perhaps he should just push on and snag a third. According to Dylan discographer Michael Krogsgaard, this is exactly what he did, recording eleven takes of "The Groom's Still Waiting At The Altar" at a Rundown session the following day, March 27th. However, no such tape exists in either the Sony or the Dylan archive; Jimmy Iovine did not produce *any* sessions at Rundown, as Krogsgaard suggests.

And yet it is possible Dylan *did* record said song in the four days that separate the "Shot Of Love" session/s from one at Studio 55. He appears to have recorded at least one contemporary pillar of wisdom in the interim, "Every Grain Of Sand," though the recording itself has (also) been mislaid.[51] It seems he really was ticking off the songs he intended as the central ballasts to a major new Dylan record.

Which is why, on March 31st, his standing band assembled at Studio 55, augmented by some familiar names from the 1978 tour—David Mansfield and Bobbye Hall, providing violin and percussion respectively—plus new second guitarist, Steve Ripley, and The Heartbreakers' keyboardist, Benmont Tench. For producer Jimmy Iovine, it was something of a dream to work with the great Dylan—having already cut his teeth engineering Springsteen and producing Patti Smith. He couldn't wait to get started, once he heard the song they were planning to record:

Arthur Rosato: I think that I brought a cassette of "Caribbean Wind" to him a day or two before the session and gave it to him or [the engineer] Shelly Yakus. We worked with him the day of the recording and never saw him after that. I think Bob managed to shatter him in one session.

The song Iovine and Yakus heard was the 1980 version—probably the one from the Warfield—but if the person standing at a state-of-art Studio 55 microphone was "the same man" who had sung *le merde* out of "Caribbean Wind" back in November, this was not the same song:

Arthur Rosato: Instead of that version, he [had] turned it into this country and western thing, like boomchika kinda stuff... Then they had these backing vocalists singing this train whoosh, and that was really bad.

Even surrounded by old Dylan hands like Rosato, Mansfield and Keltner, Iovine seemed none the wiser as to his role in proceedings. Mansfield, though, recognized the

[51] "Every Grain Of Sand" is the second song listed, after "Shot Of Love," on what Arthur Rosato, its compiler, calls "a composite list of every song or part of a song we recorded," at the sessions between March 25th and April 2nd. Hence, my conviction such a tape exists.

signs, "He was auditioning producers the way he used to audition drummers back in '78." In which case, Iovine failed the audition the minute that a baffled Dylan walked in and saw all the musicians had been isolated and he was expected to record the track with everyone separated by fiberglass and plywood:

Fred Tackett: They knew Bob was looking for an old sound studio, so they told him—and this was a very slick studio where a lot of disco records and stuff were cut now—"Bob, this is the studio where they cut the song, 'White Christmas.'" They want[ed] him to know this is an old-time studio . . . Jimmy Iovine was producing it . . . All the musicians got there early, and [so did] Jimmy Iovine. Bob always liked to just have everybody in a room together and just amps, no baffles, nothing separating, just all the music. Put a couple of mics up and record it live, a real raw live sound . . . In Bob's style [of recording], you couldn't take anything in or out, it was just all in the room. It's the way they used to do it—old style. So we get there early and Jimmy Iovine puts us all in little boxes. I was back in a closet somewhere, literally in a closet, with my mandolin.

The closet was possibly the safest place to be as the new "Caribbean Wind" howled in pain from the crude insensitivity of an unsympathetic producer dealing with an artist who didn't think of himself "as being told what to do all the time."

The fact that Dylan had decided to completely rework the lyric, replacing some once-incandescent verses with damp squibs too clever for their own good—"She was the Rose of Sharon from Paradise Lost/ Mistress of the fortress, from the city of the cross"—didn't help.

But the real travesty on the recording that ended up on 1985's *Biograph* was the arrangement, which seems to have been largely worked up in the studio. In fact, there is one near-complete runthrough of the song early on that, like the Warfield version, only really breaks down as the band play out, and which is done straight, i.e. minus the "boomchika kinda stuff" and "these backing vocalists singing this train whoosh."

By take eight Dylan had gone the whole nine yards with a messy, fussy arrangement augmented by the girls making whooshing noises—which was the one he mixed a week later and released four and a half years later. Yet it had never even been short-listed for *Shot Of Love* (as a version from later that spring was). For the musicians, the session was turning into a bust:

Jim Keltner: He struggled with ["Caribbean Wind"] and I could never figure out why. He could never figure out why. It was just one of those songs—it had great potential. The song was fantastic to play, but every time you'd hear it back, there was something missing.

Keltner knew better than to interfere, as he watched the relationship between Dylan and Iovine deteriorate to the point where Dylan turned to Rosato and suggested, "Get me the music to 'White Christmas,' 'cause that's the only song we're gonna be able to cut in this studio. We're not gonna be able to record any of *my* music here."

But Dylan knew the studio was booked for eight hours and was determined to get his money's worth.[52] He might have been joking about doing "White Christmas"—a song Iovine had actually recorded with Patti Smith, who released it as a semi-official bootleg single—but he was not adverse to cutting some standards, and after a half-hearted stab at "Dead Man, Dead Man," he suddenly found his voice on Leon Russell's "A Song For You" before showing the beat pulsing through "Cold, Cold Heart."

Perhaps there was hope yet, especially when Dylan suggested they return to "Carribean Wind" and this time, "Let's play it the old way." Collective hearts sank, though, as the girls began whooshing and Dylan sang the new lyrics to the old arrangement. Even Bobbye Hall whipping up a storm on the congas couldn't save the rose of Sharon. By now Dylan had had enough:

Fred Tackett: [Dylan] shouts, "Fred, where are you?" And I'm like, "I'm over here, in this little room back here with the mandolin." And he says, "Well, get your electric guitar and get out here." And he goes around everybody, and next thing you know, the whole set up is just taken *apart*, and he's got all of us . . . in the room together, with our amps and stuff hastily set up, and then we just started doing what we normally did . . . I remember, we were doing "Groom's Still Waiting At The Altar"—and I look up at the control room, and Jimmy Iovine and his engineer, they've just *gone*. They have just *left*. The second engineer was the only guy left in there recording stuff. [DL]

Finally given room to breathe, after dismantling all those goddamn baffles, Dylan decided there was time for one more song. With the second engineer rolling tape, they launched into "The Groom's Still Waiting" and in five minutes and thirty-eight seconds brought Claudette back from the dead.

[52] Michael Krogsgaard's discography only references eight takes of "Caribbean Wind" but the complete Studio 55 reels reveal a great deal more.

Taken at the same stately pace as previous live performances, the slower tempo allows Dylan to attack the vocal with relish and jam words into lines where even the long arm of the law couldn't reach. So, on this occasion, "I see empty-headed fools whose-time-has-come/ Standing 'round like furniture." Out of nowhere he also wonders aloud if he "could have been a lawyer fighting for justice in a police state . . . [or] a country singer 'n got into Nashville real estate"; before returning to the fate of Claudette, now that "John Wayne's dead, the phone's out of order." He saves the most unequivocal couplet in a while for last:

> Communists are falling, capitalists are crawling,
> The hand of God is moving, Jesus is calling!

The whole performance sails effortlessly between Jordan and the rock of Gibraltar, and after a day down a coalmine with a producer looking to work with a pop idol to bolster his CV rather than make good records, it turned out that pressing record and sitting back was the way to make magic. Dylan hadn't captured "Caribbean Wind," but he left Studio 55 with the best studio "Groom" to date.

The hunt for the right studio, though, would go on—and if the studio didn't come with a producer/engineer, Dylan could always ask Rosato to run the desk as he had done so ably for the past three years, resisting the impulse to repeat himself by bringing a truck down the dirty Boulevard:

Arthur Rosato: The only time we had a truck at the studio was when we recorded *Street-Legal*. We never brought in outside gear unless we were rehearsing for a tour, and then Stan Miller would bring in a monitor system and FOH [front of house] board to practice with. [But] no multitrack recording was done with that equipment. We did a studio "tour" to try and see if there was anything "better." or different, from our studio. We went from some of LA's great studios to converted garages in the Valley. Bob really liked the Santa Monica studio the best and the converted garage a close second.

That "converted garage" went by the name of Cream Studio. And it was to Cream that Dylan and the band relocated—minus Mansfield and Hall—the day after Studio 55 for another marathon session, recording thirty-plus takes in a single day while Rosato ran tape on terrific versions of "Wild Mountain Thyme," "I Wish It Would Rain" and a nailed-on "Cold, Cold Heart."

But this was only after warming up with an endless series of jams, some of which mutated into tunes with a discernible song structure—like "Borrowed Time," "Rockin' Boat," "I Want You To Know That I Love You" and "Is It Worth It?." Others simply stayed in riff form, before being assigned titles like "Straw Hat," "It's All Dangerous To Me," "Well Water" and "My Oriental Home" and then forgotten until 1985, when belatedly copyrighted:

Jim Keltner: He was looking for a vibe. He went to more length to find one than a lot of people. Some people will go to a studio and settle for it. He tried out quite a few different [ones] . . . He didn't want to fall into that trap he got trapped into with *Saved*. So he was looking to do something more alive than that.

Fred Tackett: We were jamming a lot. Bob was looking for a studio, so we were [just] going around . . . Bob was always looking for . . . old studios and guys that knew how to record [in the] old style . . . He would just start singing a song and we'd just follow him along. Musically, they weren't so complicated that you couldn't figure out what he was doing.

Probably the oddest of the Cream recordings was a seven-minute instrumental version of "Gonna Love You Anyway," recorded early in the day. A song Dylan had been rehearsing at length, it already had working lyrics. But instead of working some vocals into the song, he was led into temptation, playing "I Wish It Would Rain," one of at least three Motown classics he toyed with at these "demo" sessions.[53]

Just as at the previous session, it would take Dylan most of the day to work up enough steam to tackle actual candidates for the album he was supposedly assembling from this random series of sessions.

Three of these were finally addressed as shadows started lengthening, including an exuberant workout for "Need A Woman" which, despite its title, seemed more concerned with analyzing the narrator's failings than "her" virtues. The minute he sang about "that unseen eye is watching you/ So you gotta be cool all day long," while looking "into the mirror this morning/ I saw a man without a face," the narrating "I" did not seem like A.N. Other.

The seven-minute workout even got a proper ending. But again, rather than get the song right, he changed tack, teaching the girls the arrangement for another new song, "In The Summertime." It was immediately apparent that this was an

---

[53] The others were "My Girl," only ever an instrumental, and "Reach Out I'll Be There."

idea with some promise but only dummy lyrics; before Dylan elected to drive "I Want You To Know That I Love You" and "Is It Worth It?" into the ground. No, it wasn't worth it.

Just when it seemed the session was petering out, the girls galvanized Dylan into tackling a version of "You Changed My Life" in which "passion and pity . . . swept into the city," before revisiting "Need A Woman." Just as at Studio 55, Dylan saved his best for last, turning the screw on a song that had at least two sets of lyrics, this one containing the message: "My heart feels like it's on fire/ But my clothes ain't burning yet."

"I Wish It Would Rain" concluded a day that had taken the Rundown aesthetic for a spin around the block. And it continued idling in gear until Dylan and the band resumed their studio tour the following day at United Western Studios. Again, the singer seemed determined to not look back, preferring to spend most of the day on one song-idea, "Yes Sir, No Sir (Hallelujah)," that barely warranted the energy expended. Not that he gave up easily.

Further confirmation of a well-documented penchant for jamming on song ideas came when he spent a goodly chunk of time (and tape) on "Is It Worth It?," a song on which he would still be noodling away at the first and last Clover sessions, when he was supposed to be recording the album for real. For now *Self Portrait Vol. 2* was still on the cards, Dylan revisiting "A Song For You," done at Studio 55, "Reach Out I'll Be There," rehearsed at Rundown, and "Let It Be Me," a song he had recorded—perhaps definitively—for *Self Portrait Vol. 1*.

And still he found the energy to retackle "You Changed My Life," as well as throwing himself into another throwaway song, "Fur Slippers," that actually had a proper set of lyrics and was dispatched in a single take.

Yet nothing save the title track—not the "Need A Woman" from Cream, the "Angelina" from Rundown, the "Groom's Still Waiting" from Studio 55, nor the "You Changed My Life" from United Western—would be possible candidates for the album, even after Arthur Rosato drew up a master list for Dylan's benefit of the songs they had recorded in the sessions to date, bracketing the ones "that were more complete and [which we] were going to try to record in a session."

In fact, of the ten songs he bracketed in this way, three were never revisited— "Borrowed Time," "Gonna Love You Anyway" and a song recorded a couple of times at United Western but never finished (listed as "Movin"/ "Wait and See"). Five more would be recorded for *Shot Of Love* only to be omitted to make room for the likes of "Lenny Bruce" and "Trouble": "You Changed My Life," "Need A

Woman," "Angelina," "Is It Worth It?" and "The Groom's Still Waiting." Not even bracketed was "Caribbean Wind," suggesting Dylan felt he had tried and failed to capture this defining song.

If Dylan was in despair, it was as nothing to the state his New York lawyer, Naomi Saltzman, was in, wondering what exactly was happening out in La-La land. With a massive European tour in the works, and CBS expecting an album any day now, Saltzman duly dispatched Debbie Gold, fresh from working for Springsteen in his New York office, to LA to find out what the fug was goin' on. Almost immediately, the ebuillient Gold suggested putting "this old man" in touch with the tag team of producer Chuck Plotkin and engineer Scott[54]:

Toby Scott: Debbie was someone who [would think,] "Something needs to be done. So let me help out." She was the first person I noticed [w]as a facilitator . . . She was just [about] putting people together. She didn't work at the studio, but she was around for all the Laura Allen sessions and got to know Chuck. Then she got to meet Bruce [Springsteen] through [him]. So Debbie used Clover as her home base [when in LA] . . . [I'm sure] she was the one who said, "Hey Chuck, you wanna come over with me to a Bob session? They're working over at Studio 55."

In fact, they were working over at Rundown, on the title track, when Plotkin arrived to find Bumps "standing there, sort of conducting Bob and the band." Scott and Plotkin had been working with Springsteen for the past year and a half on that mind-numbing smorgasbord *The River*, an album which proved that Bruce really was the New Dylan, as he managed to compile an all-original double-album which omitted the best half-a-dozen songs recorded. Quite a trick.

If the sound-conscious producer needed a refresher course in how to make a proper record, in a week or less, perhaps Dylan could provide it. When the fateful day arrived for Plotkin and Dylan to meet, there were already a few crossed wires, as Dylan's favorite promotion-man later learned:

Paul Rappaport: I [heard] this story [about Bob] coming into Chuck Plotkin's studio in LA. He just walked in, "Hi, I'm Bob Dylan." "Yeah, I know." "I got songs in my head. Can we just put up some tape?" "Sure." Bob plays two, three songs. "Sounds good. I think I'm gonna make an album. Can we do that [here]?" "Sure, yeah. [But] Bob, so long as you're here, why don't we do those [songs] again, 'cause

---

[54] Plotkin seems to think it was David Geffen who first brought up his name to Dylan, hence perhaps the "special thanks" on the *Shot Of Love* sleeve.

they're not in perfect time?" Bob looked at him and said, "Chuck, people aren't in perfect time."

But just as with the 1978 tour, where Dylan had allowed the clock to run down to the point where he had no choice but to take drummer Ian Wallace along, when the music finally stopped on this game of musical chairs with LA studios, it was Chuck Plotkin who was left holding the producer's stool. Dylan did his best to put Plotkin in the picture:

Chuck Plotkin: I found out afterwards that he was sort of interviewing possible producers. . . . People were coming by, and they would hear a bit of a rehearsal, and have a bit of conversation . . . I'm not sure what happened with Jimmy [Iovine]. But Bob was experimenting. One of the things he said to me, when we talked on the phone, [was], "If you know my work, you'll know that I'm not a reliably effective record-maker. Record-making is not my fundamental thing." [DL]

Dylan had been here before, having aborted at least four albums after an initial session or two went awry, only to try something completely different. Those four albums were *Blonde On Blonde, New Morning, Blood On The Tracks* and *Desire*. In each case, a one-song residue was left on the intended record, a reminder of what might have been.[55]

In the case of *Shot Of Love*, the title track would stand as the one unrepresentative sampler to a very different "lost" album, one that had been conceptualized around "Caribbean Wind," "The Groom's Still Waiting" and "Angelina." Unlike the record he would ultimately release.

---

[55] In the case of *New Morning*, that one-song residue was the May 1st "If Not For You" with George Harrison, which was actually replaced at the last minute, but I'd like to think the point still holds.

11. COVERED IN CLOVER
[April 23 – May 1, 1981]

CLOVER
6232 SANTA MONICA BLVD
HOLLYWOOD CALIF. 90038
463-2371

Reel _29 / Sequence #1A_

Date _5·12·81_

Company _____

Artist _Bob Dylan_

Producer _B. Dylan / C. Plotkin_   Speed _15 ips_   Trks _2_

Engineer _Toby Scott_   Level _+3_   Noise Red. _NO_

Tones _See Reel·14_   Master ___   Copy

– SIDE One –

No.	Title	Remarks	Time
1)	Shot of Love – ORIGINAL MIX FROM 16 TRK OFF 24 / FADE OK? — Pulled		
2)	Heart of Mine – ORIGINAL 'SLOW' VERSIN		
3)	Property of Jesus – ORIGINAL		
4)	Lenny Bruce – ORIGINAL – BUZZ RT SIDE		
5)	Pure Love WATER DOWN LOVE – ORIGINAL MIX – NO BASS & NO FADE		

TO ALBUM MASTER
6·1·81

Working in a studio has always been very difficult for me . . . I approach record-making in the way that I learned . . . when I started recording, when I recorded for John Hammond. And we work the same way, which is [by] going into the studio and making a record. Right then and there . . . I'm not interested in that aspect of recording [of] laying down tracks and then coming back and perfecting those tracks and then perfecting lyrics . . . Songs are created in the recording studio . . . I have to play songs which're gonna relate to the faces that I'm singing to. And I can't do that if I was spending a year in the studio, working on a track. It's not that important to me. No record is that important.

—BOB DYLAN TO DAVE HERMAN JULY 2, 1981

I like the old sound, but it's done. It's never going to come back. So you just have to deal with what the modern way is. A lot of my records have been made because it's—quote—time to make a record. "When's your new record going to be delivered?" "Oh, next month." Time for me to go in and make a record. I never used to think about it during the year. I had other things to do. Some of the Seventies records were made on just one block of time. "This month I'm going to block all this time out, write the songs, record the songs, mix 'em, press 'em, get a cover together, and it's all out in a month or two." It took me a long time to get off that particular style.

—BOB DYLAN TO BILL FLANAGAN, 1985

I learned later that there was some confusion/miscommunication about what we were actually doing at Clover. I think Chuck thought we were rehearsing and selecting songs for the actual album-recording to take place after these sessions. Bob seemed to be of the opinion we were recording the record.

—TOBY SCOTT, ENGINEER ON SHOT OF LOVE, TO AUTHOR, 2017

In order to get the record made at all, I had to relinquish a lot of control over things that I ordinarily would have a lot of control over.

—CHUCK PLOTKIN TO DAMIEN LOVE, 2014

It was a little looser on the Shot Of Love *sessions compared to the* Saved *sessions. We had not played the songs as much as we had on the* Saved *record. This was good because there was . . . more spontaneous stuff going on.*

—FRED TACKETT TO SCOTT MARSHALL.

I'd say over the course of a year, [I spend] maybe six days in the studio. That's probably it. (Laughs). If I can't make a record in six days, I don't.

—BOB DYLAN TO PAUL VINCENT, NOVEMBER 18, 1980

Sometimes you just have to rip it up and start again. Dylan had to do so on April 23rd, 1981. I, dear reader, have to do the same now. So can I ask that any preconceptions you have about what happened across the three weeks Dylan spent in Clover in spring 1981, you check at the door. And please, any previous session-listing you may have to hand—"for reference only"—place in the bin provided.

I could claim the tapes are a mess, but they're not; that we're missing some key "multis" (as is the case with *Slow Train Coming* and *Saved*), but we're not. The simple fact is that the *Shot Of Love* session listings that abound on the Internet come from two sources so fatally flawed as to be worse than useless: a log of the two-track tapes they ran throughout the sessions at Clover, and the American Federation of Musicians session listings, both unimpeachable resources were it not for the fact they're not worth the paper they are written on.

In the case of the latter, guitarist Fred Tackett (under)stated it best in suggesting, "Musician contracts, union contracts for recording sessions are usually done after it's all over and a lot of times they're not accurate." The AFM sheets for *Shot Of Love*, referenced twice in Michael Krogsgaard's oft-cited sessionography, turn out to be works of fiction, as do the AFTRA contracts used for the girlsingers' fees. As for the two-track tapes the Danish doctor located (but did not hear), they had a specific—but wholly ancillary—purpose:

Arthur Rosato: There was always a two-track tape running, even if it was just rehearsing before an actual take. You have to record it, no matter what. That's pretty common in studios. Tape is cheap. [But] I wasn't in charge of tapes. That was left to Chuck and his crew.

Toby Scott: On the first day Bob showed up, I think [we realized] there was a thing that we began to call Dylan time. Which is whatever time you think he's going to be there, add three hours and that's when he may actually be there. When Bob would roll in, all the players would be sitting around and ready. Bob would walk in and Arthur would sort of appraise [the situation and decide], does he want to start playing or does he want to talk to Chuck [etc.]? Sometimes he would come in and Arthur would be there with his acoustic guitar [or] his electric guitar, and Bob would put it on and walk over to the microphone and start playing. So I think it was early in the first day that we realized [he was not gonna] say, "Okay, everybody," count [in, and then] start playing. That was not gonna happen. Bob would just start playing and the band would sort of fall in. Sometimes Jim [Keltner], or someone who knew him better, would say, "Okay Bob, are you ready to do it? One-two. . ." So we started running two-track quarter-inch [tape] just for the sake of that Troggs moment. One could never tell when some gem of inspiration would come out of Bob so we ran a quarter-inch tape of the Monitor send [signal] whenever Bob was in the room and with an instrument. The multitrack ran whenever he looked like he was about to start a song. That was always sketchy because if Bob had a guitar in his hands, at any instant he would start playing, the band would join in and he'd get to a microphone (maybe) and start singing the song. This was so spontaneous that on one song Chuck ran from the control room and picked up the vocal mic, stand and all, and followed Bob around the studio pointing the mic at Bob's mouth. He seemed unaware that he would have to sing into the microphone to be recorded properly.

The two-track would indeed pick up a couple of "Troggs moments."[56] At the very outset of that first session, it captured Dylan and the band running through "Shot Of Love," "Mystery Train," "Half As Much," "The Groom's Still Waiting" and "Dead Man, Dead Man," none of which were captured on multitrack and one of which ("Half As Much," another Hank Williams cover), Dylan never did again.[57]

Probably, these were the songs with which Dylan warmed up before the real business of the day started. As Scott suggests, the primary purpose of recording on two-track was to ensure that nothing went unrecorded. At no point, though, did Dylan, Plotkin or Scott ever intend to use such tapes for the album. That was what multitrack tape was for, and as Scott says, "The multitrack ran whenever he looked like he was about to start a song."

---

[56] The famous "Troggs tape" comprised studio dialogue recorded at a Troggs recording session that was, shall we say, a little un-P.C.

[57] If the five-song "warm up" on the 23rd only exists (on cassette) because Rosato kept a copy, the original of that reel has been lost in the tape shuffle. But the remaining two-track reels from the 23rd and 24th are extant.

So, fascinating as such tapes can be, the two-track reels do not in any way constitute the *Shot Of Love* session tapes. And after the first two sessions, things get even sketchier at the Scandinavian Institute of Rock Research, for the simple reason that most of the two-track tapes from April 28th through May 1st seem to have been lost.

After the 28th, only two reels—both from the April 30th session—appear to have survived in this form. Thankfully, these capture impromptu takes of "The Girl From Louisville," a la the Louvins, and Peter LaFarge's "Ballad of Ira Hayes," both of which the multitrack tape operator was too slow to catch.

So one set of two-track reels has queered the pitch on what was really done at Clover. But there is yet another set of such reels. Engineer Scott would use the stereo monitor mixes to make rough mixes at the end of the day—some of which *did* figure ultimately in the scheme of things:

Toby Scott: We'd go through a day—record a few songs. Chuck would go, "Could we do that one more time, Bob?" "Yeah, sure, okay." So either during the day or at the end of the day we'd go, "Okay, this seems good. Well, let's put this mix down on tape"—[usually] when Bob was out of the room. Bam, I'd hit the two-track and this would be our monitor mix. We went through the week of recording [doing this].

Unfortunately for Scott's (and Plotkin's) sanity, these were the mixes Dylan got to hear as the sessions progressed—and he was liking what he heard. But on a technical level they were all wrong. To start with, they were missing some instruments:

Toby Scott: Our API console originally had twenty-four inputs. The twenty-four inputs were . . . what we would send to tape. [But] over on the other section was what we called the jukebox—all the Nieve consoles had it—which had short faders and two knobs, left and right . . . So during the course of [the sessions] we were monitoring over there, [with] all the faders in a nice long line. [Every now and then] I'd make a little adjustment. [But] what was coming off the monitor was what was going to the two-track. That way, if someone soloed, I could hear it in the room but it wouldn't go on the two-track. So that was the setup . . . But this was a passive console. We used to [wonder] why did the monitor mixes sound incredible and the mixes off the console—where we're adding EQ [etc.]—not sound as good. It was because the monitor section had no transformers and no amplification. It was strictly [from the] tape machine through this little fader, which was only an attenuator, and reverb.

Needless to say, no distinction was made between the various two-track tapes. They were all filed away together. So disentangling rough mixes from takes unique to the two-track can be a challenge. But so can tallying the "master" reels with the multitrack session-reels.

Because the multitracks from the Clover sessions—all fifty of them, only one of which appears to have gone missing—are not the tapes from which the album itself would be compiled. Rather, in keeping with standard practice when working with analog tape, they were merely the raw ferric material, from which master takes would be physically extracted and reassembled on a series of "master reels." Ordinarily, it would be from these—and these alone—that an album recorded in the pre-digital era would come.

But not everything that warranted review at Clover was necessarily "pulled to master." If one was relying on the immediate impression of a maverick like Dylan on a particular take to decide what was worthy of promotion to a master reel, some worthy things were bound to slip through the cracks.

F'rinstance, two takes of "Angelina" recorded at the April 28th session were "starred" on the multitracks reels [#12-13], suggesting they were worthy of review at a later date, but neither was pulled to master—unlike the fourth and final take that day (the one on *Bootleg Series Vols. 1-3*).

Yet it is take three—the one time where the band refuse to let Dylan get away from them—that really delivers the goods. Here is an ensemble performance that in the true sense of the word complements the vocal of a man who has once again raised his game. "Angelina," though, was one of two songs where only one take was "pulled to master." The other, "Magic," was a single take, rather obviating its selection.

If the decision as to what was pulled to master was usually done at the end of the day, such decisions were based on what Dylan was hearing in the room and the rough mixes he was referencing—the equivalent of the "rushes" a film director will review daily. For now, he seemed to be taking things in his stride:

Toby Scott: During the sessions I didn't hear any comment from Bob regarding the sound or mixes. He seemed comfortable with the progress of everything. As I said, the "mixes" we played back for him were what we called "roughs."

A taciturn Dylan usually meant a happy Dylan. And for now it seems Scott's ingenious way of overcoming his personal phobia for headphones had endeared him to the man, who was delighted to be able to record everything live, just as nature intended:

Chuck Plotkin: Bob didn't want to wear headphones while he was recording. And that was the first time that I had ever run into that . . . And so, we had to figure out some way to organize a little kind of mini-sound system inside the studio, so that nobody had to wear headphones. And that was a big challenge . . . I [soon] realized: this is not a guy who wants to even think about going through the business of doing, like, seven takes. Forget seven takes. Once he's got the words right: that's your take, right there. [DL]

Toby Scott: One day Chuck said, "Hey, we're gonna be doing a Bob Dylan record, but it's gonna be a lot of people and it's all gonna be in one room. And Bob doesn't wanna use headphones. But everybody's got to be able to hear what everybody else is doing." So I got the run down of players and I found a small speaker system that I could mount on small short microphone stands and they would take the mix that would usually go into the headphones, [and put it] into the speakers. I had them [placed] around so that people could hear what everyone else was playing. You could turn it up and hear the cue mix. And that was back in the day when you didn't have individual mixing. You get whatever we give you, often times the stereo mix right off the console. So I set it all up and we had two drum sets. Jim Keltner was the primary drummer. Tim Drummond was the bass player. "Kootch" was one of the three guitarists. And then we had "Smitty" Smith on B-3 [organ] and then there was a piano player with Steve Douglas on sax. [The girls] are behind the B-3 in a corner. And Bob was in the middle of things . . . The room was about thirty foot wide and about twenty-five feet long. There was a little indent which sometimes we used as a little vocal booth . . . We're only talking 24-track. [So it was a case of,] "Four background singers? Here's a mic. Adjust yourself. Be on it."

The setup Scott had devised still allowed the option of overdubs, and both him and Plotkin fully expected to get the opportunity to subtly overscore final takes, à la Springsteen, once the live sessions were over; correcting obvious errors or simply punching in a new vocal on a fluffed line of an otherwise perfect take.

But if they were under such an illusion, it was not for long. An incident involving the usually reliable Tim Drummond convinced them all the rumors were true: Dylan was someone who made music as primitivist and impressionistic as the paintings that hung in his garage in Malibu:

Toby Scott: We [did] very few overdubs. Chuck would go, "Oh, we oughta replace that guitar solo or maybe you could resing that?" and Bob would go, "You wanna overdo that?" He had this tactful, but not tactful way of [putting things]. The one occasion when that did become a requirement was when we had been working on a song and we had taken a break. Now Clover was situated in the middle of the block, and at the corner was Ernie's Burrito House, the only place to get something to eat. Anyway, we came back and they were trying to get this song. We recorded it two or three times and [took a break]. We came back, Bob starts to play, "Okay, let's go." I don't know whether they did it once or twice [but it] sounds good. [So] everyone comes into the control-room and Bob comes in and we listen to it. [He] goes, "Great, that was a good take." Following studio protocol, I lean over to Chuck and go, "Tim Drummond wasn't in the room." "What?!" I say, "There's no bass. Tim's still down at Ernie's having a burrito." Then Tim walks in the room, "Hi guys, what's going on?" Chuck goes, "We can overdub it." Bob goes, "You wanna overdo it?" Chuck says, "It's bass, it's on a direct. No problem. Won't be an issue." Bob says, "I don't see why. We said it sounds good. It seems okay." Chuck goes, "No, no, no. We gotta put the bass on it." Tim goes in and plays his bass part a couple of times. Bob [listens back and] goes, "Nope, I think it sounds fine without it. If it was meant to be there, he woulda been there. So let's just move on." So I believe there's a song on the record that does not have bass. That was the first aghast moment [for] Chuck with Bob.[58]

And if Dylan still wanted the first impressions of musicians who had come to know his working methods well, he had long perfected a way of ensuring this would happen, springing brand-new songs on them in the studio at an album session, when stakes were high. He had previously informed Plotkin he "felt uncomfortable making [*Slow Train*] because the first thing I did when I got down there was, I had to sit down and play them all my songs."

Predictably, he arrived at the very first Clover session with at least three entirely new songs he wanted to try out—all probably written in the three-week break that the musicians had been bequeathed after the United Western session had proven a bust.

And there was a fourth item attempted mid-session, though the jury is still out on whether "Be Careful" ever really was a song. I'm not sure even twelve angry men could agree, but there it sits between "Is It Worth It?" and "You Changed My Life." Co-opting a line from an early draft of "Need A Woman," Dylan and the girls trade

---

[58] Benmont Tench confirmed that there was a song missing the bass, identifying it as "Watered-Down Love," but claimed less plausibly to Damien Love it was "because, we were all done, long done for the day, and almost everybody had packed up and gone home," including Tim Drummond, the bass player.

off its repeated refrain, "Be careful, baby, what you say and do/ That unseen eye is watching you," while the band work up a gelatinous groove. The verses abound with nonsensical sequiturs that ensured the song was soon quietly forgotten.

The same, however, cannot be said for the other three new numbers, "Magic," "Trouble" and "Don't Ever Take Yourself Away," all of which Dylan cut in single takes. Perhaps Dylan's methodology was not such a bad way of working, after all.

Both engineer and producer probably assumed Dylan would overdub some proper lyrics to "Magic," which makes "I'm Not There" sound finished, or redo the song at a later date, taking advantage of what was a great hook and a groovy band by including some bona fide verses. He did neither. Yet not only was the song "pulled to master" but it would appear on at least one provisional album sequence in its sung-in-tongues form. (When finally copyrighted, Dylan's music publisher wisely used a tape, not a transcript.)

Although take one of "Trouble" was also "pulled to master," it was a song he would revisit at subsequent sessions. Even on this showing, "Trouble" barely warranted such trouble, being little more than a rabid rant from the "Are You Ready?" family, to a staccato four-note blues riff. Once again, though, it gave Dylan an excuse to register rage at a world gone wrong.

As if to prove familiarity often breeds multiple attempts, the song that occupied most tape and time at this first session was "You Changed My Life," a song cut previously at Cream and United Western, having been rehearsed and reworked since early March. When the tenth of thirteen attempts was pulled to master, Dylan had three songs with which he was happy. Not that any of the trio would end up gracing the album, a state of affairs both Dylan and Plotkin seemed to take in their stride; the former, because he knew how the arc of his own albums usually went; the latter, because he couldn't imagine any of these takes being released in Dylan's name:

Arthur Rosato: Chuck used to spend a lot of time resting or whatever on the couch out front. I think we all thought that this was odd for a producer, but [maybe] he was thinking that this was rehearsal for the later "actual" recording. Inside the studio we were actually doing the record.

The point at which Plotkin started to suspect this might not be a dry run probably dawned during the second session, which was far more focused. Although only one song made it to *Shot Of Love*—"In The Summertime," in desiccated form—four songs took shape that day with surprising ease.[59]

All three rejects could, and indeed should, have been accomodated somewhere. But none of them clocked in at under six minutes. Here, in fact, was one side ready to go: "Dead Man, Dead Man" at 7.34, "Need A Woman" at 6.32 and "In The Summertime" at 6.15. Instead, as every *Shot Of Love* owner knows, a paltry three minute thirty-two of "In The Summertime" features on the album—with even that take having forty seconds remmoved from the harmonica coda.

If that particular take should have run to the end, a longer, more powerful version was cut earlier in the day. The second of three full takes, it was a performance that had the same touching vocal mannerisms and mastery of the mouth-harp that made 1979 versions of "What Can I Do For You?" more than the sum of their poetic parts.

Even more radical was take one of "Dead Man, Dead Man," a song he had been flirting with since early March and now had the requisite lyrical clout to bring many mansions down. Whipping himself and the already slightly hysterical girls into a frenzy with a pair of frenzied harmonica breaks, he unfurled verse after verse written with a poisoned pen till it ran out of ink.

He even referenced the last song on his debut album, Blind Lemon Jefferson's "See That My Grave Is Kept Clean," in one verse, "The silver spade that waits for you to throw dirt upon your tomb/ Ooh I can't stand it, ooh I can't stand it, you're running out of room"; as well Presley's 1969 comeback album, *From Elvis In Memphis*: "Killed his body some place else/ And dumped it in a long black limousine."

Once again, he had grabbed a song by the gonads on take one. But then he doubted himself, even as he pulled the take to master. He would try the song four more times on the 24th and a dozen times more on the 28th and 30th without coming close to the spirit caught on tape here.

Nonetheless, buoyed by the punchy performance, he sprung another new song on the band at day's end, "Watered-Down Love." Invariably introduced in concert with a glossary, "You don't want a love that's pure, you want a drowned love, you want a watered-down love," it was a song he was still trying to knock into shape six days after the "final" *Shot Of Love* sequence. For now, he just gave the band a glimpse of what the future held when he returned to Clover, which he would not do for another four days.

[59] None of the four songs recorded on the 24th were "Magic," the one song listed in Krogsgaard's sessionography. As already noted, "Magic" was recorded just once at these sessions, and it was on the 23rd.

What happened to Dylan between the evening of the 24th and the afternoon of the 28th—noting that the 25th and 26th was a weekend—has stayed a mystery until now. But it seems he really did go walkabouts, returning on the 28th wholly oblivious to the fact that he had left at least a dozen people clock-watching at Clover, some of whom were starting to think maybe it was time to call the cops:

Toby Scott: I remember one time on the sessions we expected him and he didn't show up for a couple of days. And Arthur was getting sort of panicked. Finally, he [re]surfaced. And we were [asking,] "Bob, where were ya?" And he had gone down to Laguna Beach. I [had already] got the impression that Bob walked around in a fog a lot of the time, and he said, "Yeah, I was down in Laguna and I was in a phone booth, and some kids saw me and said, 'Hey, what are you doing?' And I just got talkin' to 'em and I ended up spending the day and the night and the next day with them and finally I decided to come back."

Dylan's 2004 memoir, *Chronicles*, contains a similarly wild and woolly story— of questionable provenance—in which he leaves the *Oh Mercy* sessions in New Orleans at midpoint and heads into the swamps of Louisiana on a motorcycle, to clear his head and collect his thoughts, before returning to finish what he had begun.

Evidently, he did something similar here. When he did return, having put down just two tracks to date which would make the final album, he set about finishing the record across consecutive daily sessions from April 28th to May 1st. And he had another new song he later claimed it took him five minutes to write. It sure sounded like it.

On his return, he duly carried on where he had left off, flaying the corpse of "Dead Man, Dead Man" till it bled pure bile. Despite the odd invigorating new line—like, "Selling eyeglasss to the blind"—the song resolutely refused to rise again, and not one of thirteen takes that day were pulled to master.

Instead, "Angelina" was the day's star turn, even if the eight-minute epic he pulled to master appeared with much of its original instrumental palette scrubbed clean. (One suspects the version on *Bootleg Series Vols. 1-3* is another monitor mix in disguise—and all the worse for it.) The dame deserved better, but such was the fate of any song still in contention for the album at the time of mixing.

If "Angelina" was treated like some half-forgotten remnant from Rundown, another noticeable absentee so far had been "Every Grain Of Sand," which until April 29th was missing in action. In fact, he had been treating the song with kid gloves ever since September 1980, refraining from rehearsing it and save for that single stubborn line, "I am hanging in the balance of" either "the perfect, finished plan" or "the reality of man"—toss a coin—leaving the lyrics well alone.

When he did finally muster the requisite commitment to deliver this salvo of salvation, it lasted long enough for him to deliver three impressive, word-perfect takes, all of which were pulled to master for review at a later date.[60]

It was a good day, all in all. Dylan—in a scripturally inspirational zone—also nailed "Heart Of Stone" (i.e. "Property Of Jesus") in two muledrivin' moments. From somewhere deep inside, he summoned the evangelist energy to rekindle some of that post-Newport phlegm in the service of the Lord. After months of playing the doubting Thomas, the singer was hitching himself to that baptismal bandwagon and nonbelievers best get out of his path.

Two other songs from the 29th would also be pulled to master, though neither really warranted such exalted company. Dylan had finally put a set of words to "Bolero," the instrumental he had been trying to make into a song. Now called "Heart Of Mine," it was a disappointment—hardly good enough to supercede "Need A Woman" and/or "Don't Take Yourself Away."

But true to type, having finally bent the blasted thing into shape, Dylan now insisted on trying it at every remaining session, searching for some elusive groove, like that was the problem for a song which began, "Heart of mine be still/ You can play with fire, but you'll get the bill," and never left Cliché Central.

The other new song done that day was even more inconsequential. The two-minute "You're Still A Child To Me," like "Magic," had yet to get a set of lyrics, yet would still figure on a provisional album sequence. Even at this stage, it seemed like Dylan was mixing and matching songs with no fixed sequence in mind, even as he continued holding back on the songs that could really tie an album together.

The penultimate session, on the 30th, suggested he had lost his way, despite five of the day's takes being pulled to master. Now his choices really were starting to muddy the waters, with two takes of "Dead Man, Dead Man" picked almost at random from the eleven versions recorded. Not so fortunate was a version he recorded with honking sax, Steve Douglas from the 1978 world tour band having been reenlisted.

If Douglas was used to Dylan's working methods, he hadn't been required to sax up songs this trivial since working for Elvis. A song about Lenny Bruce that Dylan sat at the piano and taught to the band while tape rolled was a waste of a

---

[60] Plotkin has told a story of following Dylan around the studio with a microphone while he sang the one and only take of "Every Grain Of Sand," but the studio logs suggest he is wholly mistaken.

good melody, as Dylan tried myriad ways of saying "he had the gift of vision/ You can say he had the gift of the gab." My, oh my.

Even after twelve minutes of tape were expended on a miscellanous medley of instrumental ideas, he would not give up on "The Ballad Of Lenny Bruce" (as it was originally logged). It was his first real life narrative since "Joey," another misguided soul put to song. If Douglas thought that song was perfunctory, rock's greatest poet also asked him to inject life into "Heart Of Mine." He almost succeeded, just not to Dylan's mind. Neither sax take got pulled.

This left just May Day to complete the comeback, reflecting Dylan's usual six-day attention span when it came to the studio, and he still hadn't constructed an album that delivered the goods. And yet he had been here before, many times, and was convinced he could pull it out of the bag. When he arrived that Friday the plan was to capture all the songs previously recorded in a half-assed way and then sail away.

He chose to start with "Caribbean Wind," which he had reexamined in the interim—having mixed the best of a bad lot from Studio 55 in a way that pushed the girls into the nearest siding. Wisely, he had put a series of red lines through that earlier draft, trying to rekindle the spirit that blew through the song the previous fall. But something told him he was fighting a losing battle:

Bob Dylan: The saddest thing about songwriting is when you get something really good and you put it down for a while, and you take for granted that you'll be able to get back to it with whatever inspired you to do it in the first place. Well, whatever inspired you to do it in the first place is never there anymore. So then you've got to consciously stir up the inspiration to figure what it was about. Usually you get one good part and one not-so-good part, and the not-so-good wipes out the good part. [1985]

The problem was not really the lyric, it was the arrangement, as Dylan again self-sabotaged what should have been the album's centerpiece. By ending each and every verse with a stop-start time change that sent the song lurching off the rails, he applied the brakes just when the band was preparing for warp drive. Nonetheless, he began proceedings with three complete takes, two of which were pulled to master.

But just like in June 1965, at the fabled "Like A Rolling Stone" session, he carried on cutting versions of the song long after he thought he had it down. And just like "Rolling Stone," it resolutely refused to lie down until the band simply played through the time-signature change and hoped the singer didn't notice, as they did on the twelfth and last take.

At last the wind roared again. For all its flaws, the sheer energy with which Dylan flung himself at these over-familiar words and the sense of desperation from the musicians made this take (#12) the one. But Dylan couldn't hear the roar no more and when it came time to review the shell of a song, its power and the glory passed him by.

Thankfully, the energy of that take, led by a slightly desperate Dylan, carried him and the band through the longest day at Clover. And at the end of it, there would be a general sense of relief—and release:

Arthur Rosato: I'm sure that Bob thought the sessions were over. That's as much time Bob ever put into recording anything. The most takes that I recall for any session was about fifteen and that was usually the first day, after that it was down to around three for the rest of the run. Bob always put as much into performing any song the first time as the last, so "record it in earnest" is what he does from the beginning.

Dylan threw himself into the songs he now sought to record right, right at the death. And it was quite a unique list he had compiled. He first returned to "Trouble," "Is It Worth It?" and "Don't Take Yourself Away," all songs he thought he had captured on day one. He had changed his mind. Or maybe he was simply covering his bases.

Also on that wish list were two songs he had been struggling with since his unscheduled mid-sessions break. "Heart Of Mine" and "Watered-Down Love" were given mouth-to-mouth, then "pulled to master" alongside "Caribbean Wind" and another dose of "Trouble," which in the process lost one not-so-life-affirming verse: "Meditate on the mountaintop/ Stick a needle in your vein/ You can't depend on anything/ It'll become a ball and chain."

He even found time to indulge in an eight-minute segue of semi-ideas, flitting from "Wind Blowing On The Water," apparently an old scrap, to a fragment of slow blues #115, before going "All The Way Down" for four whole minutes. If this was meant to be mood music, perhaps he was simply trying to reach the requisite state needed to tackle "The Groom's Still Waiting" for the very last time.

If so, the trick worked. He immediately felt an injection of adrenalin as the bludgeoning intro kicked in, investing real intensity to a song that always seemed to bring out the best in him and the band. This time, as with "Every Grain Of

Sand" two days earlier, he stapled its words to the studio wall three times and stuck a pin in the resulting map. If the first take was merely a test lap, on take two Steve Douglas drugged all guest-guitarists in order to find out if the saxophone worked better.

Still feeling he had something left, Dylan turned on his last reserve tank of lung-power for a final take that was deemed "Smokin'!" by someone in the band, possibly an awestruck Benmont Tench, subbing on organ and taking a break from his day job with the Heartbreakers.

But if Tench was bowled over by two of the originals he got to play on that day, he was taken aback—at the end of a session that had already seen Dylan record nine original songs he later copyrighted, five of which he pulled to master—when the band leader decided to indulge his passion for the music with which he grew up, cutting another side of *Self Portrait Vol. 2*—or perhaps side four of *Shot Of Love*.

It could have been some side. Here was Dylan on a roll, refusing to go home, asking, is it rolling, Chuck? As per previous album sessions, he was just getting into it as the window of opportunity was closing shut. It all started with a nearly-eight-minute version of Junior Parker's "Mystery Train" that would have left Sam Phillips questioning whether Elvis really was the best white singer of R & B he ever heard.

What followed was a "Price Of Love" that went on so long, the tape op. had to change reels mid-song, before Dylan took Clydie King to one side and suggested they prove once and for all that the *Self Portrait* version of "Let It Be Me" was not the best he could do. Though he hid it away on a European-only B side, he made his point.

Yet he was not done, not by a long chalk, as he called out to the band—most of whom had been taking a much-needed breather during "Let It Be Me"—"Do you know 'Work With Me, Annie?'" A 1954 hit for Hank Ballard & The Midnighters, the twelve-bar blues was hardly from their own era. But hey, it was a twelve-bar blues. How hard could it be?

Anyhow, enough of them knew the more famous "answer song," "Annie Had A Baby," to busk along as Dylan pulled them every which way. It was a glorious, life-affirming blast from the past and the perfect way to bring the curtain down on one of the most challenging set of sessions for rock's greatest musical maverick. Whither now?:

Toby Scott: I don't know if [Dylan] had a list [of songs he wanted], but they picked out ten or twelve songs. Chuck [says to Dylan,] "Can you come in tomorrow?

Why don't we take a list to everything we've got, to see how to proceed, and what we wanna follow up with." . . . Chuck [then] uses the ill-advised words, "We'll see if we've got a record or not." That afternoon or evening Chuck has me pull our chosen mixes off the various reels and put them on the [master] reels for the next day . . . Twelve songs from the rough mixes I had done off the monitor panel for playback at the end of the day's recording . . . were assembled into the end "album" [and] that was played for Bob.

Suffice to say, the album the engineer and producer now compiled, along lines outlined by Dylan, was not the one the singer had expected to make six weeks earlier. That no longer mattered. The question that urgently needed answering was altogether more straightforward: Was it "a record or not?"

12. D.N.U.

[May 4 – June 4, 1981]

CLOVER
6232 SANTA MONICA BLVD
HOLLYWOOD CALIF. 90038
463-2371

45

Reel _____ #1 4 trk _____

Date _____ 5/18/81 _____

Company _____

Artist _____ BOB DYLAN _____

Producer _____ DYLAN/PLOTKIN _____   Speed _____   Trks _____

Engineer _____ TOBY SCOTT _____   Level _____   Noise Red. _____

Tones @ HEAD 1K SET TO Ø _____   Master _____   Copy _____

No.	Title		Time
	SHOT OF LOVE		
	PROPERTY OF JESUS		
	WATER DOWN LOVE		
	HEART OF MINE		
	EVERY GRAIN OF SAND		
	DEAD MAN		
	IN THE SUMMERTIME		
	TROUBLE		
	LENNY BRUCE		
	CARRIBIAN WIND		
	ANGELINA		
	MAGIC		

Make CD
of this
in house
(Last 3 songs
priority)

CUSTOMER
N G 4

Usually I've been working quickly in the studio and for one reason or another I just get locked into whoever's producing, their sound, and I just wanna do it and get it over with . . . I'm not sure this album hangs together as a concept because there were some real songs on it that we recorded, a couple of really long songs . . . [that] we left off . . . but when I came down to putting the songs on the album we had to cut some, so we cut those.

—BOB DYLAN TO NEIL SPENCER, JULY 1981

Usually my records are turned in on some kind of a contractual deadline. If they didn't want me with the company, they wouldn't continue to give me a contract. They're just records that are fulfilling my contract . . . To me, though, there's something about all of them that I get something out of. They're not just all filler . . . [Sure,] there's songs that aren't performed as good as they could be for all kinds of reasons. There's some songs buried on my records that are good songs that just aren't performed well, and then there's some songs that are performed well that aren't necessarily very good songs."

—BOB DYLAN TO JOE QUEENAN, 1991

I've been asked: "So how come your such a bad judge of your material? You don't put the best stuff on your record?" Well, I don't know who judges what the best stuff is or not but, basically, I'm not judging my material. I just don't think some of my stuff was recorded right.

—BOB DYLAN AT THE ROME PRESS CONFERENCE, 2001

<u>Plus</u> ça <u>change,</u> <u>plus</u> <u>c'est</u> <u>la</u> <u>même</u> <u>chose</u> (to quote a phrase). Across twenty years, interrogated by three different writers with three very different agendas—in Queenan's case, proving Dylan was a fraud and that Joe knows best—Dylan found himself called on to explain what exactly he was playing at when he took a cleaver to three albums in three years—*Saved, Shot Of Love* and *Infidels* (outside our remit)— each of which could, and should, have stood alongside his best studio work.

And rereading his various defenses, one can't help feeling sorry for the guy. Because when he says, "I just don't think some of my stuff was recorded right," he hits the historical hammer on its hindsight-filled head.

With *Shot Of Love*, it was certainly not for want of trying. When Dylan, Plotkin, Scott and probably Rosato assembled, on Monday, May 4th, 1981, to review the Clover tapes, they must have known there was a quality album there. The songs under contention at this stage were as follows:

Need A Woman [2 takes]/ Angelina [1 tk]/ Caribbean Wind [2 tks]/ Trouble [2 tks]/ Magic [1 tk]/ In The Summertime [3 tks]/ Every Grain Of Sand [3 tks]/ Dead Man, Dead Man [2 tks]/ Lenny Bruce [2 tks]/ The Groom's Still Waiting [3 tks]/ Property Of Jesus [2 tks]/ Heart Of Mine [2 tks].

Already the recollection of Scott's that "twelve songs from the rough mixes . . . were assembled into the end 'album' that was played for Bob," starts to break down. He appears to have conflated two separate occasions—selecting the album takes and then playing a "final" sequence, eight days later. In both cases, there were twelve songs, but in the former case there was the more pressing issue of picking the take which made the final cut.

Immediately deemed surplus to requirement were two original songs Dylan had worked on extensively at the sessions: "You Changed My Life," which had actually been pulled to master, and "Don't Ever Take Yourself Away," which had not. This didn't necessarily help a great deal.

If he had included those songs, he would have had enough for a double-album because there were two other songs also in the frame, both of which Dylan already knew would be on the album, the Bumps Blackwell "Shot Of Love" and "Watered-Down Love," two versions of which were added to the selection process the following day, after some fix-up work had been done.

That made for sixteen songs in total, including more than "a couple of really long songs." "Angelina" nudged past seven minutes; "Caribbean Wind" and "Every Grain Of Sand" were both around the six and a half-minute mark, as was "Need A Woman"; while both a six-minute "In The Summertime" and a seven-minute "Dead Man, Dead Man" had made it all the way to the master reels. Throw in two cover versions he had pulled to a separate "singles" reel—a seven-minute "Mystery Train" and the five-minute "Let It Be Me"—and he probably had enough to cut "Trouble" and "Lenny Bruce" adrift.

A double-album idea was never even countenanced, which meant Dylan would have to find a way to whittle down fourteen songs, some quite long, to the nine or ten he could fit on a 12-inch album and not dilute the impact by cramming the grooves, as he had on *Blood On The Tracks* (52 minutes) and *Desire* (56 minutes).

Worryingly, the first two songs to bite the dust were "Need A Woman" and "The Groom's Still Waiting," two of the ballsiest things recorded that week, but both pretty long songs. Length of track soon became a criteria at every turn as Dylan selected—and then trimmed—inferior, shorter takes of "Dead Man, Dead Man" and "In The Summertime." At this stage he was still trying to find room for "Angelina," "Caribbean Wind" *and* "Every Grain Of Sand"—a laudable goal, hamstrung by a commensurate desire to include ephemera like "Heart Of Mine" and "Magic."

According to Dr. Krogsgaard, a sequence was reached by May 12th, one which already omitted one notable casualty: "Caribbean Wind." That sequence was listed as follows (the asterisked songs supposedly being the same takes as the final record):

Side 1: *Shot Of Love / Heart Of Mine / *Property Of Jesus / *Lenny Bruce / *Watered-Down Love.
Side 2: Dead Man, Dead Man / *In The Summertime / Magic / Trouble / *Every Grain Of Sand / Angelina.

Was this "the end 'album' that was played for Bob?" It was not. In fact, no such sequence was ever under serious consideration. (No alternate version of "Dead Man, Dead Man," nor "Trouble," ever made it to a provisional *Shot Of Love* sequence.) What was assembled that day was essentially the album as we know it,[61] but with an alternate "Heart Of Mine" (for reasons we will come to), an unedited "Watered-Down Love" (with an extra verse) and the addition—after "Every Grain Of Sand"—of "Caribbean Wind."

"Caribbean Wind" would also appear on the next sequence, six days later. So it was clearly Dylan's intention to include the track, come what may, and unhappy as he clearly was with the final result. ("Maybe I got it right, I don't know. I had to leave it . . . Sometimes that happens." —Bob Dylan, 1985.)

On the end of that sequence—later pulled from the master reel—were two more songs, "Angelina" and "Magic," possibly intended as single B sides, or even held over for the next album (a habit Dylan hadn't indulged since "Mr. Tambourine Man"). This was the record, as far as Dylan was concerned. It was not, however, quite what the producer had in mind and when they listened back to it on that day, an almighty fight erupted:

[61] I mean, of course, the proper nine-track album not the fake ten-track album that has been allowed to supercede the original in recent years, with "The Groom's Still Waiting" added to the start of side two for a 1985 vinyl reissue on the grounds that it makes for a "better" album. By the same criteria, we should presumably add "Positively 4th Street" to *Highway 61 Revisited* and "Strawberry Fields Forever" and "Penny Lane" to *Sgt. Pepper*.

Toby Scott: [So] Bob shows up and we sit down. Arthur was probably around but [otherwise] it was just Bob, Chuck and I. And Chuck says, "Well, I've put these into what feels like a sequence. We'll see if these'll work." Then he plays the first reel and then he plays the second reel, and Bob goes, "Sounds like a record." And Chuck goes, "Yeah, it sounds like a record. I think we've got some great material there to make a record. I should probably book out studio time here at Clover, where we can record the record." And Bob goes, "Whaddya mean?" Chuck says, "Well, we gotta record it now in earnest." Bob replies, "You just said it sounds like a record. Sounds like a record to me! Master it and send me a copy." There wasn't a big exchange. Chuck is like, "Wait a minute!" Bob [continues], "We've been in here [a while]. It's a record. We're done." . . . The [following] day he says, "Look, do what you wanna do. You've got a week, and then present it to me and I'll decide whether it's an improvement. Otherwise, this is the record."

Scott's recollection sounds slightly fanciful and one might be inclined to discount it. Yet evidence is there to support it. There is an alternate sequence logged six days later, parts of which have been subjected to a remix, while during those six days a series of mix reels were made—real ones, not from some Danish dream. So it would appear that Dylan *did* cut Chuck some slack. The delay allowed Dylan the opportunity to review some of his own choices, and in another bizarre twist, convinced him to go back and recut two songs he seemed particularly set on including, just not as they stood.

That neither really warranted the effort was neither here nor there. He wanted "Heart Of Mine" and "Watered-Down Love" on there, somehow convinced he had two hit singles in waiting. In the latter's case he might have had a point. After all, its riff had provided a big hit for Betty Wright when applied to "Clean-Up Woman", and if Dylan didn't feel he could include an actual Motown cover on the record, he was determined to have the spirit of soul somewhere in the grooves.

And so it came to pass that on May 15th the musicians reassembled for a seventh Clover session on what should have been a day of rest. Adding to the surreal nature of the occasion, Dylan invited along Ringo Starr, Ronnie Wood and Donald "Duck" Dunn, the bassist on so many classic Stax tracks, as if their presence would give him the looseness he was looking for. What it really provided was a sloppiness he alone found endearing.

Three years later, he explained his reasons for including this version of "Heart Of Mine" on *Shot Of Love* to another set of musicians he had thrown in the deep end of his garage studio, hoping they would learn to swim before the Pacific washed them away:

> **Bob Dylan:** ["Heart Of Mine"] was done a bunch of different ways . . . but I chose for some reason a particularly funky version of that—and it's really scattered. It's not as good as some of the other versions, but I chose it because Ringo and Ronnie Wood played on it, and we did it in like ten minutes.

According to guitarist Fred Tackett, it was the session's ostensible producer, Plotkin, who "actually got behind Ringo Starr's drum set and was playing drums. Ringo's standing over next to me by the wall, with Barbara Bach, his wife, and he can't believe this guy's playing . . . He's a terrible drummer . . . Ringo's playing a tambourine—that's why [the sleeve] said he's playing percussion . . . Finally he went up and said, 'Hey, mate, can I have my kit back?'" Both engineer Scott and producer Plotkin dispute this version of events, suggesting it was Dylan who gave Chuck the green light, with Starr's blessing:

> **Chuck Plotkin:** We were crammed like sardines in the place. But for some reason, they were having trouble finding the right tempo, the right groove. So, we're taking a break, and people spread out . . . and I'm alone in the studio, and I sit down at Ringo's set, it's just a rented set of drums, and try to see if I can find the right groove . . . I'm playing, trying to locate the tempo, and Ringo walks back in, and he says, "There! That's it. That's the right feel, right there.' And so I start to get up for him to take over, and he says, "No, no, no. Don't you get up. Don't stop. You just stay right there and keep that going . . . and I'll play the toms and the cymbal." [DL]

> **Toby Scott:** I do remember Chuck playing drums and Ringo staying in the control room. It wasn't a case of Chuck taking over the drums . . . When it got going and the other players joined in, Chuck was ready to defer to Ringo, but Bob nodded for Chuck to continue playing, indicating Chuck was doing fine and it was what needed to be played. There was no ego or other issue between the two drummers . . . Chuck was very much into rhythms, rhythmic patterns, [the idea that] it doesn't need to be 1-2-3-4 . . . He'd got people into [the beat] and Bob decided, "Let's go with it."

The edited version extracted from this rather protracted "Heart Of Mine" jam session ran to just over five minutes, but some other takes that afternoon ran to double figures as Plotkin played behind, between and around but never actually on the beat. It seemed he had finally discovered what the artist himself wanted, "a particularly funky version" of the gospel-soul sound.

After nine largely instrumental takes, Plotkin had found that off-kilter groove people who "aren't in time" make. Perhaps he could now relax—but not for long. Dylan thought now was the time to get a full-blooded "Watered-Down Love." The version on the May 12th sequence was still a little too sedate for his liking, especially for an album that to his mind would be "a breakthrough point . . . the kind of music I've been striving to make."

So, rather than calling it a day, he suggested they stick at it. Once again, it felt like someone starting from scratch. And so the rules, laid out by Rosato the wise prevailed, "The most takes that I recall for any session was about fifteen and that was usually the first day." On this occasion Dylan would do nearly two dozen takes of "Watered-Down Love."

His only distraction from the task at hand was a single protracted attempt at a song logged as "In A Battle," but which should really be called "Winning A Battle," because that is what he sings. Only the two-track caught it, but it was clearly something Dylan had been working on as he plonked away at the piano, calling out the lines to the girls off-mic, while the band picked up the essential idea. A song of devotion, it showed how much was lost when Dylan didn't use the piano himself to communicate his song ideas.

But it was soon back to "Pure Love" (the original title of "Watered-Down Love") for seventeen more attempts at grasping at straws, only three of which were deemed complete. By session's end, they were no closer to striking the right chord and Dylan would have to make do with the one they had recorded on the first, just before he went into "oldies but goldies" mode, riding the "Mystery Train" back to the cradle of R & B.

Hoping to go out on a similar high on the 15th, Dylan decided to see if he could ride the "Mystery Train" till the wheels fell off. At fourteen minutes and forty-six seconds, this "Train" was ready to do exactly that, even if this time the groove was more Allman Brothers than Junior Parker. The earlier version, though, retained its ascendancy, an edit of it being short-listed for a 45 B sides reel (only to be superceded by "The Groom's Still Waiting" after Debbie Gold refused to let the matter of that song's unalloyed brilliance drop until Dylan relented).

So, after another day when Dylan refused to lay down his tune until everyone was bone-weary, they had a "Heart Of Mine" with which both producer and artist were happy. By now, though, Plotkin was in "insanity mode," to use a phrase of

Scott's, trying to construct an album that would show Dylan just what the tapes really could sound like. One particularly disastrous day that the engineer recalls was spent at Wally Heider's studio:

Toby Scott: Chuck wanted to change the key of one of the songs. So we kept the drums and the percussion instruments, [but] anything that had tonality we ran through a harmonizer to bump it up a half-step, and it came out hideous sounding. I think it was "Heart Of Stone."

All too soon, though, Plotkin's time was up and he had to present his vision for *Shot Of Love* to the final decision-maker. He had sacrificed "Lenny Bruce," replacing it first with "You're A Child To Me"—a song described on the tape notes as "a mariachi flavored instrumental with brief vocal"—and then "Heart Of Mine," which at 5.10, was pushing side one into dangerously extended territory.

He was scrabbling to find a way for the two obvious closers to conclude a side each. The sequence he seems to have played Dylan on the eighteenth was as follows:

Side 1: Shot Of Love [4:24]/ Property Of Jesus [4:44]/ Watered-Down Love [5:15]/ Heart Of Mine [5:10]/ Every Grain Of Sand [6:17].
Side 2: Dead Man Dead Man [4:04]/ In The Summertime [3:42]/ Trouble [4:45]/ Caribbean Wind [6:28].

Even taken in isolation, the new sequence was a lot better than the old and despite a single song-exchange, it made for a noticeably better balanced album. It also meant a twenty-five-minute side one, though the shorter playing time on side two allowed Dylan an opportunity to reexamine the crude fadeouts utilized on "Dead Man, Dead Man" and "In The Summertime."

Rather than do that, Dylan decided to trim a minute and a half—including a whole verse—out of "Watered-Down Love" and forty seconds from the end of "Heart Of Mine," which had originally wound down of its own accord. If Plotkin (rightly) felt he had found a solution which saved "Caribbean Wind" from the chop, gave the album a smoother mix and produced a more natural successor to *Saved*, he had been pissing in the wind:

Toby Scott: [At the end] of that week, Bob [just] said to Chuck, "No, none of this stuff is working for me. Just gimme the tapes. I will take them and I will do what needs to be done." This was on a Friday night and Chuck, being somewhat maniacal, was like, "No, I'm producing this. It ain't gonna happen." I remember living in Clover Studio [that weekend] with back doors barred with two by fours; front doors barred, Bob having sent men to retrieve all the tapes over Saturday and Sunday, [them] pounding on the door, and Chuck going, "We're not giving up the tapes."

A face-off that soon became the stuff of legend in LA studio circles, reinforcing both Plotkin's and Dylan's burgeoning reputations for going ever-so-slightly nuts when entering a studio, was only ever going to have one outcome. In the end Plotkin "relented and we gave Bob the tapes."

The album Dylan ended up okaying, and releasing to CBS, was the exact same sequence he had approved on the 12th—*minus* "Caribbean Wind." The only substitution was a "particularly funky" "Heart Of Mine." This replaced the version that had something resembling a tune. The mix was, if anything, even more stripped than the rough mix Scott and Plotkin had played him on the day. Scott realized in a heartbeat what had happened:

Toby Scott: One positive point of th[is] section of the console—the microphone input, where level, equalization and any compression or effects were done—was there were no additional "electronics" involved; amplifiers, transformers, or circuitry, so the signal was very simple but very clean and clear . . . The playback from the multitrack tape was through another section that [had] twenty-four faders with provision for assignment to left, right, or both stereo channels . . . [So] at the end of each day we [always] did a "monitor (rough) mix" from this [microphone input] section of the console . . . When the album came out, it was all the monitor mixes. It [taught me] that whenever you press record on that tape machine, you'd better be prepared to live with [the results].

Chuck Plotkin: The mixes that got released on the record . . . are all just the monitor mixes that we'd get at the end of each night. We'd do a tune, get a track we liked, and we'd just run off a rough monitor mix. And those are the mixes you hear. I *tried* to mix the record. The engineer Toby and I, we tried to squeeze some little level of aural finesse in there. But every time we did a finished mix and took it to Bob, he went: "Naw, naw, no. The other mix. The ones I've been listening to—that's the record." [DL]

Dylan was delighted. It was the album sound he had been searching for since

March 25th, 1981—actually, since November 20th, 1961. Required to promote the forthcoming shows in Europe—a return to large arenas and nostalgic audiences—with a series of radio interviews, he spoke about the album he had just handed over to the label with a rare enthusiasm, telling Capital Radio's Tim Blackmore, "I got tired of making records that didn't come out the way that I had planned it to be, but this time, this album, it sounds pretty much the way I hear my music."

Which is as close to an explanation as he is ever likely to provide for how he ended up approving the atrocity that is the released *Shot Of Love*.

13. OLD AND NEW TESTAMENTS
[June – July 1981]

```
                      Chicago, Ill.
                      Deal:

THUR/JUNE 11 ⌐        Pine Knob

Fri/JUNE 12  ⌐        Pine Knob
                      Deal:


SAT/JUNE 13           OFF

SUN/JUNE 14           Merriweather Post
                      Deal:


MON/JUNE 15

TUE/JUNE 16

WED/JUNE 17

THUR/JUNE 18

FRI/JUNE 19

SAT/JUNE 20           Toulouse/France              :      40,000 seats
                      Tix:  60 FF or $12.00
                      Deal:


SUN/JUNE 21           OFF

MON/JUNE 22           Stade de Colombes/Paris             40,000 seats
                      Paris, France
                      Tix:  60 FF or $12.00
                      Deal:

TUE/JUNE 23           Alternate day for Paris

WED/JUNE 24

THUR/JUNE 25          MOVE

FRI/JUNE 26           Earls Court open
                      Tix:  $19.35/18.25
                      Deal:
                      Nine  shows, i.e.   shows in Earls Ct. &
                                          shows in Birmingham

SAT/JUNE 27           Earls Court

SUN/JUNE 28           Earls Court         NOTE:  If 6 shows in Earls Court sell
                                                 out right away, Barry Clayman
MON/JUNE 29           Earls Court                will add a show there and deduct
                                                 one show at Birmingham.  Earls
TUE/JUNE 30           Earls Court                Ct. has larger gross so it would
                                                 be more beneficial to do one
WED/JULY 1            Earls Court                more there.

THUR/JULY 2           OFF

FRI/JULY 3            Birmingham

SAT/JULY 4            Birmingham

SUN/JULY 5            Birmingham closes
```

Yves Bigot: When can we expect a new album?

Bob Dylan: Very, very soon. In fact, maybe in the next few weeks, I hope . . . It should be out as soon as they can get it to the stores.

—FRENCH RADIO INTERVIEW JUNE 12, 1981

We're gonna try a song off this new album of ours—forthcoming, so-called new album . . . This is the main title song, called "Shot Of Love." We ain't done this before, outside of the aeroplane.

—SONG INTRODUCTION, EARL'S COURT JULY, 1981

Whatever the contrary aesthetics behind the recent shennanigans at Clover, the fact remains they left Dylan at least three weeks behind schedule in delivering the album to the label. (The tapes were shipped on or around June 4th.) With a European tour due to start in less than three weeks, there was no way CBS could get the record out in time for what was Dylan's first arena-tour in three years. Continual comments from the man himself on stage and in the press implied this was somehow CBS's fault.

But then, as the Laguna Beach incident illustrated, not only did he really have no sense of time, he had form. A last-minute decision to do his own mix for *Blonde On Blonde* had meant it appeared after the 1966 world tour; a late change in artwork had meant that *Planet Waves* appeared not at the outset, but partway through, his 1974 comeback tour; the pre-Christmas release of *Blood On The Tracks* became a post-Christmas release when he decided to rerecord half the album; and the need to rerecord "Hurricane" for legal reasons necessitated *Desire* being put back till after the first Rolling Thunder tour, also missing the Christmas rush. Like I say, the man had form.

In this instance, he really did seem intent on sabotaging *Shot Of Love*'s commercial chances any which way he could. With barely ten days in which to rehearse the band before four warm-up shows in the Midwest, and with the scars from the battle of the *Saved* sleeve still there, he turned the production of a sleeve over to short-suffering sidekick, Debbie Gold:

Paul Rappaport: He does *Shot Of Love* and he has to leave for a tour. So he's getting ready to leave and Debbie says, "Well, what about the album cover." And Bob goes, "Just make one up." "I can't just make one up. You're Bob Dylan!" "I don't care . . . what you put on it. You're smart, Debbie. Just make one up." "You can't do this, you can't leave me to make this album cover." He goes, "Bye!" and leaves.

Rehearsing the band was a greater priority. He had one new band-member who had been partly blooded at the *Shot Of Love* sessions—guitarist Steve Ripley, who had got the gig ahead of the less stable Danny Kortchmar. Ripley had a two-hour-plus set to learn, little of which had been given an airing in the pre-Clover Rundown rehearsals.

Previous patterns once again pushed to the fore as Dylan spent valuable rehearsal time working on versions of "Pastures Of Plenty" (evidently intended as part of the second band-set), "I'm Leaving It Up To You" (surely a nod to Don and Dewey's 1957 version, not Donny & Marie Osmond's musical manslaughter), "Your Cheatin' Heart," "Big River," "Vaya Con Dios" (a number one for Les Paul in 1953), "Guess Things Happen That Way," and "Smoke Gets In Your Eyes" (a Thirties standard The Platters rearranged in 1958), not one of which would feature in a single 1981 show, all of which suggested Dylan's nostalgia for the Fifties was not confined to the sound of the records released back then.

It seems it wasn't only his audience who yearned to hear some old songs. In fact, Dylan admitted as much when introducing "a real old song" at the first London show, talking about how "people [in the] last few years, they've been asking me to sing an old song. There's a whole lot of people that love to live in the past. I do it some times myself."

But when it came to his own work, he generally preferred old things to pass away. He intended to continue the precedent *Saved* had set, previewing *Shot Of Love* extensively at the forthcoming shows. In fact, when pressed by Tim Blackmore as to whether he would be playing mostly gospel material, as he had been, he insisted, "You won't be hearing any more of those songs . . . Over a period of time all of those songs become old songs. And we've just finished a new album and I think it's really good . . . [so] we'll be playing some stuff off that album."

The foolish hoped this might mean he would not be playing *anything* from *Slow Train Coming* or *Saved*. He actually meant he wouldn't be performing "any *more*" of those songs—or indeed, any less. It meant no place for "Property Of Jesus." But according to the rehearsal list for the tour, Dylan fully intended to perform 'Trouble'—though he never did—the slight "Heart Of Mine" and the transparent "Lenny Bruce," a song introduced almost apologetically at the first London show, "I don't know why, [but] sometimes I write these [kind of] songs. This song I decided to keep. I wrote this in about two minutes. I figured, Well, if it's that easy I should keep it."

It all meant Dylan had decided the way to promote his new album was to play three of the most disposable ditties he had written in many a long year. At least the tremendous title track was also in the frame. Thankfully, he thought better of this less-than-perfect plan, and rather than fans hearing a whole lot of "Trouble"'s, barnstorming versions of "Dead Man, Dead Man" and "Watered-Down Love" instead debuted at four US warm-up shows.

These shows also showed he had yet to forgive CBS for the tardiness with which they had released *Saved*, introducing "Dead Man, Dead Man" at the second US show in Clarkston, Michigan, with, "This is a new song we just recorded a couple of weeks ago. Should be out in a couple of years." Two shows later, "Watered-Down Love" was introduced as "a new song we just . . . recorded. Should be our next single. If anybody wants to know when it's really gonna come out, you could call the record company and they can tell you more specifically."

Minor point—"Watered-Down Love" was not actually his next single. "Heart of Mine" was, which CBS had already put into production. It was a safe choice and a doomed one, even with alternate unreleased B sides, both essential, on the respective European and the US editions.[62] It would have to wait until July 1st to make its live debut, alongside "Shot Of Love."

By then, "Dead Man, Dead Man," "In The Summertime" and "Watered-Down Love" were outstanding nightly. In fact, for a while there, he carried on where he had left off in Portland, Oregon, the previous December. Indeed, the summer 1981 live set had carried on where the fall 1980 tour left off, the first US show seeing not just the introduction of three songs from the now-completed *Shot Of Love* but also three standards he had sung nightly in 1974 and 1978, his two most recent "greatest hits" tours: "Ballad Of A Thin Man," "Maggie's Farm" and "Forever Young."

If anything, the larger venues seemed to push him to make the shows yet more intense, while he himself, at least for the first two weeks of touring, was as animated as he had been in 1966, when previously under attack from disaffected fans.

Fortunately, the furor the gospel tours had caused in the media a mere eighteen months earlier had now retreated firmly into the past tense, and Dylan seemed to like it that way. So did the US press. When he played the final warm-

---

[62] The European single would feature "Let It Be Me," and hats off to CBS, they managed to get it into the shops while Dylan was still touring Britain.

up show at the Merriweather Pavilion, in Maryland, a delighted Geoffrey Himes, long-standing rock critic at the *Washington Post*, thought he was the first reviewer to notice a major sea change in approach:

> There were signs during the [Merriweather] show that Mr. Dylan is growing restless with his recent persona as a born-again convert. He obviously still believes strongly in Christianity, but his religion doesn't overwhelm everything else as it did just a year ago. Last summer in Hartford, CT, he sang nothing but religious songs in a solemn manner. Last night in Columbia, spirituals were less than half the show and flashes of the impish iconoclast shone through . . . Halfway through the show, Bob Dylan and Clydie King [even] sat on the piano bench and sang "Abraham, Martin And John," with just Mr. Dylan's accompaniment. When he sang, "Has anybody here seen my old friend, Bobby? Can you tell me where he's gone?" the crowd buzzed. It was a question they'd been asking themselves.

"Masters Of War," with a similar heavy-metal arrangement to 1978, when it had received unwarranted plaudits, was introduced at the second show in Clarkston, and stayed for the duration. Otherwise, the Stateside shows were a snapshot of the late 1980 shows, so much so that Dylan tried to raise the roof on the Pine Knob Music Theater with two stand-out covers from his former Warfield residency, "Fever" and "Rise Again," only to notice he was playing one of those outdoor amphitheaters Americans like to build, with lawn seating for the many and pavilion seating for the few.

Unfortunately, "Fever," apparently a request from a friend who lived in San Francisco, was not one of the songs they had rehearsed in the past few days. When Dylan asked, off-mic, for the key to the song, fans might have feared the worse. But even if the tempo was a little off, Dylan soon raised the temperature on this Midwest musical oasis. Sliding straight into a no-holds-barred "Ballad Of A Thin Man," all was well again in the Dylan world, leaving even a reluctant reviewer like Lynn Van Matre, of the *Chicago Tribune*, with little choice but to spread the good news:

> These days, Dylan has apparently made peace with his past, or at least come to the conclusion that audience expectations must be served along with his convictions. Of the seventeen or so songs in the approximately two-hour show, about a third could be considered old Dylan.

A woman who couldn't count (Dylan played twenty-four songs at the show she saw, ten of which were pre-1979 Dylan originals), Van Matre was busily renewing her application for the tone-deaf society by voicing the risible notion, "Dylan has never been a particularly impressive live performer," making her widely-syndicated review a rather begrudging thumbs-up. Thankfully, for once, the other US reviews were universally positive.

The *Baltimore Sun*'s Tom Basham caught the final show in Merriweather, and thought "Dylan was dynamite. Sunday's concert was the best Dylan concert I've seen . . . He [even] did two songs from outside his own body of work . . . Dave Mason's "We Just Disagree" [and] "Abraham, Martin And John," [which] was an eerie hymn. The question about "my old friend John" could have been referring to two people.[63] The line about my old friend Bobby seemed to find an answer in the presence of a revitalized Bob Dylan . . . This time he chatted with the audience between songs, then would rock hard to the point where droplets of sweat were falling from his face."

Dylan was once again upping his game, even if he occasionally had to fight an underrehearsed band. With a week separating that final US show from the opening night in Europe—an open-air show to 20,000 French fans at Toulouse's Stade Municipal Des Minimes—a couple more days' rehearsals were surely in order. But no such option existed as the day after Maryland the band went their way and Dylan went his.

The band seemed to have got the better of the deal, flying direct from Washington to Paris and onto Toulouse for three days of rest and recreation, Rioja and repasts from a region famous for both; while Dylan flew three thousand miles the wrong way, to LAX, for what one must presume were pressing business matters, possibly to do with an ongoing dispute with ex-manager Albert Grossman over royalties, or even the not-so-imminent release of *Shot Of Love*.

Once again, he found himself having to compromise on artwork as the original rear-sleeve—a gas-guzzling Cadillac with a license plate that included the number of the beast (see photo section)—was replaced by an anodyne shot of the artist stopping to smell the flowers. Taking the "red-eye" on the eighteenth, Dylan gave himself a day to acclimatize before doing a 7 pm soundcheck with the newly-bronzed band, the night before his first-ever French show outside the Ile-de-France.

---

[63] Basham is referring to J.F.K. and John Lennon, the latter being murdered four days after Dylan ended a tour where he sang the song every night, giving the song an added if unintentional resonance when sung in 1981.

A week off had done wonders for all concerned. While the band had been given time to swap stories about their boss and become comfortable with life on the now-continental road, Dylan just seemed relieved to be an ocean away from those pressing business matters, doing what he loved best.

The Tolouse show even saw him slip in a good-humored, reggae-inflected "Knockin' On Heaven's Door" before "Slow Train," while from somewhere he found the "Solid Rock" that had been hiding if not since the foundation of the world, certainly for the past year. A fuel-injected Dylan began testifying for real, forgetting that French TV cameras were there filming the animated artist in full flight.

After "Solid Rock," Dylan's first stadium show since 1978 rarely let up, even if Dylan couldn't resist suggesting his new album "might be out by next spring." All doubts that he might struggle to project his post-conversion performance-art in the arenas and stadia of Europe were dispelled in the Pyrenean air.

The near-blackout on overseas coverage of Dylan's extensive touring activities since that original Warfield residency, back in November 1979, had left many ticketholders uncertain as to what they might hear, obliging Dylan to remind radio-listeners, "We've kinda been on tour for the past two years, [so] you'll be seeing the result of [those] shows . . . [as well as] a few new things."

The fact that he was playing a smattering of old hits was still deemed newsworthy this side of the pond a full eight months after he abandoned the all-gospel format, especially in so-called "quality dailies" like *The Guardian* and *The Times*, who dispatched two veterans of the English music weeklies, Mick Brown and Richard Williams respectively, to the second French show in Paris, two nights on from Tolouse.

Having played five arena shows in gay Paree in 1978, Dylan—and the French promoter—were probably being a tad optimistic hoping to fill the 40,000 capacity Stade Yves-du-Manoir, but even the half-filled stadium seemed more comfortable with the songs he sang three years earlier than the ones which were entirely new to them, helped no doubt, as Williams suggests, by Dylan's "ability to evoke the various stages of his own progress [in a way] quite virtuosic [thanks to] the now almost exaggerated elasticity of his phrasing," a rather convoluted way of saying Dylan had never sung some of these songs better.

As for the mildly disappointing attendance, it turned out to be more indicative of the success of the riot police at keeping at bay those Parisians who considered paying for a concert an affront to *liberté* and égalité than any actual Gallic aversion to Dylan's current work.[64] Their *centime*-pinching merely meant they missed a one-off Dylan/ King duet on "Let It Be Me" as well as two dozen other examples of an artist who, as Brown noted, "gave no sign of being a spent musical force."

With no other tabloid-friendly story to hand—and unwilling to discuss the kind of performance art a hundred thousand-plus Brits were willing to invest £7.50 to witness—the rest of the English media preferred to report apparently sluggish sales of the six shows at Earls Court and two shows (originally intended to be three) at Birmingham's National Exhibition Centre.

Promoter Harvey Goldsmith, on the eve of the first London show, pointed out that he had sold 110,000 tickets (out of a capacity of 120,000). He also pointed out that he didn't "know of any other act who could have sold as many tickets as Dylan has in three weeks and still have people call him a stiff." One might have believed him, too, if his company hadn't been selling tickets from the back of both arenas on a first-come, worst-seat basis.

If Goldsmith displayed a lack of faith in English audiences, Dylan himself insisted he had no such concerns, telling Blackmore, "People in England react more spontaneously to the stuff that I do than the people here [in America]." The proof would be in the pudding. Should this genuinely be what he believed, then the set list at the six Earls Court shows would be an ever-changing carousel of songs, like the twelve Warfield shows the previous November.

Well, there were certainly surprises every single night. On night one, an electric "Barbara Allen" came out of nowhere, Dylan prefacing it by admitting, "I don't do this too often any more, but I'll try it anyway," afterwards suggesting, "I used to sing that at the Troubadour Club. I don't know if it's still there."

On night two, "I Don't Believe You" was the main-set surprise—a song they had actually rehearsed Stateside, but which tonight Dylan unwisely sang without a lyric sheet—while the return for a third encore, "Knockin' On Heaven's Door," after a tender "It's All Over Now Baby Blue," convinced the audience they were in the *Before The Flood* cover-shot.

At both shows he seemed overly—one might say, uncharacteristically— anxious to let the audience know he was doing his best to mix it up. On night one at the end of "In The Garden" he expressed the "hope we played something that you came to hear. I know I've written a lot of songs, so I know I must have left something out. I hope I put something in." The following night there was more of a sarcastic edge to comments he made at a similar juncture, reflecting a difficult night for him and every singer on stage:

[64] As recently as 1979, he'd had a French hit with "Man Gave Names To All The Animals."

I hope that we played something that you came to hear. If not, we're gonna be here tomorrow night, and the next night and the night after that. You're bound to hear something that you know one of the nights.

Take that, those of you who booed the girls' set. It being a Saturday night London crowd, there had been a quite vociferous group who had no time for the girls, and having paid for their tickets, felt they had the right to complain. (*The Observer* review of Friday also suggested, "Sections of the crowd on the first night began to whistle, slow-hand clap and call for Dylan during the girls' set," but it was as nothing to Saturday's reaction.)

The immediate result was a Dylan who had just stepped off the time machine he left standing outside the Albert Hall on May 27th, 1966, Prowling the front of the Earls Court stage like a predatory panther while the band extended the "Gotta Serve Somebody" intro to Forest Hills "Ballad Of A Thin Man" proportions, he then delivered his vocal like the Four Horsemen were waiting in the wings. The viewpoint of the "Thin Man" narrator remained on his mind throughout the first set, culminating in the most finger-pointing "Thin Man" of all time and a "Slow Train" that was sung like a judgement from on high

Dylan had calmed down some by the time Carolyn Dennis stopped walking around heaven all day, but the Saturday show had a consistent intensity that broached no argument and breached no Golden Rule. The remaining London shows would still scale the heights, but Dylan was starting to realize he needed to take the odd vocal breather if his voice was going to survive a month-long onslaught on the stadia and arenas of Europe. A man who had once said no performer should ever give 100%, was giving 101%, and sandpapering precious vocal cords into the bargain.

Yet still he kept singing like his life—and his soul—depended on it, even when a depressingly large number of critics stuck their fingers in their ears and made la-la noises whenever a "religious" song showed its face. Predictably, Phillip Norman, the man later responsible for one of the worst rock biographies ever—which its subject liked to call *Shite*, not *Shout*—wrote a breathtakingly ignorant review of opening night for the *Sunday Times*, in which he implied Dylan might as well hang up his rock 'n' roll shoes after "Bruce Springsteen, a month ago, altered forever the principles of rock performance," by going on for too long and playing too many bad songs from his overwrought new album, at the expense of the good stuff he used to write.[65]

[65] For a fuller account of The River Tour, and Springsteen's entire fall from grace, I refer readers to my *E Street Shuffle*.

Dylan was still seething about the Norman review—and those who followed his blinkered lead[66]—when tackled about his own live performances by the editor of the world's leading music weekly, three weeks after the *Sunday Times* piece, "I feel very strongly about this show. I feel it has something to offer. No one else does this show, not Bruce Springsteen or anyone."

That the comparison stuck in his throat is confirmed by an occasion later that summer when he called in to CBS to see his old friend, Paul Rappaport, only to see a signed poster from Bruce on the wall, "He looks at me and he looks at a poster of Bruce and he goes, 'That guy still driving that stolen car?'"[67]

If anyone doubted he had digested Norman's diatribe, the singer's band introduction on Sunday the 28th, in which he described bassist Tim Drummond as "the walls of Jericho," dispelled them (Norman had described the bass as being "as thick as the walls of Jericho"). Unable to name a single song from the last two albums, which become collectively "the songs from *Saved* and *Slow Train Comin'*[sic]," Norman made no mention of any new material, not even "Lenny Bruce," perhaps prompting an extended intro to one of those new songs on Sunday night:

> *This is a new song off [my] forthcoming record album. I hope it's on the album, anyway. It's called "Dead Man, Dead Man When Will You Arise." I wrote quite a few new songs. I thought I'd play them because I don't know how much longer I'll be playing new songs. People wanna hear the old songs. I was thinking of cutting out all the new songs. I'm gonna play just older stuff. [But] this time here in London I'm gonna play all the new songs, just in case they never get heard again.*

It was a stinging rebuke to reviewers and nostalgists alike. Also played on the Sunday—at the expense of "Lenny Bruce"—was an exquisite live debut for "In The Summertime," which on first hearing certainly sounded like a major statement (and a major disappointment when the album appeared). The fifth night saw a hen's-teeth rare "Just Like Tom Thumb's Blues," sung with passion and precision, and a "Forever Young" with an extended harmonica coda designed to compensate for some sound problems, for which Dylan later apologized: "I hope you heard something that you came to hear . . . Hard to judge how we're doing by these monitors on stage."

---

[66] Of which, Patrick Humphries' wide-of-the-mark *Melody Maker* review must loom large.
[67] Still not his best quip at Bruce's expense, which surely has to be his greeting at their first meeting, "I hear you're the new me."

In fact, the sound had generally been excellent at the shows, which had gone down a lot better with the fans than an out-of-touch English media. And just as at the Warfield, Dylan pulled out all the stops for the final show, attended by his friends Eric Clapton and George Harrison (and luminaries like Kate Bush, who told me afterwards that she found it "wonderful").

As a nod to his old friend George, Dylan even attempted "Here Comes The Sun," reverting to "Girl From The North Country" after he realized he only knew the first verse. He also gave live debuts to two songs, "Shot Of Love" and "Heart Of Mine," and threw in "We Just Disagree," in case the critics were still jotting down notes. The earlier English reviews still stuck in his craw and at the end of "In The Garden" his "hope you heard something you like'" rap turned into a straw poll on the band:

> We tried to play a whole lot of stuff when we were here . . . but I know we left some
> things out. If we come back, we'll do those. I wish we were going to be here tomorrow,
> we could do all the stuff we left out. Anyway, . . . I think this band's one of the best ever,
> what do you think? [Loud cheers.] I get tired of reading things I don't like. I sometimes
> like to ask you what _you_ think.

The third encore was a now wholly reggaefied "Knockin' On Heaven's Door," which must have made Clapton crack a grin, having had a hit four years earlier with this exact combination. It convinced Clapton to suggest another collaboration after the show, unaware there was anyone else listening:[68]

Paul Rappaport: We see the show, which is great. I go backstage. I'm hungry and at the back there's food. I'm trying to figure out how to make [a snack] and I turn around and Eric Clapton walks in. They start talking and I don't think I'm supposed to be hearing this conversation . . . [So] this is the conversation. Clapton: "Great to see you, Bob. You know, we really should get together and do something." We're deep in this Christian thing [now]. I [just] want him to come back into form. And here's Clapton saying, "Let's do something together." I'm thinking, "[This is] manna. Thank you, God!" And Dylan goes, "I don't know, man. I'm trying to do my own thing." I'm thinking, just say something positive. Clapton's [really] pushing him, "Bob, look, I'm here, you're here, let's do something." The guy's blowing off Eric Clapton!

---

[68] Clapton had played on Dylan sessions in 1965 and 1975; Dylan had played on Clapton's in 1976.

"Rap" had come to London with Debbie Gold and a New York DJ called Dave Herman, to do a crucial recorded interview with the artist, which had been set up before the tour ostensibly to promote *Shot Of Love*. The interview was scheduled for the following day, at Dylan's hotel, the ever-popular White House, meaning that it was a working day for the bandleader. For the rest of the crew it was, as the tour itinerary baldly stated in capital letters, "AT LAST—A DAY OFF!!!!!" The plan was to do a lengthy spoken interview and syndicate it to US radio stations. But the interview did not go as smoothly as the veteran CBS rep. had hoped:

Paul Rappaport: I was in . . . charge of promotion. So I called Bob—by this time I knew him and was semi-comfortable talking to him—and I said, "Look, I wrote down twenty ideas. I know you're very particular. I'm gonna run down the twenty and you're gonna go, yes, no, yes, no. I expect a lot of noes." "All right. Go ahead." "You rarely do interviews. Would you go with me to see Scott Muni at [W]NEW. We wouldn't have to advertise that you were gonna come, you would just show up on NEW and talk about the record." "Oh man, I don't like to push my stuff that way. I feel funny. I don't want to do it." So I'm going down [the list]—no, no, no, a long list of noes until I get to number twenty, "You haven't done an interview in years. Would you just do one interview?" "Yeah, okay." "So who do you want to interview you?" "Ah, maybe Dave Herman, the morning guy." I said, "Great, can I tape the interview and send it to the radio?" "Okay." [So] I['d] got a Bob Dylan interview! . . . I got a call from Jeff [Rosen], "Bob will do the interview with Dave in England." I'm going, "The easy thing to do is when Bob's in New York and Dave's in New York, go some place in the Village and do the interview." "What can I tell you, man?" So we [have to] fly to England—Dave, Debbie and I . . . I tell David, "Look, Bob's obviously in this Christian phase. I'm promoting his music, I'm not promoting the fact he's born again. I don't wanna know about it. He's welcome to do what he wants, but do not ask him about The Bible, do not ask him about being Christian." . . . But Dave is as intimidated as anybody talking to Bob. In the interview [Dave] comes [across] as a guy who's afraid to ask the hard questions, a guy who wants to be liked by Bob, everything you don't want. And damn if the guy doesn't ask him [about his faith] . . . So Bob does his Bob thing. He can see that Herman is like a toy, and Bob takes him down the road. [He] starts talking to him about The Bible and the "beasts." There's twenty minutes on the beasts in the Bible. The weirdest shit in the world, and David's [just] going, "Really." . . . So I go in with Debbie into CBS Studios [to edit the tape] . . . I'm trying to get something that matters, in between all the talk of the beasts, ['cause] Bob's going, "Dave, you know all about the beasts?" Dave's going, "No, tell me about the beasts." So Debbie and I sat in that studio for two fuckin' days . . . trying to take the things that matter, to make an interview. I was so looking forward to the interview and when I heard the raw tape, it was [like], "Oh." But at least we had an interview.

Editing the interview so that it could be put onto a promotional album—later released as *The London Album*–would prove no simple matter either, as Dylan's mind games didn't simply extend to discussing the arcania of St. John the Divine's dramaturgical visions. For some reason, he kept playing his acoustic guitar throughout the conversation, picking out little riffs every time Herman tried to get the conversation back on track. "Rap," as mystified as anyone, called him up:

Paul Rappaport: "Hey Bob, I need to edit this interview a little bit 'cause it's very long. I need to ask you, why are you playing guitar? It's actually kinda cool, but I don't get it." And he goes, "I tell you why, man. It's a trick I learned from Mary Travers. If you play guitar while you're doing an interview, it's very difficult for someone to edit it and make you say something you didn't say. That's why I did it."

Herman was hardly the only interviewer on the tour to be caught unprepared by some of the stuff coming out of Dylan's mouth, proof positive that no matter what songs he played nightly, he was still traveling on the holy slow train, no mistake. He gave a better—if briefer—interview to *NME* editor Neil Spencer as a potential cover story to promote the album (only for it to appear in the same issue as a "slam" for *Shot Of Love* from the once-mighty pen of Nick Kent), in which Dylan talked at length about his decision to omit "Angelina" and "Caribbean Wind" from the album, as well as "the politics of sin", the world's Spiritual crisis and the Second Coming. Spencer, whether he knew it or not, had caught Dylan in a remarkably expansive mood, a million miles away from the one Herman found him in:

Neil Spencer: Looking back, I think I was a bit naive when I did that interview. I assumed Bob's "conversion" was to a kind of cosmic Christianity, the kind distilled in "Every Grain Of Sand" . . . In the same vein, I have long been fascinated by the English painter, Stanley Spencer . . . [So] I took along to the interview some postcards of Spencer's paintings of "Christ in the Wilderness," which I gave to Bob. Lord knows what he made of them . . . I was big into reggae at that time, and liked the spirituality of Rasta . . . an[other] unconventional strand of Christian tradition

... [So] I therefore saw Bob's "conversion" as part of his spiritual quest. He had already checked out his Jewish roots. What I absolutely didn't realize was that, far from Christianity being another station in Bob's quest, he had been "converted" by ... some kind of dumb Sunday school for addled coke heads. I would have been shocked—aghast—if I had known ... Bob was very civil, but evasive ... I should have asked him more about "Angelina" and "Caribbean Wind." His mention just came out of the blue ... I got a very short time with Bob, forty minutes maybe, PR listening at [the] open door. The chap from *Oor* got cut out, and was really upset. I think what swung it in my favor was [reminding him] I had met him in [1978 at] the 100 Club on reggae night.

Whether or not Dylan was touched by the postcards of the paintings, he seemed to relate to this other Spencer (a man who can legitimately claim to have "discovered" the Sex Pistols), and talked up a storm, even as his onstage remarks became curtailed, even curt, and any pronouncements to the European press became terse to the tenth.

The only other time the gregarious believer broke cover on the mainland leg was on July 13th when, between shows in Denmark and Germany, he called an impromptu press conference in Travemünde, incensed by a fake interview that had appeared in some European papers,[69] but with the bizarre instruction not to bring any tape recorders.

The few reports of the conference suggest it was another strange affair, during which he discussed the merits of two 1970 albums: *Plastic Ono Band* (the one Lennon once signed for him) and his own *Self Portrait* (which he admitted was released "to get people off my back, so they wouldn't like me no more"), as well as what Jesus continued to mean to him:

Bob Dylan: There are so many religions around. Some religions say you have many lives. Some religions say you come back again. Other religions say just sit there and stare at the wall, and you'll find total peace. So what! Jesus is not a religion. I could talk about it for days and days.

By mid-July the twenty-six song set he had delivered at his first show in Birmingham on Independence Day was long gone. His first provincial British show in fifteen years had been where for the first time since 1978 he had chosen

---

[69] Presumably this was the so-called Sandra Jones interview, published in various European papers, which does not read like any Dylan I know.

not to begin with "Gotta Serve Somebody." But he was not backsliding—rather, he was promoting his most recent album by making "Saved By The Blood Of The Lamb" the evening's opening message, addended to "Solid Rock," "What Can I Do For You?" and "In The Garden" all present and correct. The man was still not for turning. And at the second Birmingham show he threw non-tape-collectors the biggest curve-ball of all, replacing "Blowin' In The Wind" with an eyes-on-the-prize "City Of Gold."

However, the large arena shows were starting to wear on his vocal chords, and when he got to Sweden—after a much-needed two-night respite—he decided to rein in both his full-on vocals and the sledgehammer start to proceedings, easing himself into the Stockholm show with two acoustic goldies, "She Belongs To Me," last performed in 1974, and "The Times They Are A-Changin'," the first song he ever released that (almost) quoted The Bible ("So the last will be first and the first will be last"—Matthew 20:16).

Nonetheless, he was still keen to reinforce the message, singing the words "Jesus Is The One" over a two-chord riff for four minutes in Oslo, while also applying the sandblaster to "Serve Somebody," "Slow Train" and "Solid Rock," still trying to be heard above the female Wailers. By the time to got to the gates of Vienna, he was insisting, "All these singers make me sound good. I can't sing for nothing." In fact, the girls were starting to get in the way, perhaps a reaction to having a whole lot less to do, and a whole lot less opportunity to sing about Jesus all day.

By the time Dylan got to Germany, for his first-ever shows in one of the real strongholds of support for his kind of music, he was having to save his voice and conserve his energy as the shows came thick and fast—nine in twelve days.

Starting in Bed Segeberg, on July 14th, Dylan dropped the girls' opening set, accepting that he was making a rod for his own back in countries whose first language was not English, and where entire audiences were seeing Bob Dylan for the very first time. Dylan dropping "It's Gonna Rain" from the show, though, didn't mean he'd stopped singing about the End Times. When, at the show in Vienna, another 12,000-seater, it really did start raining, he almost apologized, "I know it's raining, but I hope somebody's seen the light. I know I have."

Whether a show that promised jam tomorrow and jam yesterday, but never jam today, was suited to the stadiums of Europe was a question he never fully resolved. The final European show was another outdoor stadium in France, completing at least one circle. But the Avignon show would be marred by two deaths in the audience, the second caused by the darkness that fell when the first fatality fell on a electric cable and shut out the lights.

The electrical failure may not have been directly responsible for the poor sound at this final concert, but it was unfortunate that this show had been chosen as the one Dylan recorded on multitrack and had videoed by his friend, Howard Alk, and a small film crew, for the soon-come TV special that never came.

Fortunately, Dylan had already decided to put the Otari to the use for which it was intended. Ever since the first Earl's Court show, they had been making eight-track recordings of most every show.[70] So, there was no need to champion the overamplified, underenergized Avignon show over those from earlier in the tour. He had taped a handful of outstanding shows from England and France, as well as the three Norwegian and Danish shows, the latter of which were a welcome return to relative intimacy, being staged in auditoriums catering to four or five thousand of the fortunate few.

The arena voice that Dylan had begun to revive—first documented on the 1974 official live album, *Before The Flood*, seven years earlier—was one he had gotten away from in the gospel years. Its unwelcome return was doing the band no favors, nor Dylan. It was time to regroup and review, to hold a moratorium on how and why he was shouting over the most musical band he ever had.

Perhaps he really had started to believe his was a voice in the wilderness, and that the message was being diluted at every turn by the choices he and his label made. He still had things he wanted to say, though, and an audience back home he wanted to reach. He would have to rise again. Whatever the cost to those vocal cords.

---

[70] The eight-track tapes from Mannheim (July 18) to Basel (July 23) seem to have gone missing, but were almost certainly recorded.

14. THE END OF THE ROAD
[September – November 1981]

Revel Travel Service

BONDED AND
AUTHORIZED AGENTS

WORLD WIDE
REPRESENTATION

CABLE ADDRESS: REVTRAV
TELEX: 69-8156

SAM REVEL
President

P. O. Box 3068
449 South Beverly Drive
Beverly Hills, California 90212
(213) 553-5555 • (213) 879-4454

AIR TICKETS
STEAMSHIP TICKETS
TOURS
CRUISES

HOTEL AND RESORT
RESERVATIONS

JACK REVEL
Executive Vice President

THE FENNELL GROUP

DAY	DATE	CITY	HOTEL	SHOWS
THURS.	OCT. 15	MILWAUKEE, WI	HOTEL WISCONSIN	OFF
FRI.	OCT. 16	MILWAUKEE, WI	HOTEL WISCONSIN	1
SAT.	OCT. 17	MILWAUKEE, WI	HOTEL WISCONSIN	1
SUN.	OCT. 18	MADISON, WI	NO HOTEL	1
MON.	OCT. 19	MERRILLVILLE, IN	NO HOTEL	1
TUES.	OCT. 20	BOSTON, MA	HOWARD JOHNSONS-REVERE	OFF
WED.	OCT. 21	BOSTON, MA	NO HOTEL	1
THURS.	OCT. 22	PHILADELPHIA, PA	QUALITY INN	OFF
FRI.	OCT. 23	PHILADELPHIA, PA	NO HOTEL	1
SAT.	OCT. 24	STATE COLLEGE, PA	NO HOTEL	1
SUN.	OCT. 25	BETHLEHEM, PA	NO HOTEL	1
MON.	OCT. 26	SEACAUCUS, NJ	PLAZA MOTOR INN	OFF
TUES.	OCT. 27	SEACAUCUS, NJ	NO HOTEL	1
WED.	OCT. 28	TORONTO, ONT.	HAMPTON COURT	OFF
THURS.	OCT. 29	TORONTO, ONT.	NO HOTEL	1
FRI.	OCT. 30	MONTREAL, QUE.	NO HOTEL	1
SAT.	OCT. 31	KITCHNER, ONT.	NO HOTEL	1
SUN.	NOV. 01	OTTAWA, ONT.	SHERATON-EL MIRADOR	OFF
MON.	NOV. 02	OTTAWA, ONT.	NO HOTEL	1
TUES.	NOV. 03	CINCINNATI, OH	CARROUSEL INN	OFF
WED.	NOV. 04	CINCINNATI, OH	CARROUSEL INN	1
THURS.	NOV. 05	CINCINNATI, OH	NO HOTEL	1

SINCE 1933 • TRAVEL TIME IS REVEL TIME

*The record had something that could have been made in the Forties or maybe the Fifties . . .
There was a cross element of songs on it . . . [But] the critics—I hate to keep talking about them—
wouldn't allow the people to make up their own minds . . . All they talked about was Jesus this
and Jesus that, like it was some kind of Methodist record. I don't know what was happening
[musically] . . . but* Shot Of Love *didn't fit into the current formula.*

—BOB DYLAN TO CAMERON CROWE, 1985

Back in 1987, Dylan's current art director was working in publicity for the
independent label I.R.S., home of R.E.M. and a variety of hip indie artists, and
was looking forward to promoting the forthcoming Tom Verlaine solo album,
Flash Light, being something of a fan of the ex-TV man. Leading up to the record's
release, he had been having almost daily conversations about commercial strategy
with the guitarist-singer, as I.R.S. prepared to release his first album in three years.
On the day of its release, Verlaine phoned up the man-fan, and said, "Don't call me
for the next three months."

Although Verlaine could teach Dylan a few things about the art of career-
suicide, even he would struggle to match the perversity Dylan displayed
"promoting" all three volumes in his so-called gospel trilogy, the last of which
would finally hit the stores on August 12th, 1981—three weeks after the end of a
really quite successful European tour.

Delivered three weeks late, *Shot Of Love* had been released three weeks too
late; barely a fortnight after the label's head of promotions—with two decades
behind him in radio promotion—drip-fed the FM stations a four-track EP of
songs from the album—"Shot Of Love," "Heart Of Mine," "Trouble" and "Every
Grain Of Sand," just as he had done with a similar three-track promo for *Saved*.[71] It
was a great idea, and it was one of his:

Paul Rappaport: [The 12-inch promos] would have come from me. That's what
I did to get radio play going before the album was delivered . . . I believe that I

---

[71] The three songs on the promotional *Saved* 12-inch were "Solid Rock," "Are You Ready?" and "What
Can I Do For You?"

invented the 12-inch [format]. For many years we'd send the albums to the station and they'd play whatever they want. And [so] the life of the album was only a couple of months, because they got played out. I began to think, "Suppose I gave them one or two songs, and they put them in heavy rotation." Now its got a longer life. I'm asking the [pressing] plant, "Can you make me a disc with only one [or two] songs on it?" "Yes." . . . [So now] it's like, "Here's two, three songs from Bob Dylan's [forthcoming] album, knock yourself out."

The 12-inch format also meant higher fidelity and the option to play the title-track real loud. The patchier the album, the more the ruse worked, concentrating DJs and listeners' attention on the tracks with the most immediacy—like a well-edited movie trailer for a so-so movie.

The reviewers, though, would still have to be sent the whole record, and nothing but. In the case of *Rolling Stone* and *Shot Of Love*, it would land on the desk of "good critic Paul," as Dylan called Paul Nelson in a letter he wrote to *Sing Out* back in 1964, when Nelson was a staff writer there.

Nelson struggled to make head nor tail of the record, missing deadline after deadline to deliver his review, which finally appeared in the magazine in mid-October, when the record was already sliding down *Billboard*'s Hot 100 from its peak position of thirty-three, the joint-equal worst chart position for an album of original Dylan songs in the post-electric era (1965-2012).

Although Nelson and Dylan had a personal history that went all the way back to BNY (Before New York), and Nelson's critical support back in 1965 had ensured him of a decade and a half of Dylan's undying gratitude, the good critic found little to praise in the merely awful album (to his ears) placed before him by Wenner, perhaps in the hope he might give the once-great artist a break. He would not:

> To know him is to love him, as they say, [but] it's pretty difficult to do either these days . . . Because [of] the man's past achievements . . . we tend to give his newest work the benefit of every doubt. No more . . . The singer [on *Shot Of Love*] often seems to think that he and Jesus are interchangeable on that mythic cross. Ultimate victims. And, of course, it's all our fault . . . [which means] each and every one of us can go to hell. Well, fuck that . . . On *Shot Of Love*, the soft rockers stay in your head and the hard ones stick in your craw . . . If it wasn't for "Every Grain Of Sand" . . . I doubt if I'd ever resurrect *Shot Of Love* again . . . You do wonder, though, if Bob Dylan is so full of God's love, why is he so pissed off at the rest of the world?

This was the bitterest critical pill Dylan had been forced to swallow recently—that it was Nelson cast in the role of Brutus made it doubly troubling. But at least this time he received due warning of what the review contained, ahead of publication, while preparing for his first American tour in a year.

Debbie Gold had called into *Rolling Stone*'s offices and been shown Nelson's piece, which she knew would cut Dylan to the quick. Forgetting any advice her new employer had ever relayed re wicked messengers, Gold phoned him up and read him the review over the phone.

Dylan cracked a joke suggestingt an article in the magazine about gun control had been put there to stop an artist coming down to the office and shooting staff-writers, but it still felt like a knife to the heart. Rather than live out his lil fantasy, he penned a new song, a cross between "When The Ship Comes In" and "Ballad Of A Thin Man," that directly addressed some unnamed "jerk that writes for *Rolling Stone*." The song would still linger among the sheaf of lyrics for the follow-up to *Shot Of Love*, which he would not even start recording until April 1983.

As Dylan knew well, he had been doling out free passes to Nelson for live shows for the past fifteen years, so when he played just outside of New York, at East Rutherford's brand spanking new Brendan Byrne Arena at the end of October he thought maybe the magazine had organized a group trip to the show. Before the apposite "When You Gonna Wake Up" he wanted to "say hello to all the editors of *Rolling Stone* magazine. All the writers and editors are here tonight, I think, checking me out. They're gonna come backstage later, [and] I'm gonna check them out."

There is no evidence that any of the guilty men were in attendance. The fortnightly certainly did not review the show. But it was all part of a rather belated attempt on Dylan's part to help promote an album that was slipping from the charts just as he was rousing himself to push it.

For the third year running Dylan had waited till the reviews were in and radioplay had tapered off, before announcing a US tour. And yet each time he revived this strategy, the album in question seemed to fare worse; *Slow Train Coming* staying on the charts for twenty-six weeks, *Saved* for eleven, *Shot Of Love* for just nine.

For the poor promoters, it required an act of faith they were not so sure—on recent form—would be repaid in kind. But it might be their last chance. Dylan had retired from the road for eight years at the height of his fame. He might do it again. Indeed, the fall 1981 shows would turn out to be his last US tour for "five long years." When he was asked on a May 1986 New York radio show where he had been all that time, his reply showed a man whose recall of detail remained very much intact:

Bob Dylan: I haven't stopped working . . . Seems the last time we were in the East Coast we played Hartford and Meadowlands . . . But . . . you can only play where people want you to play and I was only doing regional tours. But I've never stopped working, you know. It just seems like there's more of a demand for this show [with Tom Petty's Heartbreakers] . . . Nothing's changed around here. You all missed my gospel tours!

What Dylan called a "regional tour" was more like the "Rhyme Nor Reason Tour." Avoiding the West Coast and New York, two long-standing strongholds, the tour started in the Midwest, zipped across to Boston for a single night, took in Pennsylvania and New Jersey, before heading up to Canada, then dropping down to the South, taking in Louisiana, Texas, Tennessee and Georgia, before ending with a series of shows in Florida.

The size of venues also ran the full gamut, including shows at notorious acoustic graveyards like The Spectrum in Philadelphia, the new Meadowlands arena, Toronto's Maple Leaf Gardens, Montreal's Forum and Houston's Summit, every one of which seated seventeen thousand-plus. Yet he was also due to play four-thousand seat theaters in Ann Arbor, New Orleans and Fort Lauderdale, for two nights apiece. Dylan had come to realize, "You can only play where people want you to play," but a couple of cancellations late in the tour and a decision to play Nashville again, rather than Savannah, would play havoc with the schedule, and color Dylan's mood.

Perhaps he already sensed they were probably going to the end of the line when, during tour rehearsals, he chose to dispense with Willie Smith's services. According to one guitarist, it was over something as insignificant as a dubious taste in shirts:

Fred Tackett: [In Europe] Bob would go over to [Willie Smith's] wardrobe case . . . and take one of his Hawaiian shirts and put it on, and wear it on the show. He would get it all sweaty and [then] put this thing back. So when we started to do the next tour, Smitty went to Bob and said, "Hey, Bob, I've got all these expensive silk Hawaiian shirts and they all got ruined on this last tour, because you were wearing them and [then] I was wearing them and they didn't get cleaned. So I need you to replace those shirts for me. Otherwise I can't do the tour." Bob would kinda laugh and say, "Oh, yeah." And so it got to be the day or so before we were going to leave

... and Smitty says, "Well, Bob, I'm not going to do the tour unless you give me ... a thousand dollars for the shirts." ... So he calls Al Kooper up the day before we left and said, "Al, come and play organ with us."

Kooper confirmed to me that his recruitment was very last minute, and seemed rather proud of the fact that he had stuck it to his old friend on the fee he extracted to come to his aid. So evidently the dispute with Smith was never about the money. It was about him complaining in earshot of the rest of the band. Just not done.

Smith was at a double disadvantage, having never been through the baptism of fire that had been the gospel tour. In that sense he had always been a man apart. But Kooper was an ill-judged and ill-prepared replacement who had last played with Dylan live when the show was ninety minutes and his bit was forty-five:

Al Kooper: The shows were long. We did like two and a half/three-hour shows. It was brutal. One of the first nights we played "Like A Rolling Stone" so slow it must have taken him twenty minutes to go through the whole song. So, after the show I put my arm around him and said, "You can't play 'Like A Rolling Stone' that slow. Or if you do, let's do it really slower and then we won't have to do any more songs."

It seems Dylan was at least partly indulging Kooper. "Rolling Stone" was meant to be his party piece, as was the version of "I Want You" that followed it—which Dylan dropped mid-tour, seemingly tired of it. But their presence in the set also highlighted the fact that Kooper had very little he could offer on a lot of the songs "Smitty" had made his own.

After all, Al's patented "fumbling for a light switch" way of playing hardly suited the delicacy of a "Girl From The North Country" or an "In The Summertime" and he was hardly an ensemble player. As compensation for the thinner, more mercurial texture Kooper gave the sound, Dylan now made the strange decision to beef up the drums, partly as a way to keep his righthand man on side:

Arthur Rosato: I was talking to Bob before the start of the tour, telling him that I was burned out. I [said I] would do all my usual pre tour stuff, getting everyone ready, the production and stuff, then send them on their way. I had plenty to do at the studio and could just stay there and be the home base guy. I told him that I would fly out to the first gig to make sure things were okay, and then go home. He was very understanding and it seemed that was the plan. At the first gig, Bob was talking to me and Keltner about how great it would be to have an additional drummer. Keltner told him that [it] could be a good idea and would be easy to do. Bob, knowing that I played drums, turned to me and said, "Do you want to do it?" That was it, hooked and landed. I called back to the studio and they arranged to have my drums shipped to the next gig. So, with no rehearsal, I was the additional drummer. Keltner said that we should work out some parts, but we never had time. I was doing all the regular pre-show production, the lights would go down, I would play the show, and then would go out with Howard and Bob and film all night. I did the audio. I played on every gig.

Soon enough, Dylan himself wanted in on the whole garageband aspect of this new live sound and his notoriously reedy rhythm-guitar was bumped up in the mix, with rather discordant results, especially on songs he was trying out live for the first time in a while. A last-ever "When He Returns," a song he'd not played in a year and a half, one night in Cincinnati was played on the guitar, not the piano, and without recourse to lyrics he could no longer readily recall (a telling confirmation of how detached he had grown from some of the gospel material). The result was painful to behold.

From night one, in Milwaukee on October 16th, it was obvious that something was not right and it wasn't just the set-list. The show was essentially the same as in Europe. There were just three additions, two of them songs held over from the fall 1980 set, perhaps because Dylan felt they suited American audiences—"A Hard Rain's A-Gonna Fall" and "Señor." The other addition was Kooper's platinum *Blonde* party piece.

But Dylan also decided to rearrange the likes of "I Believe In You" and "Solid Rock," the latter of which was particularly disastrous. Denuded of the one thing it had always had—momentum—it became a fraction of its former self. As for the two-drum experiment, it might have worked if it had been applied a little more judiciously, but it made the most dexterous drummer in LA part of a tag team, reducing his role to a subsidiary one, just when Dylan needed Keltner's dexterous kit-pounding the most. Some reviewers of the October shows were baffled by his reasoning, one of whom was the *New York Post*'s Ira Mayer:

> After a dull two-hour, 25-song recital, during which the band sounded as though it were first learning the material, Dylan reeled off names like Al Kooper, Jim Keltner, Tim Drummond . . . The only logical explanation for their combined poor showing seemed to lie in the new arrangements Dylan was applying to his songs.

The arrangements emphasized melody and rhythm to a degree that rendered the lyrics meaningless . . . It took several choruses before "Mr. Tambourine Man" was even recognizable, while all the pain and tenderness of "Just Like A Woman" or the anthem-like appeal of "The Times They Are A-Changin'" were sapped out of them.

In fact, Dylan was about to be on the receiving end of some of the worst reviews of his career, and this time they were fully warranted, the criticisms being directed at the music, not any shift in his eschatalogical worldview.

There were some particularly biting attacks in Canada, where the gospel shows had been largely well-received. It turned out that taking this show—and band—back to Toronto and Montreal eighteen months after some magical gospel shows was pushing his luck. John Griffin in the *Montreal Gazette* was unsparing:

A lifeless clone appears to have replaced the Dylan of old . . . [He] has capitulated to an audience that wants to hear him grind out a pasteurized medley of his greatest hits . . . Although Dylan and his nine-piece band did work over many of his better-known songs last night, few sparkled with the flame of spontaneous creation.

If Dylan could place the blame, at least partly, on the Forum's notoriously poor acoustics, he was not allowed to invoke any such excuse by local reviewer John Kiely after he played Kitchener's seven-thousand seat Memorial Auditorium on Halloween. Instead Kiely took him to task on his whole attitude:

Bob Dylan's performance Saturday night at Kitchener Auditorium was plagued by sound problems that were gruesome even by the Aud's bargain-basement standards, but the failure of Saturday's concert cannot be placed conveniently on technical foul-ups. Dylan, appearing listless, apathetic, bored and lazy, gave a performance that never got out of neutral except when it appeared to be a parody of itself . . . For all the musicians on the stage, the band, taking its cue from Dylan, was sloppy. If not exactly ragged, it never converged on anything approaching power or even interest.

The tour had actually started out quite promisingly. After a typically ramshackle out-of-town opening, things audibly improved on night two, at a second show at Milwaukee's relatively intimate 6,000-seat Mecca Auditorium. Dylan was already mixing up the set order, moving "Hard Rain" to after an acoustic "The Times They Are A-Changin'," a nice juxtaposition lyrically and musically, which led into "Slow Train" immediately afterwards. He also threw a couple of seemingly impromptu cover versions into the set, usually a good sign, both with a Van Morrison connection.

Roscoe Gordon's "Just A Little Bit," a song covered back in 1966 by Van's second band of Belfast cowboys, Them, was one song that suited two drums and three guitars, all playing the rhythm. Sadly, it was a one-off for the song and the spirit it contained. "It's All In The Game" was another fifties standard that had recently been revived by Morrison on his own 1979 Christian rock album, *Into The Music*. Dylan did it as a duet with Clydie King, replacing "Let's Begin," a song of a similar hue.

Perhaps one or both were requests from Divina Infusino, a local journalist who had been granted what she called "a ten-minute audience" after the opening show and, as she was leaving, was told, "Listen, if you come to any more shows and you want to hear some particular song, just drop me a note before the show and I'll do it." Surely, this was a propitious sign.

But that second night in Milwaukee was as good as it got, its twenty-seven song set being trimmed back to twenty-three the following night, in Madison. Set variations also became a rare and not always wonderful thing. Save for two Dylan/ King duets on "Let It Be Me" for lucky French-Canadians, and the introduction of a real purty honky tonk "I'll Be Your Baby Tonight" into the regular set at Bethlehem, PA, a dozen October shows passed without revelation or renewal. Dylan's performance art was on the line, and for the first time since his conversion he was found wanting.

Maybe it was all CBS's fault. Dylan was certainly still apportioning blame in their direction for the poor sales of *Shot Of Love* and "Heart Of Mine," which he introduced in Boston by suggesting it "sold about three copies. I think two of them were sold about here, [in the] Combat Zone." (He was not talking allegorically. The Combat Zone was Boston's red light district.)

The Boston show on the 21st was at the Orpheum, a gorgeous deco-style downtown theater that held just 2,800. And Dylan had taken a nine hundred mile detour from Merrillville, Indiana, to play there. A second show had originally been scheduled but was later canceled, though it is hard to believe that this was because Dylan couldn't sell out two nights at the Orpheum. Logistics surely played their part on a tour where basic geography had to take second place.

Not that Dylan was doing himself any favors, slighting himself and his own singing voice—which was in the worst shape it had been in a decade (ever since a bad cold almost wrecked the *New Morning* sessions)—by introducing "It's All In The Game" to Bostonians as "a song we used to do when things got rough. People always can relate to this. I don't know, I can't seem to sing on key tonight. Nobody minds though, do you?" If audiences *were* happy, he was a lucky man. His singing only got worse, the longer the tour endured.

To partly compensate, at least some of the time, he got real talkative onstage. The show at Meadowlands' Brendan Byrne Arena saw a Dylan almost as chatty as the last time he played the Eastern Seaboard. Perhaps he had heard about the long between-song raps local nemesis, The Boss, had indulged in when he opened the Arena as a concert venue that summer. Unlike Dylan, he had not only sold out Meadowlands, he had sold it out half a dozen times.

Just being in the land of Tweeter and the Monkey Man put Dylan in a weird mood, as he explained to the largely New York-based crowd after the fifth song, "I might be acting a little strange right now. That's because this is a mighty strange place. Oh yes, it is. I ain't seen nowhere like this. Back in the dressing room there, I got a black mirror in my room!"

As the show went on, it became apparent he was a little ticked off, and it wasn't just the *Rolling Stone* staff who were on the receiving end. After a desultory "Hard Rain," he asked the mystified many, "What happens when the hard rain falls? You get watered-down love. This is off [my] big hit selling album. I don't know if it's still out. I'm not sure if it's still in print!"

Dylan also seemed rather reluctant to name the star organist, whose parents came to the show only to hear their son introduced as "Mr. and Mrs. Kooper's relative on keyboards . . . I'm not gonna tell you his name but that's him on keyboards . . . Played with me twenty years. Maybe some of you heard of him, maybe some of you haven't."

Kooper may well have been in on the joke, as he surely was a fortnight later when Dylan introduced "Ballad Of A Thin Man" in Music City USA by describing "the first time I ever came to Nashville. I think it was about 1965. My record producer had the bright idea to go down to Nashville. They hadn't seen anybody in Nashville with long hair. Does anybody remember that? Nobody had seen anybody with long hair. And when we walked down the street you had to either run or hide. Anyway I went back to my hotel room. The Ramada Inn, and instead of going out dancing I sat down and wrote this song."

Kooper had described exactly this phenomenon in his own fanciful memoir, *Backstage Passes*. But even he knew Dylan wrote "Thin Man" at least six months before he ever visited Nashville.

By the time Dylan got to Nashville, on November 14th, he was no longer sure why he was doing this. He wasn't even convinced he had got the balance of gospel to non-gospel material right, even though most of the reviewers seemed happy enough with the mix. Cliff Radel, writing for the *Cincinnati Enquirer*, thought he had struck a shrewd balance:

> Blessed are the born-again folk singers. For they shall have the best of both worlds. They can fill halls on the strength of their secular hits, as Bob Dylan did at Music Hall Wednesday night. And, while they have a captive audience, they can slip in a sacred tune or two. In Dylan's case, it was eleven . . . out of 26 numbers . . . That's a healthy tithe in anybody's collection plate.

What Radel did not fully appreciate was that opening night in Cincinnati was something of an exception. It was the one and only night he crucified "When He Returns," thus drawing on his last three albums for nine of the twenty-nine songs. A week earlier, Ira Mayer thought there was a surprising lack of passion where he expected it most, "There was neither vitality nor conviction in his renderings of the newer religious numbers inspired by his acceptance of Christianity."

Perhaps Dylan was even feeling a little guilty at the concessions he was making, as every now and then he threw in the odd ecumenical encore, like "Are You Ready?" in Kitchener (Oct 31st) or "Jesus Is The One" in Ottawa (Nov 2nd).

But the two most surprising additions to the November shows came in New Orleans—at a show he was recording on multitrack—and in Lakeland on the last night of the tour. Back in New Orleans for the first time in five years, Dylan chose to record both nights at the three-thousand capacity Saenger Theatre, an intimate setting that brought out a degree of subtlety most shows to date had been lacking.

The Louisiana locals also saw Dylan debut the first new song of the tour, which bore one of his most double-edged titles, "There's A Thief On The Cross." There were, it seems, two potential candidates: the "thief in the night" himself, who was "on the cross," or Barabbas, the thief pardoned by Pilate, who was not. Neither seem to entirely fit the song's brief. Whomever Dylan had in mind, he seemed particularly keen to "talk to him."

At least he was still writing songs with dual layers, if not multiple meanings. The two New Orleans shows also received another much-needed injection of good will when two of the band convinced Dylan to let a full-time drummer play second fiddle to Keltner for a change:

Bruce Gary: I'd just left The Knack. Keltner and Kooper, [using] the same phone, called me up from New Orleans and said, "Listen, we know you're depressed. We spoke to Bob and we asked him if it would be okay for you to come and play, because there's two drum sets anyway." The drummer roadie [sic] was playing on the second drum set because Bob liked the idea of two drums at the time. So Kooper says, "All you gotta do is get on a plane and get to New Orleans, and we'll take care of everything from there." So I jumped on a plane and the following night I played at the Saenger Centre, two nights in a row . . . He was mixing his religious songs in with his hits, but he was still very much into the Jesus thing. It opened my eyes. I remember joining in on a little [praying] session before a show. Every show anybody that was into it would get together in Bob's dressing room, and all put arms around each other and recite the Lord's Prayer. I joined in. And I sensed a wonderful energy amongst everyone and it carried with us onto the stage, and it made those shows that much more special . . . [Afterwards,] Bob came up to me. [He] wanted to thank me, [saying] that I'd breathed some new life into the shows.

Gary had auditioned for the drummer slot on the 1978 world tour, before riding the "My Sharona" bandwagon to the bitter, band-at-war end, so he was almost as burned out as the band he now joined for three nights, leaving after a big show at the Houston Summit.

According to Gary, he "was invited to come down to Clearwater [sic] but . . . I could see that everyone was crusty around the edges." (Rosato thinks, "He was fishing for the gig, but that didn't happen.") Whatever the case, at least Gary got to witness (and indeed contribute to) the last major set change of the tour, as Dylan replaced the wild mercury of "I Want You" with the protest prince who once wrote "The Lonesome Death Of Hattie Carroll."

More worryingly, the Houston show confirmed Dylan was having problems selling out the larger Southern shows, much as he had five years earlier, on the second Rolling Thunder Tour—the so-called Gulf Coast leg—where he ended up playing commensurate conurbations with similar results—half-empty auditoriums and canceled shows. The *Houston Post* reviewer, Bob Claypool, felt that what the semi-full Summit got was a half-great show:

> The Summit show drew only a smidgen over 7,000 . . . [But] what followed in the next two hours and two minutes was something totally unexpected—a show that mixed both oldies and new gospel songs, mixing them in sometimes bizarre ways . . .
> The end result, for me, was something akin to emotional whiplash . . . At final count, Dylan did 27 songs and nine of those were gospel numbers. But it was the other two-thirds that drew all the whoops and cheers . . . If the show proved anything, it

was that Dylan's old material is still powerful and incisive and that the new material is totally forgettable. Except for a really good, dynamic version of "Shot Of Love," the gospel material was wretched.

Dallas Times Herald reviewer Sean Mitchell heard more nuance, delighted by what he called, "Dylan deliver[ing] many of his standards in updated versions. He seems to enjoy reworking the rhythms of old songs and there were many examples on view." There certainly were, as Dylan gamely tried to freshen things up by playing around with time signatures and line-breaks.

But by the time the tour got to Florida on November 17th, there was a palpable sense that the end was nigh. Just as in 1976, a couple of Sunshine State shows now fell by the wayside, one of them in Gainesville on the 18th, which left a two-day hole in the schedule. Then came news that the final show of the tour in Talahassee had gone the way of all flesh.

Originally, optimistically, they had been scheduled to play the ten-thousand-plus Civic Center but it had been switched to the Florida State University, with a capacity of just 3,900, a perfect way to wind up proceedings in front of a presumably-appreciative student crowd, only for a student newspaper to apparently print a letter highly critical of Dylan's religious stance.

Quite why this should have led to the show's cancellation is not clear, but a decision was made with just four days to go, leaving the promoter $2500 out of pocket and reportedly "very bitter." It meant that the final show would now be at the eight and a half thousand capacity Lakeland Civic Center on November 21st, the very venue where Dylan had embarked on his original Gulf Coast tour, five years ago.

That show had become the stuff of legends in collector circles, as Dylan had delighted in deconstructing the set local Lakeland students had come expecting to hear, taking the songs apart into the bargain. The so-called "hate version" of "If You See Her, Say Hello" that April night showed a man genetically predisposed to reinventing himself nightly. Whereas the November 21st, 1981 show was a dispiriting end to three whole years when Dylan had made such reinventions the veritable crux of a whole new brand of Christian rock.

By now, Dylan sensed the time was out of joint. As he said after an acoustic "Times" at the penultimate show, in Sunrise, "The times are changing fast. Not changing fast enough for some people, changing too fast for others."

Feeling that Lakeland might well be it, he decided to slip into the final show, between "Ballad Of A Thin Man" and "All Along The Watchtower," the song everyone—even those not partial to *Shot Of Love*—had been waiting for him to play for the past year, "Every Grain Of Sand." And in "the fury of the moment," he crystallized everything that had happened in the past year which had inexorably taken him away from the "circle of ice and the furnace of desire."

Sung with a rare precision, but with precious little passion, the song was a pale shadow of its original self as Dylan continued to clang away on rhythm-guitar, resolutely refusing to raise the mouth harp to his lips, and then cut the song short just as Fred Tackett threatened to play the kind of lead break the song deserved.[72]

A six-song encore to a twenty-two song main set might well suggest Dylan was starting to enjoy himself. But when, for the final encore, he made "Jesus Is The One" go face-to-face with "Knockin' On Heaven's Door," the joy of salvation disappeared off the entire band's radar, leaving only a hollow feeling and a half-empty auditorium.

For the band, those final shows had become something of a slog, particularly for the now-restored second drummer, who found he was expected to "play and then go out and shoot [film] all night. We were doing skits, and Bob was writing them after the fact. We'd go out and shoot things, and he'd give some lines to somebody to say."

Perhaps Dylan was trying to recapture the spirit of the 1975 Rolling Thunder Revue, when he had been shooting the disastrous *Renaldo & Clara*, with his *cinema-vérité* enabler, Howard Alk, in tow. Instead, he had revived the spirit of the 1976 Rolling Thunder Revue, which had come to a full stop somewhere out in Utah, on the road to nowhere, with Dylan's domestic life in tatters as his wife of ten years saw in person what the road had done to him, and would continue doing to him, if s/he did not apply the brakes.

Clydie King, his new partner, also feared that the road down which Dylan was heading had no slip roads and only one destination, and she wasn't gonna go to hell for anybody. Not even him. In order to rescue him, she would have to first convince him it was time to lay low. And that meant taking the band off retainer, shutting up Rundown (even though the lease still had a good nine months left to run) and to break the news to Arthur it was time to travel on:

Arthur Rosato: The last major conversation I had with Bob in that period, Bob said he was gonna close the studio down [and] he wasn't gonna go out on the road until 1984 . . . Bob realized it was the end of an era. We just all packed up and said goodbye.

---

[72] The board tape recording of this performance is on *Bootleg Series Vol. 13*.

There would be no final blaze of glory. But neither would there be a last hairpin curve. And at least he could say, "I can't believe I'm alive." This journey through dark heat had left him a whole lot wiser, and left the world of song a better place. Now he just needed to find a place where he could be Just Bob; somewhere the Caribbean winds still howled. Time to disappear into the mist again . . .

OUTRO:
AFTER THE FLOOD

Everything passes, everything changes,
Just do what you think you should do . . .

—"TO RAMONA," 1964

Could I have been used, played as a pawn,
It certainly was possible . . .

—"CARIBBEAN WIND," 1980

If the Bible is right, the world will explode.

—"THINGS HAVE CHANGED," 1999

It was some time in the mid-nineties, possibly the last time the great poet and I had
dinner together. The macrobiotic Teri Yaki had probably left me spoiling for a fight. So
when the man whose poetry had defined a generation began to insist that anyone could
sing "In The Garden," and mean nothing by it, my hackles were up. This time it was not
the poet who felt a need to howl the truth, it was the critic:

"Are you seriously suggesting, Allen, that an apostate—not an aethiest, not an
agnostic, an apostate—would sing a song called, to give it its full title, "When They Came
For Him In The Garden," and sing it like he still meant it, and have it mean nothing? I
don't believe you!"

It is one of the few things that Dylan and I probably have in common—every
now and then we are called upon to explain, or indeed, defend his so-called

religious period. As if what happened between 1979 and 1981 was a phase he was just passing through, some kinda abberation that he had thankfully gone beyond. Of course, I wasn't usually called upon to defend Dylan to his own friends, let alone poets of the stature of Allen Ginsberg. But hey, if that's my cup, I gotta drink it.

It sure felt like much of the time some pretty smart people simply weren't listening. It must have felt that way to the man himself, too, when he sang rare-but-not-unknown Never Ending Tour versions of "I Believe In You" and "Every Grain Of Sand"—with as much passion as 1980—at the last night at the Minneapolis Orpheum in September 1992, while his mother Beattie and brother Dave sat in the fifth row; or when he played "Dead Man, Dead Man" every night at his first-ever New York theater residency in 1989; or when he told Martin Keller in 1983 that if he wanted to know who Bob Dylan was, he should listen to "Shot Of Love"; or informed Gary Hill in 1993 that, "A person without faith is like a walking corpse." Are we supposed to believe that on each of these occasions he was just killing time, talking (or singing) bull?

That he had moved on by 1983 was not in doubt—it was and is in his nature—but he wasn't about to ever apologize for his gospel period or the records he made then. As he told steadfast supporter Robert Hilburn after he emerged with the double-edged *Infidels* in 1983:

Bob Dylan: I don't particularly regret telling people how to get their souls saved. I don't particularly regret any of that. Whoever was supposed to pick it up, picked it up. But maybe the time for me to say that has just come and gone. Now it's time for me to do something else . . . Jesus himself only preached for three years.

At no point did Dylan ever renounce the views he expressed between 1979 and 1981—he just modified them, shaped by the weft and warp of fate and circumstance in life and life only. After all, he was hardly running out of things to rail against in the modern world.

And in 1984, when he briefly returned to the road for a month-long European tour repromoting *Infidels*, he went out of his way to reinforce previously stated views when asked, "Do you actually believe the end is at hand?"—as he was at least twice that spring. To *Rolling Stone*'s Kurt Loder, one of the many who had not been bowled over by *Saved*, he set out to describe a kingdom where ye shall be changed:

Bob Dylan: I believe in the Book of Revelation. The leaders of this world are eventually going to play God, if they're not already playing God, and eventually a man will come that everybody will think is God. He'll do things, and they'll say, "Well, only God can do those things. It must be him." . . . [When] the new kingdom comes in, people can't even imagine what its gonna be like. There's a lot of people walkin' around who think the new kingdom's comin' next year, and that they're gonna be right in there among the top guard. And they're wrong. When it comes in, there are people who'll be prepared for it, but if the new kingdom happened tomorrow and you were sitting there and I was sitting here, you wouldn't even remember me.

The *Sunday Times'* Mick Brown, a more subtle scribe, was also on the receiving end of an evangelical exposition that would not have been out of place in Hartford, Connecticut, on a fine May evening:

Bob Dylan: I believe that ever since Adam and Eve got thrown out of the garden that the whole nature of the planet has been heading in one direction—towards Apocalypse. It's all there in the Book of Revelation, but it's difficult talking about these things ['cause] most people . . . don't want to listen. [1984]

Such occasions became rarer and rarer as the years passed, but only—one suspects—because of the reaction they garnered. Dylan simply grew tired of being asked to define his religious position, even rebuffing Hilburn in 1985, claiming, "I feel like pretty soon I am going to write about that. I feel like I got something to say, but more than you can say in a few paragraphs in a newspaper."

He never did write it down, or at least not for the printing press, but that comment about "a few paragraphs in a newspaper" says it all. He had been judged in a few paragraphs by people who took his conversion personally and let him know it. He was now saying, if the time ever came for him to judge and be judged, it would be based on a somewhat more nuanced deposition than the one his accusers gave. It might even be delivered "face-to-face in the rain."

As it happens, it would be 1986 before Dylan toured America again, with a band that at least warranted a mention in the same breath as the consummate musicians who had been led into the greener pastures by a galvanized Dylan between 1979 and 1981—Tom Petty's Heartbreakers. A tour of Japan and Australia had prepped anyone paying attention, but still the questions kept coming:

Toby Creswell: The difference between the gospel records and the recent stuff seems to be that earlier you were laying down the law.

Bob Dylan: Every so often you have to have the law laid down, so that you know what the law is. Then you can do whatever you please with it. I haven't heard those albums in quite a while. You're probably right.

If Dylan wasn't playing a lot of "recent stuff," he was still ending every main set on the so-called True Confessions Tour with "In The Garden"—the song Ginsberg insisted to me could retain its inner meaning when sung by a former believer— and Dylan was prefacing it with a rap that should have left no one in any doubt where the man was at; especially after he insisted on putting the song, preceded by a variation of this rap, at the very start of a one-hour HBO In Concert special, broadcast later in the year. Toronto 1980 it was never going to be. But he was still telling us: he hadn't changed. He was the same man:

Before I get out of here I gotta sing you all this one song. This is a song about my hero. Everybody got heroes, right? For lots of people Mohammed Ali's a hero. And Albert Einstein, he sure was a hero. I guess you could say even Clark Gable was a hero. Michael Jackson, he's a hero, right? Bruce Springsteen! I care nothing about them people, though. None of those people are my heroes. They don't mean nothing to me. I'm sorry, but that's the truth. I wanna sing a song about my hero . . .

When they came for him in the garden, did they know?
Did they know he was the Son of God,
did they know that he was the Lord?

APPENDIX I
THE GOSPEL YEARS: A CHRONOLOGY.

MONTH ___JULY___ YEAR __81__ BOB DYLAN TOUR

SUNDAY	MONDAY	TUESDAY	WEDNESDAY	THURSDAY	FRIDAY	SATURDAY
			1 15,000 LONDON, ENG. EARL'S COURT 8:00 PM 110 mi	**2**	**3** TO BIRMINGHAM	**4** BIRMINGHAM, ENG. N.E.C. (8:00 PM)
5 BIRMINGHAM N.E.C. (8:00 PM) 300 mi	**6** TO STOCKHOLME	**7** OFF	**8** 9,500 STOCKHOLM, SWE. JOHANNESHOV ICESTADIUM 7:30 PM 350 mi	**9** 5,725 OSLO, NORWAY DRAMMENSHALLE 7:30 PM	**10** 5,725 OSLO, NORWAY DRAMMENSHALLE 7:30 PM 390 mi	**11** TO COENHAGEN
12 4,467 COPENHAGEN, DEN. BROENDBYHALL 7:30 PM 180 mi	**13** TO BAD SEGEBERG	**14** 12,000 BAD SEGEBURG, GERMANY OPEN AIR AMPH. (8:00 PM)	**15** 12,000 BAD SEGEBURG, GERMANY OPEN AIR AMPH. (8:00	**16** TO LORELEY	**17** 16,000 LORELEY, GERM. OUTDOOR (8:00 PM) 85 mi	**18** 25,000 MANNHEIM, GERM. FOOTBALL STAD. 7:30 PM) OUTDOOR 230 mi
19 11,000 MUNICH, GERM. OLYMPIC HALL (9:00 PM)	**20** 11,000 MUNICH, GERM. OLYMPIC HALL (9:00 PM) 270 mi	**21** 11,119 VIENNA, AUSTRIA STADTHALLE 7:30 PM 500 mi	**22** TO BASEL	**23** 9,000 BASEL, SWITZ. SPORTSHALLE (8:00 PM) 400 mi	**24** TO AVIGNON	**25** 25,000 AVIGNON, FRANC STADIUM (OUTDOOR) 8:00 PM
26 TO LYON	**27** TO U.S.A.	**28**	**29**	**30**	**31**	

All underlined tracks are featured on the deluxe eight-disc edition of *Trouble No More: The Gospel Years* *(The Bootleg Series Vol. 13).*

1978
Municipal Auditorium, Nashville, TN, December 2
Soundcheck includes "<u>Slow Train</u>."
Interviewed by Lynne Allen. Published in part in June 1979, *Trouser Press.*

Greensboro Coliseum, Greensboro, NC, December 7
Soundcheck includes "<u>Help Me Understand</u>" and "<u>Do Right To Me, Baby</u>"

Hollywood Sportatorium, Miami, FL, December 16
Set includes "Do Right To Me, Baby"

1979
Muscle Shoals Sound Studio, Sheffield, AL, April 30
Song recorded: "<u>Trouble In Mind</u>."

Muscle Shoals Sound Studio, Sheffield, AL, May 1
Songs recorded: "Precious Angel" and "<u>No Man Righteous (No Not One)</u>."

Muscle Shoals Sound Studio, Sheffield, AL, May 2
Songs recorded: "When You Gonna Wake Up," "Gonna Change My Way Of Thinking," and "<u>Ye Shall Be Changed</u>."

Muscle Shoals Sound Studio, Sheffield, AL, May 3
Songs recorded: "No Man Righteous (No Not One)," "I Believe In You," and "Slow Train."

Muscle Shoals Sound Studio, Sheffield, AL, May 4
Songs recorded: "<u>Gotta Serve Somebody</u>," "Do Right To Me Baby (Do Unto Others)," "<u>When He Returns</u>," and "Man Gave Names To All The Animals."

Muscle Shoals Sound Studio, Sheffield, AL, May 4
Overdub session: "I Believe In You," "Slow Train," "Gotta Serve Somebody," "Ye Shall Be Changed," and "When You Gonna Wake Up."

Muscle Shoals Sound Studio, Sheffield, AL, May 11
Overdub session: "When You Gonna Wake Up," and "I Believe In You." [new vcls.]

Rundown Studios, Santa Monica, CA, September 11
Fred Tackett audition.

Rundown Studios, Santa Monica, CA, September 12
Wayne Perkins and Rick Ruskin audition.

Rundown Studios, Santa Monica, CA, September 13
John Pechickjian audition.

Rundown Studios, Santa Monica, CA, September 25
Songs rehearsed: "When You Gonna Wake Up" and "Slow Train."
Rundown Studios, Santa Monica, CA, September 26
Songs rehearsed: "Covenant Woman," "Gonna Change My Way of Thinking," "Precious Angel," "Do Right To Me Baby," "Ye Shall Be Changed," "Solid Rock," "In The Garden," "When You Gonna Wake Up," "Gotta Serve Somebody," "Slow Train," "Man Gave Names To All The Animals," "Blessed Be The Name," "Hear Jesus Calling," "<u>Stand By Faith</u>."

Rundown Studios, Santa Monica, CA, September 28
Songs rehearsed: "Solid Rock," "This Train," "Covenant Woman Precious Angel," "Ye Shall Be Changed," "I Believe In You," "What Can I Do For You?," "Blessed Be The Name," "In The Garden," "Gotta Serve Somebody," "When You Gonna Wake Up," "Pressing On."

Rundown Studios, Santa Monica, CA, October 2
Songs rehearsed: "When You Gonna Wake Up," "Precious Angel," "<u>Slow Train</u>," "<u>Gonna Change My Way of Thinking</u>," "Solid Rock," "Blessed Be The Name," "In The Garden," "Pressing On."* [*w/ horns]

Rundown Studios, Santa Monica, CA, October 8
Songs rehearsed: "Slow Train,"* "Change My Way of Thinking,"* "Covenant Woman,"* "Gotta Serve Somebody,"* "Blessed Be The Name,"* "Knockin' On The Door (Callin')," "I Believe In You," "When You Gonna Wake Up," "Do Right To Me Baby," "Precious Angel," "In The Garden," "Slow Train," "Pressing On," "Solid Rock,"* "Barbara Allen," "No Man Righteous." [* w/ horns]

Rundown Studios, Santa Monica, CA. October 9
Songs rehearsed: "Covenant Woman," "Solid Rock,"* "When You Gonna Wake Up,"* "Ye Shall Be Changed," "Blessed Be The Name."* "Do Right To Me Baby." "Covenant Woman."* "<u>Gotta Serve Somebody</u>,"* "Knockin' On The Door (Callin')," "Pressing On," "In The Garden."* [* w/ horns]

Rundown Studios, Santa Monica, CA, October 10
Songs rehearsed: "What Can I Do For You?," "Blessed Be The Name,"* "Covenant Woman,"* "Pressing On,"* "Solid Rock,"* "In The Garden,"* "When You Gonna Wake Up,"* "Slow Train,"* "Gotta Serve Somebody,"* "Blessed Be The Name," "Covenant Woman." [* w/ horns]

Rundown Studios, Santa Monica, CA, October 11

Songs rehearsed: "You Don't Have To Get Into Trouble." "Solid Rock."* "In The Garden."* "When You Gonna Wake." "Precious Angel."* "Slow Train."* "Pressing On."* "Gotta Serve Somebody."* "What Can I Do For You?" "Covenant Woman." [* w/ horns]

Rundown Studios, Santa Monica, CA, October 12
Songs rehearsed: "Blessed Be The Name," "When You Gonna Wake Up," "Precious Angel," "In The Garden," "Slow Train," "Pressing On," "Solid Rock," "Saving Grace," "Man Gave Names To All The Animals," "What Can I Do For You?," "Covenant Woman," "Gotta Serve Somebody," "I Believe In You."

Saturday Night Live, NBC Studios, New York, NY, October 20
Songs performed: "Gotta Serve Somebody," "I Believe In You," "When You Gonna Wake Up"

Rundown Studios, Santa Monica, CA, October 23
Songs rehearsed: Gotta Serve Somebody," "I Believe In You," "When You Gonna Wake Up," "When He Returns," "Saved," "Precious Angel," "Pressing On," "Slow Train," "Man Gave Names To All The Animals," "Saving Grace," "Solid Rock," "What Can I Do For You?" "In The Garden," "Do Right To Me Baby," "Covenant Woman," "Change My Way of Thinking," "Blessed Is The Name."

Rundown Studios, Santa Monica, CA, October 24
Songs rehearsed: "Gotta Serve Somebody," "I Believe In You," "When You Gonna Wake Up," "When He Returns," "Man Gave Names To All The Animals," "Slow Train," "Precious Angel," "Saved," "What Can I Do For You?," "Covenant Woman," "Change My Way of Thinking," "Saving Grace," "Solid Rock," "Do Right To Me Baby."

Rundown Studios, Santa Monica, CA, October 25
Songs rehearsed: "Gotta Serve Somebody," "I Believe In You," "When You Gonna Wake Up," "When He Returns," "Man Gave Names To All The Animals," "Slow Train," "Precious Angel," "Saved," "What Can I Do For You?," "Covenant Woman," "Gonna Change My Way of Thinking," "Saving Grace,"

Rundown Studios, Santa Monica, CA, October 29
Songs rehearsed: "What Can I Do For You?," "Saved," "Slow Train," "Solid Rock," "Covenant Woman," "No Man Righteous," "In The Garden."

November

1	San Francisco, CA	Fox Warfield Theatre

Reviews cited: Joel Selvin, *Melody Maker*, Nov 17, 1979; Leslie Goldberg, "No More Blowin' In The Wind," *San Francisco Bay Guardian*, Nov 8, 1979; Gail S. Tagashire, "New Dylan," *San Jose Mercury News*, Nov 3, 1979; Michael Goldberg, "Heaven Can't Wait," *NME*, Nov 17, 1979; Robert Palmer, "The Gospel According to Bob Dylan," *Rolling Stone*, Dec 13, 1979; Mark Cooper, "Oh Christ It's Dylan," *Record* Mirror, Nov 17, 1979.

2	San Francisco, CA	Fox Warfield Theatre

Reviews cited: Robert Hilburn, "Fundamental Lights Still Shineth," *LA Times*, Nov 6, 1979; Leslie Goldberg, "No More Blowin' In The Wind," *San Francisco Bay Guardian*, Nov 8, 1979.

3	San Francisco, CA	Fox Warfield Theatre

Reviews cited: Robert Hilburn, "Fundamental Lights Still Shineth," *LA Times*, Nov 6, 1979.

4	San Francisco, CA	Fox Warfield Theatre
6	San Francisco, CA	Fox Warfield Theatre

Inc. "Pressing On" and "Saving Grace."

7	San Francisco, CA	Fox Warfield Theatre
8	San Francisco, CA	Fox Warfield Theatre
9	San Francisco, CA	Fox Warfield Theatre
10	San Francisco, CA	Fox Warfield Theatre
11	San Francisco, CA	Fox Warfield Theatre
13	San Francisco, CA	Fox Warfield Theatre
14	San Francisco, CA	Fox Warfield Theatre
15	San Francisco, CA	Fox Warfield Theatre

Inc. "Gotta Serve Somebody."

16	San Francisco, CA	Fox Warfield Theatre

Inc. "No Man Righteous" and "Slow Train."
Reviews of entire residency cited: Paul Williams, *What Happened?* (Entwistle Books, 1980) [entire text reproduced in *Bob Dylan: Watching The River Flow* (Omnibus Press, 1996)].

18	Santa Monica, CA	Civic Auditorium

Reviews cited: Harvey Kubernik, "Holy Bob," *Melody Maker*, Dec 8, 1979; Robert Hilburn, "Dylan's Evangelicalism Goes On," *LA Times* Nov 20, 1979; Sylvie Simmons, "God-awful," *Sounds*, Dec 15, 1979.

19	Santa Monica, CA	Civic Auditorium
20	Santa Monica, CA	Civic Auditorium

Inc. "Covenant Woman" and "Blessed Be The Name."

21	Santa Monica, CA	Civic Auditorium
25	Tempe, AZ	Gammage Center

Reviews cited: "Liner Notes," *Arizona Republic*, Nov 29, 1979.

26	Tempe, AZ	Gammage Center
27	San Diego, CA	Golden Hall

Inc. "Solid Rock" and "What Can I Do For You?"
Reviews cited: Janet Huck, "The (New) Word According to Dylan," *Newsweek*, Dec 17, 1979; John Mood, "Beautiful Raucous Dirty," *San Diego Reader*, December 22, 1994.

28	San Diego, CA	Golden Hall

December

4	Albuquerque, NM	Kiva Auditorium, Convention Center
5	Albuquerque, NM	Kiva Auditorium, Convention Center

Inc. "When He Returns."
Reviews cited: Denise Tessier, "Powerful, Moving Show," *Albuquerque Journal*, Dec 6, 1979.

7	Interviewed by KMGX's Bruce Heiman from his Tucson hotel room.	
8	Tucson, AZ	Music Hall, Community Center

Reviews cited: Pam Parrish, "No Oldies, Just Dylan At His Best," *Arizona Daily Star*, Dec 9, 1979.

9	Tucson, AZ	Music Hall, Community Center

1980
January

7[-8]	Rundown Studios, Santa Monica, CA	

Songs rehearsed include "Allow Me," "Gotta Serve Somebody," "Drinkin' Out of Two Cups" and "In The Garden." [Only tape two appears to be extant.]

11	Portland, OR	Paramount Theatre

Reviews cited: John Wendeborn, "Crowd pleased with new Dylan," *The Oregonian*, Jan 12, 1980.

12	Portland, OR	Paramount Theatre

Inc. "Saved."

13	Seattle, WA	Paramount Northwest Theatre

Reviews cited: Patrick MacDonald, "Brilliant, heartfelt but unmoving Dylan concert," *The Seattle Times*, Jan 14, 1980; Patrick MacDonald, "Three different days of Dylan," *The Seattle Times*, Jan 20, 1980.

14	Seattle, WA	Paramount Northwest Theatre

Reviews cited: Patrick MacDonald, "Three different days of Dylan," *The Seattle Times*, Jan 20, 1980.

15	Seattle, WA	Paramount Northwest Theatre

Reviews cited: Patrick MacDonald, "Three different days of Dylan," *The Seattle Times*, January 20, 1980.

16	Portland, OR	Paramount Theatre

Inc. "Man Gave Names To All The Animals."

17	Spokane, WA	Opera House
18	Spokane, WA	Opera House
21	Denver, CO	Rainbow Music Hall
22	Denver, CO	Rainbow Music Hall
23	Denver, CO	Rainbow Music Hall
25	Omaha, NE	Orpheum Theater

Reviews cited: Chuck Nash, "Dylan Draws Together Old and New," *Omaha Daily Reporter*, Feb 4, 1980.

26	Omaha, NE	Orpheum Theater
27	Kansas City, MO	Uptown Theater

Inc. "In The Garden."
Review cited: Leland Rucker, "Dylan: Uptown Theater," *Kansas City Times*,
Jan 29, 1980.

28	Kansas City, MO	Uptown Theater

Inc. "Do Right To Me."

29	Kansas City, MO	Uptown Theater
31	Memphis, TN	Orpheum Theater

Inc. "Gonna Change My Way of Thinking."

February

1	Memphis, TN	Orpheum Theater
2	Birmimgham, AL	Jefferson Civic Center
3	Birmimgham, AL	Jefferson Civic Center
5	Knoxville, TN	Civic Auditorium

Reviews cited: Kathy Byrd, "Dylan's Message Positively Clear," *University of
Tennessee Journal*, February 1980.

6	Knoxville, TN	Civic Auditorium
8	Charleston, WV	Municipal Auditorium

[1st performance of "Are You Ready?"]

9	Charleston, WV	Municipal Auditorium

Muscle Shoals Sound Studio, Sheffield, AL, February 11, 1980
Song recorded: "Covenant Woman"

Muscle Shoals Sound Studio, Sheffield, AL, February 12, 1980
Songs recorded: "Solid Rock," "What Can I Do For You?," "Saved," "A Satisfied Mind."

Muscle Shoals Sound Studio, Sheffield, AL, February 13, 1980
Songs recorded: "Saving Grace," "Pressing On," [+ ?"Solid Rock"].

Muscle Shoals Sound Studio, Sheffield, AL, February 14, 1980
Songs recorded: "In The Garden" and "Are You Ready?"

Muscle Shoals Sound Studio, Sheffield, AL, February 15, 1980
Songs recorded: "Covenant Woman" [+ ?"Saved"].

Grammy Awards, Shrine Auditorium, Los Angeles, CA, February 27, 1980
"Gotta Serve Somebody"
Quoted in *LA Times*, Feb 28, 1980.

April

9-11	Rundown Studios, Santa Monica, CA	

Songs rehearsed: "Coverdown Breakthrough," "I Will Love Him," "Ain't Gonna
Go To Hell," "Solid Rock," "In The Garden," "Do Right To Me Baby,"
"Gotta Serve Somebody," "When You Gonna Wake Up," "Precious Angel,"
"Slow Train," "Pressing On," "Saved."

17	Toronto, Ontario	Massey Hall

Reviews cited: Michael Lawson, "Dylan Disappoints Rock Fans," *Ottawa Citizen*,
April 18, 1980; Jonathan Gross, *Toronto Sun*, April 18, 1980; Peter Goddard,
"The Times, They've Changed," *Toronto Star*, April 18, 1980; Paul McGrath,
"Old-Time Religion But No Old-Time Dylan," *Toronto Globe & Mail*, April, 19,

1980.

18	Toronto, Ontario	Massey Hall

Inc. "Gotta Serve Somebody," "I Believe in You," "When You Gonna Wake Up," "Ain't Gonna Go to Hell for Anybody," "Slow Train," "Saving Grace," "Pressing On."

| 19 | Toronto, Ontario | Massey Hall |

Inc. "Covenant Woman," "Cover Down," "Pray Through," "Man Gave Names to All the Animals," "Precious Angel," "What Can I Do for You?," "Are You Ready?," "I Will Love Him."

| 20 | Toronto, Ontario | Massey Hall |

Inc. "When He Returns," "Do Right to Me Baby (Do Unto Others)," "Solid Rock. In The Garden."

| 22 | Montreal, Quebec | Le Theatre Saint-Denis |

Reviews cited: "Canadian Briefs," *Montreal Gazette*, April 23, 1980; Bruce Bailey, "Born Again Bob Forsakes The Past," *Montreal Gazette*, April 24, 1980; Stephen Gauer, "Reborn Dylan Sings Religion," *The Ottawa Journal*, Arpril 24,

1980.

23	Montreal, Quebec	Le Theatre Saint-Denis
24	Montreal, Quebec	Le Theatre Saint-Denis

Inc. "Ain't Gonna Go To Hell."

25	Montreal, Quebec	Le Theatre Saint-Denis
27	Albany, NY	Palace Theater
28	Albany, NY	Palace Theater
30	Buffalo, NY	Kleinhans Music Hall

Inc. "Are You Ready?"

May

1	Buffalo, NY	Kleinhans Music Hall

Inc. "Cover Down (Pray It Through)."

2	Worcester, MA	Memorial Theater
3	Worcester, MA	Memorial Theater
4	Syrcause, NY	Landmark Theater
5	Syrcause, NY	Landmark Theater
7	Hartford, CT	Bushnell Memorial Hall

Inc. second and last "No Man Righteous"
Reviews cited: Karen Hughes, "Dylan Presses On," *Village Voice*, May 19, 1980; Colin McEnroe, "Born-Again Dylan Shines in Bushnell Concert," *The Hartford Courant*, May 9, 1980.

8	Hartford, CT	Bushnell Memorial Hall
9	Portland, ME	City Hall
10	Portland, ME	City Hall
11	Providence, RI	Ocean State Performing Arts Center
12	Providence, RI	Ocean State Performing Arts Center
14	Pittsburgh, PA	Stanley Theatre

Reviews cited: Pete Bishop, "Dylan's Back But Religion's Got Him," *Pittsburgh Press*, May 15, 1980; Bernard Holland, "Born-Again Dylan Leaves Audience Behind," *Pittsburgh Post-Gazette*, May 15, 1980; Rex Rutkoski, "Dylan's Second Coming," *Pittsburgh New Sun*, May 22, 1980.

| 15 | Pittsburgh, PA | Stanley Theatre |

Interviewed in the foyer of the Hilton Hotel by KDKA-TV's Pat Crosby.

| 16 | Pittsburgh, PA | Stanley Theatre |

Inc. "I Believe In You"

| 17 | Akron, OH | Civic Theater |

Reviews cited: Mark Faris, "Dylan's gospel image shines on at the Civic," *Akron Beacon Journal*, May 18, 1980.

18	Akron, OH	Civic Theater

Inc. only live performance of "I Will Sing."

20	Columbus, OH	Franklin County Veterans Memorial Auditorium

Reviews cited: Natalie J. Carter, "Dylan Rolls New Stone,"
The Ohio State Lantern, May 22, 1980.

21	Dayton, OH	Memorial Hall

Interviewed by Karen Hughes.

Rundown Studios, Santa Monica, CA, September 18
Songs rehearsed: "Blue Blue River," "Makin' A Liar," "What About You, Babe?," "The Groom's Still Waiting At The Altar," "Yonder Comes Sin," "Every Grain of Sand," "Caribbean Wind," "A Couple More Years," "She's Not For You."

Rundown Studios, Santa Monica, CA, ?September 19 [listed as reel 2]
Songs rehearsed: "Sad Songs & Waltzes," "Somewhere Over The Rainbow," "If You Could Read My Mind," "Every Grain Of Sand," "Yonder Comes Sin," "Caribbean Wind," "Willin'," "Gotta Serve Somebody," "What Can I Do For You?," "Change My Way of Thinking," "Let's Keep It Between Us," "Like An Airplane Going Down," "Fourth Time Around," "Easy and Slow," "The Groom's Still Waiting."

Rundown Studios, Santa Monica, CA, September 23
Songs rehearsed: "Coverdown Breakthrough," "Rainbow Connection," "The Groom's Still Waiting At The Altar," "<u>Caribbean Wind</u>," "Every Grain Of Sand," "Yonder Comes Sin."

Rundown Studios, Santa Monica, CA, September 24
Songs rehearsed: "Caribbean Wind," "Let's Keep It Between Us," "Coverdown Breakthrough," "The Groom's Still Waiting At The Altar," "Gotta Serve Somebody," "Bo Diddley Riff (Price of Love?)," "Slow Train," "Makin' A Liar."

Rundown Studios, Santa Monica, CA, September 26
Songs rehearsed: "<u>Every Grain Of Sand</u>," "Let's Keep It Between Us," "Willin'," "Yonder Comes Sin," "Caribbean Wind," "<u>Makin' A Liar</u>," "If You Could Read My Mind."

Rundown Studios, Santa Monica, CA, September 30
Songs rehearsed: "Blue Blue River" "Caribbean Wind," "Yonder Comes Sin," "If You Could Read My Mind," "Let's Keep It Between Us."

Rundown Studios, Santa Monica, CA, October 1
Songs rehearsed: "<u>Yonder Comes Sin</u>," "Caribbean Wind," "If You Could Read My Mind," "She's Not For You," "A Couple More Years," "Fourth Time Around," "The Groom's Still Waiting At The Altar," "Simple Twist of Fate," "Rainbow Connection," "Somewhere Over The Rainbow," "In The Garden," "When You Gonna Wake Up," "Gotta Serve Somebody," "Ain't Gonna Go To Hell."

Rundown Studios, Santa Monica, CA, October 3
Songs rehearsed: "Sweet Caroline," "Untitled Song," "If It Had Not Been For The Lord."

Rundown Studios, Santa Monica, CA, October 8
Song rehearsed: "We Just Disagree."

Rundown Studios, Santa Monica, CA, October 9
Songs rehearsed: "We Just Disagree," "The Groom's Still Waiting At The Altar," "Blowin' In The Wind," "Like A Rolling Stone," "Señor (Tales of Yankee Power)," "Don't Think Twice It's Alright," "Let's Keep It Between Us," "Heatwave" (instrumental), "This Night Won't Last Forever," "Lay Lady Lay" (instrumental), "To Ramona."

Rundown Studios, Santa Monica, CA, October 10
Songs rehearsed: "Ain't Gonna Go To Hell," "Let's Keep It Between Us," "To Ramona," "Man Gave Names To All The Animals," "Slow Train," "Do Right To Me Baby," "Just Like A Woman," "Caribbean Wind," "Goin' On," "Gotta Serve Somebody," "Blowin' In The Wind," "When You Gonna Wake Up," "Solid Rock," "We Just Disagree," "In The Garden."

Rundown Studios, Santa Monica, CA, October 14
Songs rehearsed: "Heatwave," "Covenant Woman," "The Groom's Still Waiting At The Altar," "Tangled Up In Blue," "I Believe In You," "Simple Twist of Fate," "Just Like A Woman," "We Just Disagree," "Is Your Love In Vain?," "Maggie's Farm."

Rundown Studios, Santa Monica, CA, October 15
Songs rehearsed: "Goin' On," "Yonder Comes Sin," "To Ramona," "Caribbean Wind."

Rundown Studios, Santa Monica, CA, October 16
Songs filmed: "Abraham Martin and John," "Rise Again," "Mary From The Wild Moor," "I Believe In You," "Jesus Met A Woman At The Well."
Songs rehearsed: "Radio Medley" and "City of Gold."
Songs allegedly rehearsed: "Yonder Comes Sin," "Saving Grace," "I Believe You," "She's Not For You," "Man Gave Names To All The Animals," "Blowin' In The Wind," "Slow Train," "Let's Keep It Between Us," "When You Gonna Wake Up," "Just Like A Woman," "Solid Rock," "Caribbean Wind," "In The Garden."

Rundown Studios, Santa Monica, CA, October 22
Songs rehearsed: "Every Grain Of Sand," "She's Not For You," "Gotta Serve Somebody," "Fever," "Goin' On," "City Of Gold."

Rundown Studios, Santa Monica, CA, October 27
Songs rehearsed: "Show Me The Way"/"Like A Rolling Stone," "Gotta Serve Somebody," "Covenant Woman," "Ain't Gonna Go To Hell," "To Ramona," "Fever," "Man Gave Names To All The Animals," "Slow Train," "Blowin' In The Wind," "Solid Rock."

Rundown Studios, Santa Monica, CA, October 28
Songs rehearsed: "Señor (Tales of Yankee Power)," "Blowin' In The Wind," "Caribbean Wind," "In The Garden," "Simple Twist of Fate," "Solid Rock," "Gotta Serve Somebody," "To Ramona," "When You Gonna Wake Up," "Ain't Gonna Go To Hell," "Precious Angel," "Abraham Martin and John," "Let's Keep It Between Us," "Slow Train."

Rundown Studios, Santa Monica, CA, October 29
Songs rehearsed: "Blowin' In The Wind," "Heat Wave," "Gotta Serve Somebody," "Girl From The North Country," "Ain't Gonna Go To Hell," "In The Garden," "The Groom's Still Waiting At The Altar," "Precious Angel," "Like A Rolling Stone," "Man Gave Names To All The Animals," "Let's Keep It Between Us," "Slow Train," "Solid Rock," "What Can I Do For You?," "Simple Twist of Fate," "When You Gonna Wake Up."

Rundown Studios, Santa Monica, CA, October 30
Songs rehearsed: "Like A Rolling Stone," "Ain't Gonna Go To Hell," "Girl From The North Country," "Let's Keep It Between Us," "Abraham Martin and John," "Slow Train," "Señor," "What Can I Do For You?," "When You Gonna Wake Up," "Just Like A Woman," "In The Garden."

Rundown Studios, Santa Monica, CA, October 31
Songs rehearsed: "Caribbean Wind," "Covenant Woman," "The Times They Are A-Changin'"

November

9	San Francisco, CA	Fox Warfield Theatre

Reviews cited: Robert Hilburn, "Bob Dylan On His Own Terms," *LA Times*, Nov 11, 1980.

10	San Francisco, CA	Fox Warfield Theatre
11	San Francisco, CA	Fox Warfield Theatre

Interviewed by Robert Hilburn, for the *LA Times*'s *Calendar*, Nov 23, 1980.

12	San Francisco, CA	Fox Warfield Theatre

Inc. "Caribbean Wind."

13	San Francisco, CA	Fox Warfield Theatre

[w/ Carlos Santana]
Inc. "The Groom's Still Waiting At The Altar"

15	San Francisco, CA	Fox Warfield Theatre

[w/ Mike Bloomfield]

16	San Francisco, CA	Fox Warfield Theatre

[w/ Jerry Garcia]

17	San Francisco, CA	Fox Warfield Theatre
18	San Francisco, CA	Fox Warfield Theatre
19	San Francisco, CA	Fox Warfield Theatre

[w/ Maria Muldaur]
Interviewed by KMEL-FM's Paul Vincent backstage before the concert.

21	San Francisco, CA	Fox Warfield Theatre
22	San Francisco, CA	Fox Warfield Theatre

[w/ Roger McGuinn]
Inc. "City of Gold"
Reviews of entire residency cited: Ron Gluckman, "Bob Dylan In San Francisco: The Myth & The Message," The *Redwood Rock Review*, ?December 1980; "Newsreels," *BAM*, Nov 21, 1980; Paul Williams – *One Year Later* (privately circulated monograph)[entire text reproduced in *Bob Dylan: Watching The River Flow* (Omnibus Press, 1996)].

24	Tucson, AZ	Community Center
26	San Diego, CA	Golden Hall
29	Seattle, WA	Paramount Northwest Theatre
30ᵗ	Seattle, WA	Paramount Northwest Theatre

December

2	Salem, OR	The Armory

Inc. "Ain't Gonna Go To Hell."

3	Portland, OR	Paramount Theatre
4	Portland, OR	Paramount Theatre

1981

Rundown Studios, Santa Monica, CA, March 3
Songs recorded: "Jim's Tune," "Where Are You Tonight?," "Pretend It Never Happened," "It's Alright"/"Gonna Love You Anyway," "Israel."

Rundown Studios, Santa Monica, CA, March 4
Songs recorded: "Every Little Bit Hurts," "Adelita," "Dead Man Dead Man," "Gonna Love You Anyway," "Need A Woman," "She's Already Gone," "In The Garden," "Solid Rock," "The Dark Road Is A Hard Road," "Old Man," "A Million Miles Away," "You've Got A Friend."

Rundown Studios, Santa Monica, CA, March 10
Song recorded: "You Changed My Life."

Rundown Studios, Santa Monica, CA, March 11
Songs recorded: "Shot of Love" and "You Changed My Life."

Rundown Studios, Santa Monica, CA, March 20
Songs recorded: "Need A Woman," "Reach Out I'll Be There," "Heart Of Stone (Property Of Jesus)," "A Song For You."

Rundown Studios, Santa Monica, CA, ?March 21-24, 1981 or March 27-30.
Songs recorded: "Bolero (Heart Of Mine)," "Every Grain Of Sand," "Yes Sir, No Sir," "Is It Worth It?," "Let's Begin."

Rundown Studios, Santa Monica, CA, March 25-26
Song recorded: "Shot of Love," 2 instrumental jams, "Angelina."

Rundown Studios, Santa Monica, CA, ?March 27-30 Songs recorded: ?"The Groom's Still Waiting At The Altar" and "Every Grain Of Sand."

Studio 55, Los Angeles, CA, March 31
Songs recorded: "Caribbean Wind," "Dead Man Dead Man," "A Song For You," "Cold Cold Heart," "The Groom's Still Waiting At The Altar."

Cream STudio, Los Angeles, CA, April 1
Songs recorded: "Straw Hat," "Gonna Love You Anyway," "It's All Dangerous To Me," "Need That Woman," "Well Water," 3 unlisted instrumentals, "My Girl (It's Growing)" [instrumental], "My Oriental Home" [instrumental], "Wild Mountain Thyme," "Borrowed Time," "I Want You To Know That I Love You," "Rockin' Boat," "I Wish It Would Rain," "Cold, Cold Heart," "In The Summertime," "You Can't Make It On Your Own" [instrumental], "Is It Worth It?," "You Changed My Life," "Almost Persuaded."

Studio A, United Western Studio, Los Angeles, CA, April 2
Songs recorded: "Yes Sir, No Sir (Hallelujah)," Instrumental—Mid Tempo, Instrumental—Up Tempo, "Movin'," "Is It Worth It?," "A Song For You," "You Changed My Life," Unknown song, "Reach Out," "Fur Slippers," "Let It Be Me," "Ah Ah Ah."

Clover Studio, Los Angeles, CA, April 23
Songs recorded: "Shot of Love" [inserts], "Trouble," "Magic," "Bolero (Heart Of Mine)," "Don't Ever Take Yourself Away," "You Changed My Life," "Is It Worth It?," "Be Careful."

Clover Studio, Los Angeles, CA, April 24
Songs recorded: "Dead Man, Dead Man," 2 Ska instrumentals, "Need That Woman," "In The Summertime," "Watered-Down Love."

Clover Studio, Los Angeles, CA, April 28
Songs recorded: "Angelina," "Dead Man Dead Man," Bob instrumental, Blues instrumental.

Clover Studio, Los Angeles, CA, April 29
Songs recorded: "Watered-Down Love," "You're Still A Child To Me," "Property Of Jesus," "Heart Of Mine," "Every Grain Of Sand."

Clover Studio, Los Angeles, CA, April 30
Songs recorded: "The Girl From Louisville," "The Ballad Of Ira Hayes," "Dead Man, Dead Man," "Lenny Bruce," Misc. instrumental(s), "Heart Of Mine."

Clover Studio, Los Angeles, CA, May 1
Songs recorded: "Caribbean Wind," Instrumental Jam, "Trouble," "Is It Worth It?," "Wind Blowing On

The Water," "Blues," "All The Way Down," "The Groom's Still Waiting At The Altar," "Heart Of Mine," "Watered-Down Love," "Don't Ever Take Yourself Away," "Mystery Train," "The Price Of Love," "Let It Be Me," "Work With Me Annie."

Clover Studio, Los Angeles, CA, May 4
Songs pulled to master: "Need A Woman" (April 24 – 2 takes); "Angelina" (April 28 – 1 take); "Caribbean Wind" (May 1 – 2 takes); "Trouble" (April 23 + May 1 – 2 takes); "Magic" (April 24 – 1 take); "In The Summertime" (April 24 – 3 takes); "Every Grain Of Sand" (April 29 – 3 takes); "Dead Man Dead Man" (April 24 + April 30 – 3 takes); "Lenny Bruce Is Dead" (April 30 – 2 takes); "The Grooms' Still Waiting At The Altar" (May 1 – 3 takes); "Property Of Jesus" (April 29 – 2 takes); "Heart Of Mine" (April 29 + May 1 – 2 takes].

Clover Studio, Los Angeles, CA, May 15
Songs recorded: "Watered-Down Love," "Dead Man Dead Man," "Heart Of Mine," "J.A.C." (instrumental), Unknown instrumental, "Magic" (instrumental), "In A Battle," "Mystery Train."

Rundown Studios, Santa Monica, CA, 1st week of June
Songs rehearsed: "I Don't Care," "Saving Grace," "It's Alright Ma," "Man Gave Names To All The Animals," "Ballad Of A Thin Man," "City of Gold," "We Just Disagree," "Just Like A Woman," "Señor," "Like A Rolling Stone," "What Can I Do For You," "When You Gonna Wake Up," "Shot of Love," "Heart Of Mine," "All Along The Watchtower," "Solid Rock," "I Believe In You," "To Ramona," "I Don't Believe You," "Let It Be Me," "Leaving It All Up To You," "Dearest," "Your Cheatin' Heart," "Big River," "Voyez Con Dios," "Guess Things Happen That Way," "Mansion Builder," "I Ain't Never," "Slowly," "Smoke Gets In Your Eyes," "Seven Days," "Pastures of Plenty," "Trouble," "Gotta Serve Somebody," "Rise Again," "In The Garden," "Lenny Bruce," "Simple Twist of Fate," "Masters of War," "I'll Be Your Baby Tonight," "Song To Woody," "Girl Of The North Country," "Love Minus Zero," "It's All Over Now Baby Blue," "It Ain't Me Babe," "Knockin' On Heaven's Door," "Blowin' In The Wind," "Mr. Tambourine Man," "Hard Rain's A Gonna Fall," "Forever Young."
Note: This track-listing was derived from a typed list made at the time by Arthur Rosato. However, the tapes of these rehearsals appear to have been mislaid.

June

10	Chicago, IL	Poplar Creek Music Theater,
	Hoffman Estates	

Reviews cited: Lynn Van Matre, "Born-Again Dylan Resurrects Some Older & Better Songs," *Detroit Free Press*, June 12, 1981.

11	Pine Knob Music Theatre	Clarkston, MI
12	Pine Knob Music Theatre	Clarkston, MI

Inc. "Watered-Down Love."
Interviewed by Tim Blackmore for London's Capital Radio, by Paul Gambaccini for BBC Radio One and Yves Bigot for Radio Europe No. 1.

14	Columbia, MD	Marjorie Merriweather Post Pavilion

Reviews cited: Tom Basham, "Guess Who's The New Dylan," *The Sun* 6/19/81; Geoffrey Himes, "Dylan Shows Signs of Restlessness," *Baltimore Sun*, June 15, 1981.

21	Tolouse, France	Stade Municipal des Minimes

Inc. "Dead Man, Dead Man"

23	Colombes, France	Stade de Colombes

Reviews cited: Mick Brown, "Dylan At Forty," *The Guardian*, June 26, 1981; Richard Williams, "Applause For The Singer Not The Song," *The Times*, June 26, 1981.

26	London, England	Earls Court

Reviews cited: Peter Deeley, "Dylan Changes With The Times," *The Observer*, June 28, 1981; Phillip Norman, "Dylan And The Angels," *The Sunday Times*,

	June 28, 1981.	
27	London, England	Earls Court
	The entire concert is included on *TROUBLE NO MORE*.	
28	London, England	Earls Court
29	London, England	Earls Court
	Inc. "Slow Train"	
30	London, England	Earls Court

July

1	London, England	Earls Court
	Inc. live debuts of "Shot Of Love," "Heart Of Mine" and a one-off	
	"Here Comes The Sun."	
2	Interviewed by WNEW-FM's Dave Herman in his London hotel-room,	
	the interview will be released as a promotional album, called *The London Interview*.	
4	Birmingham, England	International Arena, NEC
5	Birmingham, England	International Arena, NEC
8	Stockholm, Sweden	Johanneshovs Isstadion
9	Drammen, Norway	Drammenshallen
	Inc. "When You Gonna Wake Up."	
10	Drammen, Norway	Drammenshallen
12	Copenhagen, Denmark	Brøndby-Hallen
14	Bad Segeberg, Germany	Freileichttheater
15	Bad Segeberg, Germany	Freileichttheater
	Inc. "Gotta Serve Somebody"	
17	Loreley, Germany	Freileichtbühne
	Inc. "Jesus Is The One"	
18	Mannheim, Germany Eisstadion	
19	Munich, Germany	Olympiahalle
20	Munich, Germany	Olympiahalle
	Interviewed by Neil Spencer for the *New Musical Express*, August 15, 1981.	
21	Vienna, Austria	Stadthalle
23	Basel, Switzerland	Sporthalle St. Jakob
25	Avignon, France	Palais des Sports
	Inc. "Shot Of Love."	

October

16	Milwaukee, WI	Mecca Auditorium, University of Wisconsin
17	Milwaukee, WI	Mecca Auditorium, University of Wisconsin
	Reviews cited: Divina Infusino, "The Unpredictable Dylan," *Milwaukee Journal*,	
	October 18, 1981.	
18	Madison, WI	Dane County Memorial Coliseum
19	Merrillville, IN	Holiday Star Music Theater
21	Boston, MA	Orpheum Theatre
	Inc. "In The Summertime."	
23	Philadelphia, PA	The Spectrum
	Inc. "Solid Rock"	
24	State College, PA	Recreation Building, Pennsylvania State University
25	Bethlehem, PA	Stabler Arena, Lehigh University
27	East Rutherford, NJ	Meadowlands Brendan T. Byrne Sports Arena
	Reviews cited: Ira Mayer, "Dylan: The Times They Sure Do Change,"	
	New York Post, October 29, 1981.	
29	Toronto, Ontario	Maple Leaf Gardens

| 30 | Montreal, Quebec | Forum de Montreal |

Reviews cited: John Griffin, "Bob Dylan's Old Pop Fire Is Rapidly Fadin," *Montreal Gazette*, October 31, 1981.

| 31 | Kitchener, Ontario | Kitchener Arena |

Reviews cited: John Kiely, "Listless Dylan In A Sad Show," *Kitchener-Waterloo Record*, November 2, 1981.

November

| 2 | Ottowa, Ontario | Civic Centre |
| 4 | Cincinnnati, OH | Cincinnati Music Hall |

Reviews cited: Cliff Radel, "Dylan Offers Mixed Bag," *Cincinnati Enquirer*, November 6, 1981.

5	Cincinnnati, OH	Cincinnati Music Hall
6	West Lafayette, IN	Elliot Hall Of Music, Purdue University
7	Ann Arbor, MI	Hill Auditorium, University Of Michigan
8th	Ann Arbor, MI	Hill Auditorium, University Of Michigan
10th	New Orleans, LA	Saenger Theater, Saenger Performing Arts Center

Inc. "Thief On The Cross."

| 11 | New Orleans, LA | Saenger Theater, Saenger Performing Arts Center |
| 12 | Houston, TX | The Summit |

Reviews cited: Sean Mitchell, "Just Like A Showman', *Dallas Times Herald*, November 14, 1981; Bob Claypool, *The Houston Post*, November 13, 1981.

14	Nashville, TN	Municipal Auditorium
15	Atlanta, GA	The Fox Theater
16	Atlanta, GA	The Fox Theater
19	Miami, FL	Sunrise Musical Theater
20	Miami, FL	Sunrise Musical Theater
21	Lakeland, FL	Civic Center Theatre

Inc. "Every Grain Of Sand."

APPENDIX II
SOME ALTERNATE RAPS

All the raps in this book have been compared with existing transcripts, done by Bob Pook (whither thou, Bob?) or myself in the eighties, or for Olaf Bjorner's website in the last twenty years; and in most cases have been re-transcribed from superior audio sources.

Perhaps surprisingly, a comparison between those used in my three-decades–old three-part series in *The Telegraph* (later reconstituted as the Hanuman Book, *Saved–The Gospel Speeches*) and those on the All About Dylan website confirm that the earlier transcripts are generally more accurate. Indeed, little reference to this resource seems to have been made when the raps were redone by Bjorner.

I have returned the favor by almost never preferring a reading of his to one Pook or I made in the eighties on those few occasions when I have had to rely on those original transcripts from oft-challenging audience tapes. Below are a selection of transcripts from November 1979 to May 1980 which do not fit in the main text but are nonetheless revealing of Dylan's state of mind—and/or oratory skills—at the time. Enjoy. . .

Before "In the Garden" – November 27, 1979
John the Baptist said, when he saw Jesus coming, "Behold, the lamb of God who taketh away the sins of the world." He said the "lamb of god" because, when Moses went back to the land of Egypt, to get the Hebrew children out, he told Pharaoh to let the people go—Pharaoh didn't want to do it. So . . . God told him to tell Pharaoh, he'd send all kind of plagues into this country—a lot of different plagues too: hail, frogs, wind, just all kind of plagues came. Anyway, the last plague was, "God told Moses to go to tell Pharaoh that all the first born sons are going to die." Moses was wondering about the Hebrew children, and God told Moses: "You put the sign of blood on every door. Kill a lamb and put the sign of blood on every door and those children won't die." So if they had the sign of blood on the door, they lived. And that's why John the Baptist, when he saw Jesus coming, said, "Behold, the lamb of God who taketh away the sins on the world." If you don't know Jesus, you better check into it. He's real. [Girls scream: "He's real!!!"]

Before "God Uses Ordinary People" – December 5th

Mona Lisa's gonna come and sing a song called, "God Uses Ordinary People." You know he does use ordinary people. He doesn't use big superheroes or strange mystical people, he uses ordinary people. That's right. Moses was an ordinary person. Did you know Moses didn't even want to go down to Egypt-land and get those people out. But God said, "Moses, you go down there and you get those people out." Now Moses couldn't talk very well, [but] he went down there and told Pharaoh let the people go. But Pharaoh did not want to do it. He did not want to let those people go. Pharaoh was what you could call, rebellious. He had a rebellious spirit. And God told Moses, "Well, Moses, you go tell Pharaoh, hail's gonna strike." So Moses went and he told Pharaoh that the hail was gonna come and Pharaoh didn't believe him. You know he wasn't gonna believe him. But the hail came anyway and the rivers dried up and all kinds of plagues came. You can read about it yourself, if you want to. Anyway, Pharaoh still did not want to let those people go. He would not let them go because they were working for him. They were what you call slaves. Anyway, the last time, God told Moses, "You go tell Pharaoh that all the first-born sons in Egypt are going to die tonight." God does that, you know, God will just use his judgment, however he sees fit. Anyway, Moses said to God, "Well, how will this destroying angel know the Hebrew children?" And he said, "Well, if you go kill a lamb and you put the sign of the blood on every door." And that's what Moses did. And the blood was on every door. And you know you need that blood on your door.

Before "Solid Rock" – January 12, 1980

You know, the enemy is powerful. But God is more powerful. Once I didn't have Jesus within me I didn't know I had an enemy. But you can't be victorious unless you do have an enemy. And as this present world we know is coming to a close, you need something strong to hang on to, like a solid rock. Lots of people don't understand that. Sometimes I think maybe even God's people are not supposed to understand that, I just don't know. But we'll pray for them anyway. Because God is calling His people back.

Before "When He Returns" – April 20

Well, I'm very happy to say we have Ronnie Hawkins here tonight. Yeah. I don't know where he is, I know he's here somewhere. Ronnie and I go back a long ways. I hear he's gonna be doing movies now. Was it a movie a year now, Ronnie? Well, you know, I gave Ronnie his first part in the movies. That's right. Ronnie was in a little movie we made called, Renaldo and Clara, a few years back. Ronnie played the part of Bob Dylan. Interesting movie. Anyway, I guess there's no place to go but up now, hey Ron?

Before "Solid Rock" – April 4
You know this is a desperate time right now. You gotta have something to hang onto. I'd guess you'd say it's getting kinda confusing. What's gonna happen after this? Does anybody know? Does anybody think they know? Well, the Bible says specifically what's gonna happen. I know lots of you don't read the Bible any more. I never used to read it much myself, up till a couple of years ago. But I found it very interesting, to say the least. I don't want to see you without something to hang on to. I hope you had good education to hang on to, or a lot of knowledge and experience to hang on to. But you know it's not gonna do you any good. Because the Devil's got a plan too, and he's put it in effect. Ever since Adam and Eve. But I'm not gonna tell you any more about it. I'm gonna let you find out for yourself. You know the truth, it's called the truth, the light and the way. There is only one. There can't be but one. Satan will tell you there's all kinds of ways. But there's only one way. And which kinda way do you think that is?

Before "Are You Ready?" – April 28
Remember the girl earlier, who told you about Jesus? Remember that name now! Don't matter what your friends say, it won't be some eastern religion you never heard of before [that'll save you]. Okay? He who is free is free indeed.

Before "Are You Ready?" – April 30
Young girl who told you the story about Jesus earlier, remember that story? Remember that name now. You might not ever hear that name again, but I know you wanna be free. We all wanna be delivered don't we? Well, Jesus will deliver ya! You want a doctor, He'll cure you. You want a lawyer? He'll fight your battles. What ever you want, He's all that. You know John the Baptist he baptized with water. Jesus He baptized with fire and the Holy Spirit.

Before "Saved," May 1
Thank you. Yeah. Lot of people have heard that name Satan. Not too many people know who he is. Satan is the God of Self. Called the God of Self. He's a defeated foe. Jesus is saying there isn't any self, it's just a big bluff. So if you're descended with Adam . . . Anybody here descended with Adam? Well, Adam gave the Devil keys over you. And Jesus Christ went to the Cross and took those keys back.

[73]*Before "Are You Ready?" – May 2*

Remember the young girl that told you about Jesus earlier? Wasn't that long ago, about six hours or so? Yeah. We all got a lot of food, but you ain't missing food, you need spiritual food. And you might never hear that name again but remember you heard it. Jesus is a part of yourself. You got a health problem, you got a money problem, you got love problems. John the Baptist baptized with water, Jesus baptized with the Holy Spirit, it's a little different.

Before "Solid Rock" – May 3

Lot of people pray and wonder why they don't get what they pray for. They're praying all week, praying all year. They just ain't got it. There's a reason for that. The Bible says, "You ask amiss [and receive not] to consume it upon your unGodly lust." If that's the only reason you're praying, you probably won't get it. But God got other things in store for you. And I know He's calling his people now. Some of you out there are God's people. Maybe some of you aren't, I don't know who is who. But in the last days He's gonna pour out His spirit on all flesh. Now you know if you're called or not, I don't. *

Before "Are You Ready?" – May 7

Remember that girl who told you the story about Jesus before. Her dad is a preacher. She knows all about Jesus. Remember that name now. I can't impress it upon you enough, I really can't. If you got troubles, He'll take [away] your troubles. If you got to be delivered, He will deliver you. If you've got money problems, health problems, confusion, deception, medical problems of any kind.

Before "Are You Ready?" – May 8

Remember the girl who told us the story about Jesus quite a while ago. Remember that name. I know some of you are on the verge of committing suicide! Others here think you got it all together. Don't matter. Heaven and Earth are all gonna pass away. If you wanna be alive, go look into Jesus. He'll give life and life more abundant. He who is set free is free and easy.

Before "Slow Train" – May 9

It's sooner than you think. Much sooner. I know some of you out there are on the verge of committing suicide. Others of you think you got it all together. Well,

---

* James 4:3 says, "Ye ask, and receive not, because ye ask amiss, that ye may consume *it* upon your lusts."

it don't matter. Anybody know who the God of this world is? I'm just curious to know. Satan is called the God of this world. Some of you know that, some of you don't. You got confused if you think somebody else is the God of this world. Satan is the God of this world. Jesus has overcome that power. Just about two thousand years ago at the Cross. I used to think there were all kinds of ways to get to glory, y'know. Eastern religion. Transcendental meditation. But all those ways, they fail. They only go so far. They help you deal with this world. You can't overcome this world with those kinda things, however. No, you need the power of God in you. Power of God manifested in the flesh, justified in the Spirit, preached out in the world, believed on in the nations. Raised on up into glory. You need that kind of power. Or you ain't gonna make it. You'll die alright. You'll live and you'll die. I know you might look at me and say, "Wow he's just lost his mind!" But I never did lie to you, and I never told you to vote for nobody. I never told you what to eat. Never told you which records to buy, what programs to watch, how to live, any of that stuff. I'm telling you the truth now, but it's like trying to tell somebody what a piece of bread tastes like. So it's just one of them things you gotta either do or not do by yourself. Don't let your friends mispersuade you now, because they're not gonna go with you. You come into this world alone, and you leave with nothing.

After "Ain't Gonna Go To Hell For Anybody" – May 9
We're talking about Jesus tonight. That's the only way to salvation. So if you've got demons about, they're not gonna like that name Jesus. They're gonna run from that man.

After "Ain't Gonna Go To Hell For Anybody" – May 11
I ain't gonna go to hell for anybody. I know it's not fashionable. It's not fashionable to be thinking about Heaven and Hell. I know that. But God's always in fashion. So we're gonna be talking about Jesus tonight. And I warn you right now, that if you got any demons inside of you at all they're not gonna like that name, Jesus. They're gonna rebel against that. I know a lot of you think of yourselves as rebels. But let me tell you something, you ain't no rebel at all unless you rebel against the Devil.

Before "Solid Rock" – May 12
We're hanging onto a solid rock. I don't know what you're hanging onto. Solid rock made before the foundation of the world. Nobody said it was going to be easy. Anyway, I guess we're gonna cast out seeds. I don't know how many of ya know anything about farming but when you cast out seeds, you [sometimes] cast 'em out

onto hard rock or you cast 'em out onto the wayside, or you cast them into thorns, or you can cast them into fertile ground. Now I know some of you are gonna hear this tonight and it's gonna be like casting seeds onto the wayside. Now you know who you are. You're living on the wayside and it's not gonna mean nothing to ya, and the Devil's gonna snatch you right up. Others of ya are living on some kind of rock. When you hear it, you're gonna rejoice 'cause eternal life does sound good, don't it? I mean who wants to die? [But] without firm rooting, the seed's gonna die. Also you cast them among thorns . . . Growing up amongst thorns, the riches and the cares of this world they're thorns, they're gonna strangle that seed. And it's gonna die. But I also know and I believe that there's fertile ground out there. I know that I know that I know.

Before "Ain't Gonna Go To Hell For Anybody" – May 14

Thank you. I see they got a lot of new books now. One new book, I saw a review of it in the newspapers, *How To Commit Suicide A Hundred Different Ways*. They don't tell you each one of those ways leads straight to Hell. Anyway, we're gonna be talking about Jesus tonight. If you got any demons inside you, they're not gonna like that name. So if you wanna leave, you can leave right now, leave your money behind.

Before "Solid Rock" – May 14

I seen a lot of people in my time who do exactly what I do. I've known Jimi Hendrix, I knew Janis Joplin and I knew Jim Morrison and I knew Lowell George, and if they knew then what I know now, they'd still be here. [off-mic] Hit it!

Before "Slow Train" – May 15

The last animal, in case you haven't guessed, is a snake. The same snake that was in the Garden of Eden. The same snake that was Satan, Lucifer, God of this world. Prince of power of the air, that's the same person. And just like he deceived Adam and Eve he's out there to deceive us right now. They say "Bob don't preach so much." They always say "Bob do this, Bob do that." But that's all right. You see, I will do whatever I please anyway, I don't have any friends to lose.

Before "Slow Train" – May 15

I know not too many people are gonna tell you about Jesus. I know Jackson Browne's not gonna do it, he's running on empty. I know Bruce Springsteen's not gonna do it, 'cause he's born to run and he's still running. And Bob Seger's not gonna do it 'cause he's running against the wind. Somebody's got to do it, somebody's got to tell you you're free! You're free because Jesus paid for ya! And that's the only reason you're free. Now pick up your bed and walk.

Before "Are You Ready?" – May 15
Remember the girl that told you the story about Jesus? Can you hear me now? You got to remember that name, you may never hear it again. But anytime you need it, remember it's there. 'Cause all that believe even on that name have become sons of God even on their name. He's real. John The Baptist baptized with water, Jesus he baptized with fire and the Holy Spirit. Once you get baptized that way, you've been baptized.

Before "Solid Rock" – May 16
Right, you know what time it is? It's the midnight hour. Right. Well now, you know I don't know how many of you know anything about farming. Farming is like throwing out seeds, you know. We can throw seeds out on the wayside. Just like throwing it on the wayside, the enemy comes and snatches it right away. Well, you can throw them on rock. Hear the word, and rejoice and be glad, but you won't know yourself well enough to receive it. The enemy will get you there too. You cast those seeds amongst thorns. But the cares and the riches of this world have to be out there in the thorns. So you receive the word among them kind of thorns, them thorns are gonna smother it. They entangle it. And they'll snatch it from you. But I know that there's fertile ground out here. And we are living in the End Times now, these are the final days. And God is calling His people. I know many of you out there don't think you are God's people, but you are. And I know the name Jesus scares a lot of you but it's not you that's scared it's the demons inside you that are scared. They don't want you to be free. They wanna control you, and if you can't control your tongue, they're doing a pretty good job.

Before "Slow Train" – May 16
Well, it's our last night here. I wanna thank all of you that have just been really encouraging at this time. 'Cause we know the doctrine is strong. Doctors can't abide with love. Anyway, as everybody has guessed, the animal in the last song was a snake. Same snake that was in the Garden of Eden that deceived Eve and deceived Adam, and still running around loose right now, deceiving the Nation. See, Lucifer put his spirit inside that snake. Lucifer was a high angel of God before he became the Devil. Anyway, Adam gave him the keys to this world, and he owns it. He

owns everything about it. He owns the newspapers, he owns the political parties, he owns the doctors and he owns the lawyers. He owns the educational system, he owns it all. But Jesus Christ went to the Cross to defeat that power. I know that's a secret that Satan keeps. Jesus went to the Cross not only for forgiveness of sins but to destroy the works of the Devil, and he accomplished just that. Something no man has ever done.

After "Man Gave Names To All The Animals" – May 17
All right, if you haven't guessed, the name of that last animal, I know you got it, was a snake. Same snake that was in the Garden of Eden. Same snake that Lucifer put his spirit into to deceive Eve, to deceive Adam. Who gave him the keys to this world. Lucifer was a high angel of God, he's not one of these Devils with pitchforks. Do you believe in the power of the Gospel? That Jesus Christ [went to] the Cross for the forgiveness of sins, but also to destroy the works of the Devil. Now that's something you should talk about.

Before "Solid Rock" – May 18
Now spreading the word of God is a tricky thing. First of all, you plant seeds; I don't who many of you know anything about farming, I know I don't, ha-ha-ha. However, you can't plant seeds on the wayside and I know I'm looking out on the wayside. I'm gonna plant seeds. They're gonna be received with gladness. You're gonna rejoice, but as soon as you walk out the door, you'll forget all about it. They do plant seeds out on a rock and that seed will [be] received with gladness . . . but you may not know yourself well enough for it to grow. And the Devil's gonna snatch it from you, I hope otherwise, but that's the way it is sometimes. And then there's lot of thorns out there, I know that too. I'm telling you Jesus is Lord and I know about the thorns. You're gonna receive them with gladness but you got so many cares in this world, it's gonna be tangled with all the cares of this world. They're gonna strangle that seed and not let it grow no further. But just as much as I know all that, I also know there is fertile ground out there. Now we are in the last days, God is calling his people. Some of you don't know you're God's people. Some of you don't know the Devil's already been defeated for. All you gotta do is accept it. Be baptized with the Holy Ghost. You will have the power. I'm not talking about water baptism, I'm talking about the Holy Ghost baptism.

Before "Are You Ready?" – May 20
You remember the girl that told you the story about Jesus? Can you hear me now?

Put no other name before that name. That name will still be here when this Heaven and Earth pass away. John the Baptist baptized with water, Jesus he baptized with fire and the Holy Ghost. If you ain't baptized like that right now, you just run out of here and get baptized like that.

Before "Slow Train" – May 20
In case you didn't guess, that last animal was a snake. I know some of you knew that already. Same snake that was in the Garden of Eden. Back then snakes walked on their legs. Well, actually they still do. Same snake that was in the Garden of Eden, same snake had previously been Lucifer, High angel of God . . . When Adam and Eve gave the keys to this world over to the Devil. Well, that's why Jesus Christ had to go to the Cross right? Not only for the forgiveness of sins but to destroy the works of the Devil. So that's why it says, I think it's Romans 8[74], if that same spirit that raised Christ from the dead, dwells in you, shall quicken your mortal life. And you can be alive, lots of dead people walking around today, thinking they got to be alive.

Before "Slow Train" – May 21
All right. If you haven't already guessed the name of the last animal was a . . . monkey. Not really, it was a snake. That's right, it was a snake. You got any poisonous snakes out here? I mean those that crawl on the ground, I don't mean the two-legged kind.

Before "Ain't Gonna Go To Hell For Anybody" – May 21
Ain't gonna go to Hell for anybody. You know, the Devil is all around us. Anyway, I gotta tell you about Jesus. 'Cause I don't know anyone else who'll do it. Bruce Springsteen, he's born to run, and he's still runnin'. Jackson Browne now, he's running on empty, God bless his soul . . . Bob Seger, he's . . ., what's he doing now? He's running against the wind. And The Eagles, they're on that long run. Sooner or later all those boys gotta come home. I don't care who they are.

Before "What Can I Do For You?" – May 21
How many out there know you have eternal life? How many of you don't? I'll tell you a sad thing I saw one time. I saw a drowning man pull down a man who was trying to rescue him, and they both drowned. Do you hear me now?

*Romans 8:11 reads, "If the Spirit of him that raised up Jesus from the *dead dwell in you*, he that raised up Christ from the *dead shall* also *quicken your mortal* bodies by his Spirit that dwelleth in you."

Before "Are You Ready?" – May 21

Remember the girl that told you the story about Jesus. You remember that name now. You may not hear it again. Some of you I know are on the verge of committing suicide. Others of you think you got it all together. Don't matter. Jesus is for everybody. He came to save the world not to judge the world. Education's not gonna save you. Law not gonna save you. Medicine's not gonna save you. Don't wait till it's too late now. Lot of people they wait till they're old. A lot of people they wait till they're behind bars. Lot of people wait till they're at the end of the line. You don't have to wait that long. Salvation begins right now. Today.

INTERVIEWS CONSULTED

(i) w/ Dylan (1983 –present):

Martin Keller	– *NME* August 6, 1983.
Robert Hilburn	– *LA Times* October 30, 1983.
Kurt Loder	– *Rolling Stone* June 21, 1984.

Verona press conference transcript May 29, 1984. (*Talkin' Bob Dylan* . . . 1984).
Hamburg press conference transcript May 29, 1984. (*Talkin' Bob Dy*lan . . . 1984).

Antoine De Caunes (Antennes II)	– June 17, 1984. (*Talkin' Bob Dylan* . . . 1984).
Robert Hilburn	– *LA Times* August 5, 1984.
Mick Brown	– *Sunday Times* July 1, 1984.
Bono Vox	– *Hot Press* August 26, 1984.
Bill Flannagan	– *Written In My Soul* (Contemporary, 1986).
Bob Coburn	– (*Rockline* June 17, 1985) – transcript.
Cameron Crowe	– *Biograph* sleeve notes (CBS, 1985).
Scott Cohen	– *Spin* December 1985 & *Interview* February 1986.
Charles Young on MTV September 1985	– transcript.
Bob Brown on *20/20* 9/19/85	– transcript.
Robert Hilburn	– *LA Times*, November 11, 1985.
Denise Worrell	– *Icons: Intimate Portraits* (Atlantic, 1989).
George Neegus on *60 Minutes* 1/86	– transcript.
Toby Creswell	– *Rolling Stone* (Australia) January 16, 1986.

Sydney press conference February 10, 1986 – transcript [RTS #1].

Charles Kaiser	– *Boston Review* April 1986.

Westwood press conference April 10, 1986 – transcript.

Bob Fass on *WBAI* 5/21/86	– transcript.
Mikal Gilmore	– *Rolling Stone* July 17, 1986.
Kathryn Baker	– *The State* September 16, 1988.
Edna Gundersen	– *USA Today* September 2, 1989.
Edna Gundersen	– *USA Today* September, 1990.
Joe Queenan	– *Spy* July 1991.
Paul Zollo	– *Song Talk* Winter, 1991.

Elliott Mintz on Westwood One's *The Beatle Years*, January 18, 1993 – transcript.

Gary Hill	– *Isis* #52.
John Dolen	– *Fort Lauderdale Sun-Sentinel* September 28, 1995.
David Gates	– *Newsweek* October 6, 1997.
Rome press conference July 23, 2001	– transcript.
Robert Hilburn	– *LA Times* September 16, 2001.
Mikal Gilmore	– *Rolling Stone* November 22, 2001.

Austin Scaggs   – *Rolling Stone* on-line November 17, 2004.
Ed Bradley on *60 Minutes* December 5, 2004 – transcript.

(ii) w/ Those Who Were There:
Barry Beckett   – Scott Marshall (*The Bridge* #37)
Terry Bortwick   – Scott Marshall, in *Bob Dylan: A Spiritual Life* (WND, 2017).
Tim Drummond   – Scott Marshall (transcript from interviewer).
Bill Dwyer   – Joel Gilbert, *The Gospel Years* DVD (2006).
Dan Fiala   – Scott Marshall (*The Bridge* #52).
Allen Ginsberg   – Steve Lake *Melody Maker* January 3, 1981.
Mitch Glaser   – Joel Gilbert, *The Gospel Years* DVD (2006).
Kenn Gulliksen   – *Buzz*, November 1980.
Bruce Heiman   – Scott Marshall (transcript from interviewer).
Scott Huffstetler   – Scott Marshall (*On The Tracks* #23).
Dave Kelly   – Chris Cooper *Isis* #22.
Dave Kelly   – Scott Marshall, in *Bob Dylan: A Spiritual Life* (WND, 2017).
Regina McCrary   – Joel Gilbert, *The Gospel Years* DVD (2006).
Regina McCrary   – Scott Marshall (*On The Tracks* #18).
Regina McCrary   – *On The Tracks* #23.
Larry Myers   – Scott Marshall (*The Bridge* #47).
                                       – *On The Tracks* #4.
Simon Napier-Bell   – *The Guardian* January 20, 2008.
Spooner Oldham   – Scott Marshall (*On The Tracks* #17).
Chuck Plotkin   – Damien Love, conducted in 2014, posted online May 2017.
Helena Springs   – Chris Cooper, *Endless Road* #7.
Fred Tackett   – Damien Love, conducted in 2014, posted online May 2017.
                                       – Scott Marshall (transcript from interviewer).
                                       – Masato Kato (*The Bridge* #4).
Benmont Tench   – Damien Love, conducted in 2014, posted online May 2017.
Paul Wasserman   – Scott Marshall (*The Bridge* #49).
Jerry Wexler   – Joel Gilbert, *The Gospel Years* DVD (2006).
                                       – *Rhythm & The Blues* (Knopf, 1993) w/ David Ritz.
                                       – *Rolling Stone* November 2, 1980.
Tony Wright   – *The Telegraph* #43.

Interviews with David Mansfield, Jim Keltner, Arthur Rosato, Raymond Foye, Robert Hilburn, Harvey Kubernik, Paul Rappaport, Toby Scott, Debbie Gold, Neil Spencer, Al Kooper and Bruce Gary were conducted by the author.

ACKNOWLEDGMENTS:

TROUBLE IN MIND represented a very different challenge to last year's shameless cash-in, *JUDAS!* Where the focus of that book was primarily on the reaction to Dylan's conversion to electric, this book is very much about Dylan's *own* response to both his newfound religious beliefs and the reaction it engendered by a cynical media.

My unabashed concentration on the music—much of it magnificent—that Dylan made in the three years of his Christian odyssey was only possible because of the manifold kindnesses of Jeff Rosen, Parker Fishel and Steve Berkowitz, who kept me in the loop while they worked tirelessly on the fine new Bootleg Series, *TROUBLE NO MORE.*

Likewise, Glenn Korman proved again to be a meticulous archivist and thoughtful annotator, allowing me access to his own notes on the transfers of a tsunami of Dylan rehearsals and soundboard tapes and helped me decipher session logs that were at times as arcane as the Rosetta Stone.

I was able to draw on my own archive for interviews with David Mansfield, Arthur Rosato, Jim Kletner and Al Kooper, as well as with two old friends, now passed, Debbie Gold and Bruce Gary.

It was a delight to be able to add to these dusty tapes new interviews with Raymond Foye, Robert Hilburn, Harvey Kubernik, Paul Rappaport, Toby Scott and Neil Spencer; and to resume a correspondence with Arthur Rosato, whose memory remains impressively intact, and who responded to every query with his usual generosity of spirit.

Thanks, too, to Bob Pook, who tenaciously transcribed the raps from some challenging audience tapes back in the 1980s and fully deserved his "thanks" in the Hanuman book, *Saved! The Gospel Speeches* (unlike Messrs. Bauldie and Gray!).

And I continue to treasure my conversations with the late Paul Williams and the indefatigible Joel Bernstein about this period, these shows and the various recordings over the years.

Marty Katz and Chris Bradford were generous enough to allow me to illustrate my treatise with terrific photos from the two Warfield residences.

Also their usual industrious and reliable selves on my behalf, rustling up reviews and lost interviews, were those Dylan scholars (1st class): Mitch Blank, Ian Woodward and Rod McBeath; as well as rock historian par excellence, Peter Doggett.

I also give a nod here to the work of Dave Percival and Chris Cooper in the *Wanted Man*-era, and to Joel Gilbert and Damien Love for the interviews they did for their own projects, but invaluable to me, too.

I dispense my usual thanks to Barney Hoskyns and Erik Flannagan for helping me connect the dots with names from their contact books.

Finally, thanks to Scott Marshall for sharing his own interviews with key players in the unfolding drama, while fighting the good fight with his own publisher.

And, lest I forget, none of this would have been possible—or ever realized in print—without the input and perseverance of my editors, Ian and Isabel Daley at Route Books and Jacob Hoye at Lesser Gods.

Praise be, one and all. Till the next time,

—Clinton Heylin, July 2017.

.. MYSTERIOUSLY "SAVED"

AN ASTROLOGICAL INVESTIGATION

INTO BOB DYLAN'S CONVERSION TO

AMERICAN FUNDAMENTALISM

Photo: Joyce George

Clinton Heylin is one of the leading rock historians in the world, with over two dozen books to his name. These include biographies of Bob Dylan (*Behind The Shades*), Van Morrison (*Can You Feel The Silence?*), Bruce Springsteen (*E Street Shuffle*) and Sandy Denny (*No More Sad Refrains*), as well as his acclaimed pre-punk history, *From the Velvets To The Voidoids*, and the one and only history of rock bootlegs, *Bootleg*. His highly acclaimed titles *It's One For The Money: The Song Snatchers Who Carved Up A Century of Pop* and *Anarchy In The Year Zero: The Sex Pistols, The Clash And The Class of '76* were nominated for the Penderyn Book Award. He lives in Somerset, England.

www.dylantroubleinmind.wordpress.com

JUDAS!
From Forest Hills To The Free Trade Hall
A Historical View Of The Big Boo
Clinton Heylin

"Judas, the most hated name in human history! If you think you've been called a bad name, try to work your way out from under that. Yeah, and for what? For playing an electric guitar?"
—Bob Dylan

In 1966 there was… the sell-out tour to end all tours. Bob Dylan and The Hawks found themselves at the epicenter of a storm of controversy. Their response? To unleash a cavalcade of ferocity from Melbourne to Manchester, from Forest Hills to the Free Trade Hall. For the first time, the full story can now be told from eye-witnesses galore; from timely reports, both mile wide and spot on; and from the participants themselves. And what better tour guide than Clinton Heylin, the esteemed Dylan biographer and one of the world's leading rock historians. The price of admission? Thirty pieces of silver. The password? Play fucking loud.

"The definitive written account of Dylan's historic and pivotal 1965-66 world tours."
—Bobdylan.com

"A complementary delight. Everything is explained." —Mojo

www.dylanjudas.wordpress.com
www.lessergodsbooks.com/book/judas/